Data Center Virtualization Certification: VCP6.5-DCV Exam Guide

Everything you need to achieve 2V0-622
certification – with exam tips and exercises

Andrea Mauro
Paolo Valsecchi

BIRMINGHAM - MUMBAI

Data Center Virtualization Certification: VCP6.5-DCV Exam Guide

Commissioning Editor: Vijin Boricha
Acquisition Editor: Rahul Nair
Content Development Editor: Arjun Joshi
Technical Editor: Sayali Thanekar
Copy Editor: Safis Editing
Project Coordinator: Kinjal Bari
Proofreader: Safis Editing
Indexer: Tejal Daruwale Soni
Graphics: Jisha Chirayil
Production Coordinator: Arvindkumar Gupta

First published: August 2018

Production reference: 1240818

Published by Packt Publishing Ltd.
Livery Place
35 Livery Street
Birmingham
B3 2PB, UK.

ISBN 978-1-78934-047-1

www.packtpub.com

`mapt.io`

Mapt is an online digital library that gives you full access to over 5,000 books and videos, as well as industry leading tools to help you plan your personal development and advance your career. For more information, please visit our website.

Why subscribe?

- Spend less time learning and more time coding with practical eBooks and Videos from over 4,000 industry professionals

- Improve your learning with Skill Plans built especially for you

- Get a free eBook or video every month

- Mapt is fully searchable

- Copy and paste, print, and bookmark content

PacktPub.com

Did you know that Packt offers eBook versions of every book published, with PDF and ePub files available? You can upgrade to the eBook version at `www.PacktPub.com` and as a print book customer, you are entitled to a discount on the eBook copy. Get in touch with us at `service@packtpub.com` for more details.

At `www.PacktPub.com`, you can also read a collection of free technical articles, sign up for a range of free newsletters, and receive exclusive discounts and offers on Packt books and eBooks.

Contributors

About the authors

Andrea Mauro has 20 years of experience in IT, both in industry and the academic world. He currently works as a solution architect at Assyrus (an Italian IT company). He is responsible for infrastructure implementation, architecture design, upgrades, and migration processes.

He is a virtualization and storage architect, specializing in VMware, but also Microsoft, Citrix, and Linux solutions. His first virtualized solution in production was built around ESX 2.x several years ago.

His professional certifications include several VMware certifications (VCP-DCV, vSAN Specialist, VCIX-DCV, VCIX-NV, VCDX-DCV), but also other vendor-related certifications. He is also a VMware vExpert (2010-18), Nutanix NTC (2014-18), and Veeam Vanguard (2015-18).

I would like to thank my wife and my son for their patience (this book has taken a lot of my free time for three long months), my friends from VMUG.IT for their support, and my co-author (Paolo) for his support, without whom this book would not have been possible.

Paolo Valsecchi has more than 20 years, experience in the IT industry, and he currently works as a system engineer mainly focused on VMware vSphere, Microsoft technologies, and backup/DR solutions. His current role involves covering all the tasks related to ensuring IT infrastructures' availability and data integrity (implementation, upgrade, and administration).

He holds the VMware VCP5/6.5-DCV and Veeam VMCE professional certifications, and he has been awarded the VMware vExpert title (2015-18) and the Veeam Vanguard title (2016-18).

I would like to thank my family and friends for their support and help with finalizing the project. The patience they had during the writing of this book was a constant encouragement in the last tough months, and it made this book possible. A big thanks to my co-author, Andrea, for involving me in a fascinating challenge like this, providing me the opportunity to improve my experience as author and also as technician.

About the reviewer

Karel Novak has 17 years of experience in the IT world. He currently works as a senior virtual infrastructure engineer at Arrow ECS, the Czech Republic, responsible for implementation, design, and complete consultation of VMware and Veeam. As an instructor of advanced VMware and Veeam, he has delivered many courses. He specializes in VMware DCV and NSX and, of course, Veeam. He is a VMware vExpert 2012-2018, VMware vExpert NSX 2016-2017, and a Veeam Vanguard 2015-2018. His highest certifications are VCI-Level2, VCIX6-NV, VCIX6-DCV, VMCT-Mentor, and VMCA. He is also a VMware Certification Subject Matter Expert.

He was a co-author of *Mastering VMware vSphere 6.5*.

> *I would like to say thank you, Andrea and Paolo, for your trust. I was honored to help you with this book. My dear wife is an amazing supporter of all the projects that I do. Amazing wife, thank you very much.*

Packt is searching for authors like you

If you're interested in becoming an author for Packt, please visit `authors.packtpub.com` and apply today. We have worked with thousands of developers and tech professionals, just like you, to help them share their insight with the global tech community. You can make a general application, apply for a specific hot topic that we are recruiting an author for, or submit your own idea.

Table of Contents

Preface

The **VMware Certified Professional** (**VCP**) 6.5 Data Center Virtualization certification demonstrates your skills and your ability to successfully install, configure, and manage a VMware vSphere 6.5-based infrastructure, including all of its components and layers: vCenter Server, ESXi hosts, and virtual machines.

This book describes the various paths to reaching this industry-standard certification (which is still one of the most sought-after and best-paying certifications to have), and prepares you for the whole journey along whichever path to the certification you choose.

The main part of this book is focused on the VCP65-DCV exam (2V0-622), but much of what you will learn can also be applied to the delta exam (2V0-622D). The book follows the related *VMware Certified Professional 6.5 - Data Center Virtualization Exam Preparation Guide* (`https://mylearn.vmware.com/lcms/web/portals/certification/exam_prep_guides/ Exam_Prep_Guide_2V0-622_3Oct2017.docx.pdf`), and it is structured using the same objectives.

The different chapters are grouped in different sections, according to the preparation and schedule being discussed. The aim of this book is to provide a reference point that can help your preparation for the exam in a timeframe of four weeks.

Who this book is for

The book is focused on the VCP6.5-DCV exam, covering all the required objectives outlined in the exam preparation guide.

For this reason, the expected readers for this book are vSphere administrators and IT architects who want to achieve the VCP6.5-DCV certification and have already gained some experience with the vSphere platform.

The book can also be used to learn more about the VMware vSphere 6.5 product, but this book does not provide a complete overview and is definitely not targeted at those who want to learn about the product from scratch.

For those wishing to start down a path toward the VMware certification for the first time, one requirement is to attend to an official course, which can provide the right information for those who are starting from scratch.

What this book covers

Everything outlined in the official *VMware Certified Professional 6.5 - Data Center Virtualization Exam Preparation Guide,* as well as what you will need to know for the VCP6.5-DCV certification exam, is covered in this book. The book is composed of 10 chapters, which cover the following topics.

Chapter 1, *Configuring and Administering vSphere 6.x Security,* looks at the various aspects to consider when securing the vSphere environment, such as roles, permissions, encryption, authentication, and patching.

Chapter 2, *Configure and Administer vSphere 6.x Networking,* is completely dedicated to vSphere networking. It explains standard and distributed virtual switches and covers the design, management, and optimization of the virtual network.

Chapter 3, *Configure and Administer vSphere 6.x Storage,* is focused on vSphere storage, covering the different connectivity options and protocols, such as NFS, FC, FCoE, and iSCSI. Datastore options and use cases are also discussed.

Chapter 4, *Upgrade a vSphere Deployment to 6.x,* covers the upgrade and migration procedures of vSphere from version 5.5 and 6.0 to version 6.5.

Chapter 5, *Administer and Manage vSphere 6.x Resources,* explains resource pool management and DRS configuration, describing the use of affinity and anti-affinity rules. It also discusses the new network DRS capability used to prevent migration recommendations to saturated host networks.

Chapter 6, *Backup and Recover a vSphere Deployment,* covers the backing up and restoration of the vCenter Server Appliance, as well as the backing up, recovery, and replication of virtual machines using vSphere Protection Data and vSphere Replication.

Chapter 7, *Troubleshoot a vSphere Deployment,* walks through the troubleshooting part of a virtual environment, providing a short overview of some topics and possible use cases.

Chapter 8, *Deploy and Customize ESXi Hosts,* covers the management and the configuration of the vSphere Auto Deploy and Host Profile features for optimizing and automating the ESXi host's deployment.

Chapter 9, *Configure and Administer vSphere and vCenter Availability Solutions,* goes into the configuration settings for vSphere HA and the **vCenter Server Appliance** (**VCSA**) HA setup.

`Chapter 10`, *Administer and Manage vSphere Virtual Machines*, covers some advanced features available for virtual machines, the configuration and use of content libraries, and the consolidation process using the vSphere vCenter Converter tool.

To get the most out of this book

For the topics and the procedures covered, the book is oriented to experienced vSphere administrators and IT architects who have achievement of the certification as their goal. The purpose of this book is to provide the information and the procedures you need to prepare for the exam.

This book uses the VMware vSphere 6.5 Update 1 platform (ESXi, vCenter Server) as a reference, as well as some optional components, such as VMware vCenter Converter 6.2. These are the minimum software requirements to use in a lab to follow the topics covered in the book.

 The software version used as a reference during the writing process is VMware vSphere 6.5 Update 1, which reflects the requirements for the exam preparation. The Flash-based vSphere Web Client was used to document all the procedures and screenshots, since not all of the functionalities have been implemented in the new HTML5 vSphere client. The HTML5 client is still not 100% complete and some functions may be missing. For an up-to-date list of unsupported functionality, see functionality updates for the vSphere Client at `http://www.vmware.com/info?id=1413`.

To practice the configuration procedures used through the various chapters, it is strongly recommended that you build a small lab environment to test and practice what you read through the chapters. VMware vSphere 6.5 Update 1 can be downloaded as a 60-day, fully working trial (during the trial period, it will be an Enterprise Plus version) to experiment with and learn how vSphere works.

Also, be sure to understand the limits of the available vSphere 6.5 features. The exam was very rich in the past, with those numbers now you must remember just the main limits. For more information, see this site: `https://configmax.vmware.com/`.

Each chapter is accompanied by some review questions at the end, which you should answer to verify that you have understood the content presented in the chapter. Take your time to practice and study the book to successfully achieve the VCP6.5-DCV certification.

Download the color images

We also provide a PDF file that has color images of the screenshots/diagrams used in this book. You can download it here: `https://www.packtpub.com/sites/default/files/downloads/DataCenterVirtualizationCertificationVCP6Dot5DCVExamGuide_ColorImages.pdf`.

Conventions used

There are a number of text conventions used throughout this book.

`CodeInText`: Indicates code words in text, database table names, folder names, filenames, file extensions, pathnames, dummy URLs, user input, and Twitter handles. Here is an example: "`StackName` is the name of the new TCP/IP stack."

A block of code is set as follows:

```
<config>
 <vpxd>
  <network>
    <rollback>false</rollback>
  </network>
 </vpxd>
</config>
```

Any command-line input or output is written as follows:

```
esxcli system settings advanced set -o /Net/UseHwTSO -i 0
```

Bold: Indicates a new term, an important word, or words that you see onscreen. For example, words in menus or dialog boxes appear in the text like this. Here is an example: "On the **Select name and location** page, type the name of the new distributed port group, or accept the generated name."

 Warnings or important notes appear like this.

 Tips and tricks appear like this.

Get in touch

Feedback from our readers is always welcome.

General feedback: Email `feedback@packtpub.com` and mention the book title in the subject of your message. If you have questions about any aspect of this book, please email us at `questions@packtpub.com`.

Errata: Although we have taken every care to ensure the accuracy of our content, mistakes do happen. If you have found a mistake in this book, we would be grateful if you would report this to us. Please visit `www.packtpub.com/submit-errata`, selecting your book, clicking on the Errata Submission Form link, and entering the details.

Piracy: If you come across any illegal copies of our works in any form on the Internet, we would be grateful if you would provide us with the location address or website name. Please contact us at `copyright@packtpub.com` with a link to the material.

If you are interested in becoming an author: If there is a topic that you have expertise in and you are interested in either writing or contributing to a book, please visit `authors.packtpub.com`.

Reviews

Please leave a review. Once you have read and used this book, why not leave a review on the site that you purchased it from? Potential readers can then see and use your unbiased opinion to make purchase decisions, we at Packt can understand what you think about our products, and our authors can see your feedback on their book. Thank you!

For more information about Packt, please visit `packtpub.com`.

Configuring and Administering vSphere 6.x Security

1

Security has become a critical aspect of every infrastructure, but for virtual environments, there are some advantages compared to the traditional infrastructures.

One of the main pillars of system virtualization is the **Virtual Machine** (**VM**) isolation principle, which protects a VM from other VM attacks, while also protecting the virtualization host from possible VM attacks. Of course, the isolation properties don't work for the network layer; other solutions are required to increase network security, such as VMware NSX.

While isolation protects the host level from the VM level, in some cases, it's also necessary to protect the VM level from the underlying infrastructure; for example, in a public cloud infrastructure, the consumer might have some concerns about how the provider manages the security and privacy of their data.

VMware vSphere 6.5 has introduced some important new security features, such as VM encryption, encrypted vMotion, and Secure Boot Support for VMs and ESXi.

Practicing what you learn in this chapter will be key to reinforcing your skills and your preparation for the exam. The last part of *HOL-1811-01-SDC* (vSphere v6.5 - What's New) and the lab *HOL-1811-04-SDC* (vSphere Security - Getting Started) include the encrypted VM and encrypted vMotion features.

The following topics will be covered in this chapter:

- Understanding role-based access control in vSphere
- Tuning and hardening guidelines for vCenter, ESXi, and VMs
- Working with encryption and secure VMs

Objective 1.1 – Configure and administer role-based access control

Role-based access control (**RBAC**) is a common approach to managing authorizations and permissions, based on specific roles assigned to specific users or groups.

 In VMware vSphere, roles are just sets of privileges used to authorize users (or groups) for specific vSphere inventory objects.

VMware vSphere provides the following four categories of permissions, from the most general to the most specific:

- **Group membership in the SSO domain**: Some users of the vCenter **Single Sign-On** (**SSO**) domain, such as the default administrator, have specific, implicit permissions. For more information, refer to *Objective 1.3*.
- **Global permissions**: These permissions are applied to a global root object, and can propagate to all objects. Also, they can span across different VMware products (for example, vSphere and vRealize Orchestrator).
- **vCenter permissions**: This is the main model used by vSphere Server to assign granular permissions to objects in different inventories.
- **ESXi local permissions**: Each ESXi host has local permissions, local rules, and local users. For hosts managed by vCenter, vCenter permissions are usually used. But local permissions still exist, and they are the only permission model for standalone ESXi hosts.

This chapter will mainly focus on vCenter and global permissions, as required by the exam questions. *Objective 1.3* will provide more information about SSO-related concepts. ESXi local permissions are not covered in detail, but the RBAC model is quite similar to the one used by the vCenter permissions.

 Objective 1.1 for VCP65-DCV and VCP6-DCV is the same, because there weren't any major changes in role-based access control from vSphere 6.0 to vSphere 6.5.

The official vSphere 6.5 Security Guide contains detailed information about authentication, authorization, and different permission configurations, and can be accessed at `https://docs.vmware.com/en/VMware-vSphere/6.5/vsphere-esxi-vcenter-server-652-security-guide.pdf`.

Compare and contrast propagated and explicit permission assignments

The VMware vSphere RBAC model is based on the following concepts:

- **Inventory**: A collection of multiple virtual or physical objects managed by vCenter, in a hierarchical organization. In vCenter Server, there are four different types of inventories, with different types of objects. For more information, refer to *Table 1.1*.
- **Object**: Each object in the vCenter inventory has associated permissions, or inherits them from its parent object.
- **User and Group**: In vCenter Server, users are authenticated through the SSO component; in ESXi, users are authenticated with a local authentication or AD authentication (refer to *Objective 1.3*). Note that you can only assign privileges to authenticated users, or groups of authenticated users.
- **Privilege**: This is the ability to access or execute specific functions, tasks, and operations.
- **Role**: Roles are just groups of privileges, used to make permissions management much easier.
- **Permission**: Permissions specify which role matches a specific group of users, for a specific object.

The following table summarizes the types of inventories, with the different types of objects:

vCenter inventory	Related objects
Hosts and clusters	• vCenter Servers • Data centers • Folders • Clusters • Hosts • Resource pools • vApps • VMs
VMs and templates	• vCenter Servers • Data centers • Folders • vApps • VMs • Templates

Storage (Data stores and data store clusters)	• vCenter Servers • Data centers • Folders • Data store clusters • Data stores
Networking	• vCenter Servers • Data centers • Folders • Portgroups • Distributed Virtual Switches • Distributed Portgroups • Distributed Uplinks

Table 1.1: Permission, role, user/group, and object

VMware **vCenter permissions** are assigned to objects in the vCenter inventory hierarchy by specifying which user or group has which privileges on that object. Then, to specify the privileges, you use specific roles.

 The same concepts are used for ESXi local permissions, but with some limitations; for example, the predefined roles are limited, and users/groups are limited to local ESXi and/or **Active Directory** (**AD**) domains. Also, there is only a single inventory.

The different vCenter inventories can be used to provide different levels of object hierarchies, and to group objects in different ways. Note that some objects (such as VMs) can exist in multiple inventories.

Later sections in this chapter will help you to understand how permissions are propagated through the object hierarchy.

 It is a good practice to assign only those permissions that are required to increase the security, and to have a clear permissions structure.

Global permissions are applied to a global root level, instead of a specific object. In this way, a global permission grants privileges for all objects in all inventories, but only if you assign a global permission by selecting the **Propagate to children** option. Without the propagation, a user will only have access to some global functionalities, such as creating roles. Also, remember that global permissions can span different VMware products.

Note that **vSphere tags** are a specific vCenter object type, with their own permission propagation model. This is because a tag object is not a child of vCenter, but is created at the vCenter root level. If you have multiple vCenter Servers in linked mode, then all tag objects will be shared across all vCenter Server instances. To learn how permissions are applied to tag objects, you can refer to the vSphere 6.5 Security Guide (`https://docs.vmware.com/en/VMware-vSphere/6.5/com.vmware.vsphere.security.doc/GUID-2199584C-B422-4EEF-9340-5449E1FB7DAE.html`).

View/sort/export user and group lists

User and group lists can be displayed and sorted from the vCenter Web Client in the **Users and Groups** menu, located via **Home** | **Administration** | **Single Sign-On**.

 Note that you need an SSO admin privilege to access this page. For more information about SSO, refer to *Objective 1.3*.

You can choose a specific domain (identity source, as described later). The **Users** tab will show the users, and the **Groups** tab will show the groups.

To sort a column, just click on the column heading. To change the order direction (ascending or descending), just click on it again. To show or hide a column, right-click on any of the column headings and select or deselect the name of the relevant column.

You can export the displayed list to a file (in a **Comma-Separated Values** (**CSV**) format) by selecting the **Export** button, as follows:

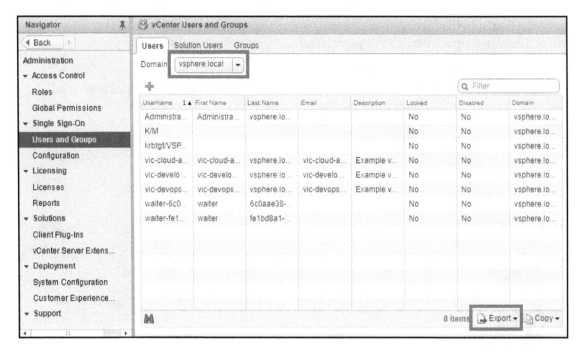

Figure 1.1: User lists in the vsphere.local domain

Add/modify/remove permissions for users and groups on vCenter Server inventory objects

As described previously, a permission is a match between an object in the vCenter object hierarchy, a user (or a group), and a role.

With vSphere Web Client, you can manage **vCenter permissions** for users or groups by selecting one object from one of the vCenter inventories and then clicking on the **Permissions** tab:

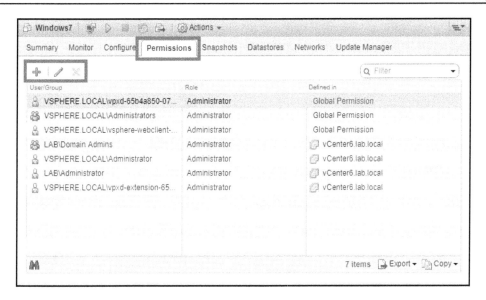

Figure 1.2: vCenter permissions on a specific object

With the selected toolbar, you can add, edit, or remove selected permissions.

For **Global Permissions**, the toolbar remains the same, but you must select the **Global Permissions** menu that is located at **Home** | **Administration** | **Access Control**:

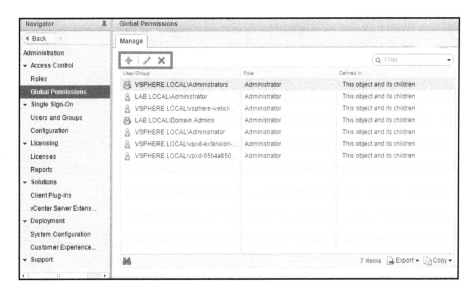

Figure 1.3: Global permissions

You will need an SSO admin privilege to access this page. For more information about SSO, refer to *Objective 1.3*.

Remember that global permissions can span more vCenter servers in the same SSO domain.

When you add or modify a permission, you need to select one or more users (or groups), a specific role, and whether the permission will be propagated in the objects hierarchy (refer to the next section for more information):

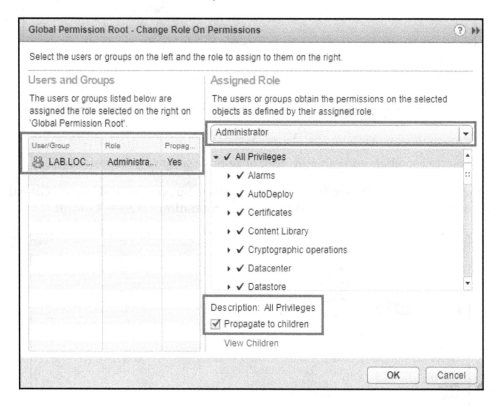

Figure 1.4: Modifying global permissions

In order to assign users or groups sets of privileges, you will need the vCenter `Modify.permissions` privilege.

For more information, refer to the vSphere 6.5 Security Guide (`https://docs.vmware.com/`
`en/VMware-vSphere/6.5/com.vmware.vsphere.security.doc/GUID-3B78EEB3-23E2-4CEB-`
`9FBD-E432B606011A.html`).

Determine how permissions are applied and inherited in vCenter Server

If you assign a permission to an object, it can be propagated down the objects hierarchy.
The propagation is enabled by default, but you can disable propagation for each permission
by checking the **Propagate to children** checkbox, as follows:

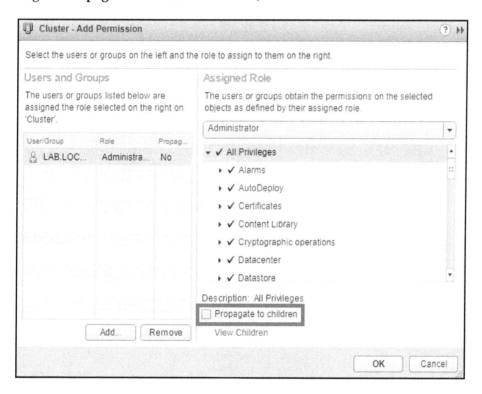

Figure 1.5: Disabling permissions propagation

VMware vCenter objects are hierarchical. This means that permissions (with the **Propagate to children** option) will be inherited (all child objects inherit from their parent objects). The following diagram, from the vSphere Security Guide, shows the entire objects hierarchy:

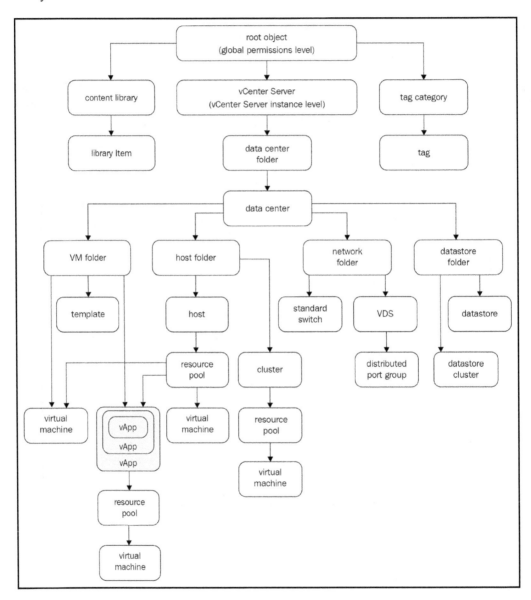

Figure 1.6: vCenter objects hierarchy

Also, the global permissions can be propagated, or not propagated, and the different inventories, which happens with the vCenter permissions in the objects hierarchy.

 Note that propagation is not necessarily enforced. The resultant permission is always more specific in the hierarchy. A permission defined at the child object level always overrides a permission propagated from parent objects.

Note that some objects can exist in different inventories (such as **VMs** in **Hosts and Cluster**, **VMs,** and **Templates** inventories). This means that different permissions can be applied in different views.

 What are the differences between global permissions and vCenter permissions applied at the vCenter object level, if you are using propagation in both cases? The vCenter object exists in all four of the inventories, so the vCenter permissions will only be propagated on specific objects of the selected inventory. With global permissions, the propagation is on all objects!

For more information, refer to the vSphere 6.5 Security Guide (`https://docs.vmware.com/ en/VMware-vSphere/6.5/com.vmware.vsphere.security.doc/GUID-03B36057-B38C-479C- BD78-341CD83A0584.html`).

Create/clone/edit vCenter Server Roles

In VMware vCenter, there are different types of roles, as follows:

- **Default roles**: These are predefined on vCenter Server, and cannot be modified or deleted.
- **Sample roles**: These are also predefined, and are used to manage certain types of tasks. They can be cloned, modified, or removed.
- **Custom roles**: These can be defined by the administrators, and are created from scratch or cloned from existing roles.

The following table summarizes the predefined roles:

Type	Role
System role	• Administrator role • No cryptography administrator role • No access role • Read-only role

Sample role	• VM power user role • VM user role • Resource pool administrator role • VMware consolidated backup user role • Data store consumer role • Tagging admin role • Network administrator role • Content library administrator role

Table 1.2: vCenter predefined roles

Usually, role names are quite descriptive about what kinds of tasks will be permitted, but you can edit them to see the complete list of privileges.

You can manage the vCenter roles using the vSphere Web Client by selecting the **Roles** menu and navigating to **Home** | **Administration** | **Access Control**:

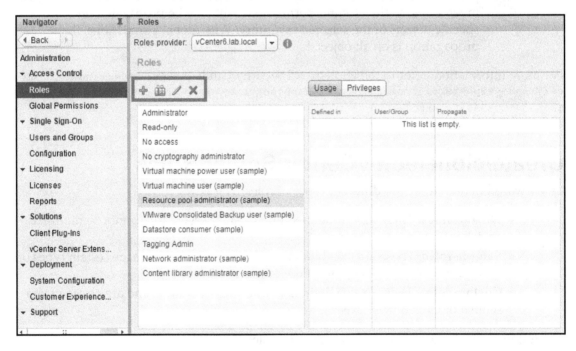

Figure 1.7: Managing vCenter roles

The selected toolbar will allow you to create, clone, modify, or delete a role.

To create a new role from scratch, just click on the Create role action icon, type a name for the new role, and then select the right privileges for the role.

To clone an existing role into a new role, just select the desired source role and click on the Clone role action icon, then type a name for the new role. At that point, you can modify it with the Edit action icon.

> Instead of creating a new role from scratch, in order to avoid potential permissions mistakes, VMware suggests cloning an existing role.

For more information, you can refer to the vSphere 6.5 Security Guide (`https://docs.vmware.com/en/VMware-vSphere/6.5/com.vmware.vsphere.security.doc/GUID-18071E9A-EED1-4968-8D51-E0B4F526FDA3.html`).

Configure VMware Identity Sources

When a user logs in to a vSphere environment, the vCenter **SSO** will validate the user's credentials through one of the configured **identity sources**.

If the user also specifies the domain name (using the `domain\user` or `user@domain` format), the authentication will match the specific identity source.

> For more information on the SSO components, you can refer to *Objective 1.3*.

Identity sources are some kind of centralized user and group system, usually some type of authentication domains, and vSphere supports the following:

- **SSO domain**: This is a default identity source, created with the configuration of the PSC.
- **AD (native)**: When the SSO is joined to an AD domain, it is possible to use the domain or the forest as an authentication source.
- **LDAP (AD)**: The users are defined on an AD domain, but you don't have to join the SSO to the AD domain.
- **LDAP (OpenLDAP)**: The users are defined on an OpenSource LDAP server.
- **Local OS**: The users are defined in the SAM file (for Windows-based SSO) or the `/etc/passwd` and `/etc/shadow` files (for Linux-based SSO).

Note that the SSO domain is always enabled, and is included in the available identity sources.

You can add new identity sources or remove existing ones, and you can also change the default source.

Note that you must have vCenter SSO administrator privileges in order to manage the identity sources.

From the vSphere Web Client, just select the **Configuration** menu, located at **Home** | **Administration** | **Single Sign-On**. Then, select the **Identity Sources** tab:

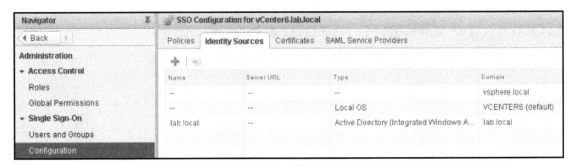

Figure 1.8: SSO identity sources

To configure a new identity source, select **Identity Sources** and click on the plus icon (+). Then, choose the proper identity source type and enter the specific identity source settings.

For example, for AD, you will see a screen like the following:

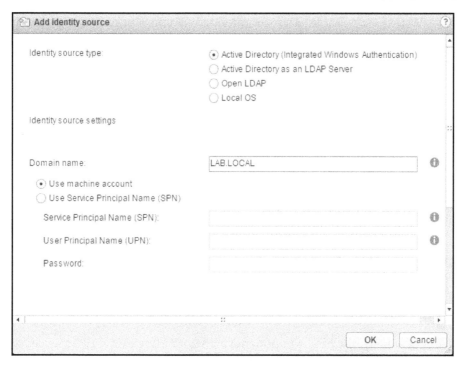

Figure 1.9: Adding an AD domain as a new identity source

 When an identity source is added, all users and groups in the new domain can be authenticated by SSO. However, in vCenter, they will have the **No access** role.

For more information about authentication, see the **Platform Services Controller (PSC)** 6.5 Administration Guide (`https://docs.vmware.com/en/VMware-vSphere/6.5/com.vmware.psc.doc/GUID-B98DF9C2-FE7D-483F-9521-C17C138B59D8.html`).

Apply a role to a user/group and to an object or group of objects

Once a role has been defined, you can use it to assign specific authorizations to authenticated users or groups.

Whenever possible, it's recommended to assign permissions to groups instead of users, for better and more flexible permissions management.

The entire procedure was described previously, in the *Adding/modifying/removing permissions for users and groups in vCenter Server inventory objects* section.

 You will need the `Permissions.Modify` privilege for the specific objects to modify the permissions and roles.

Note that some objects may reference other objects, such as VMs that include data store objects (for the virtual disk locations) and network objects (for the connected portgroups). In those cases, you will need to apply for the right roles in all of the different inventories.

Change permission validation settings

As described previously, the SSO component can have different identity sources. When a directory service (such as AD or LDAP) is used, the SSO regularly validates users and groups on the directory domain. This validation occurs at regular intervals, specified in the vCenter Server settings.

You can view or change these settings with the vSphere Web Client by selecting your vCenter Server in the vSphere object navigator and then selecting the **Configure** tab and clicking on **General** under **Settings**.

Select the **User directory** area, and view or change the values as needed:

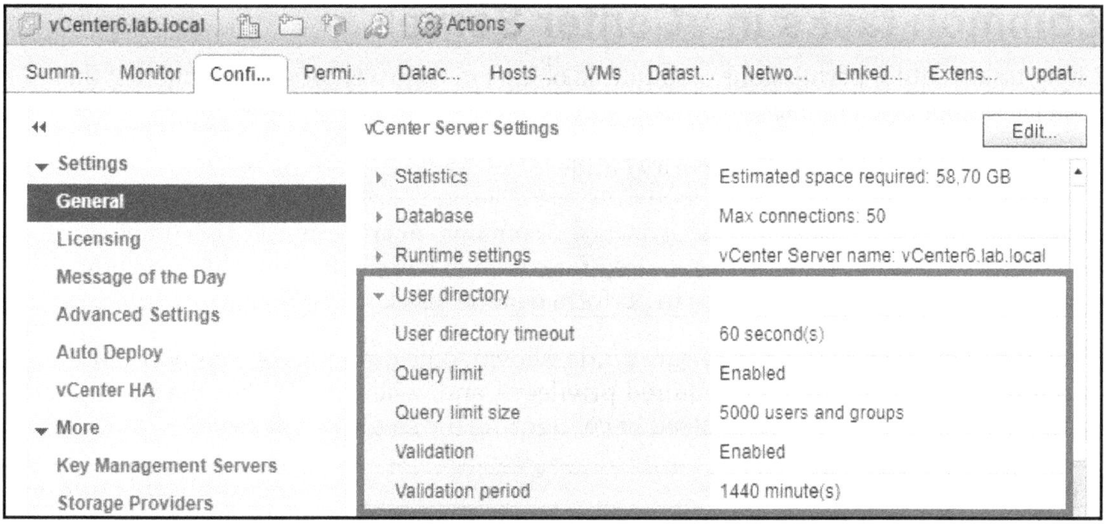

Figure 1.10: vCenter Server settings—User directory

There are different options and settings, as follows:

- **User directory timeout**: This is the maximum amount of time, in seconds, that SSO allows a search to run on the selected domain source. For large domains, this can be increased.
- **Query limit**: This helps you to define whether there must be a maximum number of users and groups that vCenter can display.
- **Query limit size**: This is the maximum number of users and groups that vCenter displays in the **Select Users or Groups** dialog box. If you enter **0** (zero) or remove the previous option, all users and groups will appear.
- **Validation**: This is used to define whether validation is enabled or disabled.
- **Validation period**: This is how often, in minutes, validation is performed.

For more information, refer to the vCenter Server and Host Management Guide (`https://docs.vmware.com/en/VMware-vSphere/6.5/com.vmware.vsphere.vcenterhost.doc/GUID-007C02A8-C853-4FBC-B0F0-933F19768DD4.html`).

Determine the appropriate set of privileges for common tasks in vCenter Server

Many tasks require permissions on multiple objects in the inventory. Without all of them, the task cannot be completed successfully.

The vSphere 6.5 Security Guide (https://docs.vmware.com/en/VMware-vSphere/6.5/com.vmware.vsphere.security.doc/GUID-4D0F8E63-2961-4B71-B365-BBFA24673FDB.html) contains several examples of combined sets of permissions required for common tasks, with some hints on how to manage permissions to perform generic tasks.

The following table, from the VMware guide, shows some examples of common VM administration tasks with their required privileges, and, where applicable, the appropriate sample roles that can be used (instead of configuring the single privileges):

Task	Required privileges	Applicable role
Create a VM	On the destination folder or data center: • **Virtual machine	Inventory	Create new** • **Virtual machine	Configuration	Add new disk** (if creating a new virtual disk) • **Virtual machine	Configuration	Add existing disk** (if using an existing virtual disk) • **Virtual machine	Configuration	Raw device** (if using an RDM or SCSI pass-through device)	Administrator
	On the destination host, cluster, or resource pool, navigate to **Resource	Assign virtual machine to resource pool**	Resource pool administrator or administrator
	On the destination data store or the folder that contains the data store, navigate to **Datastore	Allocate space**	Data store consumer or administrator
	On the network that the VM will be assigned to, navigate to **Network	Assign network**	Network consumer or administrator
Power on a VM	On the data center in which the VM is deployed, navigate to **Virtual machine	Interaction	Power On**	VM power user or administrator
	On the VM or the folder of VMs, navigate to **Virtual machine	Interaction	Power On**	

Task	Required privileges	Applicable role
Deploy a VM from a template	On the destination folder or data center, navigate to **Virtual machine** | **Inventory** | **Create from existing** or **Virtual machine** | **Configuration** | **Add new disk**	Administrator
	On a template or folder of templates, navigate to **Virtual machine** | **Provisioning** | **Deploy template**	
	On the destination host, cluster, or resource pool, navigate to **Resource** | **Assign virtual machine to resource pool**	
	On the destination data store or folder of data stores, navigate to **Datastore** | **Allocate space**	Data store consumer or administrator
	On the network that the VM will be assigned to, navigate to **Network** | **Assign network**	Network consumer or administrator
Take a VM snapshot	On the VM or a folder of virtual machines, navigate to **Virtual machine** | **Snapshot management** | **Create snapshot**	VM power user or administrator
Install a guest operating system on a VM	On the VM or folder of VMs, navigate to: • **Virtual machine** | **Interaction** | **Answer question** • **Virtual machine** | **Interaction** | **Console interaction** • **Virtual machine** | **Interaction** | **Device connection** • **Virtual machine** | **Interaction** | **Power Off** • **Virtual machine** | **Interaction** | **Power On** • **Virtual machine** | **Interaction** | **Reset** • **Virtual machine** | **Interaction** | **Configure CD media** (if installing from a CD) or **Configure floppy media** (if installing from a floppy disk) • **Virtual machine** | **Interaction** | **VMware Tools install**	VM power user or administrator
	On a data store that contains the installation media ISO image, navigate to **Datastore** | **Browse datastore** (if installing from an ISO image on a data store) On the data store to which you upload the installation media ISO image, navigate to **Datastore** | **Browse datastore** or **Datastore** | **Low level file operations**	
Migrate a VM with vMotion	On the VM or folder of VMs, navigate to: • **Resource** | **Migrate powered on virtual machine** • **Resource** | **Assign Virtual Machine to Resource Pool** (if the destination is a different resource pool from the source)	Resource pool administrator or administrator
	On the destination host, cluster, or resource pool (if they are different from the source), navigate to: • **Resource** | **Assign virtual machine to resource pool**	

Task	Required privileges	Applicable role
Cold migrate (relocate) a VM	On the VM or folder of VMs, navigate to: • **Resource | Migrate powered off virtual machine** • **Resource | Assign virtual machine to resource pool** (if the destination is a different resource pool from the source)	Resource pool administrator or administrator
	On the destination host, cluster, or resource pool (if different from the source), navigate to: • **Resource | Assign virtual machine to resource pool**	
	On the destination data store (if it is different from the source), navigate to **Datastore | Allocate space**	Data store consumer or administrator
Migrate a VM with Storage vMotion	On the VM or folder of VMs, navigate to **Resource | Migrate powered on virtual machine**	Resource pool administrator or administrator
	On the destination data store, navigate to **Datastore | Allocate space**	Data store consumer or administrator

Table 1.3: Required privileges for common tasks

These are just examples, but in most cases, you will need to build your own custom role (or set of roles).

Other software or solutions based on vSphere may specify the right privileges that are needed in order to build custom roles with minimum privileges.

Compare and contrast default system/sample roles

As described in the *Creating/cloning/editing vCenter Server roles* section, there are two different types of predefined roles:

- **System roles (cannot be modified or deleted)**:
  - **Administrator role**: With this role, you can correspond to all privileges. By default, users with this role are the SSO administrator, the vCenter `root` (or administrator) user, and ESXi `vpxuser` (used by the vCenter agent).

- **No cryptography administrator role**: This role has the same privileges as the administrator role, except for cryptographic operations privileges. This means that users cannot encrypt or decrypt VMs, or access encrypted data.
- **Read-only role**: With this role, it's possible to view the details of the object, but it's not possible to change anything.
- **No access role**: With this role, it's not possible to view or change the object in any way. By default, new users and groups are assigned to this role.

- **Sample roles (can be cloned, modified, or removed)**:
    - **VM administrator**: This role allows for complete and total control of a VM, including some related host operations.
    - **VM power user**: This role grants rights only to a VM, including changing the settings or creating snapshots.
    - **VM user**: This role grants access rights exclusively to VMs, with limited functions, such as powering on, powering off, or resetting the VM, or running media from the virtual discs.
    - **Resource pool administrator**: This role is permitted to create resource pools and assign those pools to VMs.
    - **Data center administrator**: This role permits adding new data center objects.
    - **VMware consolidated backup user**: This role is required for the old VCB framework, but is a good starting point for other backup products.
    - **Data store consumer**: This role allows using space on a data store.
    - **Network consumer**: This role allows assigning a network to a VM or a host.

For more details, see *Table 1.2* or the vSphere 6.5 Security Guide (`https://docs.vmware.com/en/VMware-vSphere/6.5/com.vmware.vsphere.security.doc/GUID-18071E9A-EED1-4968-8D51-E0B4F526FDA3.html`).

Determine the correct permissions needed to integrate vCenter Server with other VMware products

Sample roles can match specific integration requests. Also, *Table 1.3*, from the vSphere 6.5 Security Guide, showed some examples of common tasks with their required privileges, and, where applicable, the appropriate sample roles that can be used.

However, for other VMware products (and third-party products), you may need a specific set of permissions, and this list is usually provided by the related product documentation.

Also, remember that global permissions can span different VMware products. For example, for vCenter Orchestrator, you can use global permissions.

Objective 1.2 – Secure ESXi and vCenter Server 2

To increase the security of ESXi, vCenter, and other vSphere components, you will need to use different approaches, as follows:

- **Protecting the physical layer**: For example, for the networking part, use dedicated VLAN for different traffic.
- **Securing network communications**: This at least applies to infrastructural components. By default, management traffic is already encrypted. Note that one new feature of vSphere 6.5 is the ability to also encrypt vMotion traffic.
- **Applying the minimum privileges**: Limit all the services, permissions, access to minimize the attack surface.

 Objective 1.2 for VCP65-DCV and VCP6-DCV is quite different, due to the security and hardening changes from vSphere 6.0 to vSphere 6.5.

Hardening is a process that enhances the security of a system, a service, or an entire infrastructure, by reducing the attack surface and minimizing the possible vulnerabilities and related risks.

VMware has built in a set of Security Hardening Guides (https://www.vmware.com/security/hardening-guides.html), including one related to the vSphere environment. The vSphere 6.5 Security Configuration Guide is a spreadsheet file with several possible hardening actions and guidelines, each classified with a risk profile. There are also some example scripts, for enabling security automation.

> The *vSphere 6.5 Security Configuration Guide* isn't a compliance tool; it can be used to reach compliance, but it's not automatically enforced. It's a set of guidelines that attempts to explain security risks, but there are other solutions for mitigating them.

The Security Guide contains in-depth information on how to secure ESXi hosts (https://docs.vmware.com/en/VMware-vSphere/6.5/com.vmware.vsphere.security.doc/GUID-A706C6C6-DF07-455B-99B9-5B8F8580F1EB.html) and vCenter components (https://docs.vmware.com/en/VMware-vSphere/6.5/com.vmware.vsphere.security.doc/GUID-8C5F5839-37EC-409E-8C46-C8AD146CBC73.html):
https://docs.vmware.com/en/VMware-vSphere/6.5/vsphere-esxi-vcenter-server-652-security-guide.pdf

Configure encrypted vMotion

This is a new option in vSphere 6.5 (but only for the Enterprise Plus edition), in order to secure the vMotion network traffic.

The vMotion encryption feature isn't simply an encrypting of the entire network channel for the vMotion traffic; it's a per-VM setting. There aren't certificates to manage or import on the infrastructural side.

This will be discussed later, in *Objective 1.4*, because it's related to the VM options.

On the infrastructural side, you will need to configure the proper key servers (as described in *Objective 1.3*).

Describe ESXi Secure Boot

Unified Extensible Firmware Interface (**UEFI**) is a replacement for the traditional BIOS firmware, and is supported for VM from virtual hardware 7.

Secure boot is part of the UEFI firmware standard, where the UEFI firmware validates the digital signature of the operating system and its bootloader, to ensure that the bootstrap sequence starts only a properly signed system, including drivers and applications.

Starting with vSphere ESXi 6.5, it's possible to have secure boot for both ESXi and VMs.

For ESXi, the secure boot can verify each VIB by using its digital sign. At boot time, the already validated ESXi VMkernel will validate each VIB against the firmware-based certificate:

Figure 1.11: ESXi secure boot

 For more information on how to enable this feature, and also some possible issues (during the upgrade process, for example), see `https://blogs.vmware.com/vsphere/2017/05/secure-boot-esxi-6-5-hypervisor-assurance.html`.

For the secure boot options for VMs, see *Objective 1.4*.

Harden ESXi hosts

To increase the protection of ESXi hosts against possible attacks and unauthorized access, consider the following options:

- **Limit user privileges and access**: One aspect is using the RBAC model (described in *Objective 1.1*) to limit user privileges. But, you also have to use a centralized authentication, limit the authorized users, restrict access to ESXi management adapter, and enforce security policies (such as password expiration and password complexity).

- **Limit shell access**: ESXi shell and ESXi SSH access have several privileged accesses, and permit executing several commands from the CLI. For this reason, this type of access must be closed or limited. Lockdown mode (as described later) can be effective for limiting that type of access.

- **Limit services**: By default, ESXi only runs essential services, and any services that are not needed are stopped. Note that third-party services, such as some hardware vendor agents, should be limited, or at least validated.

- **Limit network connections**: ESXi has a built-in firewall (starting from ESXi 5.0), and, by default, it is closed on most ports. When you enable a service, it also opens the right ports. The personal firewall does not protect from DoS attacks, so keep your ESXi VMkernel interfaces on protected networks, and continue to use perimeter firewalls.

- **Use secure connections**: By default, most of the communications are secured by the SSL layer, and all weak ciphers are disabled (this can vary in the different builds of vSphere). Also, VMware vSphere 6.0 introduced a certification authority (described in *Objective 1.3*) to help with certification management.

- **Update your environment**: **VMware Update Manager** (**VUM**) can simplify host patching. With the VCSA, the vCenter management can also be simplified (using VAMI).

- **Check the VMware Security Advisories** (https://www.vmware.com/security/advisories.html): This site has a list of possible security vulnerabilities for VMware products, and related remediation or mitigation.

Also, in order to mitigate security risks in ESXi, there are some built-in security settings, as follows:

- **Shell access**: ESXi Shell and SSH are disabled, by default. It is usually safe to keep both ESXi Shell and SSH access disabled, preventing direct access to the ESXi CLI. Note that in this case, you can still use `esxcli` remotely, as well as other remote CLI tools!
- **Firewall**: Usually, there are a few ports open by default, and ports are automatically open on the firewall if there are some services that need specific ports. Although you can manually open ports or build custom ESXi firewall rules, try to keep the management automatic.
- **Services**: Following the minimum privilege approach, ESXi only runs required services, and new services are automatically started if a specific feature requires them.
- **Secure protocols**: By default, weak ciphers are disabled, and communications from clients are secured by SSL. Starting with vSphere 6.5, the TLS protocol versions 1.0, 1.1, and 1.2 are enabled, by default. Also, see VMware KB 2147469 (`https://kb.vmware.com/s/article/2147469`)—Managing TLS protocol configuration for vSphere 6.5.
- **Web server**: A custom Tomcat web service is used to provide access from the web client. The service has been hardened to improve its security.
- **Bugs**: VMware usually releases security patches, in case of possible security issues affecting ESXi (or other components). With VUM, you can easily apply those patches.
- **Secure Boot**: VMware ESXi 6.5 supports secure booting, as described previously.

Enable/configure/disable services in the ESXi firewall

As stated previously, only the required ports are open on the ESXi firewall. But, using the vSphere Web Client, it's possible to manage incoming and outgoing firewall rules. Usually, firewall rules are related to specific ESXi services.

It's possible to manage service settings and/or firewall rules in the **Security Profile** menu, under the **Configure** tab of each host:

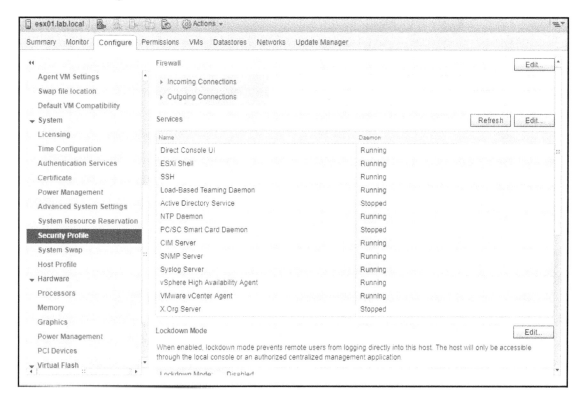

Figure 1.12 ESXi security profile

The first part (**Firewall**) shows all active incoming and outgoing rules, with their corresponding firewall ports.

Firewall rules can be modified by clicking on the **Edit** button in the **Firewall** section:

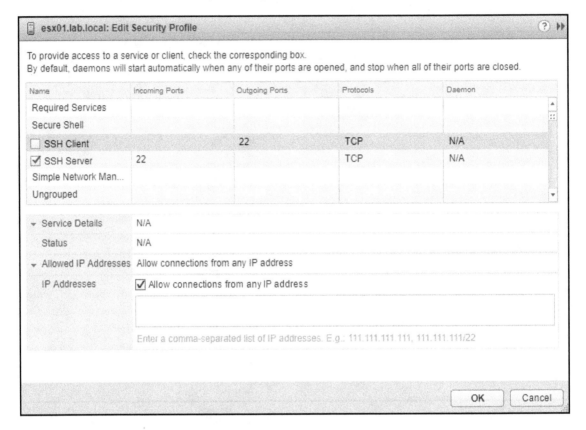

Name	Incoming Ports	Outgoing Ports	Protocols	Daemon
Required Services				
Secure Shell				
☐ SSH Client		22	TCP	N/A
☑ SSH Server	22		TCP	N/A
Simple Network Man...				
Ungrouped				

Figure 1.13 Editing the security profile—firewall rules

You can enable or disable a specific firewall rule, and you can also specify which logical network address is authorized to use the selected service.

> Until vSphere 6.0, it was also possible to build custom firewall rules, but not from the UI. For more information, see KB 2008226 (`https://kb.vmware.com/s/article/2008226`)—**Creating custom firewall rules in VMware ESXi 5.x.**

The second part (**Services**) shows all of the configured services, and their statuses. It's possible to manage them with the **Edit** button, in the **Services** section:

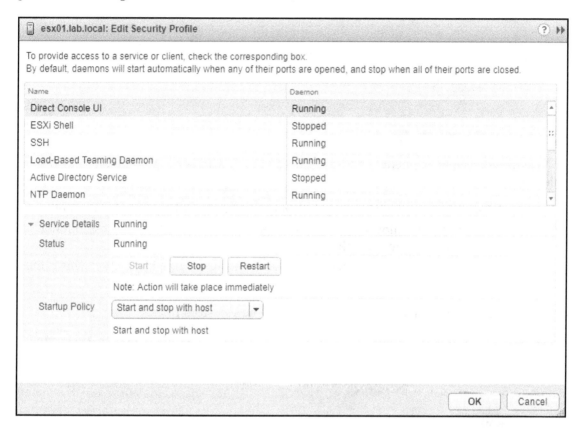

Figure 1.14: Editing security profile—services

In the **Service Details** section, you can see the status, and also perform some tasks:

- **Manage the services status**: Use the **Start**, **Stop**, or **Restart** buttons
- **Define how services are started**: With the **Startup Policy,** you can choose how each service must be started, with one of the following three startup policies:
  - **Start and stop with host**
  - **Start and stop manually**
  - **Start and stop with port usage**

Starting a service automatically opens the network ports that are required by the service.

For more information, see the vSphere 6.5 Security Guide (`https://docs.vmware.com/en/ VMware-vSphere/6.5/com.vmware.vsphere.security.doc/GUID-9C8A0CD0-1664-4F21- B75A-541C03E37233.html`).

Change ESXi default account access

ESXi permissions management has a local RBAC model, with some predefined local system roles, such as the following:

- **Administrator role**: With all privileges, like the administrator role in vCenter.
- **Read-only role**: Allows for viewing objects associated with ESXi host, but not making any changes, like the read-only role in vCenter.
- **No access role**: No privileges at all, like the no access role in vCenter. This is the default role for new users.

As with vCenter permissions, it's possible to define new custom roles.

ESXi roles and local users can be managed through the **Host** UI interface; both are located in the **Security & users** tab, in the **Host | Manage** menu:

Figure 1.15: ESXi user and role management

You can find local user management in the **Users** menu, and local role management in the **Roles** menu.

Local permissions can be managed via the **Host | Action** button, in the **Permissions** menu:

Figure 1.16: ESXi permissions

 If a user exists in both ESXi host and SSO (or one of its identity sources), there can be two different users with the same login on the different authentication sources. The full login name must be `login@domain` to avoid confusions.

On each ESXi, there are some default local users:

- **Root user**: This is a built-in user with the administrator role. You can remove or change the role of the root user, but be sure to first add another user with the administrator role. Note that this is the only built-in user that is reported in the ESXi user management interface, but there are also other users.

- **vpxuser user**: This user is used by vCenter to manage ESXi hosts, after they have been connected. Note that this user also has an administrative role. This user must be managed by the vCenter Server; don't change it in any way (such as changing its password or permissions).
- **dcui user**: The primary purpose of this user is to configure hosts for lockdown mode, from the **Direct Console User Interface (DCUI)**.

> For audit purposes, be sure to assign named accounts to all accounts with the administrator role.

For more information, see the vSphere 6.5 Security Guide (`https://docs.vmware.com/en/ VMware-vSphere/6.5/com.vmware.vsphere.security.doc/GUID-2215AADC-D4CD-49DD- AF92-65BED243D851.html`).

The next section will describe how to add an ESXi to an AD domain, in order to use external users and groups.

> Also, remember that if your ESXi host is managed by a vCenter Server, it might be better to manage authentication and authorization tasks through the vCenter permissions.

Add an ESXi Host to a directory service

To use centralized users (and groups) instead of local accounts, it's possible to join an ESXi to an AD domain. When the host is added to AD, the **ESX Admins** domain group has the administrator role on the ESXi host.

It's possible to join an ESXi host to an AD domain if it is a standalone host, or if it's managed by a vCenter Server. But, if your ESXi is already managed by a vCenter Server, authentication and authorization with the vCenter permissions might be enough; there's no need to also use ESXi roles.

If ESXi is managed by vCenter, you can use the vSphere Web Client to join ESXi to an AD domain. Use the **Join Domain** button in the **Authentication Services** menu, under the **Configure** tab of a specific host, as in the following screenshot:

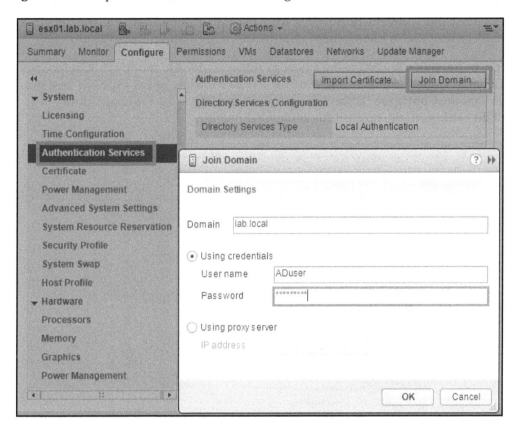

Figure 1.17: Joining an ESXi to an AD domain

Enter the full AD domain name (in a DNS format), and the credentials of an AD user with enough permissions to join a computer to the domain.

To add a standalone ESXi to an AD domain, you will need the **Host** UI. In this case, just select the **Host** | **Manage** menu, go to the **Security & users** tab, and select **Authentication**.

For more information, see the vSphere 6.5 Security Guide (`https://docs.vmware.com/en/VMware-vSphere/6.5/com.vmware.vsphere.security.doc/GUID-4FD32125-4955-439D-B39F-C654CCB207DC.html`).

Apply permissions to ESXi Hosts using Host Profiles

Host profiles are only available in the Enterprise Plus edition, and are used to provide a standard configuration for multiple ESXi hosts. You can create a new host profile from a reference host and apply the host profile to all hosts that share similar characteristics with the reference host (like a homogeneous hardware configuration).

To apply permissions to ESXi using a host profile, you need to modify it with the vSphere Web Client in **Home | Policies and Profiles | Host Profiles**. Select a specific host profile and click on the **Configure** tab, and then click on the **Edit Host Profile...** button, or select **Edit settings** in the host profile contextual menu:

Figure 1.18 Editing a host profile

The security setting and the permissions rules are in the **Security and Services** menu.

Note that, in the same menu, you can also configure ESXi firewall rules and domain service integration, as discussed previously.

For more information, see the vSphere 6.5 Security Guide (`https://docs.vmware.com/en/` `VMware-vSphere/6.5/com.vmware.vsphere.security.doc/GUID-FD142F1A-FE26-473E-` `BF09-AC2F84B15318.html`).

 Objective 8.2 will provide more information on how to create, manage, and apply host profiles.

Enable Lockdown Mode

To harden ESXi connected to a vCenter Server, one option is to use **lockdown mode**, which disables a direct connection to ESXi host. The host will only be accessible through the vCenter Server, or, depending on the lockdown mode, through the DCUI.

It's possible to modify lockdown mode in the host settings or from the DCUI (the usual method).

In vSphere 6.x, lockdown mode has different levels of protection; the following are the different configuration options available:

- **Disabled**: Lockdown mode is disabled.
- **Normal**: Lockdown mode is enabled, DCUI is not blocked, but the Host UI, ESXi shell, or ESXi SSH is disabled.
- **Strict**: Lockdown mode is enabled, and all local services are disabled (including the DCUI that is stopped). ESXi is only accessible through the vCenter Server.

You can configure ESXi lockdown mode from the vSphere Web Client, when you add a new host. It's also possible to change the setting later; in that case, select the **Security Profile** menu in the **Configure** tab of the desired ESXi.

Find the **Lockdown Mode** area (after **Services**), and click on the **Edit...** button, as follows:

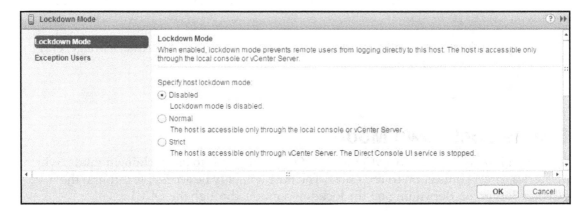

Figure 1.19: Configuring lockdown mode

In vSphere 6.x, there is a new feature for lockdown mode: the **Exception Users** list. Those users (or solutions) will be excluded from lockdown mode (if Normal mode is used). Exception users cannot be managed from the DCUI.

From the DCUI, press *F2* and log in, then select **Configure Lockdown Mode** and press *Enter*:

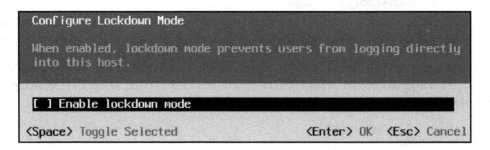

Figure 1.20: Configuring lockdown mode from the DCUI

For more information, see the vSphere 6.5 Security Guide (`https://docs.vmware.com/en/VMware-vSphere/6.5/com.vmware.vsphere.security.doc/GUID-88B24613-E8F9-40D2-B838-225F5FF480FF.html`).

Control access to hosts (DCUI/Shell/SSH/MOB)

Lockdown mode, as described previously, can be used to limit and control access to ESXi by using DCUI (in strict mode), or ESXi Shell and ESXi SSH.

There are also other ways to limit access to an ESXi host. For example, there is the **Managed Object Browser** (**MOB**) interface, which provides a view of the VMkernel objects. Usually, it's recommended to disable it in production systems.

Starting with vSphere 6.0, the MOB interface is disabled by default. However, for some specific cases, you may need to enable it again.

You can enable and disable the MOB interface by using the vSphere Web Client. Select the desired host, choose the **Configure** tab, and go to the **Advanced System Settings** menu (in the **System** section).

Check the value of `Config.HostAgent.plugins.solo.enableMob`, and change it as needed.

Harden vCenter Server

Depending on your type of vCenter deployment, you may have internal or external PSC (see *Objective 1.3*), and you may also have Windows-based servers or Linux-based virtual appliances.

 Note that, in the new major release of vSphere, there will only be the virtual appliance (or vCenter Virtual Appliance (VCSA)) option, and the Windows-based installation will no longer be available.

There are some generic security best practices that are valid for both versions, as follows:

- Use named accounts, and minimize permissions
- Monitor privileges of vCenter Server administrator users
- Limit vCenter Server network connectivity
- Verify certificates
- Keep the vCenter OS and services updated

By using the VSCA, from VMware for vSphere 6.5 and later, you can use the same VM hardening suggestions (see *Objective 1.4*). But note that the VCSA is already based on a hardened operating system (in vSphere 6.5, the VCSA is based on the VMware PhotonOS platform).

By default, on VCSA, the shell access is disabled. A remote shell with SSH can be enabled during the deployment, but note that by default this shell has a limited set of commands (but it's also easy to enable the full shell).

The PSC security best practices are quite simple:

- **Check password expirations**: Remember that the default SSO password lifetime is 90 days.
- **Use NTP for time sync**: All systems must use the same time source. Time synchronization is essential for authentication, and also for certificate validity.

For more information, see the vSphere 6.5 Security Guide (`https://docs.vmware.com/en/VMware-vSphere/6.5/com.vmware.vsphere.security.doc/GUID-8C5F5839-37EC-409E-8C46-C8AD146CBC73.html`).

Control datastore browser access

Data store browsing is provided by different roles, but it is mainly provided by the `Datastore.Browse` privilege. It can be dangerous, because users with this privilege can view, delete, copy, upload, or download files directly from data stores.

Be sure to assign this privilege only to users or groups that really need it, in order to follow the minimum privilege principle.

VM file encryption (see *Objective 1.4*) can help to minimize some risks in data confidentiality if a user can browse the data store.

Create/Manage vCenter Server Security Certificates

Network communications between vSphere components are usually encrypted using TLS/SSL protocols. At a minimum, all management traffic is secured by default.

However, in vSphere 5.5 and earlier, the TLS/SSL communications were only authenticated with a username, password, and basic certification verification (thumbprint). Starting with vSphere 6.0, vCenter uses certificates for authentication, to increase the security of communications.

VMware vSphere 6.x supports the following certificate modes:

- **VMware Certificate Authority** (default): The PSC acts as a top-level CA (or as an intermediate CA) and provisions certificates to ESXi hosts and other endpoints that require them.
- **Custom Certificate Authority**: In this case, custom certificates signed by third-party or enterprise CAs are used. Unless you change the certificate mode to Custom Certificate Authority, the PSC might replace custom certificates.
- **Thumbprint Mode**: Certificates are checked for the correct format, but without verifying the validity of the certificate. This mode was used until vSphere 5.5, but it is still available as a compatible option in vSphere 6.x.

For more information about the VMware Certification Authority, see *Objective 1.3*.

Control MOB access

MOB access was already discussed in the section on **hardening ESXi hosts**. The **Managed Object Browser** (**MOB**) is a web-based server application that can permit access to some data and represent a security risk.

Remember that, starting with vSphere 6.0, the MOB is disabled by default.

Change vCenter default account access

User management was already discussed in *Objective 1.1*.

The default role for new users or new identity sources is **No access**. However, there are also the local users (of the vCenter OS), which can have some privileges and, for example in previous vCenter Server Windows based system local administrator was also added as a vCenter Administrator.

Starting with vSphere 6.0, the local administrator of the PSC (user root for VCSA, or administrator for Windows-based) does not have the full administrative vCenter permissions.

For the VCSA, the root user (the password of which is defined during the installation) can, of course, access the VAMI interface.

Restrict administrative privileges

Due to the minimum privilege principle, not all administrative users must have the administrator role. A good practice is to create a custom role with an appropriate set of privileges, and assign it to other administrators.

For more information and an example, see *Objective 1.1*.

Understand the implications of securing a vSphere environment

During the hardening process, you have to find the right balance between security and manageability. Some changes related to increasing the security of the vSphere environment can have an impact on its manageability (for example, see the *Enabling lockdown mode* section).

Objective 1.3 – Configure and Enable SSO and Identity Sources

The SSO, introduced in vSphere 5.1, is the authentication broker of a vSphere environment.

Using a secure token mechanism, different vSphere components can communicate with each other. Both the internal components and the vSphere users are authenticated with SSO, with its different identify sources (different authentication domains, as described in *Objective 1.1*).

Objective 1.3 for VCP65-DCV and VCP6-DCV is similar, because there weren't major changes in SSO authentication from vSphere 6.0 to vSphere 6.5.

For more information about authentication, see the PSC 6.5 Administration Guide (`https:/ /docs.vmware.com/en/VMware-vSphere/6.5/com.vmware.psc.doc/GUID-B98DF9C2-FE7D- 483F-9521-C17C138B59D8.html`).

Describe PSC architecture and components

From vSphere 6.0, the vCenter components are grouped into two separated roles, as follows:

- **The vCenter Server**: Also called the management node, used to provide specific vCenter-related services.
- **The Platform Services Controller**: Also called the infrastructure controller, used to provide common infrastructure services for different VMware products:

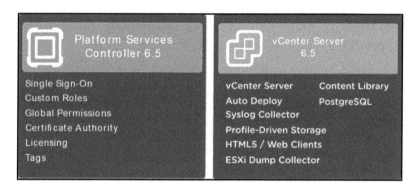

Figure 1.21: PSC and vCenter

Each role groups different types of services and functions, according to the following table:

Platform Service Controller	vCenter Server
Single Sign-On Custom roles Global permissions Certificate Authority VMware Certificate Service VMware Identity Management Service VMware Directory Service VMware License Service Tags VMware Appliance Management Service (VAMI), on VCSA only	vCenter Server Inventory Service Profile-Driven Storage HTML5 / vSphere Web Clients Server Auto Deploy Content Library Syslog Collector ESXi Dump Collector Optional: VMware Update Manager Optional: Embedded DB (PostgreSQL)

Table 1.4: PSC and vCenter node services and functions

Both components can be based on a Windows Server OS (installable version), or in a virtual appliance form (VCSA). For version 6.5, mixed environments are supported (in the future, it is likely that only the VCSA will be supported).

 Note that the PSC uses limited resources, as compared to the management nodes (just 2 vCPU and 4 GB of RAM).

The PSC is an important component in the design, providing services not only for vCenter Server and vSphere, but for the VMware products in general. SSO, for example, can be shared with other VMware products (for example, vRealize Orchestrator and vRealize Automation), to provide a centralized user authentication.

The main core services provided by the PSC discussed in this objective are:

- **SSO**: Solves the problem of mutual authentication between different components, and also the authentication in an environment with different identity sources (this will be described later). The SSO provides an internal authentication domain; in vSphere 5.5, the default name was `vsphere.local`. With vSphere 6.0 and later, you can choose the name of the SSO domain.
- **Certificate management**: Also called **VMware Certificate Authority** (**VMCA**), it manages digital certificates, and can act as a **Certification Authority** (**CA**).

Depending on your environment and infrastructure design, the vCenter Server and PSC roles can be deployed in two different ways:

- **Embedded**: The same machine has both vCenter Server and PSC. This deployment model supports a good scaling in terms of hosts or VMs, like an external deployment (with a single vCenter), but does not provide enhanced linked mode (unless using vSphere 6.5, Update 2). Note that vCenter High Availability is supported for embedded deployments in vSphere 6.5.
- **External**: The vCenter Server and PSC roles are on different machines. This is the only configuration that supports complex topology.

The following table summarizes the pros and cons of each deployment model:

	Embedded PSC	External PSC
Scalability	2,000 hosts per vCenter 25,000 VMs per vCenter (powered-on)	2,000 hosts per vCenter 25,000 VMs per vCenter (powered-on) More with linked mode

Manageability	Best	More servers to be managed
Upgrade/Patching	Simple	First update all PSCs, and then vCenter
Resiliency	No outages caused by connectivity and name resolution issues between vCenter and PSC	Possible outages caused by connectivity and name resolution issues between vCenter and PSC
Availability	VCSA: vCenter HA Windows: Failover Cluster	For vCenter, same solutions For PSC, load balancer
Multi-vCenter	VMware Cloud for AWS Enhanced linked mode (for VCSA 6.5U2 or later)	Enhanced linked mode
Multi-Site	No	Enhanced linked mode

Table 1.5: Embedded and external PSC

VMware recommends six high-level PSC topologies, as follows:

- vCenter Server with embedded PSC
- vCenter Server with external PSC
- PSC in replicated configuration
- PSC in HA configuration
- vCenter Server deployment across sites
- vCenter Server deployment across sites, with load balancer

For more information, see KB 2147672 (`https://kb.vmware.com/s/article/2147672`)—Supported and deprecated topologies for VMware vSphere 6.5.

Also, note that vCenter Server can have an embedded or external database server. And, if VCSA supports external databases, it is highly recommended to use the embedded one:

	Embedded DB	**External DB**
Scalability	For VCSA: 2,000 hosts or 25,000 VMs (powered-on) For Windows: 20 hosts or 200 VMs	2,000 hosts or 25,000 VMs (powered-on) More with linked mode
Manageability	Best	More servers to be managed
Upgrade/Patching	Simple	More dependencies

Resiliency	No outages caused by connectivity issues between vCenter and DB	Possible outages caused by connectivity issues between vCenter and DB
Availability	VCSA: vCenter HA Windows: Failover Cluster	DB requires a specific solution, such as clustering

Table 1.6: Embedded and external databases

Differentiate available authentication methods with VMware vCenter

As previously stated, SSO is an authentication broker and security token exchange infrastructure.

 In vSphere 5.1 and 5.5, SSO was a specific role, but starting with vSphere 6.0, SSO is a part of the PSC role.

As described in *Objective 1.2*, SSO supports multiple identity sources, including external directory services, such as AD.

Using AD for user authentication simplifies permission management, ensures password complexity, and allows for using the same security policies for AD, to minimize the risk of unauthorized access.

To improve authentication security, **multi-factor authentication (MFA)** is preferable to simple username/password methods. **Two-factor authentication (2FA)** is a type of multi-factor authentication that uses two components.

Starting with vSphere 6.0 Update 2, it is possible to use two-factor authentication, as follows:

- Smart card (UPN-based **Common Access Card (CAC)**)
- RSA SecurID token

Note that vCenter SSO only supports native SecurID, and does not support RADIUS authentication. For more information about authentication, see the PSC 6.5 Administration Guide (`https://docs.vmware.com/en/VMware-vSphere/6.5/com.vmware.psc.doc/GUID-ACFFCBEC-6C1C-4BF9-9971-04AEE9362AFE.html`).

Perform a multi-site PSC installation

Multi-site PSC is only possible with an external PSC deployment. In this configuration, an SSO domain will span multiple sites. You will have one single SSO domain, but with multiple sites, as illustrated in the following diagram:

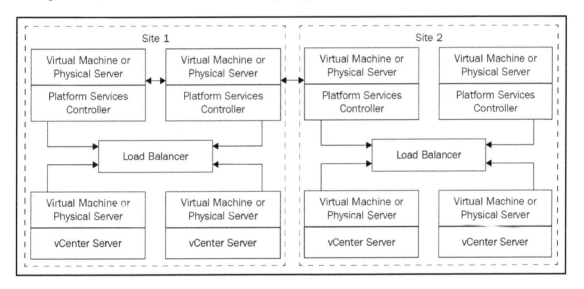

Figure 1.22: Multi-site PSC deployment

To provide high availability for the PSC, it's recommended to have at least two PSCs on each site, with a third-party load balancer.

Site membership can be specified during the installation of the PSC (**Stage 2**), as follows:

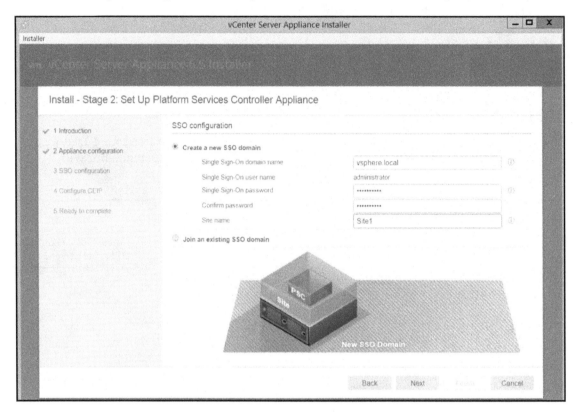

Figure 1.23: PSC deployment

Configure/manage identity sources

Consider the topic described in *Objective 1.1*; in this section, we will consider the AD case.

To assign vCenter permissions to AD users or groups, you must first join the PSC to the AD domain. This allows the AD users to log in to the vCenter Server using the Windows session authentication (SSPI).

The procedure to join the vCenter Server to an AD domain depends on how the vCenter and the PSC have been deployed:

- **Embedded PSC**: Join the vCenter to the AD domain
- **External PSC**: Join the PSC to the AD domain

Only a writable Domain Controller can be used to join the AD domain. A **Read-Only Domain Controller** (**RODC**) is not supported.

For Windows-based vCenter or PSC, just join the Windows machine to the AD domain.

For VCSA, to join the PSC or the vCenter to the AD, follow this procedure:

1. From the vSphere Web Client, log in with the right SSO admin account.
2. Select **Home** | **Administrator** | **Deployment** | **System Configuration** and choose the proper node (the PSC or the vCenter, depending on the deployment).
3. In the **Manage** tab, select the **Advanced** | **Active Directory** menu, then click on the **Join** button to enter the details to join the AD.
4. Enter the **Domain** to join, and optionally the **Organizational unit**. Specify the AD username in UPN format (`username@domain.com`), with the privileges to join the PSC to the domain.
5. After the process has completed, the joined domain will be listed in the **Domain** field, and a new **Leave...** button will be displayed:

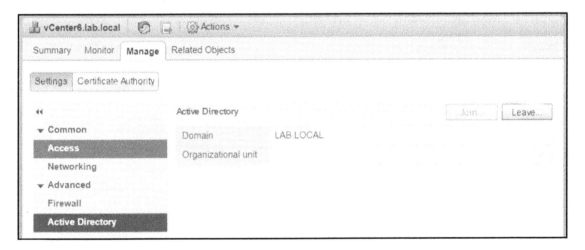

Figure 1.24: AD membership

6. You need to reboot the node to enable the changes.
7. When the node has been rebooted, navigate to **Configuration** | **Identity Sources** to add the AD domain. Click **Add** to open the **Add Identity Source wizard**.

8. Select the **Active Directory (Integrated Windows Authentication)** option, and enter the joined FQDN domain name, if it's not displayed automatically.

9. Select the **Use machine account** option to use the local machine account as the SPN. If you expect to rename the machine, don't use this option, because it will break the authentication process. Click on **OK** to confirm the specified AD domain as the new identity source.

10. On the **Identity Sources** tab, the joined AD domain is now displayed. Now, you can assign permissions to users/groups to be members of the AD domain.

 To prevent authentication conflicts, don't use a username that is used by other identity sources, such as OpenLDAP or Microsoft AD.

Configure/manage platform services controller (PSC)

The PSC appliance (like the VCSA appliance) can be managed by using the **vCenter Server Appliance Management Interface** (**VAMI**).

However, to manage specific PSC services, you can use the **Platform Services Controller UI**; or, for some tasks (such as certificates management), you can also use the vSphere Web Client. Some services, such as smart card authentication, are only configurable from the Platform Services Controller UI.

The following table summarizes the different **user interfaces** (**UIs**) available for the PSC:

Web interface	URL
VAMI (only for VCSA appliances)	`https://PSC:5480`
Platform Services Controller UI	`https://PSC/psc`
vSphere Web Client	`https://vCenter/vsphere-client`

Table 1.7: UI interfaces for PSC

In this table, "PSC" is the IP address or the FQDN of the PSC (if external) or the vCenter Server (if embedded).

Configure/manage VMware Certificate Authority (VMCA)

Starting with vSphere 6.0, the new PSC component includes not only the SSO part, but also the VMCA. The VMCA is used for the certification management of all vSphere infrastructural elements.

This not only simplifies the certification management (with auto-enrollment for expired certificates), but also improves the security of the different network connections (as described before).

Using VMCA mode (see *Objective 1.2* for different modes for managing certificates), the PSC will generate and issue all certificates needed by the different vSphere components. Certificates are stored by the **vSphere Endpoint Certificate Store** (**VECS**).

To avoid browser warnings, you need to trust VMware's CA, but first, you have to gain that certificate. You can simply download it from the vCenter home page, under **Download trusted root CA certificates**:

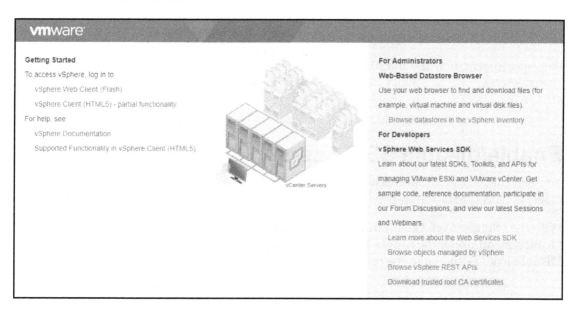

Figure 1.25: vCenter Server home page

You will download a simple `download.zip` file that contains both the CA certificate and the revocations list.

To import the certificate in a Windows system, you can use different approaches, as follows:

- **Import manually**: For Internet Explorer, Edge, or Chrome, you can simply double-click on the certificate and import it into the trusted CA. Note that Firefox has a different certificates repository.
- **Import by using GPO**: Under **Computer Configuration | Windows Settings | Security Settings | Public Key Policies | Trusted Publishers,** you can import existing certificates. Be sure to import them into the Trusted Root Certification Authorities store.
- **Trust from another CA**: Add it as an intermediate CA in your existing CA authority.

Otherwise, you can replace the CA certificate of VMCA; or, just don't use it at all, and manage all of the certificates as you did in the past.

For more information, see KB 2097936 (`https://kb.vmware.com/s/article/2097936`)—How to use vSphere 6.x Certificate Manager.

For more information about authentication, see the PSC 6.5 Administration Guide (`https://docs.vmware.com/en/VMware-vSphere/6.5/com.vmware.psc.doc/GUID-779A011D-B2DD-49BE-B0B9-6D73ECF99864.html`).

Enable/disable SSO users

You can enable and disable accounts from the vSphere Web Client or the PSC UI; in both cases, you need SSO admin privileges.

With the vSphere Web Client, from **Home | Administration**, just select the **Users and Groups** menu under the **Single Sign-On** section. Select a user account and click on the **Disable** icon, as shown in the following screenshot:

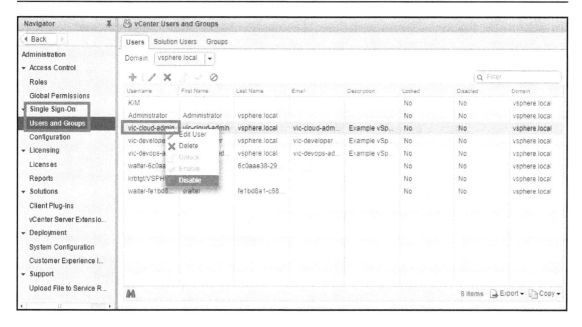

Figure 1.26: Disable SSO users

To enable the user again, right-click on the username and select **Enable**.

If you disable (or delete) the administrative user in the SSO domain, you cannot manage the SSO domain (unless you previously created another user with SSO admin privileges).

For more information about authentication, see the PSC 6.5 Administration Guide (`https:/ /docs.vmware.com/en/VMware-vSphere/6.5/com.vmware.psc.doc/GUID-AC8A1B39-8E0D-4604-82DF-C5FC92ECA50D.html`).

Upgrade a single/complex PSC installation

If you have a complex vSphere environment with more external PSCs, and perhaps with multi-site deployment, the upgrade process can be a little more critical.

To upgrade a vSphere environment, there is a general order that must be followed. For the basic vSphere components, perform the following:

1. **External PSC**: Upgrade each SSO or PSC, one by one. Applicable only in external PSC deployments.
2. **vCenter Server**: Upgrade each vCenter Server, one by one.
3. **ESXi hosts**: Upgrade each ESXi host, one by one.

 In environments with more VMware products, the upgrade/update sequence is much more complex. See VMware KB 2147289 (`https://kb. vmware.com/s/article/2147289`)—Update sequence for vSphere 6.5 and its compatible VMware products.

For the PSC components, it's usually preferable to upgrade them during the maintenance windows, to avoid authentication issues. But, if all external PSCs are configured in a high availability configuration, with external load balancers, you can perform upgrades on PSCs one by one, without interruptions.

For more information about each transitional step, including diagrams, see the *Upgrade or Migration Order and Mixed-Version Transitional Behavior for Multiple vCenter Server Instance Deployments* section in the vSphere Upgrade Guide (`https://docs.vmware.com/en/VMware-vSphere/6.5/com.vmware.vsphere.upgrade.doc/GUID-FDF1D082-36EB-41EB-9D97-A48D33A1D843.html`).

For the vCenter Server appliance (for both vCenter and PSC), the update and upgrade process can be managed from the VAMI UI. The update is quite simple (for example, using an external URL), and the upgrade requires the VCSA 6.5 ISO.

The VCSA GUI upgrade is a two-stage process (like the installation). The first stage is a deployment wizard that deploys the OVA file of the new appliance on the target ESXi host or vCenter Server instance. After the virtual appliance deployment finishes, you are redirected to the second stage of the process, which sets up and transfers the services and configuration data from the old appliance to the newly deployed appliance.

For more information, see KB 2147686 (`https://kb.vmware.com/s/article/2147686`)—Best practices for upgrading to vCenter Server 6.5.

Configure SSO policies

The vCenter SSO policies enforce security rules related to the SSO users defined in your environment. There are three main types of SSO policies: password policies, lockout policies, and token policies.

You can manage SSO policies from the vSphere Web Client (with SSO admin privileges) or the PSC UI.

With the vSphere Web Client, in **Home** | **Administration**, just select the **Configuration** menu in the **Single Sign-On** section. Then, select the **Policies** tab and choose the right category of policies, as follows:

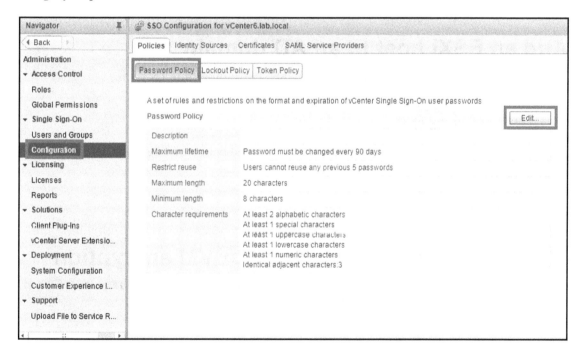

Figure 1.27: SSO policies

Note that there are password expiration rules for the virtual appliance local users, if you are using VCSA for vCenter and/or the PSC components. Be sure to check those settings. By default, vCenter Single Sign-On passwords expire after 90 days. Starting with version 6.0, the password policy only applies to SSO user accounts, not to SSO system accounts (usually `administrator@vsphere.local`).

If you are using AD users, both for hosts and vCenter, then the password policies are enforced by AD GPO.

For more information about authentication, see the PSC 6.5 Administration Guide (`https:/ /docs.vmware.com/en/VMware-vSphere/6.5/com.vmware.psc.doc/GUID-43527B09-63BB-44A6-91D3-E3A470904698.html`).

Add an ESXi host to an AD domain

This task was described in *Objective 1.2*, in the host hardening options.

For more details, see KB 2075361 (`https://kb.vmware.com/s/article/2075361`)—Configuring ESXi host with AD authentication.

Remember to synchronize the proper time between ESXi and the directory service system.

Configure and manage KMS for VM encryption

In vSphere 6.5, to encrypt VM disks, you will need to configure a **Key Management Server (KMS)**, or, better yet, a cluster of KMS.

You can use the vSphere Web Client, as follows:

1. Select the vCenter Server in the inventory, then select the **Configure** tab. Expand **More,** and select **Key Management Server** to access the KMS management section.

2. Click on the **Add KMS...** icon to add the KMS server (you must have one in your network). Specify the required parameters, and click on **OK** to save the configuration:

Figure 1.28: Adding a new KMS

3. Once the KMS server is successfully added to the vCenter Server, the **Connection Status** will be displayed as **Normal**. Having configured the KMS server, you can start encrypting VMs.

 KMS are mandatory for VM encryption, but are not required for vMotion encryption.

For more information, see the vSphere 6.5 Security Guide (`https://docs.vmware.com/en/ VMware-vSphere/6.5/com.vmware.vsphere.security.doc/GUID-78DD547A-6FFC-49F1- A5F2-ECD7507EE835.html`) or the StarWind blog post at `https://www.starwindsoftware. com/blog/encryption-of-vmware-vsphere-6-5-virtual-machines-and-vmotion- migrations-and-their-performance`.

Objective 1.4 – Secure vSphere Virtual Machines

The hardening guide describes a lot of specific VM options, but, starting with ESXi 6.0 Patch 5, many of the advanced VM settings are now set to be **Secure By Default**.

This means that the desired values in the Security Configuration Guide are the default values for all new VMs, and you don't have to manually set them anymore.

For more information, see the blog post at `https://blogs.vmware.com/vsphere/2017/06/secure-default-vm-disable-unexposed-features.html`.

For virtual networking, NSX can provide a micro-segmentation capability, to enforce network security directly at the VM virtual NIC level.

Also, at VMworld 2017, a new product was announced: **VMware AppDefense**, a data center endpoint security product that protects applications running in virtualized environments. AppDefense works inside of the VM (compared to NSX, which only works at the network level), and understands how applications are normally supposed to work, monitoring any changes that could indicate a threat.

Objective 1.4 is totally new for VCP65-DCV, but it contains some parts of Objective 1.2, from the VCP6-DCV exam preparation guide.

Enable/disable VM encryption

VMware vSphere 6.5 added the possibility to encrypt VM files (such as `.vmx` and swap files) and virtual disks (VMDK), making the stored VM data more secure. For example, they are inaccessible with a simple data store browsing operation.

To allow VM encryption, the following components are needed:

- **KMS**: Generates and stores the keys needed to encrypt and decrypt the VMs. The KMS provides vCenter and ESXi with the necessary keys by using the KMIP protocol. Multiple KMS vendors are compatible, including HyTrust, Gemalto (SafeNet), Thales e-Security, CloudLink, and Vormetric. For a complete list, see the VMware Compatibility Guide (`https://www.vmware.com/resources/compatibility/search.php?deviceCategory=kmsdetails=1releases=354page=1 display_interval=10sortColumn=PartnersortOrder=Asc`). KMS configuration was described in *Objective 1.3*.
- **vCenter Server**: The only component that can log in to the KMS to obtain the keys and pass them to ESXi hosts is vCenter Server. The different KMS keys are not stored in the vCenter; it only keeps a list of key IDs.

No additional or specific hardware is required for the encryption/decryption operations, but processors with support of the AES-NI instruction set are recommended, in order to improve the performance. AES-NI should be enabled in the host BIOS.

VM encryption is controlled by VM storage policies (see `Chapter 3`, *Configure and Administer vSphere 6.x Storage*, for more information). To change the storage policy of a VM, follow this procedure:

1. From the vSphere Web Client, right-click on the VM to encrypt. Navigate to **VM Storage Policies** | **Edit VM Storage Policies**.

2. From the **VM storage policy** drop-down menu, select the **VM Encryption Policy** option to encrypt the VM:

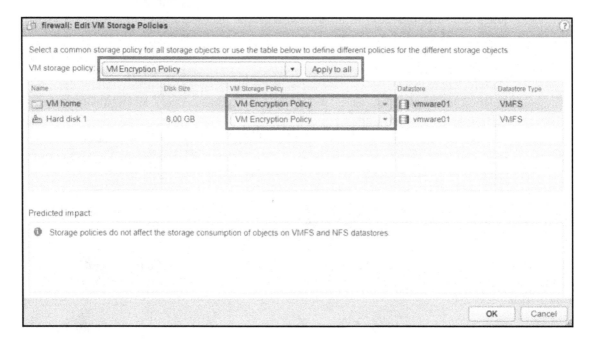

Figure 1.29: Encrypting a VM

3. When the encryption process has completed, the **VM Hardware** area in the VMs **Summary** tab will display the **Encryption** field that indicates which components are encrypted.

There are different recommendations when using encrypted VMs, but the most important are as follows:

- If PSC or vCenter are implemented as VMs, don't encrypt them.
- Never edit the `.vmx` files or `.vmdk` descriptor files of encrypted VMs; otherwise, the VMs will become unrecoverable.

To perform the preceding operations, you will need the required privileges, as follows:

- **Cryptographic operations.Encrypt new**
- **Cryptographic operations.Decrypt**
- **Cryptographic operations.Register host** (if the host encryption mode is not enabled)

Note that encrypted VMs can be a challenge for native backup programs, but there is a way to permit backup of the encrypted files in a clear format, to allow for indexing and granular restore. Several backup products already support this feature.

For more information, see the vSphere 6.5 Security Guide (`https://docs.vmware.com/en/ VMware-vSphere/6.5/com.vmware.vsphere.security.doc/GUID-5E2C3F74-38C1-44C3- ABC5-C2C9353B9DC4.html`).

Describe VM Secure Boot

As described in *Objectve 1.2*, **Unified Extensible Firmware Interface (UEFI)** is a replacement for the traditional BIOS firmware, and secure boot uses the UEFI firmware to validate the digital signature of the operating system and its bootloader.

With vSphere ESXi 6.5, you can use secure boot with both ESXi and VM. For ESXi secure boot description, see *Objective 1.2*.

VM secure boot has some important requirements, as follows:

- Virtual hardware version 13 or later
- EFI firmware in the VM boot options
- VMware Tools version 10.1 or later
- A guest operating system that supports UEFI secure boot:
    - Some examples of supported operating systems are Windows 8 and Windows Server 2012 or newer, VMware ESXi 6.5 and Photon OS, RHEL/Centos 7.0, and Ubuntu 14.04

You can enable secure boot on a VM by using the vSphere Web Client, in the **VM options** of the desired VM, as follows:

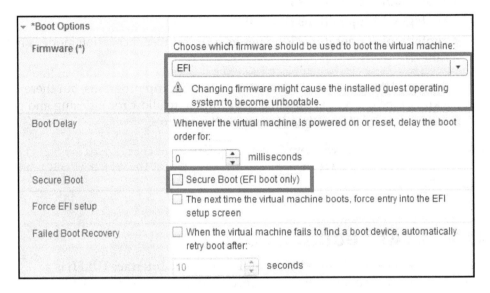

Figure 1.30: VM secure boot

 You cannot upgrade a VM that uses BIOS boot to a VM that uses UEFI boot. If a VM already uses UEFI boot and the operating system supports UEFI secure boot, you can simply enable secure boot.

You will need `VirtualMachine.Config.Settings` privileges to enable or disable UEFI secure boot for the VM.

For more information, see the vSphere 6.5 Security Guide (`https://docs.vmware.com/en/ VMware-vSphere/6.5/com.vmware.vsphere.security.doc/GUID-898217D4-689D-4EB5- 866C-888353FE241C.html`).

Harden virtual machine access

As described in *Objective 1.2*, VMware has provided some Security Hardening Guides (`https://www.vmware.com/security/hardening-guides.html`) to provide guidance on how to increase security in a vSphere environment.

VMware suggests some security best practices to increase the security of VMs running in a vSphere environment, as follows:

- **Use templates**: Instead of manually installing guest operating systems and applications, prefer templates or other provisioning systems to enforce security baselines.
- **Limit console access**: Be sure to protect and limit access to the VM console, for the confidentiality of data (by default, more users can see the same VM console sessions).
- **Limit remote access**: Remote protocols used for management (such as SSH or RDP) must be secured, controlled, and limited.
- **Limit resources**: Without proper resource management (such as resource pools), more VMs can consume most of the host resources, with a possible **denial-of-service (DoS)** scenario.
- **Minimize services**: Any service that is running in a VM is a potential target for attacks. Be sure to disable services or system components that are not necessary.
- **Minimize hardware**: Disconnect or remove unused devices, such as CD/DVD drives, floppy drives, and USB adapters. This also helps with VM migration. Note that CD/DVD drives may be needed for VMware Tools installation/upgrade.
- **Limit VMware Tools functions**: Disable unused functionality, such as unused display features or **host guest file systems (HGFSs)**. Some of those functions will be discussed in the next section.

 Because a VM is almost equivalent to a physical server, it is possible (in most cases) to apply the same security approaches and solutions.

For more information, see the vSphere 6.5 Security Guide (`https://docs.vmware.com/en/VMware-vSphere/6.5/com.vmware.vsphere.security.doc/GUID-CF45F448-2036-4BE3-8829-4A9335072349.html`).

Control VMware Tools installation

VMware Tools installation and upgrade is performed by using the virtual CD/DVD drive. This means that, without it, you cannot perform those operations from the vSphere Web Client.

Another option for disabling VMware Tools installation is to change the role and remove the privilege required to install VMware Tools (**Virtual machine .Interaction.VMware Tools install**).

Note that both tricks do not work with standalone VMware Tools if they are installed from the binaries files in the guest OS.

Control VM data access

VMware provides some functions to permit data access inside of the VM:

- **HGFS**: This is used to transfer files between the host and the VMs. Note that this capability is actually only leveraged on Workstation/Player/Fusion, and it's not implemented in ESXi.
- **Copy and paste between the guest OS and remote console**: By default, this feature is disabled, as recommended for a secure environment. If copy and paste is enabled and the VM has VMware Tools installed, you can copy and paste between the guest operating system and the remote console.

You can control those features by using the vSphere Web Client: select a VM, right-click on the VM, and click on **Edit Settings**. In the **VM Options** tab, click on **Advanced,** and click on **Edit Configuration**.

At this point, check the specific rows (if they exist) or create new rows. The following table summarizes some possible parameters:

VM advanced parameter	Recommended value	Result
`isolation.tools.hgfsServerSet.disable`	**TRUE**	Disable HGFS file transfer
`isolation.tools.copy.disable`	**TRUE**	Disable copy operations
`isolation.tools.paste.disable`	**TRUE**	Disable paste operations
`isolation.tools.setGUIOptions.enable`	**FALSE**	Disable VMware Tools options from the guest

Table 1.8: Hardening VM advanced settings

If you make changes to the preceding configuration parameters, restart the VM to load the changes.

 Note that all of those four settings are disabled by default starting ESXi 6.5 update 1, in ESXi 6.0 Patch 5 and 5.5 Update 3 Patch 11.

The vSphere 6.5 Security Guide (`https://docs.vmware.com/en/VMware-vSphere/6.5/com.vmware.vsphere.security.doc/GUID-60E83710-8295-41A2-9C9D-83DEBB6872C2.html`) reports other settings that are not exposed in vSphere, but could cause vulnerabilities, as follows:

VM advanced parameter	Recommended value
`isolation.tools.unity.push.update.disable`	TRUE
`isolation.tools.ghi.launchmenu.change`	TRUE
`isolation.tools.memSchedFakeSampleStats.disable`	TRUE
`isolation.tools.getCreds.disable`	TRUE
`isolation.tools.ghi.autologon.disable`	TRUE
`isolation.bios.bbs.disable`	TRUE

Table 1.9: Other hardening VM advanced settings

Configure virtual machine security policies

Some VM security policies have already been discussed; others, related to DoS attacks, will be discussed in the next section.

Harden a virtual machine against DoS attacks

One or more VMs may consume too many resources on a single host, causing a possible DoS scenario. To minimize this possibility, a proper configuration of the VM resource management is needed; also, remember that each VM has implicit limits, due to resources configured in the VM settings.

Other possible DoS situations are as follows:

- **Virtual disk shrinking**: Shrinking a virtual disk reclaims the disk's unused space. This operation can be performed by a non-administrative user in the guest operating system, and multiple operations can cause a DoS on the virtual disk. To disable the ability to shrink virtual disks, you must use two VM advanced settings, **isolation.tools.diskWiper.disable** and **isolation.tools.diskShrink.disable**, as described in KB 1002019 (`https://kb.vmware.com/s/article/1002019`)—Growing, thinning, and shrinking virtual disks for VMware ESX and ESXi.

 This operation is not supported in ESXi, but it is supported in Workstation/Player/Fusion.

- **Informational messages from VM to VMX files**: A DoS can happen if you do not control the size of a VMs VMX file, and the amount of information in it exceeds the data store capacity. By default, the file limit is 1 MB, and you can change it with the **tools.setInfo.sizeLimit** VM advanced option. For more information, see the vSphere 6.5 Security Guide (`https://docs.vmware.com/en/VMware-vSphere/6.5/com.vmware.vsphere.security.doc/GUID-9610FE65-3A78-4982-8C28-5B34FEB264B6.html`).
- **Unnecessary hardware devices**: Any connected device represents a potential attack channel. As described previously, it's a good practice to remove or disable all unneeded or unused devices. Note that, by default, users and processes with local privileges on a guest OS can connect or disconnect some hot-plug hardware devices (such as the virtual NIC).

Control VM-VM communications

The **Virtual Machine Communication Interface** (**VMCI**) provides a communication channel between a VM and the host, or between two or more VMs on the same host. In vSphere 6.5, VMCI is disabled by default.

Of course, each VM can talk to others by using the virtual network, so be sure to enforce network segregation with VLAN at the portgroup level, or, if possible, micro-segmentation with NSX.

Control VM device connections

As described previously, any device can represent a potential attack channel, and a good practice is to remove or disable unnecessary devices.

Using VMware Tools, it's possible to connect or disconnect devices, potentially causing a DoS, but this feature is disabled by default. For more information, see the vSphere 6.5 Security Guide (`https://docs.vmware.com/en/VMware-vSphere/6.5/com.vmware.vsphere.security.doc/GUID-F88A5FED-552B-44F9-A168-C62D9306DBD6.html`).

Note that VMware provides some devices that are hot-pluggable (such as the virtual NIC). In this case, users and processes with local guest OS privileges (root or administrator) can disconnect those types of devices from the OS. For more information, see KB 1012225 (`https://kb.vmware.com/s/article/1012225`)—Disabling the HotAdd/HotPlug capability in ESXi 6.x, 5.x and ESXi/ESX 4.x VMs.

The following table summarizes some parameters for controlling the VM device connections:

VM advanced parameter	Recommended value	Result
`isolation.device.connectable.disable`	**TRUE**	Disable the connection of devices
`isolation.device.edit.disable`	**TRUE**	Disable copy operations
`devices.hotplug`	**FALSE**	Disable device hotplug

Table 1.10: Hardening VM advanced settings

Configure network security policies

Standard and distributed virtual switches (described in `Chapter 2`, *Configure and Administer vSphere 6.x Networking*) both have specific security policies:

- **Promiscuous mode**: Promiscuous mode permits a virtual NIC to capture all frames on the virtual switch portgroup. Of course, it can represent a security risk for the confidentiality of the data.

- **MAC address changes**: The guest OS can change the MAC address of the virtual NIC, and this can be used by a spoofing attack.
- **Forged transmits**: Any outgoing frame with a source MAC address that is different from the one currently set on the VMX file.

By default, on distributed virtual switches, all of the previous policies are rejected. On standard virtual switches, only the promiscuous mode is rejected; in that case, you can change the settings with the vSphere Web Client, by selecting the **Configure** tab on the desired host, and then the **Virtual switches** menu. Then, select the desired virtual switch, click the **Edit settings** icon, and choose the **Security** menu:

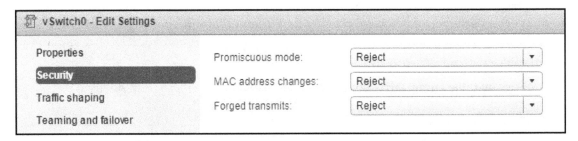

Figure 1.31: Network security policies

For more information, see the vSphere 6.5 Security Guide (`https://docs.vmware.com/en/ VMware-vSphere/6.5/com.vmware.vsphere.security.doc/GUID-9782B9AA-CB4C-40FF- AD1F-359180545D6E.html`).

Configure VM encrypted vMotion

Protecting stored data is only one element of security; you also need to encrypt the network connections. For the infrastructure part, all of the communication between vCenter and the hosts is usually encrypted. However, some other infrastructural network traffic usually is *not* protected; for example, iSCSI or NFS traffic (and also vMotion, until vSphere 6.5).

As described in *Objective 1.2*, there is now a new feature to encrypt vMotion traffic.

Encryption of vMotion traffic is per-VM; when the VM is migrated, a one-time 256-bit key is randomly generated by vCenter Server (note that it does not use the KMS).

Settings are per-VM, but only for VMs with virtual hardware 13. You can view or change the settings by right-clicking on the VM and selecting **Edit Settings...**, then selecting the **VM Options** tab in the **Encrypted vMotion** section:

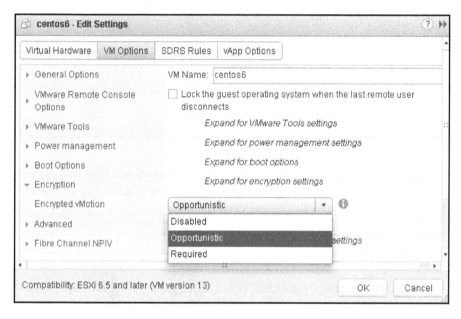

Figure 1.32: Encrypted vMotion settings

The different options are as follows:

- **Disabled**: Do not use encrypted vMotion for this VM.
- **Opportunistic (default)**: Use encrypted vSphere vMotion only if the source and destination hosts can support it (ESXi versions 6.5 and later).
- **Required**: Force the use of encrypted vMotion. If the source or destination host does not support encrypted vMotion, then the migration will not be possible.

You can disable vMotion encryption, unless the VM is encrypted; in that case, it is always enforced.

In vSphere 6.5, migration across vCenter Server systems is not supported for encrypted VMs.

For storage vMotion or vMotion without shared storage, the disks are transmitted as they are, as follows:

- For encrypted disks, the data is transmitted encrypted.
- For disks that are not encrypted, Storage vMotion encryption is not supported.

For more information, see the vSphere 6.5 Security Guide (`https://docs.vmware.com/en/ VMware-vSphere/6.5/com.vmware.vsphere.security.doc/GUID-E6C5CE29-CD1D-4555- 859C-A0492E7CB45D.html`).

What is missing

The official *VCP65-DCV Exam Preparation Guide* covers a lot of security topics, but the vSphere 6.5 Security Guide has richer information and more topics. For example, the following aspects are not considered in the preparation guide:

- Manage the Acceptance Levels of Hosts and VIBs (`https://docs.vmware.com/ en/VMware-vSphere/6.5/com.vmware.vsphere.security.doc/GUID-751034F3- 5337-4DB2-8272-8DAC0980EACA.html`)
- ESXi Passwords and Account Lockout (`https://docs.vmware.com/en/VMware- vSphere/6.5/com.vmware.vsphere.security.doc/GUID-DC96FFDB-F5F2-43EC- 8C73-05ACDAE6BE43.html`)
- SSH Security (`https://docs.vmware.com/en/VMware-vSphere/6.5/com.vmware. vsphere.security.doc/GUID-EF55F930-AC17-46EF-BF43-1DB2500F0734.html`)
- Control Access for CIM-Based Hardware Monitoring Tools (`https://docs. vmware.com/en/VMware-vSphere/6.5/com.vmware.vsphere.security.doc/GUID- 645EBD81-CF86-44D7-BE77-224EF963D145.html`)
- vCenter Password Requirements and Lockout Behavior (`https://docs.vmware. com/en/VMware-vSphere/6.5/com.vmware.vsphere.security.doc/GUID- 4BDBF79A-6C16-43B0-B0B1-637BF5516112.html`)

- Set the vCenter Server Password Policy (`https://docs.vmware.com/en/VMware-vSphere/6.5/com.vmware.vsphere.security.doc/GUID-E905038D-A5A3-401E-921D-58A4CD57B07C.html`)

- Required Ports for vCenter Server and PSC (`https://docs.vmware.com/en/VMware-vSphere/6.5/com.vmware.vsphere.security.doc/GUID-925370DD-E3D1-455B-81C7-CB28AAF20617.html`)

- Additional vCenter Server TCP and UDP Ports (`https://docs.vmware.com/en/VMware-vSphere/6.5/com.vmware.vsphere.security.doc/GUID-ECEA77F5-D38E-4339-9B06-FF9B78E94B68.html`)

- Managing TLS Protocol Configuration with the TLS Configurator Utility (`https://docs.vmware.com/en/VMware-vSphere/6.5/com.vmware.vsphere.security.doc/GUID-82028A21-8AB5-4E2E-90B8-A01D1FAD77B1.html`)

- Securing vSphere Networking (`https://docs.vmware.com/en/VMware-vSphere/6.5/com.vmware.vsphere.security.doc/GUID-9782B9AA-CB4C-40FF-AD1F-359180545D6E.html`)

- Add vCenter Single Sign-On Users (`https://docs.vmware.com/en/VMware-vSphere/6.5/com.vmware.psc.doc/GUID-72BFF98C-C530-4C50-BF31-B5779D2A4BBB.html`)

- Add a vCenter Single Sign-On Group (`https://docs.vmware.com/en/VMware-vSphere/6.5/com.vmware.psc.doc/GUID-7877D42E-9EB3-40D3-B92F-E86559966BBC.html`)

- vCenter Single Sign-On Security Best Practices (`https://docs.vmware.com/en/VMware-vSphere/6.5/com.vmware.psc.doc/GUID-0073F0C0-2987-492F-9B6B-4E998E4DBC1B.html`)

- Troubleshooting PSC (`https://docs.vmware.com/en/VMware-vSphere/6.5/com.vmware.psc.doc/GUID-24E58D0D-9138-4273-A6A5-C73F6CF379C3.html`)

- Limit Informational Messages from Virtual Machines to VMX Files (`https://docs.vmware.com/en/VMware-vSphere/6.5/com.vmware.vsphere.security.doc/GUID-91BF834E-CB92-4014-8CF7-29CE40F3E8A3.html`)

Review questions

For more questions, see `Chapter 11`, *Mock Exam 1,* and `Chapter 12`, *Mock Exam 2:*

1. What are the requirements for implementing VM secure boot? (Choose three)
   - A: Guest operating system that supports UEFI secure boot
   - B: VMware Tools version 10.1 or later
   - C: VM virtual hardware 13 or later
   - D: VM virtual hardware 10 or later
   - E: VMware Tools version 10 or later

   A, B, C - See *Objective 1.4*

2. Which sentence about virtual network security policies is true?
   - A: Only promiscuous mode is disabled on standard switches by default.
   - B: Only MAC changes are disabled by default.
   - C: Only forged transmissions are disabled by default.
   - D: All are disabled by default.

   A - See *Objective 1.4*

Summary

Following VMware's vision, the five pillars of cyber hygiene are as follows:

- **Least privilege**: This is the common, and most reasonable, approach; it applies to user accounts, service accounts, and services in general (for example, used ports).
- **Micro-Segmentation**: Using NSX, it's finally possible to bring network control to the VM level, with granular security rules. Considering the new product (AppDefense), VM security can be enforced at both the network and application levels.
- **Encryption**: Data must be protected at each level, and for the physical level, encryption is the only way to ensure good protection.

- **Authentication**: Authentication is usually the weakest part, primarily due to simple passwords (or passwords that are not changed periodically).
- **Patching**: Keeping your software components up to date is crucial for the security aspect, but it's also very important for implementing new features. Upgrading and patching will be discussed in *Objective 4*.

Chapter 2, *Configure and Administer vSphere 6.x Networking*, will check your virtual networking knowledge.

2
Configure and Administer vSphere 6.x Networking

Virtual networking is quite important for a virtualized environment—due to the isolation pillar of the system virtualization, the VMs can communicate with each other (and with the rest of the world) only through the network.

VMware vSphere virtual networking has several important concepts, but they are well explained in this document: `https://www.vmware.com/content/dam/digitalmarketing/ vmware/en/pdf/techpaper/virtual_networking_concepts.pdf`.

Starting from version 4.0, there are two different types of virtual switches:

- **Standard virtual switches (vSS)**: Available in all ESXi editions, including the free edition
- **Distributed virtual switches (vDS or also DVS)**: Available only with Enterprise Plus edition or bounded with VMware vSAN or NSX licenses

 Practicing what you learn during the chapter is a key point to enforce your skills and prepare for the exam. A useful VMware HoL for this purpose is the HOL-1810-01-SDC—Virtualization 101: Introduction to vSphere.

The reader will learn about the following in this chapter:

- Managing vSphere standard switches
- Managing vSphere Distributed Switches
- Understanding VMkernel interfaces
- VMkernel interfaces
- NIOC capabilities

Objective 2.1 – Configure policies/features and verify vSphere networking

This chapter is about the vDS switches and their functionalities. Some concepts are also valid for vSS, but the exam preparation seems to prefer the vDS-related questions. Note that the standard VMware vSphere Install & Configuration course does not cover vDS!

The vDS is based on these elements:

- **The vDS itself**: It contains some configuration parameters and some monitoring features and also contains the following elements:
    - **Uplink Port Group**: This is the physical connection to the physical switches. Each uplink will correspond to a physical NIC on each host member of the vDS.
    - **Distributed Port Group**: This is the virtual connection and provides the network connectivity for all VMs and for the ESXi VMkernel adapters.

 For more information, see the KB 1010555 (`https://kb.vmware.com/s/article/1010555`): "Overview of vNetwork Distributed Switch" concepts.

But why would you want to use a vDS (if you have the license) and why is the VCP-DCV exam mostly about vDS for the networking part?

There are a lot of features and capabilities that are available only on vDS and, anyway, some of the concepts that you learn for vDS can be valid also for standard switches.

 Objective 2.1 for VCP65-DCV and VCP6-DCV is quite the same, just because there weren't big changes in networking from vSphere 6.0 to vSphere 6.5. All that's different are the final sub-chapters that are new in version 6.5 of the guide.

The vSphere 6.5 Networking guide contains in-depth pieces of information about networking capabilities and configurations: `https://docs.vmware.com/en/VMware-vSphere/6.5/vsphere-esxi-vcenter-server-652-networking-guide.pdf`.

Creating/deleting a vSphere Distributed Switch

The vSphere Web Client in the **Networking** category can be used to create a new vDS. Just right-click on the desired data center (vDS can span clusters in the same data center) and select **Distributed Switch | New Distributed Switch....** Then, on the **Name and location** page, type a name for the new vDS, or accept the automatically generated name, and click **Next**.

Now, on the **Select version** page, you need to select a vDS version:

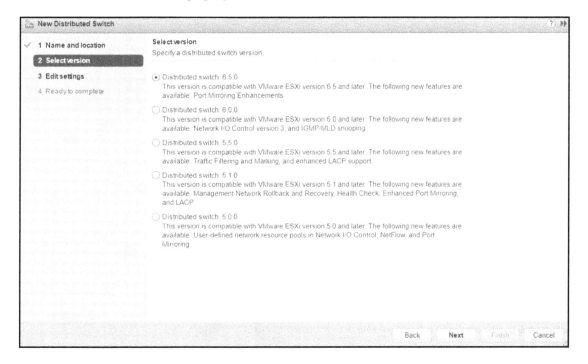

Figure 2.1: Creating a new distributed virtual switch

Each version defines a different compatibility with a different version of vSphere, but also different functions, as described in the following table:

Version	Compatibility	New functions
Distributed Switch version 6.5.0	vSphere 6.5 and later	Port mirroring enhancements
Distributed Switch version 6.0.0	vSphere 6.0 and later	Network I/O Control version 3 and IGMP/MLD snooping

Distributed Switch version 5.5.0	vSphere 5.5 and later	Traffic filtering and marking, and enhanced LACP support
Distributed Switch version 5.1.0	vSphere 5.1 and later	Management of network rollback and recovery, health check, enhanced port mirroring, and LACP
Distributed Switch version 5.0.0	vSphere 5.0 and later	User-defined network resource pools in Network I/O Control, NetFlow, and port mirroring

Table 2.1: Distributed virtual switch versions

Then, on the **Edit settings** page, configure the proper vDS settings:

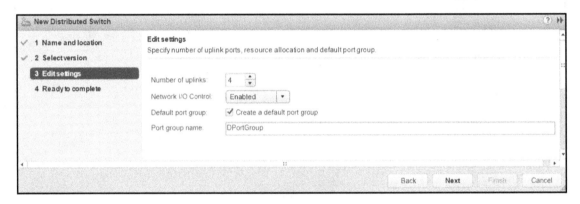

Figure 2.2: Distributed virtual switch settings

Use the arrow buttons to select the **Number of uplinks**, which is the maximum number of allowed physical connections to the distributed switch per host.

Use the drop-down menu to enable or disable **Network I/O Control** (**NIOC**). NIOC will be described and discussed in *Objective 2.2*.

Select the **Create a default port group** checkbox to automatically create a new distributed port group with default settings. Note that the port group can also be created after the virtual switch, as described later.

The vDS will be created in the selected data center. The features supported on the distributed switch, as well as other details, can be viewed by clicking the **Summary** tab of the new distributed switch.

For more information, see the vSphere 6.5 Networking guide (`https://docs.vmware.com/en/VMware-vSphere/6.5/com.vmware.vsphere.networking.doc/GUID-D21B3241-0AC9-437C-80B1-0C8043CC1D7D.html`).

Adding/removing ESXi hosts from a vSphere Distributed Switch

You can add new hosts to a vDS; in this phase, you can connect physical network adapters, VMs, and VMkernel interfaces to the switch.

 Its is important to check your environment before new hosts are added to a distributed switch and verify all the requirements. Also, migration of existing interfaces and VMs must be planned carefully.

First of all, create all needed distributed port groups for the virtual machines and for VMkernel networking. This part will be discussed later.

Also, ensure that you add enough uplinks on the vDS to match all physical NICs (for each host) that you want to connect to the switch. This part will be discussed later.

You can use the **Add and Manage Hosts** wizard in the vSphere Web Client to:

- **Add hosts** to an existing vDS
- **Manage host networking**
- **Remove hosts** from a vDS

The **Add hosts** option (or **Add host** and **manage host networking**) will guide you in adding multiple hosts at a single time:

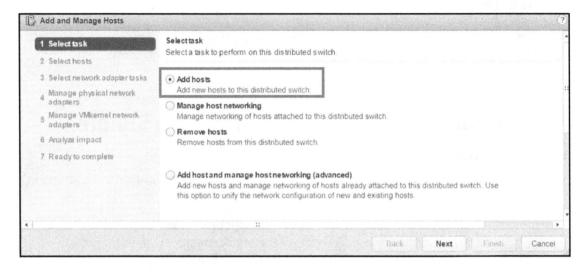

Figure 2.3: Adding hosts to a vDS

The same wizard will also migrate all the VMs, the VMkernel network adapters, and the uplinks on the hosts to the vDS at the same time, without (or with very limited) service interruptions.

We can also choose hosts from the same wizard. We will have to ensure that the network adapters that are in use are migrated before removing the hosts from a vDS.

For more information, see the vSphere 6.5 Networking guide (https://docs.vmware.com/en/VMware-vSphere/6.5/com.vmware.vsphere.networking.doc/GUID-6E51D76A-DC9F-44E2-B673-7D92384AFDE4.html).

Adding/configuring/removing dvPort groups

A **distributed port group** (**dvPort**) is a group of ports on a specific vDS that provides network connectivity to the VMs and/or the VMkernel interfaces.

The first dvPort can be configured during vDS creation, but you can create a new dvPort using the vSphere Web Client, in the **Networking** inventory, by selecting a specific vDS. Then select **Distributed port group** | **Create a new port group**.

On the **Select name and location** page, type the name of the new distributed port group, or accept the generated name.

Then, on the **Configure settings** page, set the general properties for the new dvPort as illustrated in the following screenshot:

Figure 2.4: Adding a dvPort to a vDS

The different settings are related to dvPort management and configuration:

- **Port binding**: How the virtual ports are allocated to the different network resources: VM vNICs, VMkernel interfaces, and uplinks. There are different allocation methods:
    - **Static binding**: A port is assigned statically when the resource is connected to the vDS.
    - **Dynamic binding**: A port is assigned dynamically when the VM is powered on (and, of course, it's connected to the vDS). Dynamic binding has been disapproved since vSphere 5.0.
    - **Ephemeral - no binding**: No port binding.

- **Number of ports**: How many ports are pre-allocated (by default, 8) on the vDS. Note that each dvPort has an assigned number with a range in the defined number or ports (for example, 1-8). In case of range extension, the new numbers can have a new range, depending on the port allocated before (for example, can be 81-88 if there were 80 ports allocated before).
- **Port allocation**: This defines how number of ports are allocated. There are two different methods:
    - **Elastic (default)**: All ports are pre-assigned and a new set of X ports (the number of ports) is created.
    - **Fixed**: Additional ports are not created once all the ports are assigned. You need to change the number of ports.

VLAN and network resource pools will be discussed later.

To delete a dvPort, just right-click on the selected dvPort and choose the **Delete** menu:

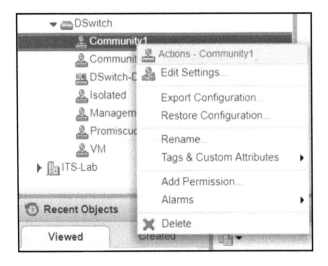

Figure 2.5: Removing a dvPort from a vDS

 Be sure to migrate your VMs to a proper port group before removing a dvPort!

For more information, see the vSphere 6.5 Networking guide (https://docs.vmware.com/en/VMware-vSphere/6.5/com.vmware.vsphere.networking.doc/GUID-69933F6E-2442-46CF-AA17-1196CB9A0A09.html).

Adding/removing uplink adapters to dvUplink groups

Physical NICs (vmnic#), used in existing uplinks on a vSS, can be easily migrated when you are adding hosts to a vDS, but you can also add or remove physical NICs later.

One way is using, again, the **Add and Manage Hosts** wizard add-on described in the previous section.

But you can also the same procedure of the vSS, host by host. Using the vSphere Web Client, you can select the desired host, then select the **Configure** tab and **Virtual switches** in the **Networking** menu.

Select the vDS and then the Manage the physical network adapters connected to the selected switch icon:

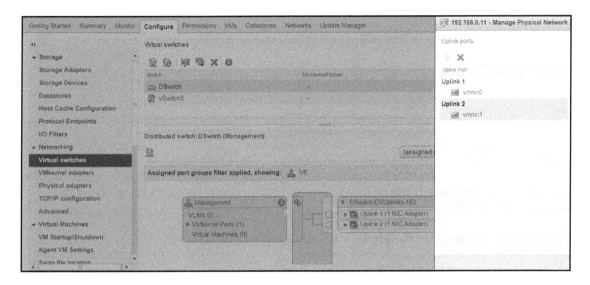

Figure 2.6: Changing the uplink configuration

For more information, see the vSphere 6.5 Networking guide (https://docs.vmware.com/en/VMware-vSphere/6.5/com.vmware.vsphere.networking.doc/GUID-0CBF12A2-1074-4514-BE36-B09565BC4620.html).

Configuring vSphere Distributed Switch general and dvPort group settings

You can change the settings of a vDS by using the vSphere Web Client and selecting the desired vDS in the **Networking** inventory.

Then right-click and choose **Settings | Edit Settings...**, or select the **Configure** tab and click on the **Edit...** button in the **Properties** menu:

Figure 2.7: vDS general settings

The **General** settings of a vDS are quite similar to what you can see during the creation of a new vDS, but now there is the ports counter and the option to assign a name for each uplink. You can change MTU and NIOC settings, and also modify the number of uplinks.

For more information, see the vSphere 6.5 Networking guide (`https://docs.vmware.com/en/VMware-vSphere/6.5/com.vmware.vsphere.networking.doc/GUID-E0FED4AB-823D-4B61-B668-9400746D52E5.html`).

To change the dvPort settings, you can right-click on a dvPort and choose **Edit Settings...**, or again use the **Configure** tab of the dvPort.

The general options are exactly the same as discussed during the creation of a dvPort.

There are several other options discussed later. But also, there is the possibility to define some possible override at the port level, using the **Advanced** menu:

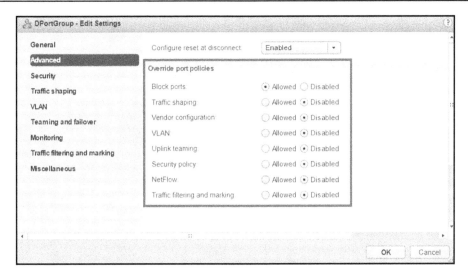

Figure 2.8: Port overrides

For more information, see the vSphere 6.5 Networking guide (`https://docs.vmware.com/en/VMware-vSphere/6.5/com.vmware.vsphere.networking.doc/GUID-FCA2AE5E-83D7-4FEE-8DFF-540BDB559363.html`).

Creating/configuring/removing virtual adapters

The **VMkernel virtual adapters** (**vmk#**) are used by the ESXi networking layer to provide connectivity to hosts and manage some core services such as the management of traffic, vSphere vMotion, fault tolerance, IP storage, vSAN, and so on.

You can migrate existing VMkernel adapters when you are adding hosts to a vDS.

But you can also easily create new adapters with the vSphere Web Client. In the **Host and Clusters** inventory, select the desired host, then, in the **Configure** tab, choose the **VMkernel adapters** menu (in the **Networking** section).

Here, you can check the existing adapters or create a new one:

1. Click on the Add host networking icon.
2. In the **Select connection type** menu, confirm the **VMkernel Network Adapter** option and click on **Next.**
3. In the **Select target device** menu, choose the desired dvPort on a vDS (it's also valid for vSS) and click on **Next.**

4. In the **Port properties** menu, define the network configuration you need (**IPv4**, **IPv6**, or **IPv4 and IPv6**), the TCP/IP stack (for more information about TCP/IP stack, see the *Creating and configuring custom TCP/IP Stacks* section) that should be used, and the type of services enabled on this new VMkernel adapter:

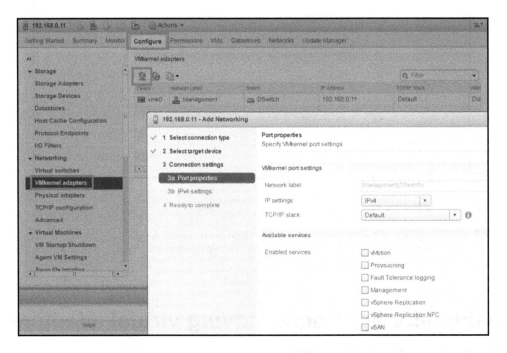

Figure 2.9: VMkernel adapter configuration

There are different types of services that can be provided by different types of VMkernel interfaces:

Type of service	Type of VMkernel	Description
Management traffic	Management	On this interface flows the management traffic between the host and vCenter Server. By default, a Manager VMkernel adapter is created during the ESXi installation. Usually, this interface is also used by vSphere HA. Note that it's possible to add other VMkernel adapters for management traffic (it's one possible way to provide redundancy to this function).

Provisioning traffic	Provisioning	On this interface flows the data transferred for virtual machine cold migration, cloning, and snapshot migration.
vMotion traffic	vMotion	On this interface flows the vMotion traffic during the live migration of VMs across hosts. If this property is not enabled for any VMkernel adapter, migration with vMotion to the selected host is not possible. Note that it's possible to have multiple vMotion interfaces to improve bandwidth and throughput.
Fault tolerance traffic	Fault tolerance logging	On this interface flows the fault tolerance logging traffic used by the vSphere FT feature. Note that you can have only one VMkernel adapter for FT traffic per host.
Storage traffic	-	IP-based storage traffic, such as NFS or iSCSI, can use one or more VMkernel interface. Note that there isn't a specific type for those kinds of traffic.
vSAN traffic	vSAN	This interface enables vSAN traffic on the host. In a vSAN cluster, this interface is mandatory, and it will also be used for vSphere HA.
vSphere Replibe usedon traffic	vSphere Replication	This interface manages the outgoing replication data that is sent from the source ESXi host to the vSphere Replication server.
vSphere Replication NFC traffic	vSphere Replication NFC	This interface manages the incoming replication data on the target replication site.

Table 2.2: VMkernel virtual adapters

As described later, there are also different TCP/IP stacks available with different settings for different VMkernel interfaces.

For more information, see the vSphere 6.5 Networking guide (`https://docs.vmware.com/ en/VMware-vSphere/6.5/com.vmware.vsphere.networking.doc/GUID-8244BA51-BD0F- 424E-A00E-DDEC21CF280A.html`).

Migrating virtual machines to/from a vSphere Distributed Switch

VM networking can be easily migrated when you are adding hosts to a vDS. But you can migrate a VM to a dvPort later with the vSphere Web Client.

One option is to right-click on a vDS and choose the **Migrate VM to Another Network...** wizard:

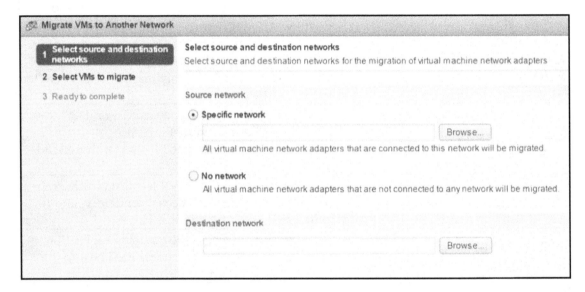

Figure 2.10: Migrating VMs to a dvPort

You can select the source network and the destination network, and also which VM will be migrated.

Another option is just to edit the VM settings and change the VM port group to a dvPort.

For more information, see the vSphere 6.5 Networking guide (`https://docs.vmware.com/en/VMware-vSphere/6.5/com.vmware.vsphere.networking.doc/GUID-3DDB651A-7C17-49E7-A911-C973A7E80402.html`).

Configuring LACP on vDS given design parameters

The **Link Aggregation Control Protocol** (**LACP**) is a standard that bundles several physical ports together to form a single logical channel. Usually, it's called dynamic link aggregation (in contrast to static link aggregation).

LACP is fully supported in vSphere 5.1 and later, but only with vDS (vSS can only support static link aggregation or EtherChannel, with the **IP hash** teaming policy).

LACP must be prepared correctly for the physical part of the networking. You create **Link Aggregation Groups** (**LAG**); every LAG group has two or more ports. You can create up to 64 LAGs.

Each LAG can be created using the vSphere Web Client, in the **Configure** tab of the selected vDS, under the **LACP** menu.

Just click on the New Link Aggregation Group icon:

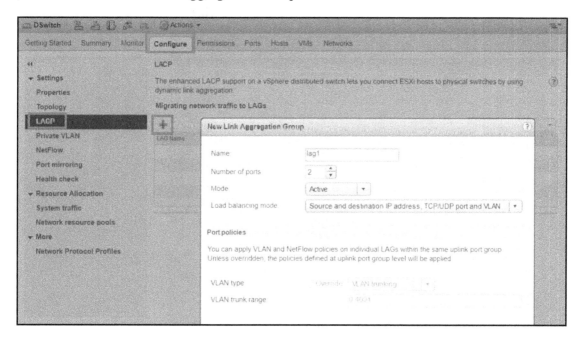

Figure 2.11: Adding a new LAG

You can choose how many physical NIC ports will be used for the LAG (minimum two) and several different parameters that must match the same setting on the physical switches.

The LAG Mode options can be:

- **Passive**: The LAG ports do not initiate LACP negotiations
- **Active**: The LAG ports initiate negotiations with the LACP Port Channel at the physical switched side

The LAG load balancing mode (LNB mode) option can be:

- Source and destination IP address, TCP/UDP port, and VLAN
- Source and destination IP address and VLAN
- Source and destination MAC address
- Source and destination TCP/UDP port
- Source port ID
- VLAN

Now you can use the **Migrating network traffic to LAGs** wizard to migrate your network to the LACP configuration:

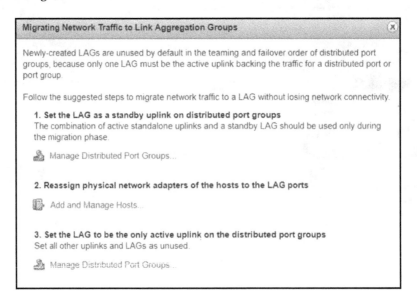

Figure 2.12: Migrating network traffic to LAGs

For more information, see the vSphere 6.5 Networking guide (`https://docs.vmware.com/en/VMware-vSphere/6.5/com.vmware.vsphere.networking.doc/GUID-0D1EF5B4-7581-480B-B99D-5714B42CD7A9.html`).

Describing vDS Security policies/settings

This was already described in *Objective 1.4* for the standard virtual switches.

By default, on vDS, all security policies are rejected on all dvPorts:

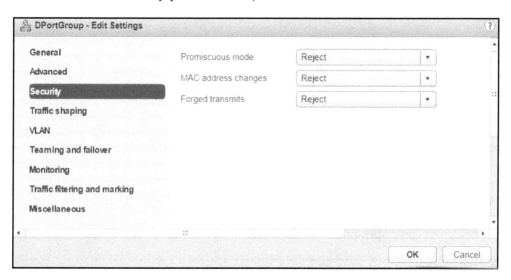

Figure 2.13: Security policies of a dvPort

For more information, see the vSphere 6.5 Networking guide (`https://docs.vmware.com/en/VMware-vSphere/6.5/com.vmware.vsphere.networking.doc/GUID-62914CF2-A6A8-4DCC-90A9-8CD4BBF50017.html`).

 There is also a BPDU filter feature (both on vSS and vDS), as described in KB 2047822 (`https://kb.vmware.com/s/article/2047822`)—Understanding the BPDU Filter feature in vSphere.

Other security policies are implemented with NSX (for example, IP Spoof Guard).

Configuring dvPort group blocking policies

Port blocking can be enabled both at port group level and port level.

To disable all the ports on a specific dvPort, just select the **Miscellaneous** menu in the dvPort settings:

Figure 2.14: Miscellaneous settings of a dvPort

To block a specific port, just select a vDS and choose the **Ports** tab. Then, select a specific port, click on the Edit distributed port setting icon, and define an override (note that you should enable override options at dvPort level):

Figure 2.15: Miscellaneous settings of a single port

For more information, see the vSphere 6.5 Networking guide (`https://docs.vmware.com/ en/VMware-vSphere/6.5/com.vmware.vsphere.networking.doc/GUID-9BB253AF-F0CD-4288-8A58-79CD7CD5405B.html`).

Configuring load balancing and failover policies

Teaming and failover settings on a dvPort are similar to the same settings on a vSS, but with an important addition.

You can view or change those settings in the **Teaming and failover** menu in the dvPort settings:

Figure 2.16: Teaming settings for a dvPort

The different **Load balancing** settings are as follows:

- **Route based on originating virtual port**: VMs are distributed according to their associated virtual port ID on the virtual switch. After the virtual switch selects an uplink for a VM, it always forwards traffic through the same uplink. Note that, in this way, one VM can only use the bandwidth of one physical uplink.

- **Route based on source MAC hash**: VMs are distributed according to a hash algorithm based on the VM MAC address. Also, in this case, one VM can only use the bandwidth of one physical uplink.

- **Route based on IP hash**: VMs are distributed according to a hash algorithm based on the source and destination IP address of each packet. In this case, one VM can use more physical uplinks, but physical switches must be configured according to this configuration (ports corresponding to the virtual switch uplinks must be in Etherchannel mode).

- **Route based on physical NIC load**: The vDS checks the actual load of the uplinks and tries to reduce it on overloaded uplinks. The vDS tests the uplinks every 30 seconds, and if their load exceeds 75 percent of usage, the port ID of the virtual machine with the highest I/O is moved to a different uplink. Note that this option is available only with vDS.
- **Use explicit failover order**: In this case, there isn't any load balancing feature, but better resiliency.

Other failover (and failback) policies are as follows:

- **Network failure detection**: How to detect an uplink failure and start a failover to another active (or standby) uplink. The available methods are as follows:
  - **Link status only**: Use only on the link status that the physical NIC provides.
  - **Beacon probing**: Sends out and listens for specific Ethernet frames sent each second using broadcast or beacon probes. Requires at least three uplinks and cannot be used with IP Hash (or LCAP). For more information, see VMware KB 1005577 (`https://kb.vmware.com/s/article/1005577`)—What is beacon probing?
- **Notify switches**: During the failover or failback of one uplink, the virtual switch sends notifications over the network to update the lookup tables on physical switches.
- **Failback**: If a failed uplink returns online, the virtual switch sends the uplink back.

To minimize failover and failback operations, you can change the following settings on the physical switch:

- Disable the **Spanning Tree Protocol** (**STP**) on physical NICs that are connected to ESXi hosts.
- For Cisco-based networks, enable PortFast mode for access interfaces or PortFast trunk mode for trunk interfaces. This might save about 30 seconds during the initialization of the physical switch port.
- If available, use the **PortFast Bridge Protocol Data Unit** (**BPDU**) guard feature to prevent specific network topology attacks (`https://kb.vmware.com/s/article/2017193`).
- Disable the trunking negotiation.

For more information, see the vSphere 6.5 Networking guide (`https://docs.vmware.com/en/VMware-vSphere/6.5/com.vmware.vsphere.networking.doc/GUID-4D97C749-1FFD-403D-B2AE-0CD0F1C70E2B.html`).

Configuring VLAN/PVLAN settings for VMs given communication requirements

Virtual LAN (VLAN) is a standard (IEEE 802.1Q) used to segment Ethernet broadcast domains in different logical networks. A specific tag (VLAN ID) is added to the Ethernet frames to identify which VLAN belongs to a packet.

On the physical switches, network ports can be configured in two different ways:

- **VLAN untagged**: All packets bounded on a specific VLAN ID (this mode is also called access or untagged mode)
- **VLAN tagged**: Multiple VLANs can flow in this port (this mode is also called trunk or tagged mode)

Some switches have a **native VLAN** option, where all packets without any VLAN ID can be tagged on the specific VLAN ID used by the native VLAN.

VMware vSphere supports different tagging options:

- **External VLAN tagging**: Physical switch ports are in untagged mode on a specific VLAN ID. No configuration is needed at the virtual switch level.
- **Virtual switch VLAN tagging**: Physical switch ports are in tagged mode on more VLANs, and each port group is configured on a specific VLAN.
- **VM VLAN tagging**: Physical switch ports are in tagged mode and also the VM port group is configured on more VLANs using the VLAN trunking option on vDS (on vSS by using VLAN ID 4095).

To configure the proper VLAN configuration on a dvPort, choose the **VLAN** menu in the settings:

Figure 2.17: VLAN settings for a dvPort

There are different available options for the VLAN type:

- **None**: Do not use VLAN.
- **VLAN**: In the VLAN ID field, enter a number between 1 and 4,094.
- **VLAN trunking**: Enter a VLAN trunk range.
- **Private VLAN:** Select a private VLAN entry. But you need to configure the PVLAN at the vDS level, as described later.

For more information, see the vSphere 6.5 Networking guide (`https://docs.vmware.com/en/VMware-vSphere/6.5/com.vmware.vsphere.networking.doc/GUID-CF00FE1E-4BA4-4949-949B-29CAD52F3A89.html`).

With distributed virtual switches, there is also support for **Private VLANs** (**PVLAN**), usually used to solve the VLAN limitations (in scalability and security) by adding a further segmentation of the logical broadcast domain into multiple smaller broadcast subdomains.

Each PVLAN is identified by two VLAN numbers (primary and secondary), and there are three different PVLAN types:

- **Promiscuous Primary VLAN**: When the primary and secondary numbers are the same. It is the same as a traditional VLAN, with a single domain broadcast there—everybody can talk with everything.
- **Community**: VMs can communicate with other VMs in the same community PVLAN and with all VMs in the promiscuous PVLAN.
- **Isolated**: VMs can communicate only with VMs in the promiscuous PVLAN.

PVLAN must be defined first at vDS level—in the **Configure** tab, expand **Settings** and select **Private VLAN**:

Figure 2.18: PVLAN settings for a vDS

For more information, see the vSphere 6.5 Networking guide (https://docs.vmware.com/en/VMware-vSphere/6.5/com.vmware.vsphere.networking.doc/GUID-A9287D46-FDE0-4D64-9348-3905FEAC7FAE.html).

Configuring traffic shaping policies

On vDS, a traffic shaping policy is applied to each port at the port group level. But it's also possible to define specific and granular options at the port level.

You can control ingress or egress traffic (with vSS you can only control egress traffic) in the **Traffic shaping** menu in the dvPort settings:

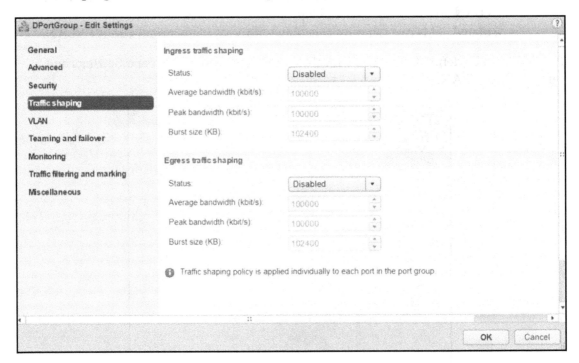

Figure 2.19: Traffic shaping settings on a dvPort

There are different settings, as follows:

- **Average bandwidth (kbits/s)**: The number of Kbps to allow, averaged over time.
- **Peak bandwidth (kbits/s)**: The maximum Kbps to allow (when it is sending or receiving a burst of traffic). This number limits the bandwidth during peaks.
- **Burst size (KB)**: Maximum number of bytes to allow in a peak. If this value is set, it's possible to have a burst bonus, limited to the maximum peak value and only the amount of data specified in the burst size.

The bursting "bonus" works in the following mode:

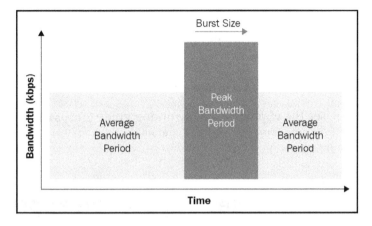

Figure 2.20: Peak on a vDS

For more information, see the vSphere 6.5 Networking guide (`https://docs.vmware.com/en/VMware-vSphere/6.5/com.vmware.vsphere.networking.doc/GUID-D3A091C0-0D0D-480D-ACE3-62524E2E0D0A.html`).

Enabling TCP Segmentation Offload support for a virtual machine

TCP Segmentation Offload (**TSO**) and **Large Receive Offload** (**LRO**) are two optimizations that can be used on physical and VM NICs. These optimizations can improve the performance of ESXi hosts by reducing the VMkernel CPU overhead for TCP/IP network operations; in this way, the host has more CPU cycles to run applications.

For more information, see KB 2055140 (`https://kb.vmware.com/s/article/2055140`)—Understanding TSO and LRO in a VMware environment.

If TSO is enabled on the transmission path, the NIC divides larger data chunks into TCP segments. If TSO is disabled, the CPU performs segmentation for TCP/IP.

 TSO is referred to as **Large Segment Offload** or **Large Send Offload** (**LSO**) in the latest vmxnet3 driver attributes.

By default, TSO is enabled in the VMkernel of the ESXi host, and in the vmxnet2 and vmxnet3 virtual machine adapters.

To disable at the host level, you can use the `ethtool` command (for each NIC), or better, the `esxcli` command:

```
esxcli system settings advanced set -o /Net/UseHwTSO -i 0
```

For more information, see the vSphere 6.5 Networking guide (`https://docs.vmware.com/en/VMware-vSphere/6.5/com.vmware.vsphere.networking.doc/GUID-E105A601-9331-496C-A213-F76EA3863E31.html`).

Enabling jumbo frames support on appropriate components

The original IEEE 802.3 specifications defined a valid Ethernet frame size from 64 to 1,518 bytes. Considering that the standard Ethernet header is 18 bytes in length, then the payload for a standard frame ranges in size from 46 to 1,500 bytes. This is the **Maximum Transmission Unit** (**MTU**).

Jumbo frames are Ethernet frames with more than 1,500 bytes of payload, typically around 9,000 bytes. Note that ESXi supports 9,000 bytes a maximum frame size, which you can configure.

You must enable jumbo frames end to end, so there are many places where you have to set the right MTU: physical switches, virtual switches, end interfaces (vNIC and VMkernel adapters). Otherwise, the performance will not increase, but rather do the opposite due to packet fragmentation.

 Before enabling jumbo frames, check with your hardware vendor to ensure that your physical network adapter supports jumbo frames.

You can enable jumbo frames both on a vSphere Distributed Switch and a vSphere standard switch by changing the MTU to a value greater than 1,500 bytes. For a vDS, just go into the **Advanced** menu in the vDS settings:

Figure 2.21: MTU settings on a vDS

Where should you enable jumbo frames? Usually, they are mostly used for IP-based storage traffic. If you plan to use jumbo frames for iSCSI or NFS traffic, see KB 1007654 (`https://kb.vmware.com/s/article/1007654`)—iSCSI and Jumbo Frames configuration on VMware ESXi/ESX.

For more information, see the vSphere 6.5 Networking guide (`https://docs.vmware.com/en/VMware-vSphere/6.5/com.vmware.vsphere.networking.doc/GUID-53F968D9-2F91-41DA-B7B2-48394D997F2A.html`).

Recognizing the behavior of vDS auto-rollback

Starting with vSphere 5.1, it is possible to prevent misconfiguration of the management network and automatically recover the previous configuration by using rollback and recovery support, available both on vDS and vSS as describe in VMware KB 2032908 (`https://kb.vmware.com/s/article/2032908`)—Understanding network rollback and recovery in vSphere 5.1 and later.

By rolling configuration changes back, vSphere protects hosts from losing connection to the vCenter Server as a result of misconfiguration of the management network.

But there are also two different types of auto-rollback options: (host) **networking rollback** and **vDS rollback**.

A vDS rollback happens when invalid updates are made to vDS, dvPorts, or distributed ports for one of these changes:

- Changing the MTU of a distributed switch
- Changing the following settings in the distributed port group of the management VMkernel network adapter:
  - Teaming and failover
  - VLAN
  - Traffic shaping
- Blocking all ports in the distributed port group containing the management VMkernel network adapter
- Overriding the policies at the level of the distributed port for the management VMkernel network adapter

Rollback is enabled by default in vSphere 5.1 and later. You can disable rollback by editing the `vpxd.cfg` configuration file of vCenter Server directly.

In the `<network>` element, set the `<rollback>` element to `false`:

```
<config>
 <vpxd>
  <network>
    <rollback>false</rollback>
  </network>
 </vpxd>
</config>
```

Note that you can connect directly to a host and use the DCUI to fix the invalid configuration of the management network.

For more information, see the vSphere 6.5 Networking guide (`https://docs.vmware.com/en/VMware-vSphere/6.5/com.vmware.vsphere.networking.doc/GUID-8BA411A4-8582-4C02-8489-D3D7D09A9BF0.html`).

Configuring vDS across multiple vCenters to support Long Distance vMotion

Starting with vSphere 6.0, you have the ability to hot-migrate VMs between vCenter Server with the support for geographical vMotion (long-distance vMotion).

There are some requirements, including some at the network side:

- **Physical network requirements**: The minimum network bandwidth is 250 Mbps with a maximum latency of 150 ms.
- **Virtual network requirements**: There should be layer network connectivity for the VM network port groups. Also, for each host there should exist two VMkernel adapters marked for vMotion traffic, and both must be reachable to each other (also with routing).
- **CPU compatibility**: Both hosts must have the same CPU generation family or must be compliant with the same EVC baseline.
- **Version requirements**: The source and destination vCenter Server instances and ESXi hosts must be 6.0 or later. Also, the cross-vCenter Server and long-distance vMotion features both require an Enterprise Plus license.
- **Time sync**: Both vCenter Server instances must be time-synchronized with each other for correct vCenter Single Sign-On token verification.

The following table summarizes the requirements for the different versions of vMotion:

Version	Bandwidth	RTT	Distance
4	622 Mbps	5 ms	~200 km
5	250 Mbps	10 ms	~600 km
6	250 Mbps	150 ms	~5000 km

Table 2.3: vMotion requirements

The vCenter servers perform network compatibility checks to prevent several possible configuration problems.

 The cross-vCenter or long-distance vMotion can be performed from the vSphere Web Client, but only if vCenter servers are in Enhanced Linked Mode and in the same SSO domain. Otherwise, you can use vSphere APIs/SDK or the Cross vCenter Workload Migration Utility Flings utility (`https://labs.vmware.com/flings/cross-vcenter-workload-migration-utility`) to migrate virtual machines.

For more information, see KB 2106949 (`https://kb.vmware.com/s/article/2106949`)—Long Distance vMotion requirements in VMware vSphere 6.0.

Comparing and contrasting vSphere Distributed Switch capabilities

A vDS provides centralized management and monitoring of the networking configuration of all hosts that are associated with the vDS.

Using vDS separates the **control plane** from the **data plane**:

- The control plane is located in the vCenter Server and it's the structure used to manage the vDS (formally, it's more a management plane, in that it includes most control plane features).
- The data plane is distributed on each ESXi and it implements basic networking features, such as package switching, filtering, VLAN tagging, and so on. The data plane section of a vDS located on an ESXi host is called a host proxy switch.

The vDS networking configuration created on vCenter Server (the management plane) is automatically pushed to all host proxy switches on the different ESXi (the data plane).

The following diagram (from the vSphere Networking guide) summarizes the entire architecture:

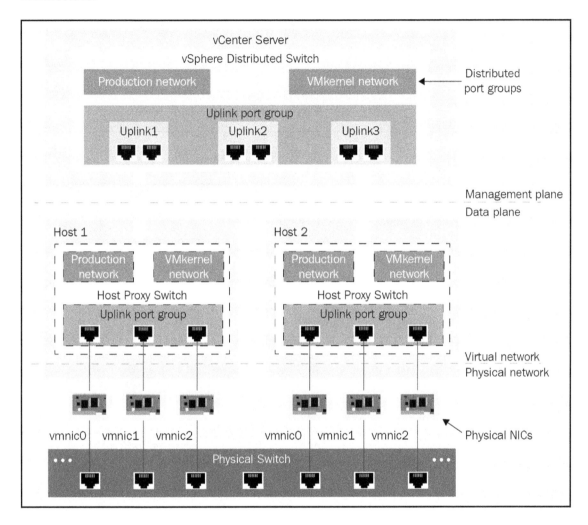

Figure 2.22: vDS architecture

With the distributed switch, you can have more features and functions:

Feature	Standard Virtual Switch	Distributed Virtual Switch
L2 forwarding	Yes	Yes
VLAN segmentation	Yes	Yes

802.1Q tagging	Yes	Yes
NIC teaming	Yes	Yes (+LACP support)
Traffic shaping	Yes (only egress)	Yes (ingress/egress)
QoS	No	Yes
Centralized and unified management	No	Yes
Private VLAN support	No	Yes
Network runtime state follows VM	No	Yes
Netflow and port mirroring	No	Yes

Table 2.4: vSS versus vDS

 Starting with vSphere 6.5 Update 1, VMware has discontinued its third-party virtual switch (vSwitch) program, and plans to deprecate the VMware vSphere APIs used by third-party switches.

For more information, see the KB 2149722 (`https://kb.vmware.com/s/article/2149722`)—FAQ: Discontinuation of third-party vSwitch program.

Configuring multiple VMkernel Default Gateways

Until ESXi 6.0, there was only one default gateway for the entire TCP/IP stack. But sometimes you need different gateways for different VMkernel services, such as vMotion or iSCSI.

One option is to add some additional static routes, but this is not supported in ESXi 6.5 (KB 2001426 (`https://kb.vmware.com/s/article/2001426`)—Configuring static routes for vmkernel ports on an ESXi host).

Another option is to use multiple default gateways, and this is possible starting with ESXi 6.0 and thanks to the **multiple TCP/IP stacks**. Each TCP/IP stack represents a different network configuration, with specific network parameters, such as a different default gateway.

You can set the different default gateway using the vSphere Web Client, in the **Configure** tab of each ESXi host. Just select the **TCP/IP configuration** menu (in the **Networking** section), choose one TCP/IP stack, and click on the Edit TCP/IP stack configuration icon:

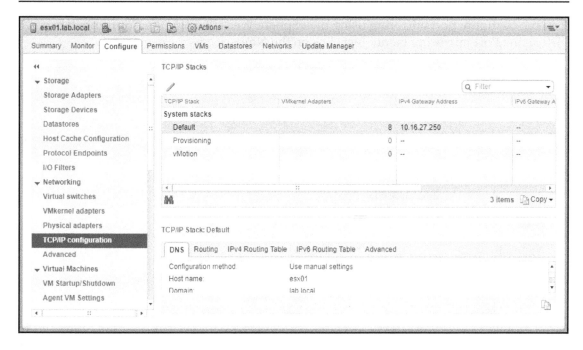

Figure 2.23: TCP/IP stacks

For more information, see the vSphere 6.5 Networking guide (`https://docs.vmware.com/en/VMware-vSphere/6.5/com.vmware.vsphere.networking.doc/GUID-44CAFD7C-6352-4993-A461-A27EE1C7D940.html`).

It's also possible to create a custom TCP/IP stack, as described later.

Configuring ERSPAN

VMware vDS provides industry-standard features to monitor the network traffic: **port mirroring (Encapsulated Remote Switched Port Analyzer (ERSPAN))** and **NetFlow** (discussed later).

Port mirroring is used on a switch to send a copy of packets seen on one switch port (or an entire VLAN) to a monitoring connection on another switch port. Port mirroring is based on ERSPAN standards.

 Certain port mirroring functionalities in vSphere 5.1 and later depend on which version of vCenter Server and vSphere Distributed Switch, and which host you use, and how you use these aspects of vSphere together.

You can configure port mirroring using the vSphere Web Client, in the **Configure** tab of a vDS, in the **Port mirroring** menu. Just click on the **New...** icon:

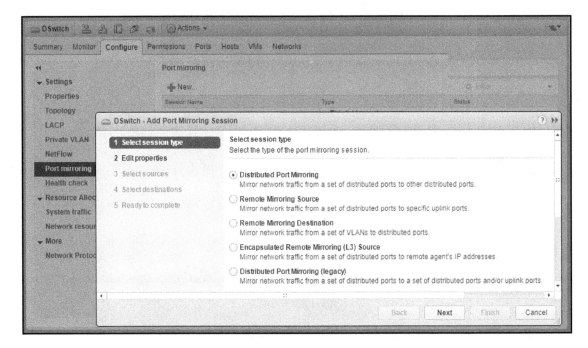

Figure 2.24: Adding a port mirror session

There are different session types for the port mirroring:

- **Distributed Port Mirroring**: Mirror packets from some VMs on one host to a VM on the same host. For more information see this blog post: `https://blogs.vmware.com/vsphere/2013/01/vsphere-5-1-vds-feature-enhancements-port-mirroring-part-1.html`.
- **Remote Mirroring Source**: Mirror packets from some VMs on one host to a specific uplink port on the same host, with an external monitor system. For more information see this blog post: `https://blogs.vmware.com/vsphere/2013/02/vsphere-5-1-vds-feature-enhancements-port-mirroring-part-2.html`.
- **Remote Mirroring Destination**: Mirror packets from VMs on one host to a VM on another host. For more information see this blog post: `https://blogs.vmware.com/vsphere/2013/02/vsphere-5-1-vds-feature-enhancements-port-mirroring-part-3.html`.

- **Encapsulated Remote Mirroring (L3) Source**: Mirror packets from a number of distributed ports to the IP addresses of a remote agent. The virtual machine's traffic is mirrored to a remote physical destination through an IP tunnel.
- **Distributed Port Mirroring (legacy)**: Mirror packets from a number of distributed ports to a number of distributed ports and/or uplink ports on the corresponding host.

For more information, see the vSphere 6.5 Networking guide (`https://docs.vmware.com/en/VMware-vSphere/6.5/com.vmware.vsphere.networking.doc/GUID-CFFD9157-FC17-440D-BDB4-E16FD447A1BA.html`).

Creating and configure custom TCP/IP Stacks

As described previously, starting with vSphere 6.0 there are multiple TCP/IP stacks.

As shown in *Figure 2.23*, the predefined VMkernel TCP/IP stacks are the following:

- **Default TCP/IP stack**: Provides networking support for the management of traffic between vCenter and ESXi, and usually for other system traffic such as vMotion, IP storage, fault tolerance, and so on.
- **vMotion TCP/IP stack**: Can be used for the vMotion traffic and could be useful to provide better isolation for the vMotion traffic or when the vMotion adapters need a different default gateway. If you use this TCP/IP stack, then the VMkernel adapters on the default TCP/IP stack are disabled for the vMotion service.
- **Provisioning TCP/IP stack**: Supports the traffic for VM cold migration, cloning, and snapshot migration but also for long-distance vMotion. The provisioning TCP/IP stack can be used to isolate the traffic from the cloning operations on a separate gateway. If you use this TCP/IP stack, then the VMkernel adapters on the default TCP/IP stack are disabled for the provisioning traffic.

 The provisioning traffic uses the **Network File Copy** (**NFC**) service, a file-specific FTP service, used by ESXi for copying and moving data. Long-distance vMotion uses this service to copy data between data centers.

You can add custom TCP/IP stacks at the VMkernel level to handle networking traffic of custom applications, but actually, this operation is possible only from the CLI, with the following `esxcli` command on each ESXi:

```
esxcli network ip netstack add –N=StackName
```

`StackName` is the name of the new TCP/IP stack.

The custom TCP/IP stack is created on the host. Now you can assign VMkernel adapters to the stack.

For more information, see the vSphere 6.5 Networking guide (`https://docs.vmware.com/en/VMware-vSphere/6.5/com.vmware.vsphere.networking.doc/GUID-660423B1-3D35-4F85-ADE5-FE1D6BF015CF.html`).

Configuring Netflow

NetFlow is a feature that was introduced on Cisco routers that provides the ability to collect IP network traffic as it enters or exits an interface. Starting with vSphere 5.1, VMware supports **Internet Protocol Flow Information Export** (**IPFIX**) to analyze VM IP traffic by collecting data from a vDS and sending it across to a NetFlow collector tool.

You can configure the NetFlow collector using the vSphere Web Client, in the **Configure** tab of the selected vDS. Just select the **NetFlow** menu in the **Settings** section. Then click on the **Edit...** button:

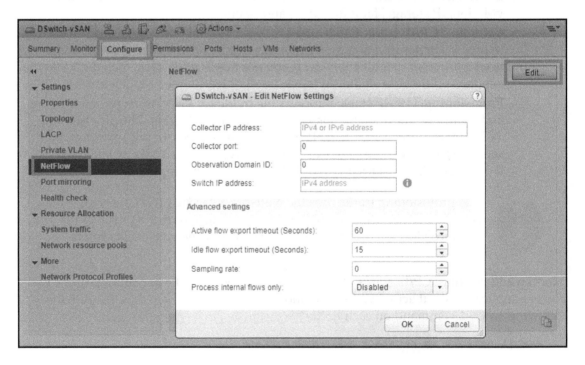

Figure 2.25: Editing NetFlow Settings

The different parameters are the following:

- **Collector IP address** and **Collector port** of the NetFlow collector. You can contact the NetFlow collector via the IPv4 or IPv6 address.
- **Observation Domain ID** identifies the information related to the switch.
- **Switch IP address** is used to see the information from the vDS in the NetFlow collector under a single network device instead of under a separate device for each host on the switch.
- The (optional) **Active flow export timeout (Seconds)** and **Idle flow export timeout (Seconds)** textboxes set the time, in seconds, to wait before sending information after the flow is initiated.
- The (optional) **Sampling rate** option is used to change the portion of data that the switch collects. The sampling rate represents the number of packets that NetFlow drops after every collected packet. A sampling rate of x instructs NetFlow to drop packets in a collection of packets: dropped packets ratio 1:x.
- The (optional) **Process internal flows only** option is used to collect data on network activity between virtual machines on the same host.

For more information, see the vSphere 6.5 Networking guide (`https://docs.vmware.com/en/VMware-vSphere/6.5/com.vmware.vsphere.networking.doc/GUID-55FCEC92-74B9-4E5F-ACC0-4EA1C36F397A.html`).

Objective 2.2 – Configuring Network I/O control (NIOC)

VMware vSphere **Network I/O Control** (**NIOC**) is a network resource control engine used to provide **quality of service** (**QoS**) capabilities to VDS; usually, it's used to guarantee the network bandwidth or manage this in a proper way for business-critical applications (or for VMkernel traffic) and to resolve situations where several types of traffic compete for common resources.

Objective 2.2 for VCP65-DCV and VCP6-DCV is exactly the same because there weren't big changes in networking from vSphere 6.0 to vSphere 6.5.

The vSphere 6.5 Networking guide contains in-depth pieces of information about networking capabilities and configurations: https://docs.vmware.com/en/VMware-vSphere/6.5/vsphere-esxi-vcenter-server-652-networking-guide.pdf.

Explaining NIOC capabilities

Starting with vSphere 6.0, the new NIOC v3 introduces a mechanism to reserve bandwidth for system traffic based on the capacity of the physical NICs on a host. It enables fine-grained resource control at the VM network adapter level similar to the model that you use for allocating CPU and memory resources.

If you have upgraded a vDS to version 6.0.0 without converting NIOC to version 3, you can upgrade NIOC to use the enhanced model for bandwidth allocation to system traffic and to individual virtual machines:

vSphere Network I/O Control	vSphere Distributed Switch Version	ESXi Version
2.0	5.1	5.1, 5.5, 6.0, 6.5
	5.5	5.5, 6.0, 6.5
3.0	6.0	6.0, 6.5
	6.5	6.5

Table 2.5: NIOC versions

For more information, see the vSphere 6.5 Networking guide (https://docs.vmware.com/en/VMware-vSphere/6.5/com.vmware.vsphere.networking.doc/GUID-98E0B3C2-52A7-4CAB-A839-4DA82A9F6D3A.html).

Configuring NIOC shares/limits based on VM requirements

One option to configure reservation for a group of VMs is using a network resource pool, but this works only to provide a reservation quota.

But with NIOC v3 there is also another option: just edit the VM settings and locate the network adapter card. You will notice the same **Shares**, **Reservation**, and **Limit** settings, typically for CPU and memory:

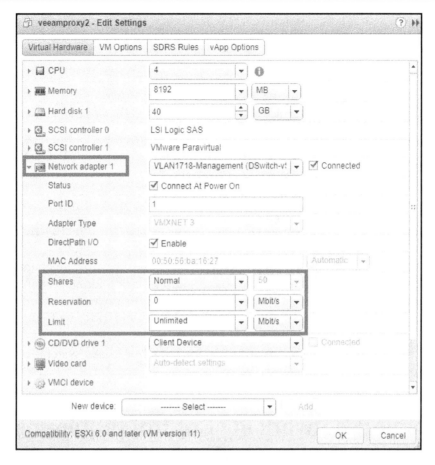

Figure 2.26: VM networking settings

To have those options, there are some prerequisites:

- **vDS version**: Must be version 6.0.0 or later.
- **NIOC version**: Must be version 3.
- **NIOC status**: Must be enabled. See the *Enabling/disabling Network I/O Control* section for information on how to manage its status.
- **VM traffic**: The VMs system traffic needs a configured bandwidth reservation. See Configure Bandwidth Allocation for System Traffic (`https://docs.vmware.com/en/VMware-vSphere/6.5/com.vmware.vsphere.networking.doc/GUID-491C1690-D32E-4940-AEA0-6E1C65D36B93.html#GUID-491C1690-D32E-4940-AEA0-6E1C65D36B93`).

For more information, see the vSphere 6.5 Networking guide (`https://docs.vmware.com/en/VMware-vSphere/6.5/com.vmware.vsphere.networking.doc/GUID-FECAC41A-2C7A-4AD6-B740-7D8D44BADB52.html`).

Explaining the behavior of a given NIOC setting

VMware recommends utilizing NIOC whenever there are multiple traffic types flowing through some shared network adapter. This situation is common with 10 GB NICs where usually two ports sustain all the network traffic.

Different parameters can be used to control the network traffic:

- **Shares**: The relative priority of a traffic type against the other traffic types that are active on the same physical adapter.
- **Reservation**: The minimum bandwidth, in Mbps, that must be guaranteed on a single physical adapter. The total bandwidth reserved for all system traffic types cannot exceed 75 percent of the bandwidth that the physical network adapter with the lowest capacity can provide. Reserved bandwidth that is unused becomes available to other types of system traffic.
- **Limit**: The maximum bandwidth, in Mbps or Gbps, that a system traffic type can consume on a single physical adapter.

Determining Network I/O Control requirements

To use NIOC v3 you need at least vSphere 6.0 and of course vDS. In order to have vDS, you need an Enterprise Plus edition, or a product (such as NSX) that adds a distributed switches feature.

SR-IOV is not available for virtual machines configured to use Network I/O Control version 3.

Differentiating Network I/O Control capabilities

You can use NIOC on a distributed switch to configure bandwidth allocation for the traffic that is related to the main vSphere features:

- Management
- Fault tolerance
- iSCSI
- NFS
- vSAN
- vMotion
- vSphere replication
- vSphere data protection backup
- Virtual machine

For the different versions of NIOC, see the *Explaining NIOC capabilities* section.

 Note that NIOC v3 does not support SRV-IO, CoS tagging, and user-defined network resource pools.

Regarding NIOC and other vSphere features, DRS can migrate VMs within a cluster of vSphere hosts to accommodate bandwidth reservations assigned to VM ports.

Enabling/Disable Network I/O Control

By default, NIOC is enabled on a new vDS. To disable it or change the settings, you can use the vSphere Web Client and select the desired vDS. From the **Actions** menu, select **Edit Settings**.

From the **Network I/O Control** drop-down menu, select **Disabled** (or **Enabled**):

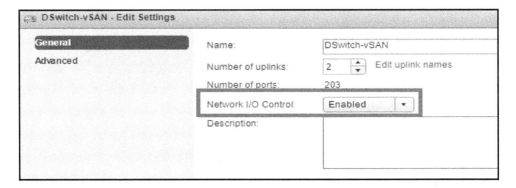

Figure 2.27: VM networking settings

For more information, see the vSphere 6.5 Networking guide (`https://docs.vmware.com/en/VMware-vSphere/6.5/com.vmware.vsphere.networking.doc/GUID-E13CC2B0-5357-4261-8C0E-8BE5BD56BD20.html`).

Monitoring Network I/O Control

To monitor the NIOC settings, you must manage resource allocation under system traffic and, if needed, the network resource pools and VMs settings. You can use the vSphere Web Client in the **Networking** inventory, select a vDS, choose the **Configure** tab and go into the **Resource Allocation** menu.

For the system traffic, some useful metrics and details are the following:

- Network I/O Control status (the state is Enabled/Disabled)
- NIOC version
- Physical network adapters details
- Available bandwidth capacity
- Total bandwidth capacity
- Maximum reservation allowed
- Configured reservation
- Minimum link speed

Another option is to monitor the traffic (as described before) or capture the packets with `pktcap-uw`.

What is missing

The official VCP65-DCV Exam Preparation Guide covers a lot of security topics, but the vSphere 6.5 Networking guide is definitely more rich, with more contents.

For example, the following aspects are not considered in the preparation guide:

- Setting Up Networking with vSphere Standard Switches (`https://docs.vmware.com/en/VMware-vSphere/6.5/com.vmware.vsphere.networking.doc/GUID-E198C88A-F82C-4FF3-96C9-E3DF0056AD0C.html`)
- Upgrade a vSphere Distributed Switch to a Later Version (`https://docs.vmware.com/en/VMware-vSphere/6.5/com.vmware.vsphere.networking.doc/GUID-330A0689-574A-4589-9462-14CA03F3F2F4.html`)
- Upgrade Network I/O Control to Version 3 on a vSphere Distributed Switch (`https://docs.vmware.com/en/VMware-vSphere/6.5/com.vmware.vsphere.networking.doc/GUID-4F40390D-E5F4-4139-AC50-FDB2C4F36B42.html`)
- Backing Up and Restoring Networking Configurations (`https://docs.vmware.com/en/VMware-vSphere/6.5/com.vmware.vsphere.networking.doc/GUID-140C6A52-F4C1-4B13-B2A3-9FFCF6000991.html`)
- Single Root I/O Virtualization (SR-IOV) (`https://docs.vmware.com/en/VMware-vSphere/6.5/com.vmware.vsphere.networking.doc/GUID-CC021803-30EA-444D-BCBE-618E0D836B9F.html`)
- Remote Direct Memory Access for Virtual Machines (`https://docs.vmware.com/en/VMware-vSphere/6.5/com.vmware.vsphere.networking.doc/GUID-9AADBB49-876E-4E44-8149-D0523D8ADA6A.html`)
- Large Receive Offload (`https://docs.vmware.com/en/VMware-vSphere/6.5/com.vmware.vsphere.networking.doc/GUID-514BC149-CDE7-4E07-A922-E3DFB663DC13.html`)
- NetQueue and Networking Performance (`https://docs.vmware.com/en/VMware-vSphere/6.5/com.vmware.vsphere.networking.doc/GUID-6B708D13-145F-4DDA-BFB1-39BCC7CD0897.html`)
- MAC Address Management (`https://docs.vmware.com/en/VMware-vSphere/6.5/com.vmware.vsphere.networking.doc/GUID-1C9C9FA5-2D2D-48DA-9AD5-110171E8FD36.html`)
- Configuring vSphere for IPv6 (`https://docs.vmware.com/en/VMware-vSphere/6.5/com.vmware.vsphere.networking.doc/GUID-A01FC824-6C68-4E11-A5CD-7652A023D9BE.html`)
- Multicast Filtering (`https://docs.vmware.com/en/VMware-vSphere/6.5/com.vmware.vsphere.networking.doc/GUID-9C4D2D07-74EC-46D3-99A5-D7C01B5AE811.html`)

- Capturing and Tracing Network Packets by Using the pktcap-uw Utility (`https://docs.vmware.com/en/VMware-vSphere/6.5/com.vmware.vsphere.networking.doc/GUID-5CE50870-81A9-457E-BE56-C3FCEEF3D0D5.html`)
- vSphere Distributed Switch Health Check (`https://docs.vmware.com/en/VMware-vSphere/6.5/com.vmware.vsphere.networking.doc/GUID-4A6C1E1C-8577-4AE6-8459-EEB942779A82.html`)
- DVS backup and restore (`https://kb.vmware.com/s/article/2034602`)
- Switch Discovery Protocol CDP and LLDP (`https://docs.vmware.com/en/VMware-vSphere/6.5/com.vmware.vsphere.networking.doc/GUID-A1B145E9-6454-45C0-8E7E-71E04A3BC9FF.html`)
- Networking Best Practices (`https://docs.vmware.com/en/VMware-vSphere/6.5/com.vmware.vsphere.networking.doc/GUID-B57FBE96-21EA-401C-BAA6-BDE88108E4BB.html`)
- MAC Address Management (`https://docs.vmware.com/en/VMware-vSphere/6.5/com.vmware.vsphere.networking.doc/GUID-1C9C9FA5-2D2D-48DA-9AD5-110171E8FD36.html`)

Review questions

For more questions, see `Chapter 11`, *Mock Exam 1*, and `Chapter 12`, *Mock Exam 2*:

1. What are the right requirements for removing a host from a vDS? (Choose three.)
     - A: Verify that physical NICs on the target hosts are migrated to a different switch
     - B: Verify that VMkernel adapters on the hosts are migrated to a different switch
     - C: Verify that virtual machine network adapters are migrated to a different switch
     - D: Verify the license of the host
     - E: Verify the vDS version

   ABC - See *Objective 2.1*

2. With NIOC, is it possible to set network reservations and limits at VM level?
   - A: Yes, but only with NIOC v3
   - B: Yes, always
   - C: No, only at network resource pool
   - D: No, never

A - See *Objective 2.2*

Summary

This chapter was dedicated to virtual networking, both with standard and distributed virtual switches, and covered the design, management, and optimization of the virtual network.

Virtual networking concepts were covered, both with standard and distributed virtual switches. Also, there were some considerations about the design, the management, and the optimization of virtual networks.

However, there are new network trends, including **Network Virtualization (NV)**, **Network Function Virtualization (NFV)**, and **Software-defined Networking (SDS)** solutions and products. VMware NSX is an NV solution that could really improve a vSphere environment, not only in terms of networking, but also by adding a lot of new functions (using NFV), especially for security.

Chapter 3, *Configure and Administer vSphere 6.x Storage*, and its objectives will check your knowledge of the storage aspects.

3
Configure and Administer vSphere 6.x Storage

Storage is usually the most critical part of a virtual infrastructure, due to the need for enough performance and capacity for the entire cluster and all the workloads inside it. In order to provide features such as vSphere **high availability** (**HA**), vSphere **Distributed Resource Scheduler** (**DRS**), and other cluster-related capabilities, you need common shared storage for all the ESXi hosts of the cluster. You can also have more storage per cluster, or use the same storage for more clusters.

 Practicing what you learn during this chapter is a key point for enforcing your skills and preparation for the exam. Different labs can help you, such as the *HOL-1808-01-HCI* (vSAN v6.6.1 - *Getting started*) for vSAN, and *HOL-1827-01-HCI* (VMware Storage - Virtual Volumes and Storage Policy-Based Management) for vVols and SPBM.

In this chapter, you will be learning the following topics:

- Learning new VMFS6 datastore capabilities
- Managing a VMFS or NFS datastore
- Configuring multi-path
- Configuring storage integration
- Learning new SIOC configuration options

Objective 3.1 – Managing vSphere integration with physical storage

VMware vSphere supports different types of storage, including traditional and software-defined solutions. For the physical storage, the three main categories are the following:

- **Direct attached storage (DAS)**: vSphere supports SCSI, SATA, SAS solutions, including (in vSphere 6.5), and also NVMe solutions.
- **Network-attached storage (NAS)**: vSphere supports NFSv3 and (starting with vSphere 6.0) NFSv4. Note that Content Library also supports the SMB protocol, but is limited to this specific function.
- **Storage area network (SAN)**: vSphere supports several FC, FCoE, and iSCSI solutions.

Each type of storage provides different capabilities and features:

Storage type	Frontend protocols	Datastore	vSphere features
DAS	SCSI, SATA, SAS, and so on	VMFS	VADP, RDM*, vSphere HA, and DRS**
SAN FC	FC, FCoE	VMFS vVols	VADP, RDM, vSphere HA and DRS, vSphere FT
SAN iSCSI	iSCSI	VMFS vVols	VADP, RDM, vSphere HA and DRS, vSphere FT
NAS	NFS	NFS vVols	VADP, vSphere HA and DRS, vSphere FT

Table 3.1

* For local storage, RDM can only be configured from command lines.

** For local storage, vSphere cluster functions can only be enabled with supported shared SAS products.

 Objective 3.1 for VCP65-DCV and VCP6-DCV are quite similar just because there weren't big changes in those storage functions from vSphere 6.0 to vSphere 6.5. The NFS part is new, but it's also repeated in *Objective 3.4*.

For more information and details, see the vSphere 6.5 storage guide (`https://docs.vmware.com/en/VMware-vSphere/6.5/vsphere-esxi-vcenter-server-652-storage-guide.pdf.pdf`).

Performing NFS v3 and v4.1 configurations

ESXi supports NFS datastore using NFS 3 or NFS 4.1 (starting with vSphere 6.0) protocols, both over TCP (by default, NFS is on the UDP transport protocol). The difference between those two types of NFS will be explained in *Objective 3.4*.

The first step is to configure on the NFS server a share and export it so that it can then be mounted on the ESXi hosts.

Like software iSCSI, to use NFS, you need to first configure the ESXi host with a proper VMkernel and virtual network configuration to access a remote NFS server.

> There isn't an NFS service that you can select in a VMkernel adapter. We will be selecting the interface with the closest routing rule (usually, this is the first in the same network).

The NFS datastore is a special type of datastore, because you do not need to format the NFS volume with a local filesystem, such as VMFS.

For more information, see the vSphere 6.5 Storage guide (`https://docs.vmware.com/en/VMware-vSphere/6.5/com.vmware.vsphere.storage.doc/GUID-9282A8E0-2A93-4F9E-AEFB-952C8DCB243C.html`).

More details on how to mount an NFS datastore will be provided later.

Discovering new storage LUNs

For block-based storage, the different logical disks are provided to the ESXi storage subsystem with a unique **logical unit number** (**LUN**) identifier.

> The same LUN cannot be presented to an ESXi host through different storage protocols, such as iSCSI and Fibre Channel.

If you are adding new LUNs (or modifying the LUNs geometry), then you might need to rescan your storage to see the changes at the ESXi level. There are two different types of storage rescan: automatic and manual.

Automatic rescan is performed directly by the vCenter Server on all the hosts in the same cluster. This feature can be turned off with a specific vCenter advanced option: `Config.vpxd.filter.hostRescanFilter`.

By default, when you perform VMFS datastore management operations, such as creating a VMFS datastore, or increasing or deleting a VMFS datastore, vCenter Server will automatically rescan and update your storage on all the hosts.

But in certain cases, you need to perform a manual rescan, and there are different levels where you can perform it: at adapter level, at host level, and also at the cluster level.

If the storage changes are limited to storage connected through a specific adapter, then you can perform a rescan at adapter level.

You can use the vSphere Web Client, select an ESXi host, then, in the **Configure** tab, select the **Storage Adapters** menu in the **Storage** section. Now, select the desired adapter and click on the rescan icon to rescan:

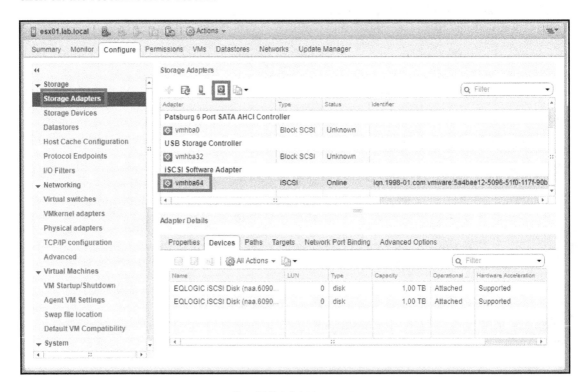

Figure 3.1: Host adapter storage rescan

It's also possible to rescan all the adapters at the same time, but not from the vSphere Web Client (for example, it's possible from the host UI or a new vSphere Client in HTML5).

When the storage changes are extended to all the adapters (and maybe to all the hosts in a cluster), you need to perform a wider storage rescan.

With the new vSphere Client, it's possible to rescan all the storage and the datastore at the host level, but this function is not available in the vSphere Web Client.

Otherwise, you can rescan the storage on all the hosts in a cluster using the vSphere Web Client by selecting a cluster and then going to the **Storage | Rescan Storage...** menu:

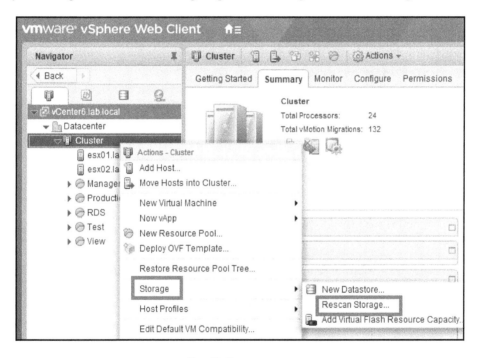

Figure 3.2: Cluster storage rescan

You must choose how to perform the rescan:

- **Scan for new Storage Devices**: Rescan all adapters to discover new storage devices. If new devices are discovered, they appear in the device list.
- **Scan for new VMFS Volumes**: Rescan all storage devices to discover new datastores that have been added since the last scan. Any new datastores appear in the datastore list:

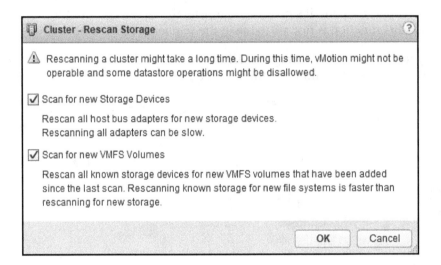

Figure 3.3: Storage rescan options

The progress of the rescan can be monitored in the `/var/log/vmkernel` file on each ESXi host.

You need to perform a manual rescan each time you make one of the following changes:

- Changes in the SAN fabric zoning
- Creation of new LUNs
- Changing of the path masking on a host
- Reconnecting a SAN (or SAS) cable
- Changing some iSCSI configuration (such as CHAP settings)
- Adding a single host to the vCenter Server after you have changed some shared storage setting

The range of scanned LUN IDs for an ESXi host can be from 0 to 16,383. ESXi ignores LUN IDs greater than 16,383.

The configurable `Disk.MaxLUN` parameter controls the range of the scanned LUN ID. The parameter has a default value of `1024`. Note that vSphere 6.x supports more than 256 LUNs and that, in most storage, LUN 256 and 257 may be used by vVols.

 vCenter automatically hides some LUNs, such as RDM LUNs; this behavior will be described later.

For more information, see the vSphere 6.5 Storage guide (`https://docs.vmware.com/en/VMware-vSphere/6.5/com.vmware.vsphere.storage.doc/GUID-D0595EB3-D20C-4951-88EF-5AFB0BF2398D.html`).

Configuring FC/iSCSI/FCoE LUNs as ESXi boot devices

Boot from SAN is an option so that you can have diskless ESXi hosts, and it's supported for FC, FCoE, and (with some limitations) iSCSI storage arrays.

There are some requirements, as follows:

- Each host must have access to its own dedicated boot LUN and should be the first LUN ID (usually 0). Multiple servers can share a diagnostic partition. You can use array-specific LUN masking to achieve this configuration.
- Enable boot both at host BIOS level and the SAN adapter (depending on the type of SAN).
- Multipathing to a boot LUN on active-passive arrays is not supported because the BIOS does not support multipathing and is unable to activate a standby path.

The configuration of the adapter varies from the type of adapter (for example, Emulex or Qlogic) enable and correctly configure the HBA, so it can access the boot LUN.

For FCoE boot from SAN (introduced in vSphere 5.1), you perform most configurations through the option ROM of the network adapter. The network adapters must support one of the following formats, which communicate parameters about an FCoE boot device to VMkernel:

- **FCoE Boot Firmware Table (FBFT)**: Intel propriety
- **FCoE Boot Parameter Table (FBPT)**: Defined by VMware for third-party vendors to implement a software FCoE boot

Note that, with FCoE, you have the following additional limitations:

- You cannot change software FCoE boot configuration from within ESXi
- Coredump is not supported on any software FCoE LUNs, including the boot LUN
- Multipathing is not supported at pre-boot
- If you are using an Intel 10Gb controller with a Cisco switch, configure the switch port to enable spanning tree (STP) and to turn off **switchport trunk native vlan**

For iSCSI, there are other additional considerations, depending also on the type of the iSCSI initiator (discussed later).

For independent iSCSI adapters, just refer to the specific HBA vendor guide.

For software-dependent iSCSI adapters, you need a NIC that supports the **iSCSI Boot Firmware Table** (**iBFT**) format. In this case, you can configure the networking and iSCSI boot parameters on the network adapter and enable the adapter for the iSCSI boot.

For more information, see the following vSphere 6.5 Storage guides:

- Booting ESXi from Fibre Channel SAN (`https://docs.vmware.com/en/VMware-vSphere/6.5/com.vmware.vsphere.storage.doc/GUID-9004389B-E2C0-4BE5-811C-E4886E3B7450.html`)
- Booting ESXi with Software FCoE (`https://docs.vmware.com/en/VMware-vSphere/6.5/com.vmware.vsphere.storage.doc/GUID-C1FD30A2-27C1-45A6-A736-E0AE76A0ADB2.html`)
- Booting from iSCSI SAN (`https://docs.vmware.com/en/VMware-vSphere/6.5/com.vmware.vsphere.storage.doc/GUID-2A66A330-A9E5-460B-8982-54A1B1C38C02.html`)

Mounting an NFS share for use with vSphere

After you have configured the networking on the ESXi host, you can add a new NFS datastore using the vSphere Web Client. On the Storage inventory, in the **Getting Started** tab, just click on **Add a Datastore**. On the **Host and Clusters** inventory, select a host and choose the **Storage | New Datastore...** menu in the contextual menu:

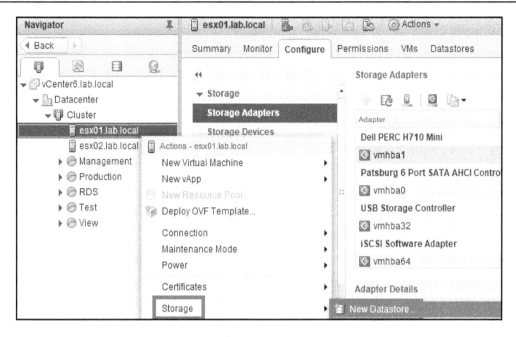

Figure 3.4: Adding a new datastore

Then, choose an **NFS** datastore type:

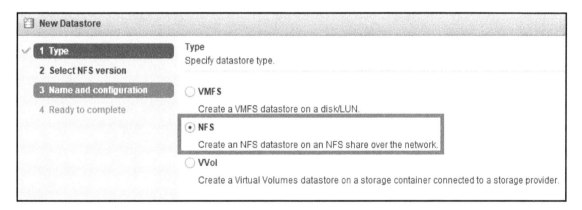

Figure 3.5: Adding a new NFS datastore

Select the proper NFS version:

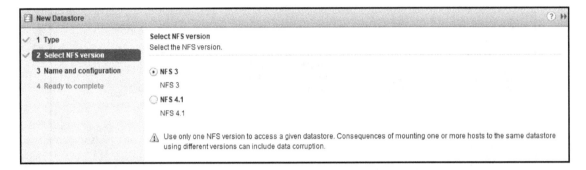

Figure 3.6: Adding a new NFS datastore—Select NFS version

If multiple hosts access the same datastore, you must use the same protocol on all hosts.

Then, enter the **Datastore name**, the server name or IP address (IPv6 or IPv4), and the mount point folder name:

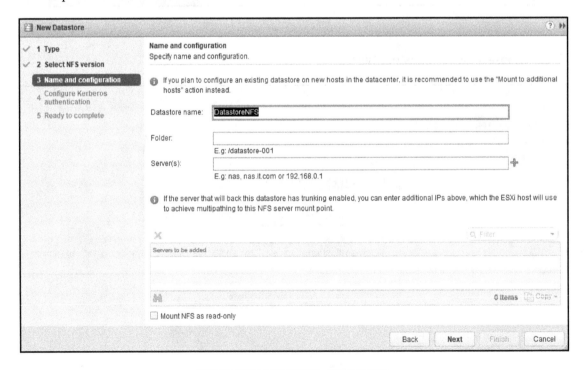

Figure 3.7: Adding a new NFS datastore—Select NFS version

The vSphere Web Client enforces a 42-character limit for the datastore name.

NFS 3 uses one single TCP connection between the client and server. For this reason, ESXi does not support multiple paths and the only solution is to work with more IPs at the storage side and use link aggregation. NFS 4.1 provides multipathing for servers that support session trunking. In this case, you can add multiple IP addresses or server names if the NFS server supports trunking. The ESXi host uses these values to achieve multipathing to the NFS server mount point.

For datastores that contain read-only data (for example, ISO), you can select the Mount NFS read-only option.

NFS 4.1 authentication options will be discussed in *Objective 3.4.*

Virtual disks created on NFS datastores are thin-provisioned by default. To also have thick-provisioned VMDK, you must have VAAI-compatible storage that supports the Reserve Space operation. VAAI will be discussed later.

For more information, see the vSphere 6.5 Storage guide (`https://docs.vmware.com/en/VMware-vSphere/6.5/com.vmware.vsphere.storage.doc/GUID-B52657D0-248D-4A99-99CC-D35B350461D5.html`).

Enabling/configuring/disabling vCenter Server storage filters

By default, vCenter Server provides some storage protection filters to avoid storage corruption and to provide only the storage devices that can be used for a particular operation.

Unsuitable devices are not displayed for selection, for example, LUNs are already used by VMFS datastore or RDM disks.

You can control these filters using the vCenter Server advanced settings:

Advanced parameter	Description
`Config.vpxd.filter.vmfsFilter`	When set to false, you are allowed to add a VMFS volume to a VM, even when in use by another VM
`Config.vpxd.filter.rdmfilter`	When set to false, you are allowed to add a LUN as an RDM, even when in use by another VM
`Config.vpxd.filter.SameHostandTransportsFilter`	When set to false, incompatible LUNs are allowed to be added as extents
`Config.vpxd.filter.hostRescanFilter`	When set to false, the auto rescan for all hosts is disabled after adding storage

Table 3.2

You can change those settings with the vSphere Web Client by selecting the vCenter Server object and then the **Configure** tab. Advanced parameters are available under **Settings** | **Advanced Settings** | **Edit**.

To disable these features, in the value textbox, enter `False` for the specified key.

You do not need to restart the vCenter Server to apply changes.

For more information, see the vSphere 6.5 Storage guide (`https://docs.vmware.com/en/ VMware-vSphere/6.5/com.vmware.vsphere.storage.doc/GUID-EC4B7E67-9802-4BFE-8041- 435C2375CF64.html`).

Configuring/editing hardware/dependent hardware initiators

ESXi can access an iSCSI storage by using one of the following iSCSI initiator types:

- **Software iSCSI initiator**: ESXi manages the entire iSCSI stack and uses one or more VMkernel adapters and a virtual network. With the software iSCSI adapter, you can use iSCSI technology without purchasing specialized hardware.
- **Dependent hardware iSCSI initiator**: iSCSI management and configuration are managed by VMware, but part of the network stack is implemented at the NIC level using some iSCSI offload capabilities. At ESXi level, those NICs are presented with two different components—a hardware iSCSI adapter and a corresponding standard networking NIC.
- **Independent hardware iSCSI initiator or iSCSI HBA**: This is the same as an FC HBA; all of the network stack is implemented in hardware inside the adapter. On the ESXi side, you just see one or more vmhba, like with all other block storage adapters. Network configuration must be performed at card level, using BIOS management, or specific tools (there are also plugins for vCenter to manage the configuration inside vSphere).

CNA cards could appear fully independent or dependent on hardware adapters, but usually using NPAR as a real HBA.

 Hardware iSCSI adapters are enabled by default.

The main difference between one mode and another is how the network is configured: only the independent hardware iSCSI adapter does not require one or more VMkernel adapters on a proper virtual network. Also, the host CPU usage will decrease from the software iSCSI to the HBA iSCSI, but performance and throughput are quite the same for all types of initiators.

For more information, see the vSphere 6.5 Storage guide (https://docs.vmware.com/en/VMware-vSphere/6.5/com.vmware.vsphere.storage.doc/GUID-7A4E3767-CB54-4E88-9BA8-298876119465.html).

Enabling/disabling software iSCSI initiator

By default, the software iSCSI initiator is disabled. To enable it, you must first add the proper adapter.

You can add the software iSCSI adapter using the vSphere Web Client. Select the host and the **Configure** tab, then, in the **Storage | Storage Adapters** menu, click on the + icon and choose **Software iSCSI adapter**:

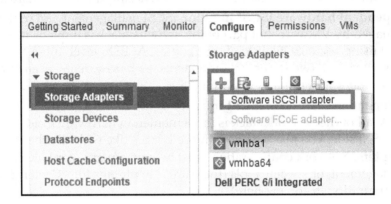

Figure 3.8: Adding a software iSCSI adapter

A new vmhba interface will be created for the iSCSI software initiator.

To disable the software iSCSI initiator using the vSphere Web Client, select the **Configure** tab once more and then the **Storage Adapters** menu. On **iSCSI Software Adapter**, click on the **Disable** button:

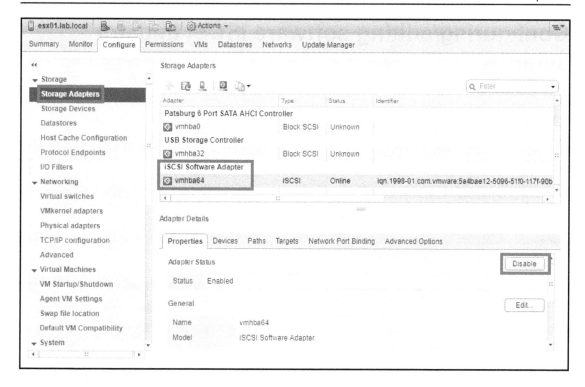

Figure 3.9: Disabling a software iSCSI adapter

 You need to reboot the host to disable and remove the adapter.

For more information, see the vSphere 6.5 Storage guide (`https://docs.vmware.com/en/ VMware-vSphere/6.5/com.vmware.vsphere.storage.doc/GUID-4FEBE089-504C-4E56-8AB3- C909E62F7D07.html`).

Configuring/editing software iSCSI initiator settings

Different software iSCSI initiator settings can be changed.

You can modify them using the vSphere Web Client by selecting an ESXi host and the **Configure** tab. Select the **iSCSI Software Adapter** in the **Storage Adapters** menu:

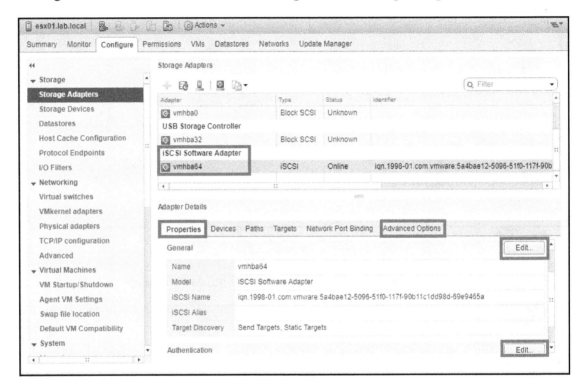

Figure 3.10: Software iSCSI initiator settings

In the **General** properties, you can change the iSCSI name or the iSCSI alias.

If you change the name of an iSCSI adapter, it will only be used for new sessions, and existing sessions aren't altered.

In the **Authentication** properties, you can configure CHAP settings (see the *Enabling/configuring/disabling iSCSI CHAP* section).

In the **Targets** tab, you can only add new targets. To make changes, remove the existing target and re-add it.

In the **Advanced Options** tab, you can change some settings, such as `ARP Redirect` or `Delayed ACK`, that specific storage can require.

For more information, see the vSphere 6.5 Storage guide (`https://docs.vmware.com/en/ VMware-vSphere/6.5/com.vmware.vsphere.storage.doc/GUID-AE007BE0-DB6E-4E0A-8FA1- F4030E0F8D9F.html`).

Configuring iSCSI port binding

As we stated previously, software and dependent hardware iSCSI adapters depend on a VMkernel networking configuration that should match the storage requirements.

Depending on the storage network interfaces, you can use multiple VMkernel adapters with multiple physical NICs with a 1:1 mapping.

The VMkernel adapters must be on the same subnets as the iSCSI storage system interfaces. If you have multiple subnets, then you will probably have multiple virtual switches. But if all the storage interfaces work in the same subnet, then you will use a single virtual switch and you must use the iSCSI port binding feature.

When you use port binding for multipathing, follow these requirements:

- iSCSI ports of the array target must reside in the same broadcast domain and IP subnet as the VMkernel adapters
- All VMkernel adapters used for iSCSI port binding must reside in the same broadcast domain and IP subnet
- All VMkernel adapters used for iSCSI connectivity must reside in the same virtual switch

To configure iSCSI port binding, first, create the VMkernel interfaces used for the iSCSI initiator. Be sure that each VMkernel adapter has only one active NIC as an uplink (the others should not be used).

Then, in the **Configuration** tab of each host, in the **Storage** | **Storage Adapters** menu, select the iSCSI adapter and then the **Network Port Binding** tab. Now, you can add desired adapters that will be used for the iSCSI initiator using the **+** icon:

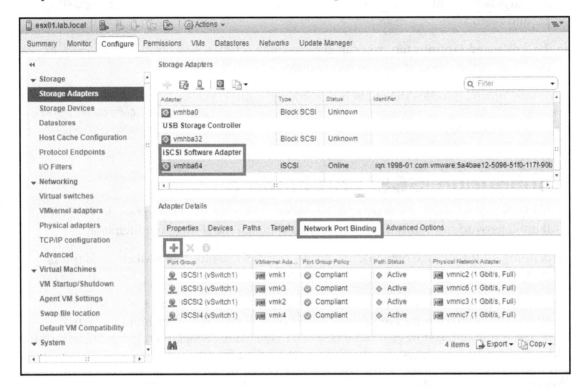

Figure 3.11: iSCSI port bindings

Finally, perform the **Rescan** and **Refresh** operations.

 Port binding does not support network routing.

For more information, see the vSphere 6.5 Storage guide (`https://docs.vmware.com/en/ VMware-vSphere/6.5/com.vmware.vsphere.storage.doc/GUID-0D31125F-DC9D-475B-BC3D- A3E131251642.html`) or the VMware KB 2038869 (`https://kb.vmware.com/s/article/ 2038869`)—considerations for using software iSCSI port binding in ESX/ESXi.

Enabling/configuring/disabling iSCSI CHAP

The iSCSI traffic requires a secure network, both for the confidentiality and for the integrity of the data. Usually, you can use an isolated VLAN to reach this scope.

But for the authentication, iSCSI implements the **Challenge Handshake Authentication Protocol** (**CHAP**), which verifies the initiators (and, if needed, the targets).

ESXi supports unidirectional CHAP for all types of iSCSI initiators, and bidirectional CHAP for software and dependent hardware iSCSI initiators.

For software and dependent hardware iSCSI initiators, you can configure the authentication in the initiator settings, as we mentioned in the previous section.

Using the vSphere Web Client, you can select a host, then, in the **Configure** tab, select the **Storage** | **Storage Adapters** menu. In the iSCSI initiator **Properties** tab, click on the **Edit...** button in the **Authentication** section:

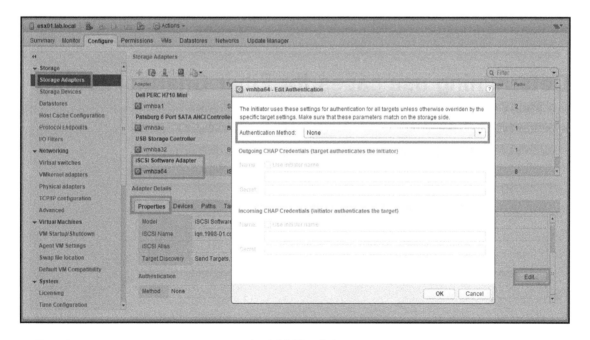

Figure 3.12: iSCSI port bindings

You can choose between these options:

- **None**: CHAP authentication is not used at all
- **Use unidirectional CHAP if required by target**: ESXi prefers non-CHAP connections but can use CHAP if required by the target
- **Use unidirectional CHAP unless prohibited by target**: ESXi prefers CHAP, but can use non-CHAP if the target does not support CHAP
- **Use unidirectional CHAP**: The target requires CHAP authentication for the ESXi initiator
- **Use bidirectional CHAP**: Both the initiator and the target require CHAP authentication

 The CHAP name cannot exceed 511 alphanumeric characters and the CHAP secret cannot exceed 255 alphanumeric characters. Some hardware adapters might have lower limits.

For more information, see the vSphere 6.5 Storage guide (`https://docs.vmware.com/en/VMware-vSphere/6.5/com.vmware.vsphere.storage.doc/GUID-AC65D747-728F-4109-96DD-49B433E2F266.html`).

Determining use cases for Fiber Channel zoning

In a **Fiber Channel** (**FC**) fabric, zoning provides the access rules to define who can talk with whom: which initiator can talk with which target.

A typical full switched FC fabric is like this one:

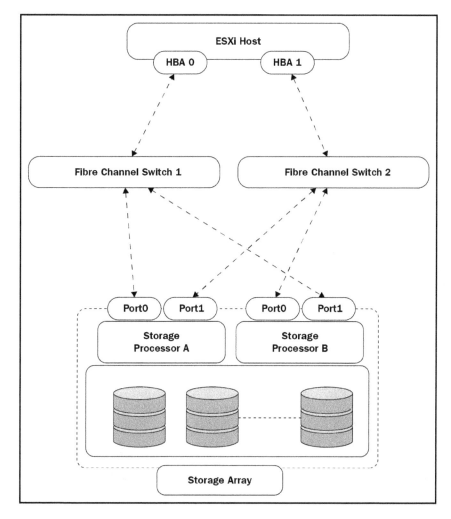

Figure 3.13: FC switched fabric

You need to configure both switch 1 and 2 with the correct zoning, with rules based on the switch port or, better, on the **World Wide Name** (**WWN**) addresses (similar to the physical address of a NIC).

Each zone defines which HBA port can connect to which **Storage Processors** (**SP**) port or ports.

A proper zoning has the following advantages:

- Reduces the number of targets and LUNs presented to a host
- Controls and isolates paths in a fabric
- Can prevent non-ESXi systems from accessing a particular storage system, and from possibly destroying VMFS data
- Can be used to separate different environments

VMware suggests that you use single-initiator zoning or a single-initiator-single-target zoning, but, of course, the best choice depends on the storage vendor's recommendations.

Note that, at storage level, there is also the LUN masking option to show or hide specific LUNs from a specific host.

For more information, see the vSphere 6.5 Storage guide (`https://docs.vmware.com/en/ VMware-vSphere/6.5/com.vmware.vsphere.storage.doc/GUID-E7818A5D-6BD7-4F51-B4BA-EFBF2D3A8357.html`).

Comparing and contrasting array thin provisioning and virtual disk thin provisioning

VMware vSphere supports two models of storage provisioning:

- **Thick provisioning**: The entire storage is reallocated, as well as if it is not used
- **Thin provisioning**: Only the used storage is allocated

Thin provisioning helps to minimize storage under utilization problems by allocating storage space in a flexible on-demand manner. But, in this case, it's very important to have an effective disk reclaim feature to free deleted blocks at the underlying level (more details will be provided in *Objective 3.4*).

VMware vSphere supports two models of thin provisioning: at array level (datastore) and at virtual disk level (VMDK).

For the **thin-provisioned virtual disk**, you have VMDKs that grow dynamically depending on the used space. VMware will report the provisioned space (that is, the "configured" space) and the used space (that is, the size of the thin VMDK).

It's possible to over allocate the datastore space and potentially block the growth of other thin-provisioned VMDKs if the datastore fills.

You can easily check the type of a VMDK in the VM properties or summaries:

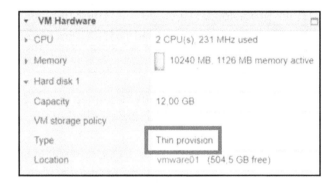

Figure 3.14: VM disk summary

Note that VM snapshot files are also "thin-provisioned" (the real format could be different, depending on the datastore type and the size of the VMDK), so VMs with an active snapshot will be affected by a full datastore.

For **thin-provisioned datastores**, when a LUN is thin-provisioned, the storage array reports the LUN's logical size (and not the real used size). Note that you risk over-allocating your storage with not enough free space to permit the proper growth of the thin-provisioned LUNs.

Using VAAI (described in *Objective 3.4*), ESXi can be aware of underlying thin-provisioned LUNs.

To check if a LUN is thin-provisioned, you need to use the `esxcli` command:

```
esxcli storage core device list -d vml.xxxxxxxxxxxxxxxx
```

And check the thin provisioned status row of the report.

And what's happened to the VMDK provisioning if you are using the thin-provisioned datastore? The following table summarizes the different cases:

Storage provisioning	VM virtual disk provisioning	Resulting provisioning
Thin provisioning	Thin provisioning	Thin provisioning
Thin provisioning	Thick provision lazy zeroed	Thin provisioning

Thin provisioning	Thick provision eager zeroed	Thick provisioning (unless there's specific storage optimization, such as compression)
Thick provisioning	Thin provisioning	Thin provisioning at VM level
Thick provisioning	Thick provision lazy zeroed	Thick provisioning
Thick provisioning	Thick provision eager zeroed	Thick provisioning

Table 3.3

 The VM provisioning could be totally redefined by the **Storage Policy-Based Management** (**SPBM**), which is described in the next chapter.

For more information, see the vSphere 6.5 Storage guide (`https://docs.vmware.com/en/ VMware-vSphere/6.5/com.vmware.vsphere.storage.doc/GUID-AC8E9C20-C05F-4FB5-A5DA- 11D0A77A291B.html`).

Objective 3.2 – Configure software-defined storage

With a traditional storage, vSphere can abstract the underlying storage capacities from virtual machines. But with a **software-defined storage** (**SDS**), vSphere can also abstract storage capabilities and provide part of storage manageability and automation.

VMware provides two different approaches for an SDS approach with vSphere:

- **Virtual SAN (vSAN)**: Implements a hyper-converged and SDS solution based on VMware software. Note that vSAN requires an additional license and has several editions. These features depend on the vSAN version and editions, and some of them are limited to the all-flash configuration only.
- **Virtual volumes (vVOLs)**: Integrates existing external storage and have the SDS flexibility. To use vVOLs, you need a certified storage with vVOLs support and at least the ESXi standard edition:

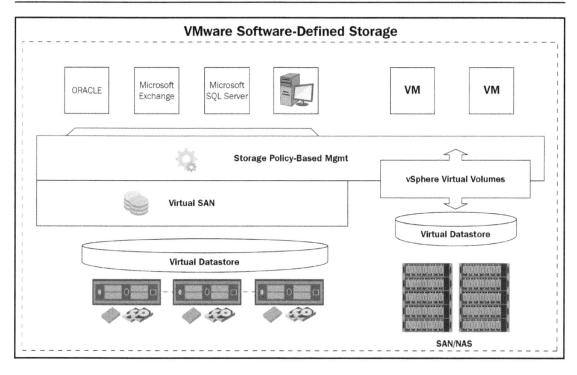

Figure 3.15: VMware software-defined storage

With the SDS model, a virtual machine becomes a unit of storage provisioning and can be managed through a flexible policy-based mechanism using SPBM.

SPBM is a framework that provides a single control panel across various data services and storage solutions, including VMware vSAN and vVOLs.

 Objective 3.2 for VCP65-DCV and VCP6-DCV is quite similar, both for the vSAN (also if vSAN 6.5 and 6.6 have more functions compared to vSAN 6.0) and vVOLs.
The topics covered in this objective are huge and covered in specific courses (at least for vSAN). Also, they are not fully necessary for the exam; you can understand just the basics and maybe learn more or make more practice later.

For more information and details, see the vSphere 6.5 Storage guide and the administering VMware vSAN 6.5 guide:

- `https://docs.vmware.com/en/VMware-vSphere/6.5/vsphere-esxi-vcenter-server-652-storage-guide.pdf.pdf`
- `https://docs.vmware.com/en/VMware-vSphere/6.5/vsan-661-administration-guide.pdf`

Creating vSAN cluster

A VMware vSAN cluster is just a vSphere cluster with compliant ESXi hosts that exports local disks in a single shared datastore.

Before creating a vSAN cluster, you must match several requirements that are described in the administering VMware vSAN guide (`https://docs.vmware.com/en/VMware-vSphere/6.5/com.vmware.vsphere.virtualsan.doc/GUID-D2AAEC0C-D5C3-4885-A2C2-789DC0212850.html`).

To create a new vSAN cluster with the vSphere Web Client, follow these steps:

1. In the **Host and Clusters** inventory, right-click a datacenter and select **New Cluster....**
2. Type a name for the cluster in the **Name** textbox.
3. Enable vSAN by selecting the **vSAN Turn ON** checkbox and click on the **OK** button. The cluster will appear in the inventory.

> If the cluster already exists, then vSphere HA must be turned off before you can turn on the vSAN feature!

4. Now, just add the proper hosts to the vSAN cluster. For the disk configuration, see the *Creating disk groups* section.

If you enable vSAN on an existing cluster, the options will be a little more complex, as in the following screenshot:

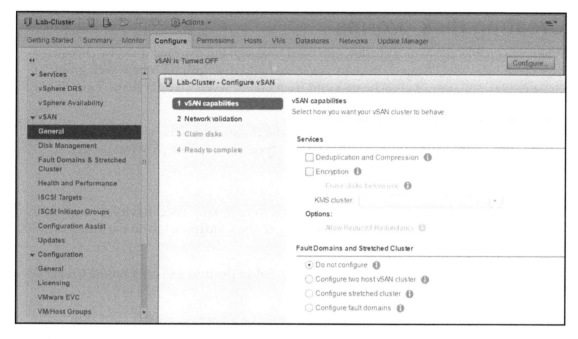

Figure 3.16: Configuring a vSAN cluster

Enabling vSAN is only the first step. Afterward, you need to configure different aspects, as follows:

- (Optional) enable compression and deduplication (only for all flash vSANs)
- (Optional) enable vSAN encryption
- (Optional) define the fault domains or stretched cluster configuration

Enabling vSAN creates a vSAN datastore and registers the vSAN storage provider. vSAN storage providers are built-in software components that communicate the storage capabilities of the datastore to vCenter Server.

For more information, see the administering VMware vSAN guide (`https://docs.vmware.com/en/VMware-vSphere/6.5/com.vmware.vsphere.virtualsan.doc/GUID-5656EA30-F7C7-494C-A356-E1471942625A.html`).

Creating disk groups

When you enable vSAN on a cluster, you need to assign the required disks by choosing a disk-claiming mode. Physical disks are organized into **disk groups**, where each group contains one (and only one) cache disk and from one to seven capacity disks. Each ESXi can have a maximum of five disk groups.

Carefully consider the ratio of cache to capacity: although the ratio depends on the requirements and type of workloads, VMware suggests usually at least a 10% ratio.

To create a disk group, define the disk group and individually select devices to include into it. You can use the vSphere Web Client by going to the **Configure** tab on the selected vSAN enabled cluster.

In the **vSAN** menu, click on **Disk Management**. Select the host and click on the **Create a new disk group** icon.

Now, select the proper disk for the cache tier (must be a flash-based disk) and then select the disks for the capacity tier. In the second case, you can use the **Capacity type** drop-down menu to match the type of disks and the type of vSAN (if you select **Flash** disks, you will have an all-flash storage; if you select **HDD** disks, you will have a hybrid storage).

For more information, see the administering VMware vSAN guide (`https://docs.vmware.com/en/VMware-vSphere/6.5/com.vmware.vsphere.virtualsan.doc/GUID-AE1E9A59-6C20-46BB-9BAA-6FF3CB310A01.html`).

Monitoring vSAN

Understanding all vSAN concepts is out of the scope of this book and the exam, where you just need to know some basics aspects.

You can monitor a vSAN with the vSphere Client in the **Monitor** tab as it has several menus for the capacity, disks usage, and the health of the storage.

Also, a powerful CLI called **Ruby vSphere Console** (**RVC**) is available that can help both in monitoring and troubleshooting tasks. For more information, see `https://blogs.vmware.com/kb/2016/10/tips-tricks-ruby-vsphere-console-rvc-managing-virtual-san-environment.html`.

For more information, see the administering VMware vSAN guide (`https://docs.vmware.com/en/VMware-vSphere/6.5/com.vmware.vsphere.virtualsan.doc/GUID-0DD0572A-0B7A-43FB-B74D-64ECCC3B4D64.html`).

Describing vVOLs

Introduced in vSphere 6.0, vVOLs are a new integration and management framework that abstracts and virtualizes existing storage (SAN or NAS) and provides an SDS approach based on vSphere SPBM.

With vVOLs, the storage can address individual VM objects. In this way, the storage gains complete control over virtual disk content, layout, and management, and can provide fine-grained features on each of them. The following diagram compares the traditional storage approach (based on VMFS or NFS datastores) with the vVOLs approach:

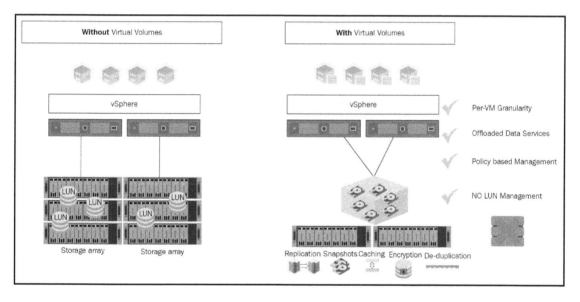

Figure 3.17: VMware vVOLs

With the new vSphere 6.5, there are some improvements:

- Support for storage replication (vVOLs replication enablement)
- SPBM for Availability
- Support for Oracle RAC on vVOLs

For more information, see the vSphere 6.5 Storage guide (`https://docs.vmware.com/en/`
`VMware-vSphere/6.5/com.vmware.vsphere.storage.doc/GUID-0F225B19-7C2B-4F33-BADE-`
`766DA1E3B565.html`) and VMware KB 2113013 (`https://kb.vmware.com/s/article/`
`2113013`)—understanding VVOLs in VMware vSphere 6.0.

Understanding a vSAN iSCSI target

VMware vSAN works as a datastore with its own filesystem (depending on the vSAN
version) and each VMDK is a file descriptor that points to a vSAN object.

But for the external physical workload, you can use the vSAN iSCSI target to "export" part
of the vSAN space as a traditional iSCSI LUN.

Supported operating systems for the vSAN iSCSI target include the following:

- Microsoft Windows 10, Windows Server 2016, 2012 R2, 2012, 2008 R2, 2008
- RedHat RHEL 7, RHEL 6, RHEL 5
- SUSE Linux Enterprise Server 12, SLES 11 SP4/SP3/SP1

 Use of the vSAN iSCSI target for providing storage directly to vSphere
ESXi is not currently supported.

For more information, see the administering VMware vSAN guide (`https://docs.vmware.`
`com/en/VMware-vSphere/6.5/com.vmware.vsphere.virtualsan.doc/GUID-13ADF2FC-9664-`
`448B-A9F3-31059E8FC80E.html`).

Explaining vSAN and vVOL architectural components

VMware vSAN and vVOLs have several technical aspects needed for a proper design,
configuration, and management, but most of them are out of the scope of this book. We will
just provide the basics that can be useful for the exam itself.

vSAN architecture

VMware vSAN architecture has several concepts, but the basics are the following:

- **Disk groups**: Already described in the *Creating disk groups* section.
- **vSAN datastore**: The datastore provided by vSAN and backed by the aggregate storage of all the host's disk groups. Note that there can be a single vSAN datastore in a vSAN cluster.
- **VM Storage policy**: Determines the component placement and provisioning and redundancy.
- **Failures To Tolerate (FTT)**: Number of hosts, disk, or network failures a VM object can tolerate.

vVOL architecture

The Virtual Volumes architecture has five major components:

- **vVOL Objects**: Can be Config- vVOL (Metadata), Data- vVOL (VMDKs), Mem-vVOL (Snapshots), Swap- vVOL (Swap files), or Other- vVOL (Vendor solution-specific).
- **Protocol Endpoint (PE)**: It's a logical I/O proxy that permits ESXi to communicate with the storage and "speak" to vVOLs. ESXi uses Protocol Endpoints (PE) to establish a data path on demand from VMs to their respective vVOLs objects.
- **Storage Container (SC)**: Unlike traditional LUN and NFS-based vSphere storage, the vVOLs functionality does not require pre configured LUNs or volumes on the storage side, but at least a designed spaced is needed. This is called a storage container, which is a pool of raw storage capacity or an aggregation of storage capabilities. A storage container is basically a vVOLs "datastore" that contains all vVOLs objects.
- **VASA Provider (v3.0)**: This is the vVOLs storage provider for the storage awareness service for vSphere. The provider mediates out-of-band communication between the vCenter Server and ESXi hosts on one side and a storage system on the other.
- **Array**: This implements vVOLs features; note that not all storage vendors implement vVOLs in the same way, so it really depends on the maturity of their solution.

For more information, see the vSphere 6.5 Storage guide (`https://docs.vmware.com/en/ VMware-vSphere/6.5/com.vmware.vsphere.storage.doc/GUID-EE1BD912-03E7-407D-8FDC- 7F596E41A8D3.html`) and the VMware KB 2113013 (`https://kb.vmware.com/s/article/ 2113013`)—Understanding VVOLs in VMware vSphere 6.0.

Determining the role of storage providers in vSAN

A **vSphere APIs for Storage Awareness** (**VASA**) provider, or a storage provider, enables communication between the vSphere stack and the storage system, providing awareness of specific storage capabilities and functions.

The vSAN storage provider reports a set of underlying storage capabilities to vCenter and reports the storage requirements of the VMs.

 VMware vSAN configures and registers a storage provider for each host in the vSAN cluster, but only one host's storage provider is active. The others storage providers that belong to other hosts are on standby. Of course, if the active storage provider fails (for a host failure), another host will bring its provider online as an active instance.

To verify that the vSAN storage provider is properly registered, use the vSphere Web Client and select the vCenter Server (the root of the inventories). On the **Configure** tab, click **Storage Providers**.

For more information, see the administering VMware vSAN guide (`https://docs.vmware. com/en/VMware-vSphere/6.5/com.vmware.vsphere.virtualsan.doc/GUID-CE1FB67B-CB88- 4AAC-9668-7A406CA443AA.html`).

Determining the role of storage providers in vVOLs

As mentioned previously, the VASA provider is a key component for vVOLS, and you need a certified VASA provider that mediates out-of-band communication between vSphere components and the storage.

After you register the storage provider, vCenter can discover all configured storage containers and their capabilities, endpoints, and relevant attributes.

The provider creates an I/O access point for a vVOL on a **Protocol Endpoint** (PE). A single PE can be the I/O access point for multiple vVOLs.

 Storage Vendors are responsible for supplying certified storage providers that can provide vVOLs support.

For more information, see the vSphere 6.5 Storage guide (`https://docs.vmware.com/en/ VMware-vSphere/6.5/com.vmware.vsphere.storage.doc/GUID-8776CF33-ECF8-4541-9221- 1F14898B121C.html`).

Explaining vSAN failure domains functionality

A fault domain is a set of elements that can fail together without causing any issue due to a proper redundancy across different fault domains.

By default, in vSAN, each host is an implicit "fault domain", but you can group one or more hosts in an explicit fault domain, according to their physical location in the datacenter.

Using vSAN's fault domains feature, it's possible to protect against rack or chassis failure if your vSAN cluster spans across multiple racks or blade server chassis.

 A minimum of **three** fault domains are required for a vSAN cluster. But, depending on the FFT value, the real required minimum number is `2*FTT+1` fault domains in a cluster.

For more information, see the administering VMware vSAN guide (`https://docs.vmware. com/en/VMware-vSphere/6.5/com.vmware.vsphere.virtualsan.doc/GUID-8491C4B0-6F94- 4023-8C7A-FD7B40D0368D.html`).

Configuring/managing VMware vSAN

Configuration and management of a vSAN cluster is out of the scope of this book, and for the exam preparation, you just need some basic information.

Remember that vSAN management is driven with VM storage policies and that the default vSAN policy has thin provision (due to the object space reservation set to 0), FTT=1 (mirror of all the vSAN objects between two fault domains), and single stripe per object (but objects bigger than 255 GB are split into multiple components).

For more information, see the administering VMware vSAN guide (`https://docs.vmware.com/en/VMware-vSphere/6.5/com.vmware.vsphere.virtualsan.doc/GUID-AEF15062-1ED9-4E2B-BA12-A5CE0932B976.html`).

Creating/modifying VMware Virtual Volumes

The vVOLs preparation and configuration depends on the storage type, but basically, you have to follow these steps:

1. Register the storage provider in the vCenter Server in order to activate the communication between vSphere and the storage.
   A VASA provider is usually a web-based service provided by the storage controller or by a management machine.
2. Use the **New Datastore** wizard to create a Virtual Volumes datastore type.
3. Create the VMs in this new "datastore" and use the proper VM storage profile (there is already a default one for vVOLs; for more information, see the vSphere 6.5 Storage guide (`https://docs.vmware.com/en/VMware-vSphere/6.5/com.vmware.vsphere.storage.doc/GUID-0CAD6480-5414-4287-9007-51A1E4635E97.html`) and the specific storage vendor guide on how configured vVOLs (if supported)).

Configuring storage policies

As stated previously, the VM storage policies are a new way to manage VM provisioning with the SPBM framework. SPBM interprets the different storage requirements and dynamically composes the different storage services, such as placing the VM on the right storage tier, allocating capacity, provide snapshots, and replication.

The following should be noted:

- Policies are stored and managed by vCenter server, but can be applied to VMs in one or more clusters.
- More vCenters in enhanced linked more will have each one its own set of policies.
- A maximum of 1,024 policies can exist per vCenter.
- Storage policies can define one or many rules around performance, availability, and space efficiency.
- A storage policy can be applied to a group of VMs, a single VM, or even a single VMDK within a VM.
- Storage policies are not additive. Only one policy (that contains one or more policy rules) can be applied per object.

To learn more, see this blog post: Understanding Storage Policy-Based Management: `https://blogs.vmware.com/virtualblocks/2017/01/16/understanding-storage-policy-based-management/`.

VM storage policies can be based on different criteria, such as the following:

- **Rules based on storage-specific data service**: Typically used by vSAN and vVOLs, but also without them. In this case, a VASA provider is usually used to discover the storage capabilities.
- **Rules based on tags**: In this case, VASA is not required, but instead, vSphere tags are used on a specific datastore.
- **Common Rule Sets**: These roles do not define storage placement but are used to activate some specific data services for the VMs, such as encryption, replication, and so on.

To create (or manage) a VM storage policy, use the vSphere Web Client, and go to **Home |
Policies and Profiles | VM Storage Policy**. Then, create a new policy or modify one:

Figure 3.18: Example VM storage policy for a Nimble Storage

After you create the VM storage policy, you can modify or clone it, or delete any unused
policies.

For more information on SPBM, see the vSphere 6.5 Storage guide (`https://docs.vmware.
com/en/VMware-vSphere/6.5/com.vmware.vsphere.storage.doc/GUID-720298C6-ED3A-
4E80-87E8-076FFF02655A.html`).

Enabling/disabling vSAN Fault Domains

Previously, we have described the scope of a vSAN fault domain and the possibility to
define explicit fault domains, usually needed for rack/enclosure awareness or mandatory
for vSAN stretched cluster configuration (in this case, each site is a fault domain).

You can configure fault domains during the vSAN creation, but also later. Using the vSphere Web Client, select the vSAN cluster in the **Hosts and Clusters** inventory. In the **Configure** tab, choose the **vSAN | Fault Domains & Stretched Cluster** menu:

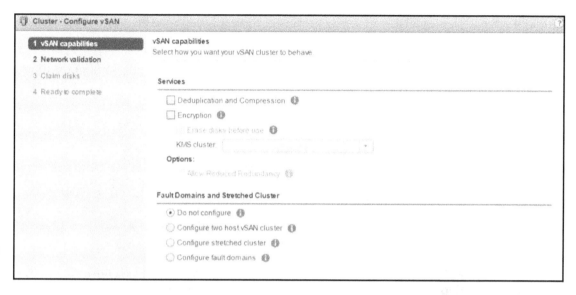

Figure 3.19: vSAN Fault Domains

Note that, depending on the configuration of the host, you have different fault domain options, especially for the 2-nodes and stretched cluster configuration.

For more information, see the administering VMware vSAN guide (`https://docs.vmware.com/en/VMware-vSphere/6.5/com.vmware.vsphere.virtualsan.doc/GUID-8491C4B0-6F94-4023-8C7A-FD7B40D0368D.html`).

Creating Virtual Volumes given the workload and availability requirements

As mentioned previously, vVOLs configuration can be managed with VM storage policies and SPBMs that "expose" the storage capabilities.

Depending on the storage, you may choose the RAID type, the disks type, the specific storage protection solutions (such as snapshots or replicas), or the different data services (such as compression or deduplication). All of these choices must match the specific workload requirements.

Collecting vSAN Observer output

VMware vSAN Observer is a web-based monitoring and troubleshooting tool that runs on RVC. This was initially the only way to have detailed information of vSAN, but now most of that information is available in vSAN graphs in the vSphere Web Client.

For more information, see VMware KB 2064240 (`https://kb.vmware.com/s/article/ 2064240`)—how to use and interpret performance statistics collected using vSAN Observer.

Creating storage policies appropriate for given workloads and availability requirements

Both vSAN and vVOLs use the SPBM framework to define the VM objects provisioning and which features should be enabled.

As mentioned previously, vSphere offers default storage policies for vSAN and vVOLs, but it's possible to define new policies and assign them to the VMs.

How to configure VM storage policies has already been discussed, but you may be interesting in understanding how to check the compliance with those rules.

You can apply the storage policy when you create, clone, or migrate the virtual machine, or after a VM has been created.

To check a policy compliance, use the vSphere Web Client, and navigate to **Home | Policies and Profiles | VM Storage Policies**. Now, select the desired policy and you can check the VM compliance in the **Monitor** tab, as in the following screenshot:

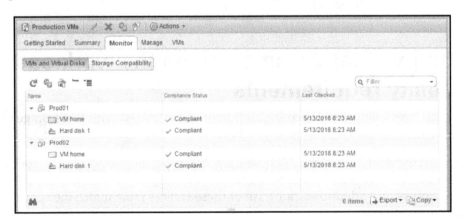

Figure 3.20: VM storage policy compliance status

Configuring vVOLs Protocol Endpoints

We discussed the function of the protocol endpoints in the previous section.

You can manage them with the vSphere Web Client by selecting a host, then clicking the **Configure** tag and going to the **Storage** | **Protocol Endpoints** menu:

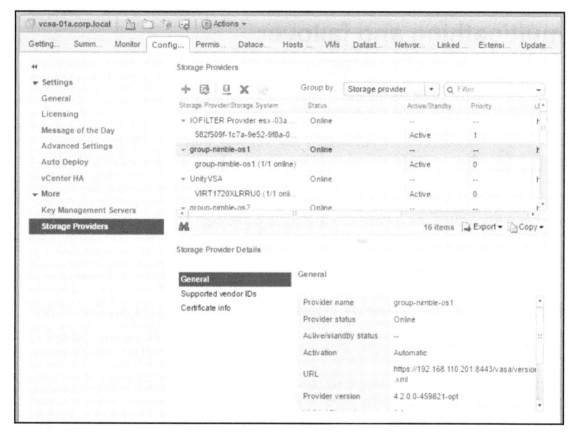

Figure 3.21: vVOLs storage providers

Use the tabs under **Protocol Endpoint Details** to access additional information and modify properties for the selected protocol endpoint.

For example, to manage the multipath option on a block-based storage, select the desired protocol endpoint and click on **Properties**, then, on multipathing policies, click **Edit Multipathing**.

For more information, see the vSphere 6.5 Storage guide (`https://docs.vmware.com/en/ VMware-vSphere/6.5/com.vmware.vsphere.storage.doc/GUID-4756CD33-8B65-4735-94D4- 94C6F9E8CC02.html`).

Objective 3.3 – Configure vSphere Storage multipathing and failover

Multipathing, also called I/O multipathing, is a typical feature in block-based storage (but usually for SAN environments) to establish and manage multiple physical paths between an initiator and the target device, basically to provide better availability and resilience (in case of path failures) but also to improve performance.

 Objective 3.3 for VCP65-DCV and VCP6-DCV are the same just because there weren't big changes in those storage functions from vSphere 6.0 to vSphere 6.5.

For more information and details, see the vSphere 6.5 Storage guide (`https://docs. vmware.com/en/VMware-vSphere/6.5/vsphere-esxi-vcenter-server-652-storage-guide. pdf.pdf`).

Explaining common multi-pathing components

Starting with ESXi 4, ESXi uses a collection of storage APIs and the **Pluggable Storage Architecture** (**PSA**) to manage storage multipathing. PSA features will be described later.

There is also an extensible multipathing module called **Native Multipathing plugin** (**NMP**). The core components are as follows:

- **Storage Array Type Plugins (SATP)**: Recognizes the type of storage architecture
- **Path Selection Plugin (PSP)**: Responsible for choosing a physical path for I/O requests
- **Multipathing Plugin (MPP)**: Provides multipath rules

The following diagram summarizes the entire architecture:

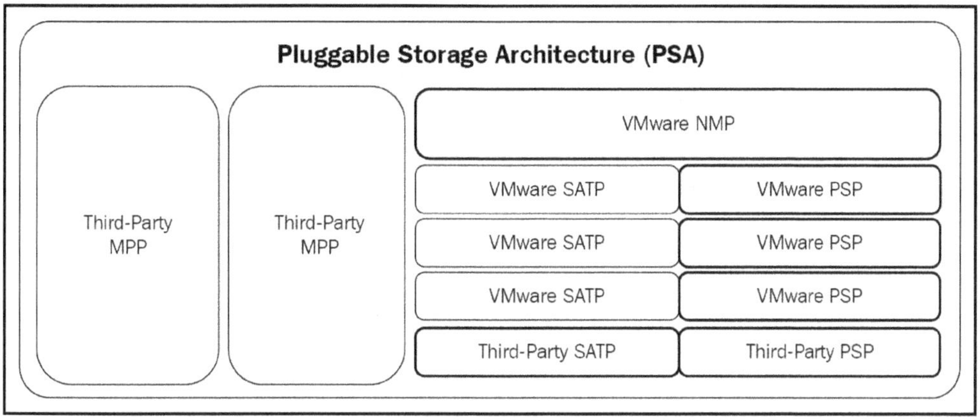

Figure 3.22: Pluggable Storage Architecture (PSA)

Note that VM storage I/O might be delayed for up to 60 seconds during path failover. For this reason, it's really important to increase the disk timeout inside the guest OS (which is automatically done during the VMware Tools installation).

For more information, see the vSphere 6.5 Storage guide (`https://docs.vmware.com/en/ VMware-vSphere/6.5/com.vmware.vsphere.storage.doc/GUID-9DED1F73-7375-4957-BF69- 41B56C3E5224.html`).

Differentiating APD and PDL states

In vSphere HA configurations, starting with vSphere 6.0, there are some new storage-related features that protect virtual machines from possible storage issues. These features are part of a new component: **VM Component Protection** (**VMCP**).

VMCP can manage two different types of faulty storage conditions:

- **Permanent Device Loss (PDL)**: Occurs when the storage array issues an SCSI sense code, indicating that a specific device is unavailable (a typical case is a failed LUN).
- **All Paths Down (APD)**: Usually, it's related to a SAN networking (or storage) issue where there is no active path to reach the target. This condition is different from PDL because the initiator doesn't have enough information to determine if the device loss is temporary or permanent.

The configuration is available in the vSphere Web Client, in the vSphere HA configuration of a specific cluster. Just select the **Failure and Responses** menu and look at the specific APD and PDL settings, as in the following screenshot:

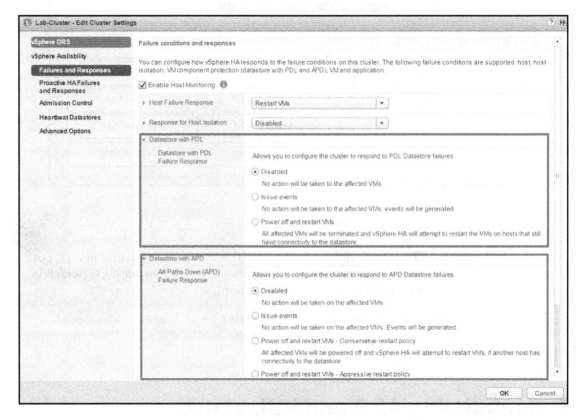

Figure 3.23: APD and PDL responses

For both of these cases, you can configure a response type from one of the following options:

- **Disabled**: No action will be taken against the affected VMs during a PDL or APD event
- **Issue events**: No action will be taken against the affected VMs, but the administrator will be notified for a PDL or APD event
- **Power off and restart VMs**: All affected VMs will be terminated on the host with the PDL or APD condition and vSphere HA will attempt to restart the VMs on different hosts that still have working connectivity to the storage device

For APD conditions, there are two different types of power off and restart VMs options: one aggressive and one conservative that first try to determine if there is another host that can restart the VMs.

For more information on APD and PDL, see the vSphere 6.5 Availability guide (`https://docs.vmware.com/en/VMware-vSphere/6.5/com.vmware.vsphere.avail.doc/GUID-F01F7EB8-FF9D-45E2-A093-5F56A788D027.html`), or this blog post (for version 6.0, but still valid): `https://blogs.vmware.com/vsphere/2015/06/vm-component-protection-vmcp.html`.

Comparing and contrasting active optimized versus active non-optimized port group states

VMware supports different types of storage architectures:

- **Active-active storage array**: All the paths are active unless a path fails. It's also possible to access a LUN simultaneously through all controllers and all available paths without significant performance degradation. One example is the Dell-EMC VMAX product.
  There are some special subcases of this type of architecture:
    - **Virtual port storage array**: Supports access to the storage services through a single virtual port. For example, with iSCSI, it is possible to work with a single virtual IP instead of each IP of each port. This storage handles port failovers and connection balancing transparently. One example is the Dell Compellent product when configured in virtual ports mode.
    - **Active-standby controllers**: Controllers are in an active-standby configuration where all the load is on the active controller and the second will just be used to migrate all the ports. On the active controller, all paths are active (on the active controller). One example is the Dell EqualLogic product.
- **Active-passive storage array**: One controller is active on a specific LUN and the second is passive on the same LUN (but could be active on another LUN). If access to the active storage port fails, one of the passive storage processors can be activated by the servers accessing it. You can change the LUN "ownership" cost time with the operation called trespass. One example is the Dell PowerVault product (at least the first versions).

- **Asymmetrical storage array**: **Asymmetric Logical Unit Access** (**ALUA**) storage has all ports that could be active, but with different levels of access per port. With ALUA, hosts can determine the states of target ports and prioritize paths; some of the active paths are primary and others are secondary. One example is the EMC VNX product.

The following table summarizes the type of storage and the default SATP and PSP:

Type of storage	Generic SATP	Default PSP
Active-active storage array	`VMW_SATP_DEFAULT_AA`	Fixed
Active-passive storage array	`VMW_SATP_DEFAULT_AP`	MRU (Most Recently Used)
Asymmetrical storage array	`VMW_SATP_ALUA`	MRU (Most Recently Used)

Table 3.4

The different paths can have different level of "optimizations":

- **Optimized**: These are the paths on the controller that owns the LUN (for active-active storage are all the paths)
- **Unoptimized**: These are the paths on the controller that does not own the LUN, on an active-passive storage
- **Active unoptimized**: These are the paths on the controller that does not own the LUN, on an ALUA storage

For more information, see the vSphere 6.5 Storage guide (`https://docs.vmware.com/en/VMware-vSphere/6.5/com.vmware.vsphere.storage.doc/GUID-4D64F3DA-9701-4210-B34A-0A44D3A0100C.html`).

Explaining features of Pluggable Storage Architecture (PSA)

The PSA framework (introduced in vSphere 4.0) is a collection of VMkernel APIs that allow partners to insert specific functions into the ESXi storage layer.

Previously, we documented the architecture of PSA and NMP, so now, let's consider its features.

When coordinating the VMware NMP and any installed third-party MPPs, the PSA performs the following tasks:

- Provides logical device and the physical path I/O statistics
- Loads and unloads multipathing plugin
- Implements logical device bandwidth sharing between VMs
- Hides VM specifics from a particular plugin
- Routes I/O requests for a specific logical device to the MPP managing that device
- Handles I/O queuing to the logical devices
- Handles I/O queuing to the physical storage HBAs
- Handles physical path discovery and removal

Note that third-party plugins are also supported, falling into one of three categories:

- **Third-party Multipathing Plugin (MPP)**: Provides new multipath rules to VMware **native multipathing** (**NMP**)
- **Third-party Storage Array Type Plugin (SATP)**: Used to recognize some storage capabilities, not recognized by the VMware SATPs
- **Third-party Path Selection Plugin (PSP)**: Similar to the previous one, but usually used to identify the default multipath rule for a new storage

For more information on PSA, see the vSphere 6.5 Storage guide (`https://docs.vmware.com/en/VMware-vSphere/6.5/com.vmware.vsphere.storage.doc/GUID-C1C4A725-8BE4-4875-919E-693812961366.html`).

Understanding the effects of a given claim rule on multipathing and failover

When ESXi is connecting to storage, it will recognize the storage and discover all available paths to the target device. Based on a set of **claim rules**, the ESXi determines which module should claim the paths to a particular device and become responsible for managing the multipathing support for that device. Each claim rule is numbered and the order defines how the rules are parsed.

By default, ESXi also performs a periodic (every five minutes) path evaluation causing any unclaimed paths to be claimed by the appropriate module.

Usually, these rules can discover and properly configure most of the certified storage, but in some cases, you need to manually edit them, as we will explain later.

For more information, see the vSphere 6.5 Storage guide (`https://docs.vmware.com/en/ VMware-vSphere/6.5/com.vmware.vsphere.storage.doc/GUID-98F0851E-12F2-4FB2-A794-7643DD2E6F9B.html`).

Explaining the function of claim rule elements

As mentioned previously, claim rules are used to identify the storage and the proper configuration, especially for multipathing.

For each physical path, ESXi runs through the claim rules, parsing in the order of the numbers.

For the paths managed by the NMP module, the second set of claim rules is applied to define which SATP should be used to manage the paths for a specific array, and which PSP can be used for each device.

Each claim rule identifies a set of paths based on the following parameters:

- Vendor/model strings
- Transportation, such as SAS, iSCSI, and Fibre Channel
- Adapter, target, or LUN location
- Device driver

Claim rules cannot be managed from the GUI. One possible way is to use the ESXi CLI. For example, to see the rules list, run the following command:

```
esxcli storage core claimrule list
```

You will see an output like this:

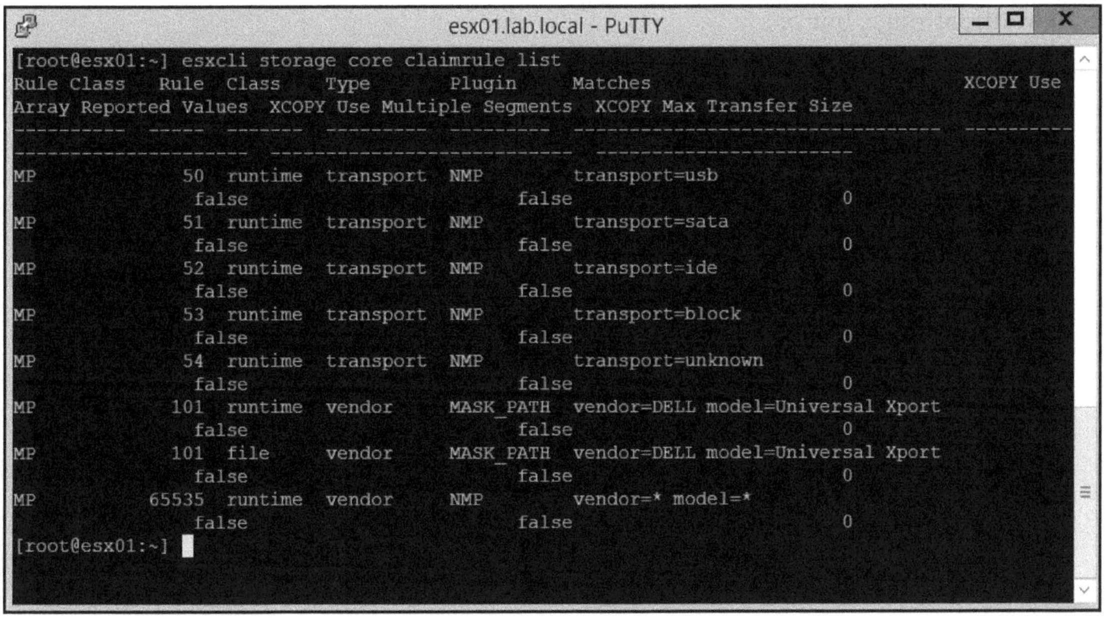

Figure 3.24: ESXi storage claim rules list

For more information, see the vSphere 6.5 Storage guide (`https://docs.vmware.com/en/ VMware-vSphere/6.5/com.vmware.vsphere.storage.doc/GUID-9B19EF2E-DA5A-43D2-B41F- 8E7C112D2E00.html#GUID-9B19EF2E-DA5A-43D2-B41F-8E7C112D2E00`).

Changing the path selection policy using the UI

Usually, there is no need to change the default multipathing settings, because ESXi will claim the right rules and the proper configuration.

However, sometimes, you may need to make changes, for example, to select a better multipath option or to select a default path.

You can use the vSphere Web Client, select a datastore, and then click the **Configure** tab. Then, in the **Connectivity and Multipathing** menu, select each ESXi host and click on the **Edit Multipathing...** button:

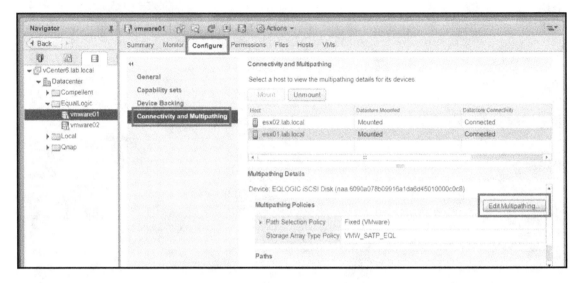

Figure 3.25: Connectivity and multipathing

The different path policies will be described later.

For more information, see the vSphere 6.5 Storage guide (`https://docs.vmware.com/en/ VMware-vSphere/6.5/com.vmware.vsphere.storage.doc/GUID-9DED1F73-7375-4957-BF69- 41B56C3E5224.html`).

Determining required claim rule elements to change the default PSP

Previously, we described how to list the claim rules. To see how they are applied to each device, you can run the following command:

```
esxcli storage nmp device list
```

It will describe all the details for each storage device, like in the following example:

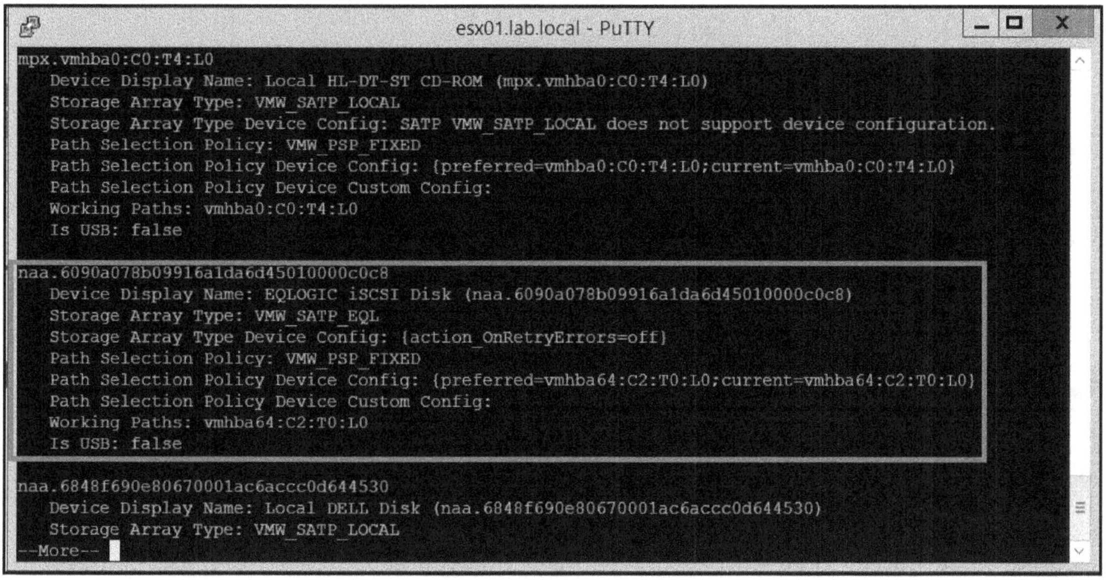

```
                              esx01.lab.local - PuTTY                    _  □  X
mpx.vmhba0:C0:T4:L0
    Device Display Name: Local HL-DT-ST CD-ROM (mpx.vmhba0:C0:T4:L0)
    Storage Array Type: VMW_SATP_LOCAL
    Storage Array Type Device Config: SATP VMW_SATP_LOCAL does not support device configuration.
    Path Selection Policy: VMW_PSP_FIXED
    Path Selection Policy Device Config: {preferred=vmhba0:C0:T4:L0;current=vmhba0:C0:T4:L0}
    Path Selection Policy Device Custom Config:
    Working Paths: vmhba0:C0:T4:L0
    Is USB: false

naa.6090a078b09916a1da6d45010000c0c8
    Device Display Name: EQLOGIC iSCSI Disk (naa.6090a078b09916a1da6d45010000c0c8)
    Storage Array Type: VMW_SATP_EQL
    Storage Array Type Device Config: {action_OnRetryErrors=off}
    Path Selection Policy: VMW_PSP_FIXED
    Path Selection Policy Device Config: {preferred=vmhba64:C2:T0:L0;current=vmhba64:C2:T0:L0}
    Path Selection Policy Device Custom Config:
    Working Paths: vmhba64:C2:T0:L0
    Is USB: false

naa.6848f690e80670001ac6accc0d644530
    Device Display Name: Local DELL Disk (naa.6848f690e80670001ac6accc0d644530)
    Storage Array Type: VMW_SATP_LOCAL
--More--
```

Figure 3.26: ESXi storage details

Now, you can match the proper claim rule.

Determining the effect of changing PSP on multipathing and failover

Instead of changing the multipathing for each datastore (or storage device), you can manage the claim rules and change them to force the changes on all the devices.

Also, you can change the default rule to simplify the configuration of newly discovered devices that will have the new settings.

Note that you can only limit the changes on specific device types, or protocols, or all other elements in the claim rules.

You can also change the default multipath behavior, for example, to use round-robin instead of Fixed for all new active/active storage:

```
esxcli storage nmp satp set -s VMW_SATP_DEFAULT_AA -P VMW_PSP_RR
```

Determining the effects of changing SATP on relevant device behavior

As mentioned previously, the default configuration provided by the different SATP match the proper multipath policy needed for a specific storage. Usually, you don't have to change them, unless required by the storage vendor or when, for a storage vendor, there are more possible multipath policies that can be used (SATP can only have one default).

Note that changing the SATP for storage may change the PSP, which might create unexpected failover results.

Configuring/managing storage load balancing

Multipathing provides not only resiliency but also load balancing by distributing I/O loads across multiple paths.

Configuration and management have already been discussed and it's performed with claim rules or the multipath policy.

Differentiating available storage load balancing options

Distributing the I/O load on multiple paths can improve performance because there can be load balancing across all storage controllers interfaces. On the ESXi side, there can be a better distribution across different storage adapters or different SAN interfaces.

Load balancing options depend on the multipathing policies.

Differentiating available storage multipathing policies

Multipathing is a technique that lets you efficiently and reliably use more than one path to transfer data between the host and an external storage array.

Depending on the storage type, you need specific multi-path criteria. VMware ESXi has three main types of path selection policies (provided by NMP):

- **Fixed**: ESXi uses the one designated preferred path if it has been configured. Otherwise, it selects the first working path discovered at system boot time.
- **Most Recently Used (MRU)**: ESXi selects the path that it used recently. When the path becomes unavailable, it selects an alternative path and does not revert to the original path when that path becomes available again.
- **Round Robin (RR)**: ESXi uses an automatic path selection algorithm, rotating through all active paths when connecting to active-passive arrays, or through all available paths when connecting to active-active arrays.
  By default, ESXi performs 1,000 IOPS on each path, but you can tune this parameter, as explained in KB 2069356 (`https://kb.vmware.com/s/article/2069356`)—`Adjusting Round Robin IOPS limit from default 1000 to 1`).

Refer to your storage vendor documentation and best practices for VMware vSphere.

For more information, see the vSphere 6.5 Storage guide (`https://docs.vmware.com/en/VMware-vSphere/6.5/com.vmware.vsphere.storage.doc/GUID-37F97D1C-4E4F-460B-ACF9-04D1347959CC.html`).

Configuring storage policies including vSphere storage APIs for storage awareness

VASA is a set of APIs (introduced in vSphere 5.0) that will enable vCenter to discover the capabilities of the datastores at storage side, making it much easier to select the appropriate datastore for VM placement.

With vSphere 6.0, a new VASA, 2.0, has been introduced to manage VVOLs.

You just need a VASA provider that exposes all of those capabilities, as already described in *Objective 3.2*.

For more information, see the vSphere 6.5 Storage guide (`https://docs.vmware.com/en/VMware-vSphere/6.5/com.vmware.vsphere.storage.doc/GUID-E65B34EF-E125-4014-94BB-8DD7F7C4E6EB.html`).

Locating failover events in the UI

Storage failover events can be located on the **Events** tab in the vSphere Web Client.

Otherwise, you can read the `/var/log/vmkernel.log` file on each ESXi, but you need to "decode" the different event, as explained in VMware KB 1003433 (`https://kb.vmware.com/s/article/1003433`)—SCSI events that can trigger the ESX server to fail a LUN over to another path.

Objective 3.4 – Perform VMFS and NFS configurations and upgrades

The following part is similar and complementary to *Objective 3.1*, with some repetition, but also with more details related to VMFS and NFS datastores.

From a logic point of view, it could be better to read both sections at the same time.

 Objective 3.4 for VCP65-DCV and VCP6-DCV are quite similar just because there weren't big changes in those storage functions from vSphere 6.0 to vSphere 6.5. It's just VMFS6 that's totally new.

For more information and details, see the vSphere 6.5 Storage guide: `https://docs.vmware.com/en/VMware-vSphere/6.5/vsphere-esxi-vcenter-server-652-storage-guide.pdf.pdf`.

Performing VMFS v5 and v6 configurations

Starting with vSphere 6.5, VMware has introduced a new VMFS version used for block-based storage: VMFS 6.

This new version adds new capabilities compared to previous filesystem versions:

Feature	VMFS-3	VMFS-5	VMFS-6
Supported ESXi versions	3.x, 4.x, 5.x, and 6.x	5.x and 6.x	6.5
Disk partitions type	**master boot record(MBR)**	**GUID partition table (GPT)** by default MBR (legacy)	GPT

VMFS datastore up to 64 TB	Yes (using extents)	Yes	Yes
VMFS hot extend	Yes (only using extents)	Yes	Yes
VMDK larger than 2 TB	No	Yes (with vSphere >5.5)	Yes
Unified block size (1 MB)	No	Yes	Yes
Atomic Test and Set (ATS) enhancements (see also the VAAI part)	No	Yes	Yes
Sub-blocks for space efficiency	64 KB (max ~3k)	8 KB (max ~30k)	64 KB (dynamic)
Small file support	No	1 KB	1 KB
Physical block size	512n	512n	512n or 512e
VMFS space reclamation (UNMAP)	No	Yes (manually)	Yes (automatically)
VMDK space reclamation	No	Yes (limited to VDI case)	Yes (virtual hardware 13)

Table 3.5

Note that you cannot create VMFS3 datastores on ESXi 6.5 or later, but it's still possible to use them (if they exist).

Creating a new VMFS datastore can also be performed with the vSphere Web Client: on the **Host and Cluster** inventory, select a host, and choose **Storage | New Datastore** in the contextual menu. Choose the proper LUN and format it with the proper VMFS version. There is a 42-character limit for the datastore name.

 During the installation process, the local datastore (if it exists) will be formatted with VMFS5.

For more information, see the vSphere 6.5 Storage guide (`https://docs.vmware.com/en/ VMware-vSphere/6.5/com.vmware.vsphere.storage.doc/GUID-5AC611E0-7CEB-4604-A03C- F600B1BA2D23.html`).

Describing VAAI primitives for block devices and NAS

The **vSphere APIs for Array Integration (VAAI)** is a set of features (introduced in vSphere 4.1) that provide hardware acceleration and offload functionalities for some types of operations.

Initially, designed only for block-based storage (with VMFS datastore), with vSphere 5.0, this has also been extended to NAS storage (with NFS datastore).

The following table shows the different primitives available for VAAI:

Functions	VMFS datastore	NFS datastore
Datastore locking	**Atomic Test and Set (ATS)** is used to improve the SCSI reservation	Not needed because NFS provides a better locking mechanism
Clone and Copy	XCOPY is used to accelerate cloning and VM storage migration	Full file clone and fast file clone
Write Same	Use to accelerate eager thick provisioning	Not available
Reserve space	Not needed	Used to provide thick provisioning
Extended statistics	Not needed	Used to provide more statistics
Storage thin provisioning	Thin provisioning OOS alarms and UNMAP	Not needed

Table 3.6

In vSphere 6.x, VAAI hasn't changed too much from the previous version, but now these features are available from the standard edition.

For more information, see the vSphere 6.5 Storage guide (https://docs.vmware.com/en/VMware-vSphere/6.5/com.vmware.vsphere.storage.doc/GUID-7A61B13D-7B3C-46F1-BF28-BFA4FDA53C88.html) and VMware KB 1021976 (https://kb.vmware.com/s/article/1021976)—Frequently Asked Questions for vStorage APIs for Array Integration.

Differentiating VMware filesystem technologies

There are four main types of vSphere datastores:

- **VMFS Datastore**: The vSphere Virtual Machine filesystem format is a proprietary VMware filesystem used for block-based storage.
- **NFS Datastore**: Used for file-based storage. ESXi 6.x supports versions 3 and 4.1 of the NFS protocol.
- **Virtual SAN**: vSAN use its own filesystem (depending on the vSAN version) and is identified as a single shared datastore with its own type.
- **Virtual Volumes**: The vVOLs datastore is the entire storage container that stores all vVOLs objects.

All of these have been described in the previous sections.

Migrating from VMFS5 to VMFS6

VMFS 5 and VMFS 6 can coexist on the same ESXi but, of course, on different datastores.

 Due to the changes done in VMFS 6 metadata structures, there is no way to upgrade from VMFS5 to VMFS6. You need to build a new VMFS6 datastore and migrate the VMs to it.

For more information, see VMware KB 2147824 (`https://kb.vmware.com/s/article/2147824`)—Migrating VMFS 5 datastore to VMFS 6 datastore.

Differentiating physical mode RDMs and virtual mode RDMs

A **Raw Device Mapping** (**RDM**) is a special VM disk provision option, where a LUN is mapped 1:1 to a VM (like in a passthrough mode) instead of being a VMDK file on a VMFS datastore. Still, a VMDK file is created on a datastore, but in this case, it's just a "pointer" to the physical LUN.

There are two different types of compatibility mode for RDM:

- **Physical mode**: Allows the guest operating system to access the hardware directly. Physical compatibility can be used for applications that are SAN-aware and have been installed on a VM. They can also be used for guest clustering.
- **Virtual mode**: RDM is managed as a VMDK, with features such as snapshots or cloning:
  - If you clone a VM with this RDM type, the LUN is copied into a VMDK file.
  - If you migrate a VM with this RDM type, you can choose to migrate the mapping file or copy the contents of the LUN into a VMDK file.

 There is no significant difference in performance for sequential I/O between the different types of virtual disks. For random I/O, thin VMDKs have the worst performance and higher latency (for lazy thick, it depends if you have to write a new block).

For more information, see the vSphere 6.5 Storage guide (`https://docs.vmware.com/en/ VMware-vSphere/6.5/com.vmware.vsphere.storage.doc/GUID-B3522FF1-76FF-419D-8DB6- F15BFD4DF12A.html`).

Creating a virtual/physical mode RDM

You can add an RDM disk to a VM using the vSphere Web Client. From the **New device** drop-down menu, select **RDM Disk** and click **Add**.

You will see all the available LUNs (LUNs that are already used for VMFS or RDM are automatically filtered).

Then, you can check all the virtual disk settings:

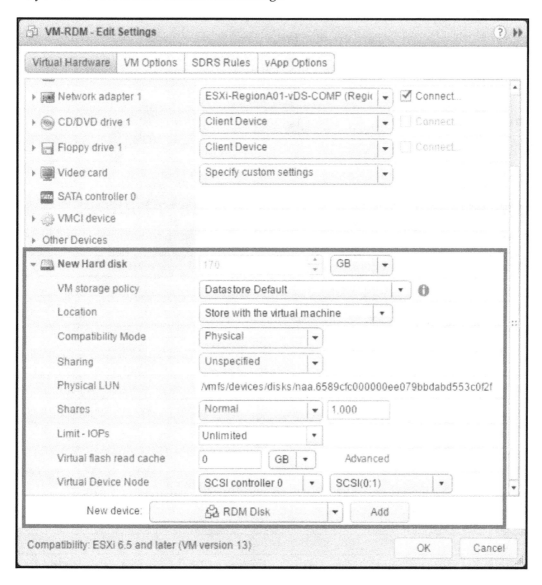

Figure 3.27: Adding an RDM to a VM

RDM can be selected in the **Compatibility Mode** menu. The other settings are the same as a traditional VMDK.

> By default, it's not possible to create an RDM using a LUN marked as "local" (typically connected to SAS storage). For more information, see VMware KB 1017530 (`https://kb.vmware.com/s/article/1017530`)—Raw Device Mapping for local storage.

For more information, see the vSphere 6.5 Storage guide (`https://docs.vmware.com/en/VMware-vSphere/6.5/com.vmware.vsphere.storage.doc/GUID-D06EC5D3-FCE6-4E07-8967-0D146A12FEA0.html`).

Differentiating NFS 3.x and 4.1 capabilities

The main differences between NFS 3 and 4.1 are summarized in the following table:

Feature	NFS 3	NFS 4.1
ESXi compatibility	Since v3	Only 6.x
NFS security	`AUTH_SYS`	`AUTH_SYS`/Kerberos
Hardware acceleration	VAAI NAS (vSphere > 5.0)	VAAI NAS
Multipath	No	Yes
IPv6 support	Yes	Yes
File locking	Files are named `.lck-file_id`	Share reservations

Table 3.7

The following table lists major vSphere solutions that NFS versions support:

vSphere Features	NFS version 3	NFS version 4.1
vMotion and Storage vMotion	Yes	Yes
High availability	Yes	Yes
Fault tolerance	Yes	Yes (only new FT)
Distributed resource scheduler	Yes	Yes
Host profiles	Yes	Yes
Storage DRS	Yes	No
Storage I/O control	Yes	No
Site recovery manager	Yes	No
Virtual volumes	Yes	Yes

vSphere Features	NFS version 3	NFS version 4.1
vSphere Replication	Yes	Yes
vRealize Operations Manager	Yes	Yes

Table 3.8

 Virtual disks created on NFS datastores are thin-provisioned by default. To have thick-provisioned VMDKs as well, you must have VAAI-compatible storage that supports the Reserve Space operation. VAAI will be discussed later.

For more information, see the vSphere 6.5 Storage guide (`https://docs.vmware.com/en/ VMware-vSphere/6.5/com.vmware.vsphere.storage.doc/GUID-8A929FE4-1207-4CC5-A086-7016D73C328F.html`).

Comparing and contrasting VMFS and NFS datastore properties

Both VMFS and NFS datastores have similar features and capabilities, but there are some differences, which are summarized in the following table:

Feature	VMFS datastore	NFS datastore
Type of storage	Block-based	File-based
Number of datastores	512 per host	256 per host
Datastore max size	64 TB	Depends on storage
Locking	SCSI Reservation	File locking (different from NFS 3 and 4.1)
Disk provisioning	Thick/thin	Thin (Thick only with VAAI)
RDM	Physical/virtual	Not supported
Multipathing	Supported	Supported only in NFS 4.1

Table 3.9

Configuring Bus Sharing

SCSI Bus Sharing is a feature of the VM's controllers to allow multiple access simultaneously to the same virtual disks connected to the selected controller.

On the **Virtual Hardware** tab, expand the SCSI controller, and select the type of sharing in the **SCSI Bus Sharing** drop-down menu:

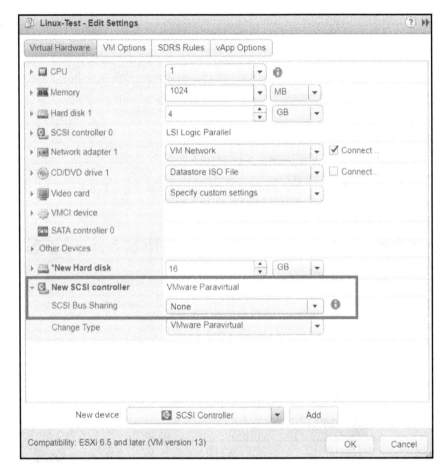

Figure 3.28: SCSI Bus Sharing

The different types of SCSI bus sharing are as follows:

- **None**: Virtual disks cannot be shared by other VMs
- **Virtual**: Virtual disks can be shared by VMs on the same ESXi
- **Physical**: Virtual disks can be shared by VMs on any ESXi

For more information, see the vSphere 6.5 Virtual Machine Administration guide (https://docs.vmware.com/en/VMware-vSphere/6.5/com.vmware.vsphere.vm_admin.doc/GUID-4FB34475-018B-43B7-9E33-449F496F5AB4.html).

Configuring multi-writer locking

Another way to share a virtual disk across two or more VMs is by using the **multi-writer** option. The multi-writer option allows VMFS-backed disks to be shared by multiple VMs.

In this case, the option is at virtual disk level and you can edit it with the vSphere Web Client in the VM settings:

Figure 3.29: Virtual disk sharing options

For more information, see VMware KB 1034165 (https://kb.vmware.com/s/article/1034165)—Enabling or disabling simultaneous write protection provided by VMFS using the multi-writer flag.

Connecting an NFS 4.1 datastore using Kerberos

Mounting an NFS datastore has already been described in *Objective 1.3*.

With NFS 4.1, you can add multiple IP addresses or server names if the NFS server supports trunking in order to achieve multipathing to the NFS datastore.

Also, NFS 4.1 supports both Kerberos and non-root user authentication. With NFS 3, remote files are accessed with root permissions, and servers have to be configured with the **no_root_squash** option to allow root access to files. This is known as an **AUTH_SYS** mechanism.

For an NFS 4.1 datastore, you can use Kerberos authentication to secure the communication between the NFS server and ESXi.

There are two different options for Kerberos authentication:

- **Kerberos for authentication only (krb5)**: Supports identity verification.
- **Kerberos for authentication and data integrity (krb5i)**: In addition to identity verification, provides data integrity services. These services help to protect the NFS traffic from tampering by checking data packets for any potential modifications.

For more information, see the vSphere 6.5 Security guide (`https://docs.vmware.com/en/ VMware-vSphere/6.5/com.vmware.vsphere.security.doc/GUID-987194A1-E4F8-470D- B28F-3B4DB9B4CCB4.html`).

Creating/renaming/deleting/unmounting VMFS datastores

After you have presented the LUN (as described in *Objective 1.3*), you can simply add a new VMFS datastore and you can choose between VMFS5 or VMFS6, as described previously.

Datastores can be renamed at any time without any issues.

But before you delete or unmount a datastore, consider the following:

- Ensure that there are no registered or running VMs on that datastore
- Check that the datastore is not managed by Storage DRS
- Verify that **Storage IO control** (**SIOC**) is disabled on the datastore
- If vSphere HA is configured, make sure that the datastore is not used for HA heartbeats

For more information, see the vSphere 6.5 Storage guide (`https://docs.vmware.com/en/ VMware-vSphere/6.5/com.vmware.vsphere.storage.doc/GUID-5AC611E0-7CEB-4604-A03C- F600B1BA2D23.html`).

Mounting/unmounting an NFS datastore

Mounting an NFS datastore has already been described in *Objective 1.3*.

Before unmounting an NFS datastore, use the same considerations that you would for a VMFS datastore.

For more information, see the vSphere 6.5 Storage guide (`https://docs.vmware.com/en/ VMware-vSphere/6.5/com.vmware.vsphere.storage.doc/GUID-B52657D0-248D-4A99-99CC- D35B350461D5.html`).

Extending/expanding VMFS datastores

In vSphere, it is possible to expand a VMFS datastore in two different ways:

- **Dynamically grow an expandable datastore extent:** In this case, the extent (a LUN partition) is increased with the adjacent free capacity
- **Dynamically add a new extent:** In this case, another extent (from another LUN) is "concatenated" to the existing extent

The recommended way is to grow an expandable datastore extent (added with vSphere 4.0).

In both cases, it is possible to use the **Increase Datastore Capacity** menu in the contextual menu of each datastore:

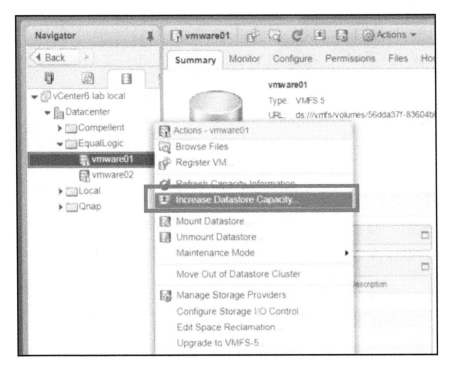

Figure 3.30: Increase Datastore Capacity

For more information, see the vSphere 6.5 Storage guide (https://docs.vmware.com/en/ VMware-vSphere/6.5/com.vmware.vsphere.storage.doc/GUID-08E082E7-59CB-4BB0-B579- 3903F14E95FC.html).

Placing a VMFS datastore in maintenance mode

By using **Storage DRS** (**SDRS**) to group datastores in a datastore cluster, it's possible to put a datastore in maintenance mode and evacuate all the VMs to other datastores in the same datastore cluster.

Just for the vSphere Web Client, go to the **Datastore** inventory and select **Maintenance Mode** | **Enter Maintenance Mode** on the desired datastore:

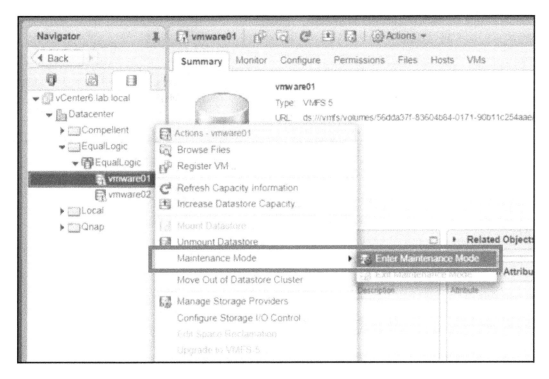

Figure 3.31: Datastore Maintenance Mode

A list of recommendations appears for datastore maintenance mode migration.

For more information, see the vSphere 6.5 Resource Management guide (`https://docs.vmware.com/en/VMware-vSphere/6.5/com.vmware.vsphere.resmgmt.doc/GUID-D229556E-C991-41BD-A378-363CC9D2B2CC.html`).

SDRS will be discussed later, in *Objective 5.2*.

Selecting the preferred path/disabling a path to a VMFS datastore

Storage multipathing has already been explained in *Objective 3.3*.

But to manage the paths, for example, in order to temporarily disable a path, or to select the preferred path (for a Fixed policy), you can use the vSphere Web Client, select a datastore in the **Datastore** inventory, and choose the **Connectivity and Multipathing** menu in the **Configure** tab:

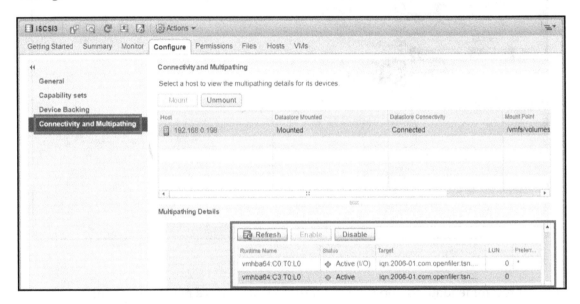

Figure 3.32: Datastore path management

For more information, see the vSphere 6.5 Storage guide (`https://docs.vmware.com/en/VMware-vSphere/6.5/com.vmware.vsphere.storage.doc/GUID-98F0851E-12F2-4FB2-A794-7643DD2E6F9B.html`).

Enabling/disabling vStorage API for array integration (VAAI)

VAAI is enabled by default and you can control it with the following ESXi advanced settings:

Advanced parameter	Description
HardwareAcceleratedLocking	ATS, which is used during the creation of files on the VMFS volume
HardwareAcceleratedMove	Clone Blocks/Full Copy/XCOPY, which is used to copy data
HardwareAcceleratedInit	Zero Blocks/Write Same, which is used to zero-out disk regions

Table 3.10

For more information, see the VMware KB 1033665 (`https://kb.vmware.com/s/article/1033665`)—Disabling the VAAI functionality in ESXi/ESX.

Determining a proper use case for multiple VMFS/NFS datastores

The use of different VMFS and/or NFS datastores can depend on performance, capacity, or data protection. It can also depend on specific storage vendor requests or requirements (for example, for vSAN, only one datastore can exist).

Objective 3.5 – Set up and configure Storage I/O Control

Storage I/O Control (**SIOC**) was initially introduced in vSphere 4.1 to provide I/O prioritization and **quality of service** (**QoS**) of VM disks running on a cluster with a shared storage. It extended the shares and limits not only at the host level, but at the cluster level. With vSphere 5.0, SIOC provides cluster-wide I/O shares and limits for NFS datastores, not only VMFS datastores.

Objective 3.5 for VCP65-DCV and VCP6-DCV are quite similar just because there weren't big changes in those storage functions from vSphere 6.0 to vSphere 6.5.

For more information and details, see the vSphere 6.5 Storage guide: `https://docs.vmware.com/en/VMware-vSphere/6.5/vsphere-esxi-vcenter-server-652-storage-guide.pdf.pdf`.

Describing the benefits of SIOC

With vSphere 6.5, there are two different SIOCs:

- **SIOC v1**: Disabled by default and can be enabled per datastore. By default, the latency threshold for a datastore is set to 30 ms. If SIOC is triggered, disk shares (aggregated from all VMDKs using the datastore) are used to assign I/O queue slots on a per-host basis to that datastore. The throttling is done by modifying the device queue depth of the various hosts sharing the datastore.
- **SIOC v2**: This can now be managed using SPBM policies. VM Storage Policies in vSphere 6.5 have a new option called common rules, which is used for configuring data services provided by hosts, such as SIOC and encryption.

SIOC v1 and SIOC v2 can co exist on vSphere 6.5.

Note that there are also some limitations for SIOC usage:

- Enterprise Plus edition is required for both versions
- SAN with auto-tiering must be certified for SIOC
- NFS 4.1 isn't supported and RDM is not supported
- VMFS datastores with multiple extents are not supported
- Datastores must be managed by a single vCenter Server

For more information, see the vSphere 6.5 Resource Management guide (`https://docs.vmware.com/en/VMware-vSphere/6.5/com.vmware.vsphere.resmgmt.doc/GUID-7686FEC3-1FAC-4DA7-B698-B808C44E5E96.html`).

Enabling and configuring SIOC

You can enable SIOC v1 using vSphere Web Client by going to the **Configure** tab of the selected datastore. In the **General** menu, just click the **Edit** button in the **Datastore Capabilities** area.

Then, select the **Enable Storage I/O Control** checkbox:

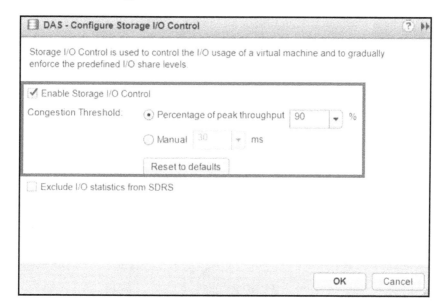

Figure 3.33: Configuring SIOC v1

Then, for each VM, set the proper storage I/O shares and an upper limit of the **I/O operations per second** (**IOPS**) allowed.

 By default, each VM virtual disk has Normal (1,000) as a share value.

For more information, see the vSphere 6.5 Resource Management guide (`https://docs.vmware.com/en/VMware-vSphere/6.5/com.vmware.vsphere.resmgmt.doc/GUID-7686FEC3-1FAC-4DA7-B698-B808C44E5E96.html`).

Configuring/managing SIOC

You can configure and manage SIOC v2 using SPBM-based policies.

There are already some predefined common rules that can be used to define a storage policy:

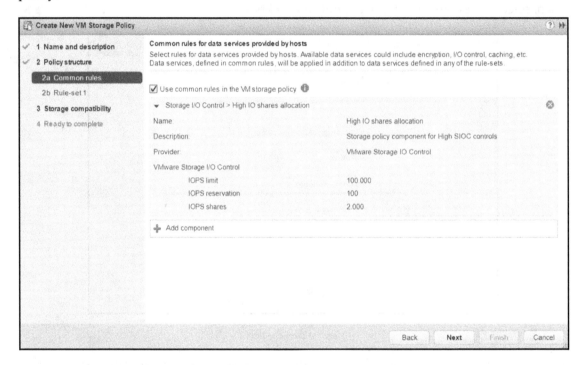

Figure 3.34: Configuring SIOC v2

Note that, compared to SIOC v1, it's also possible to define an IOPS reservation.

Monitoring SIOC

Using the vSphere Web Client, it's possible to monitor SIOC in the datastore **Performance** tab, which shows the latency, the IOPS of the VMs, and the SIOC activities:

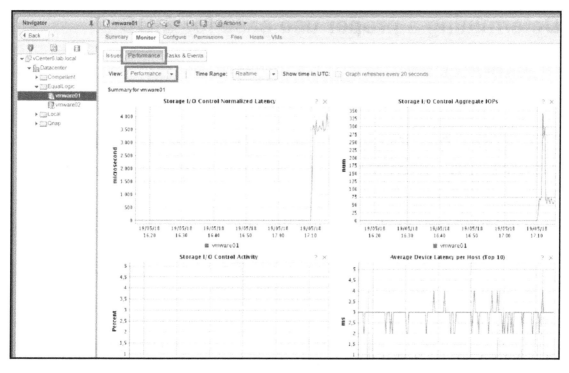

Figure 3.35: Monitoring SIOC

Differentiating between SIOC and dynamic queue depth throttling features

SIOC uses the concept of a congestion threshold that's based on latency, as described previously.

Dynamic Queue depth throttling (or Adaptive Queue Depth) is a different way to adjust the LUN queue depth by returning an SCSI Sense Code of BUSY or QUEUE FULL status.

For more information, look at the following blog post: `https://cormachogan.com/2013/01/22/adaptive-queueing-vs-storage-io-control/`.

Determining a proper use case for SIOC

In a virtual infrastructure, usually, all I/O operations from different VMs on the same datastore are totally "melted". By using SIOC, you can provide a proper storage QoS and also guarantee the expected level of services.

Comparing and contrasting the effects of I/O contention in environments with and without SIOC

Without SIOC, VM access to the datastore is "normalized" at each ESXi level only, but not at a cluster level.

With SIOC, all VMs in the cluster will receive proper I/O access to shared datastores depending on their VMDK reservations, shares, and limits.

Understanding SIOC metrics for datastore clusters and Storage DRS

As described previously, the datastore performance tab provide several graphs using the followings metrics:

- Average latency and aggregated IOPS on the datastore
- Latency among hosts
- Queue depth among hosts
- Read/write IOPS among hosts
- Read/write latency among virtual machine disks
- Read/write IOPS among virtual machine disks

For more information, see the vSphere 6.5 Resource Management guide (`https://docs.vmware.com/en/VMware-vSphere/6.5/com.vmware.vsphere.resmgmt.doc/GUID-45A22E5E-5025-4760-92E6-BAB82153F641.html`).

What is missing

The official VCP65-DCV Exam Preparation Guide covers a lot of security topics, but the vSphere 6.5 Storage guide is definitely more rich, with more content.

For example, the following aspects are not considered in the preparation guide:

- N-Port ID Virtualization (https://docs.vmware.com/en/VMware-vSphere/6.5/com.vmware.vsphere.storage.doc/GUID-E05D5E0A-89A3-4948-8F61-F86A84128446.html)
- Configuring Fibre Channel over Ethernet (https://docs.vmware.com/en/VMware-vSphere/6.5/com.vmware.vsphere.storage.doc/GUID-A9503ED6-2622-4278-890E-B869C3971A9F.html)
- Best Practices for Fibre Channel Storage (https://docs.vmware.com/en/VMware-vSphere/6.5/com.vmware.vsphere.storage.doc/GUID-0C1B4D0A-F993-4F8A-8255-EE156A85C904.html)
- Setting LUN Allocations for iSCSI (https://docs.vmware.com/en/VMware-vSphere/6.5/com.vmware.vsphere.storage.doc/GUID-62902F8C-0D28-46E3-AFFA-5E52C49B15A4.html)
- Using Jumbo Frames with iSCSI (https://docs.vmware.com/en/VMware-vSphere/6.5/com.vmware.vsphere.storage.doc/GUID-0AB1E949-8A97-425B-96E1-DC1A2BC7DC29.html)
- Configuring Discovery Addresses for iSCSI Adapters (https://docs.vmware.com/en/VMware-vSphere/6.5/com.vmware.vsphere.storage.doc/GUID-66215AF3-2D81-4D1F-92D4-B9623FC1CB0E.html)
- Best Practices for iSCSI Storage (https://docs.vmware.com/en/VMware-vSphere/6.5/com.vmware.vsphere.storage.doc/GUID-34297ED3-9D62-4869-BB9E-6EDFBEBD2E94.html)
- Scheduling Queues for Virtual Machine I/Os (https://docs.vmware.com/en/VMware-vSphere/6.5/com.vmware.vsphere.storage.doc/GUID-99C31BE3-D39D-4DA1-89A3-EC9DEA5CC24E.html)
- Mask Paths (https://docs.vmware.com/en/VMware-vSphere/6.5/com.vmware.vsphere.storage.doc/GUID-ACDB4CB6-39B8-4293-8B1F-EE4072DACAEE.html)/Unmask Paths (https://docs.vmware.com/en/VMware-vSphere/6.5/com.vmware.vsphere.storage.doc/GUID-E0534170-A21E-47C6-B989-B7615CC96FBD.html)
- Adding Multipathing Claim Rules (https://docs.vmware.com/en/VMware-vSphere/6.5/com.vmware.vsphere.storage.doc/GUID-4DF1B72D-9106-4D73-8948-3E5F37147294.html)

- Raw Device Mapping (`https://docs.vmware.com/en/VMware-vSphere/6.5/com.vmware.vsphere.storage.doc/GUID-B3522FF1-76FF-419D-8DB6-F15BFD4DF12A.html`)
- Setting Timeout on Windows Guest OS (`https://docs.vmware.vSphere/6.5/com.vmware.vsphere.storage.doc/GUID-EA1E1AAD-7130-457F-8894-70A63BD0623A.html`)
- Checking Metadata Consistency with VOMA (`https://docs.vmware.com/en/VMware-vSphere/6.5/com.vmware.vsphere.storage.doc/GUID-6F991DB5-9AF0-4F9F-809C-B82D3EED7DAF.html`)
- Managing Paths for a Mapped LUN in the vSphere Web Client (`https://docs.vmware.com/en/VMware-vSphere/5.5/com.vmware.vsphere.storage.doc/GUID-240B7639-09C7-4085-8310-4733EC1F2320.html`)
- UNMAP (`https://docs.vmware.com/en/VMware-vSphere/6.5/com.vmware.vsphere.security.doc/GUID-751034F3-5337-4DB2-8272-8DAC0980EACA.html`)
- Snapshots (`https://docs.vmware.com/en/VMware-vSphere/6.5/com.vmware.vsphere.security.doc/GUID-DC96FFDB-F5F2-43EC-8C73-05ACDAE6BE43.html`)
- Instant clones versus linked clones (`https://vinfrastructure.it/2017/08/instant-clones-vs-linked-clones/`)
- VMware vSphere APIs for IO Filtering (VAIO) (`https://code.vmware.com/programs/vsphere-apis-for-io-filtering`)
- Flash Cache (`https://docs.vmware.com/en/VMware-vSphere/6.5/com.vmware.vsphere.storage.doc/GUID-07ADB946-2337-4642-B660-34212F237E71.html`)

Review questions

For more questions, see `Chapter 11`, *Mock Exam 1*, and `Chapter 12`, *Mock Exam 2*:

1. Which kind of vSphere datastore supports the automatic space reclaim?
   - A: VMFS5
   - B: VMFS6
   - C: vSAN
   - D: NFS

   B - See *Objective 3.1 and 3.2*

2. What are two different ways to share a virtual disk across two (or more) VMs?
   - A: Use a controller with SCSI Bus Sharing
   - B: Use the multi-write option at VMDK level
   - C: Use a physical RDM
   - D: Use a vSAN datastore

AB - See *Objective 3.4*

Summary

This chapter has been dedicated to the storage part of a virtual infrastructure. We started with the local block-based storage and extended it to the shared block storage with FC, FCoE, and iSCSI protocols, and used NAS storage and NFS-based storage.

Chapter 4, *Upgrade a vSphere Deployment to 6.x*, and objective will provide information on how to upgrade a vSphere deployment to version 6.5.

4
Upgrade a vSphere Deployment to 6.x

Understanding the correct sequence of tasks to upgrade the VMware vSphere platform is an essential part of the certification path, allowing you to gain the necessary skills to successfully complete the procedure while also giving you the ability to answer any questions that you might face in the exam.

This chapter will cover all of the steps to successfully upgrade the VMware vSphere core components, such as ESXI hosts and vCenter Server, to version 6.5. Make sure that you understand how the upgrade works and the components that are involved, and take time to practice the activities provided in this chapter.

Practicing what you learn in this chapter will be key to reinforcing your skills and your preparation for the exam.

In this chapter, we will cover the following skills:

- Performing ESXI host and virtual machine upgrades
- Creating and attaching baselines and/or baseline groups to vSphere objects
- Upgrading a vSphere Distributed Switch
- Upgrading VMware Tools and virtual machine hardware
- Upgrading an ESXi host by using vCenter Update Manager
- Performing vCenter Server upgrades in Windows
- Performing a vCenter Server migration to vCSA

Objective 4.1 – Perform ESXi Host and Virtual Machine Upgrades

vSphere 6.5 Update 1 supports migration from vSphere 6.0 Update 3 and vSphere 5.5 Update 3b, and it can be performed in different ways.

The simplest method that you can use to upgrade your infrastructure is through **vSphere Update Manager** (**VUM**), a tool that centralizes and simplifies the management of patches and updates for the VMs, ESXI hosts, and vApps installed in the virtual environment.

The components of the vSphere platform can also be upgraded through scripts, using CLI commands that allow for the automation of the installation procedure, making the process faster overall.

 Before migrating your infrastructure, keep in mind that vCenter Server must be running version 6.5 Update 1 before upgrading the ESXI hosts to 6.5 Update 1.

Updating manager

vSphere version 6.5 comes with two versions of the Update Manager tool, as follows:

- **Windows-based**: The VUM component must be installed from the installation media, and it requires a supported database that resides on the same server as vCenter, or in a separate Windows-based VM
- **Part of the vCSA**: VUM is embedded in the appliance, and no longer requires the installation of an additional external Windows

To store and organize server data, the Windows vCenter Server and the vCSA need a supported database, and each vCenter Server instance must have its own database. To manage small environments (up to 20 hosts and 200 VMs), the vCenter Server and the vCSA in vSphere 6.5 come with a bundled PostgreSQL database that you can use without the need to install additional components. For larger environments, Windows-based vCenter supports Microsoft SQL Server (Express for small environments, Standard and Enterprise for large environments) and Oracle databases, while for the vCSA, Oracle is the only possible option.

The management and configuration of the Update Manager are performed through the flash-based vSphere Web Client, as are all of the tasks required for the upgrade procedure.

Configuring download source(s)

If the method used to upgrade the virtual infrastructure uses Update Manager, the vSphere upgrades can be downloaded from VMware's website or from third-party websites, shared through a repository, or manually imported as ZIP files (offline bundles). The offline bundle import feature is only supported for hosts running version 5.0 or later.

To add or modify download sources in vSphere Web Client, navigate to **Home** | **Update Manager** and select your vCenter Server instance. Select the **Manage** tab and under **Settings**, select **Download Settings**.

To add or modify the download sources, click on the **Edit...** button. Although VUM supports both HTTP and HTTPS protocols, to increase security, using HTTPS for URL addresses is recommended:

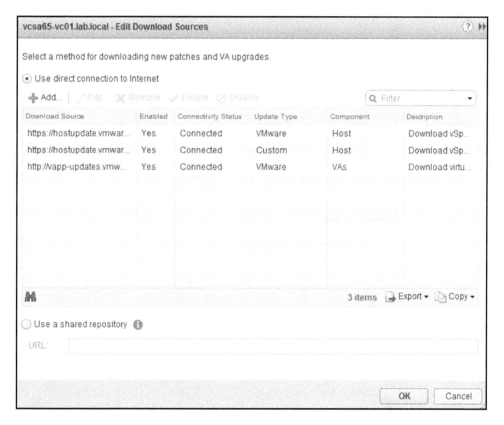

Figure 4.1: Adding or modifying download sources

Downloading updates from the internet and using a shared repository at the same time is not supported. You can only use one option.

To download all of the updates from the listed download sources, click on the **Download Now** button:

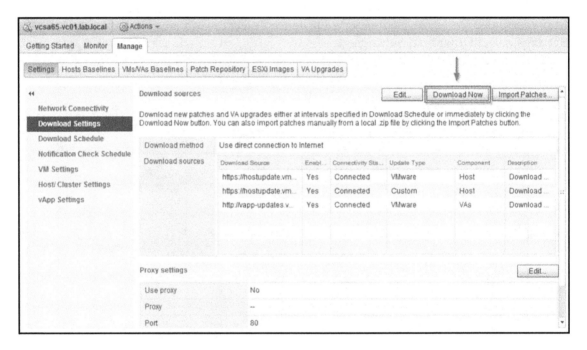

Figure 4.2: Downloading available updates from VMware's website

Setting up UMDS to set up download repository

If an internet connection is not available on the machine that has Update Manager installed, Update Manager uses an optional module called **Update Manager Download Service** (**UMDS**) to download virtual appliance upgrades, patch binaries, patch metadata, and create notifications. Available in version 6.5 for both Windows and Linux-based operating systems, the UMDS component must be installed on a machine that has internet access.

UMDS 6.5 has the ability to recall a patch, if the released patch has potential issues.

Importing ESXi images

Upgrading the ESXI host to version 6.5 can be performed by using the host upgrade baselines with the Update Manager tool. Make sure that the hardware and software used meet the minimum requirements, as follows:

- 64-bit x86 processors, released after September 2006
- At least two CPU cores
- NX/XD bit, to be enabled for the CPU in the BIOS
- A minimum of 4 GB of physical RAM
- Intel VT-x or AMD RVI, enabled on x64 CPUs to support 64-bit VMs
- 1 GB or faster Ethernet controllers

To avoid issues due to unsupported hardware (for instance, ESXI host 6.5 doesn't have the driver for Realtek NICs), it is always best to check the VMware Compatibility Guide at `https://www.vmware.com/resources/compatibility` before starting the upgrade procedure.

The upgrade of ESXi can use a standard ISO image provided by VMware (with a name formatted like `VMware-VMvisor-Installer-6.5.0.update01-5969303.x86_64.iso`), a custom ISO image based on the hardware vendor (HP, Dell, Lenovo, and so on), or an ISO image created with the VMware Image Builder. Update Manager 6.5 supports upgrading from ESXi 5.5 or ESXi 6.0 to ESXi 6.5.

To import an ESXi image, you should use the vSphere Web Client connected to the vCenter Server where the Update Manager is registered, and go to **Home** | **Update Manager**. Select the **ESXi Images** tab and click on the **Import ESXi Image...** icon:

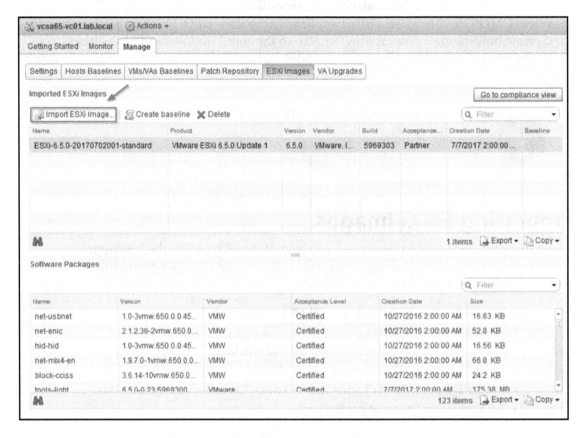

Figure 4.3: Import an ESXi image in VUM

Creating baselines and/or baseline groups

Baselines are used when scanning the VM to determine the compliancy level of scanned objects. Once the ESXi image has been imported in VUM, to upgrade the hosts in your vSphere environment you must create a baseline that will be used during the scan process to upgrade an ESXI host from a previous supported version to the current version.

Depending on the business requirements, vSphere 6.5 provides different baselines types that you can use to apply specific updates/patches to the ESXI hosts configured in your network:

- **Static baselines**: The defined content doesn't change over time, even if the repository is updated with new patches/updates. They are typically used to ensure a specific patch or update is applied to the hosts configured in your environment.
- **Dynamic baselines**: This is the configuration used most often, and it keeps your environment up to date, since patches change over time. The baselines define a set of patches that meet the criteria specified during the baseline configuration, by adding or removing patches accordingly.
- **Upgrade baselines**: These are used to perform the version upgrades of the ESXI hosts installed in your vSphere environment.
- **Host Extension baselines**: These contain additional software from VMware or third parties, and are used to provide additional features, updated drivers, and improvements to ESXI hosts.

VUM provides two predefined patch baselines and three predefined upgrade baselines:

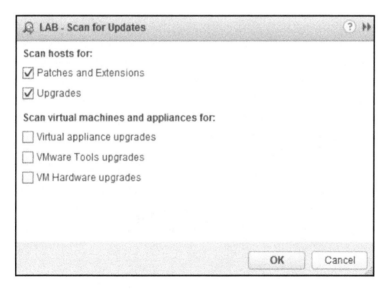

Figure 4.4: Predefined baselines

Baseline groups are used to put together different existing baselines to meet the specific needs of your environment. They can contain patch, extension, and upgrade baselines.

Predefined virtual machine and virtual appliance upgrade baselines cannot be edited or deleted.

To create a new baseline, go to the **Hosts Baselines** tab and click on the **New Baseline...** link:

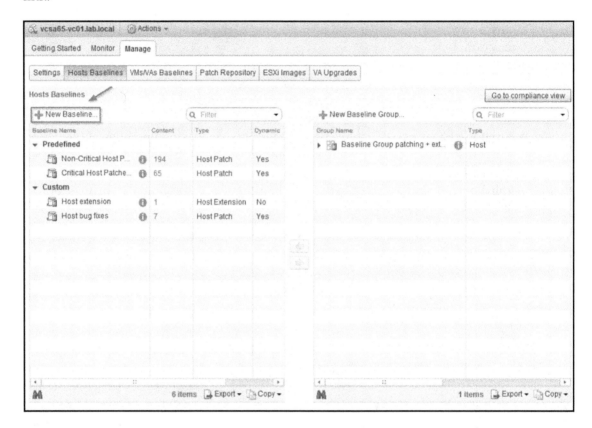

Figure 4.5: Create host baselines

After entering a name, under **Baseline Type**, select **Host Upgrade** and click on **Next**. Select the ESXi image previously imported to be used with the baseline.

Attaching baselines to vSphere objects

Having created the host baseline that you will use to upgrade the ESXI hosts, you now need to attach the new baseline for the hosts to process.

To attach baselines to objects, you must switch the Update Manager to **Compliance View**. From the **Hosts Baselines** tab, click on the **Go to compliance view** button:

Figure 4.6: Switching Update Manager to Compliance View

In the **Update Manager** tab, click on the **Attach Baseline...** button to select the host baseline to attach at the object level (vCenter, datacenter, or cluster) containing the ESXI hosts that you need to upgrade to the newer version:

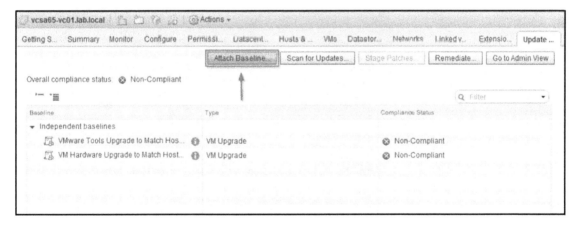

Figure 4.7: Attaching baselines from Update Manager

Under the **Upgrade Baselines** menu, select the baseline previously created and click on **OK** to confirm:

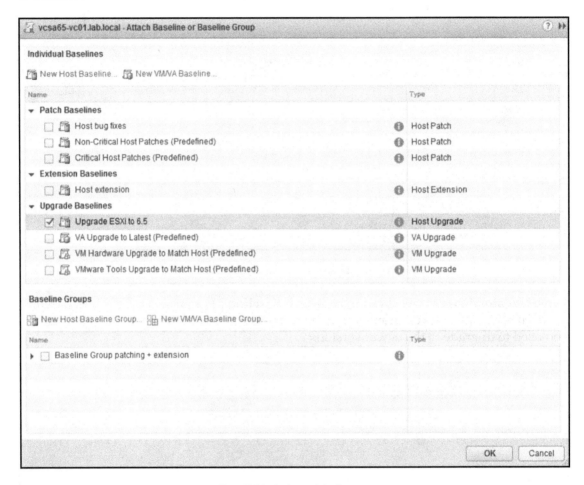

Figure 4.8: Selecting the upgrade baseline to use

Once the baseline is attached, the **Compliance Status** will show whether the attached hosts are up to date or in need of an upgrade. If a scan hasn't been performed yet, the status will be shown as **Unknown**, since the host state is unknown and needs to be scanned for compliance.

Scanning vSphere

Once the baseline has been attached to the host, you must click on the **Scan for Updates...** button to verify the host's compliance with the attached baseline. In the **Scan for Updates...** wizard, specify **Upgrades** as the scan option, then click on **OK**.

The scanning process will verify whether the processed hosts are up to date or in need of an upgrade. Once the scanning process has completed, you will have two possible ESXi states, as follows:

- `Compliant`: Hosts are up to date
- `Non-Compliant`: Hosts need to be upgraded:

Figure 4.9: ESXI hosts' statuses after scanning

Staging patches and extensions

The ESXi upgrade procedure does not consider a staging process. Staging is normally used when patching ESXI hosts or adding an extension baseline.

During the staging process, patches are copied from the Update Manager to the ESXI hosts across the network, reducing the remediation time.

From the **Update Manager** tab, click on **Stage Patches** and select the patches to be copied to the selected ESXI hosts.

 If you have hosts connected to the Update Manager over a slow WAN connection, staging patches can reduce the ESXi outage required for remediation.

Remediating an object

If the scanned hosts are marked as non-compliant, you will need to remediate them in order to perform an upgrade or apply missing patches. The remediation process applies patches and upgrades to the objects that are not compliant with the attached baseline.

In a scenario where the upgrade is applied to a cluster of hosts, if a failure occurs during the upgrade procedure, the overall process stops. To speed up a cluster upgrade, you can also upgrade host members in parallel, instead of one at a time. If an error occurs to a host during the parallel remediation, only the upgrade process for the affected host will stop, while it will continue for the other hosts.

 To figure out the reason why an error occurred during the remediation process, check the log at `/var/log/esxupdate.log`.

If you upgrade a cluster of hosts, some cluster features, such as HA, **distributed power management** (**DPM**), and **fault tolerance** (**FT**) must be temporarily disabled.

To proceed with remediation, from the **Update Manager** tab, click on the **Remediate** button and select the created baseline to apply.

After the remediation procedure has completed, the staged patches or extensions will be deleted from their cache by the hosts:

Figure 4.10: ESXI host remediation

TIP

Before starting the remediation process for the hosts, back up the current ESXi configuration to quickly restore the hypervisor, in case something goes wrong with the upgrade.

Upgrading a vSphere Distributed Switch

Before upgrading a vSphere Distributed Switch, make sure that the vCenter and ESXI hosts are upgraded first; this is a prerequisite for performing the upgrade. During the Distributed Switch upgrade process, there is no downtime for the attached virtual machines; a backup of the virtual switch configuration is recommended, in order to quickly restore the functionality of the switch if a failure occurs during the upgrade procedure.

To back up the configuration of a Distributed Switch, go to **Home** I **Networking**. Right-click on the virtual switch to back up and select **Settings** I **Export Configuration**. You can back up the Distributed Switch and all ports, or just the Distributed Switch.

To upgrade the Distributed Switch, go to **Home | Networking** and right-click on the virtual switch to process. Select **Upgrade | Upgrade Distributed Switch...**; then, from the wizard, specify the version of the Distributed Switch to upgrade. An upgrade from version 5.x to 6.0 or 6.5 is not reversible:

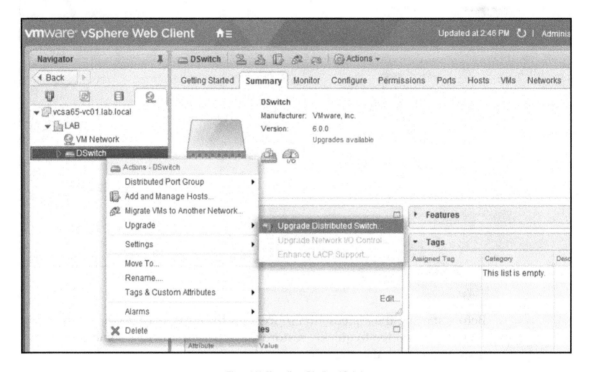

Figure 4.11: Upgrading a Distributed Switch

Upgrading VMware Tools

VMware Tools is a set of utilities installed in the guest OS that improves overall performance and provides better control of the virtual machine, making administration easier. VMware Tools is not installed by default, and some features, such as power control management (shutdown and restart, for instance), improved graphical interface, better mouse control, and the ability to copy and paste files, will not be available until you install VMware Tools.

Version 6.5 delivers two versions of VMware Tools, as follows:

- **Version 10.1**: Only available for an OEM-supported guest OS
- **Version 10.0.12**: A special version of VMware Tools provided by VMware for guests who are no longer supported by their vendors; this version won't receive further enhancements

 It is recommended to upgrade to the latest VMware Tools version included in your ESXi. VMware vSphere 6.5 Update 1 includes VMware Tools version 10.1.7.

To increase security, the ESXi 6.5 ISO images containing VMware Tools are cryptographically verified each time they are read; additional files with appropriate signatures have been included in the VMware Tools distributions to help with this verification.

The VMware Tools instance included in version 6.5 supports the most widely used guest operating systems, but VMware also provides tools for other guests (downloads are available at `https://my.vmware.com/web/vmware`).

When an ESXI host is upgraded, a new version of VMware Tools becomes available for the virtual machines, and the installation procedure may differ, depending on the installed OS. The procedure to install or upgrade VMware Tools is the same, and the virtual machines can be configured to check and install newer versions automatically. To perform an automatic upgrade, virtual machines must be powered on, with a running OS.

For Windows-based virtual machines, a yellow caution icon will show up in the Windows taskbar when a VMware Tools upgrade is available.

To manually upgrade VMware Tools for a specific virtual machine, from vSphere Web Client, right-click on the virtual machine to upgrade and select **Guest OS | Upgrade VMware Tools**.

Alternatively, you can right-click on the virtual machine and select **Edit Settings** to access its configuration. Then, go to the **VM Options** tab and enable the **Check and upgrade VMware Tools before each power on** option:

Figure 4.12: Automating the VMware Tools upgrade

It's also possible to manually upgrade multiple virtual machines at the same time. From vSphere Web Client, select the object level where the virtual machines to upgrade are located and go to the **VMs** tab. Select the virtual machines to process, then click on **Actions** and select the **Guest OS | Install/Upgrade VMware Tools...** option:

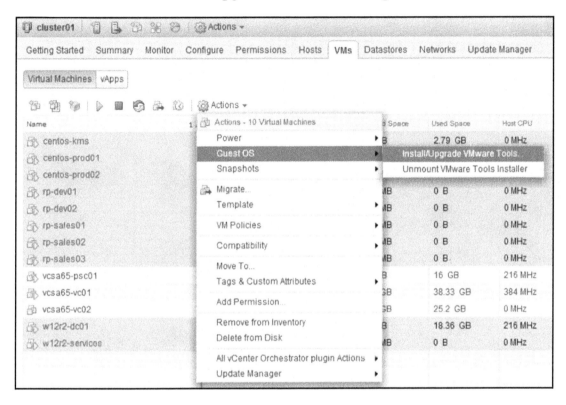

Figure 4.13: VMware Tools upgrade for multiple virtual machines

To fully automate the VMware Tools upgrade for all of the virtual machines installed in your virtual infrastructure, you can use the Update Manager tool.

From vSphere Web Client, access the **VMs and Templates** view, select the vSphere object level where the virtual machines are running, and go to the **Update Manager** tab. Attach and configure the predefined **VMware Tools Upgrade to Match Host** baseline accordingly and execute the remediation as follows:

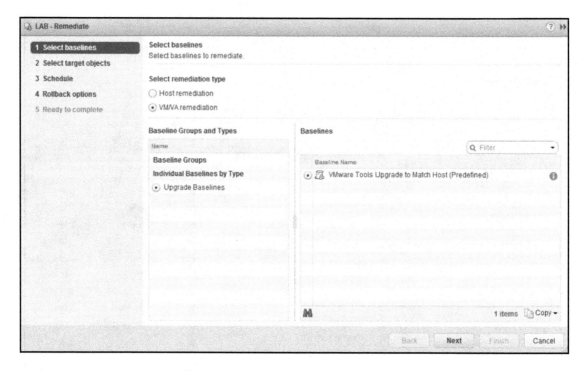

Figure 4.14: Automating the installation of VMware Tools using VUM

To determine whether a virtual machine is running an up-to-date VMware Tools version, right-click on the virtual machine and access the **Summary** tab. You can click on the **More info...** link to get additional details:

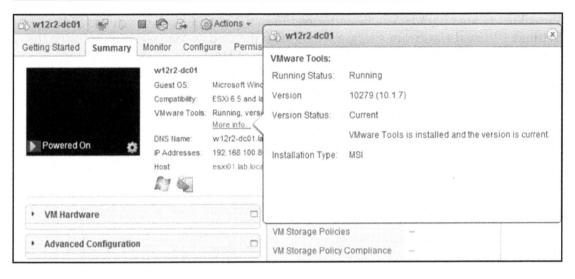

Figure 4.15: Checking the installed VMware Tools version

Upgrading virtual machine hardware

The virtual hardware version configured for a virtual machine determines the virtual hardware supported by the VM. vSphere 6.5 introduces hardware version 13 and supports VMs created with previous hardware versions.

What hardware version to use depends on the ESXi version used in your environment. If different versions of ESXi host are installed, you should choose the correct hardware version to match the lowest version host used in the infrastructure (ESXi 5.5 and 6.0 don't support hardware version 13).

A lower version has reduced functionality and it won't take advantage of the latest features. A VM with a higher hardware version won't be supported by a VMware product with a lower version.

Virtual hardware upgrades can be performed from the virtual machine settings (**Edit Settings | Virtual Hardware | Upgrade**), through the Update Manager tool, by using the predefined baseline **VM Hardware Upgrade to Match Host**, or performed from the vSphere Web Client, by right-clicking on the VM and selecting **Compatibility | Upgrade VM Compatibility**:

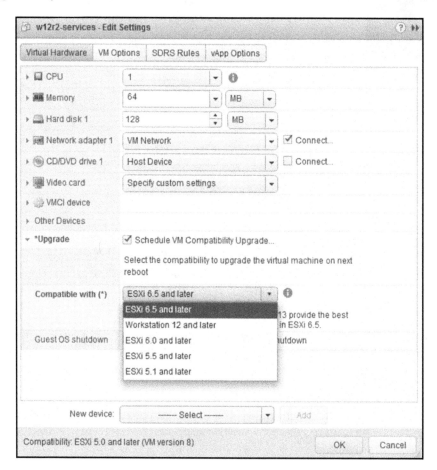

Figure 4.16: Upgrading virtual hardware from the VM's settings

You also have the option to upgrade the virtual hardware for multiple virtual machines at the same time. From vSphere Web Client, select the object level where the virtual machines to upgrade are located and go to the **VMs** tab. Select the virtual machines to process, then click on **Actions** and select the **Guest OS | Install/Upgrade VMware Tools** option:

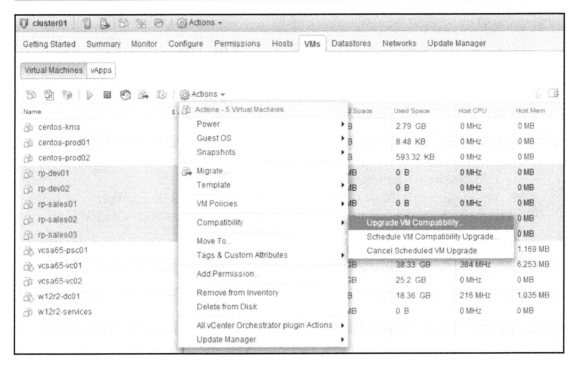

Figure 4.17: Virtual hardware upgrade for multiple virtual machines

In vCenter Server, you can define a default hardware version for VM creation on a host, cluster, or datacenter. From vSphere Client, right-click on the object to configure and select **Edit Default VM Compatibility**, then select the hardware version to use from the **Compatible with** drop-down menu.

Upgrading an ESXI host by using vCenter Update Manager

An ESXI host can be upgraded from a previous supported version to the current version through the Update Manager, using a custom baseline attached to the hosts to upgrade. If the ISO host image version used to perform the scan process is the same as that of the target hosts, VUM marks the scanned hosts as compliant; they are marked as non-compliant if the version differs.

Before proceeding with the upgrade, make sure that the ESXI hosts meet the minimum requirements.

To upgrade a host with VUM, follow this step-by-step procedure:

1. From vSphere Web Client, select **Home** | **Update Manager**, then select the vCenter Server instance to configure.
2. Go to the **Manage** | **ESXi Images** tab and click on the **Import ESXi Image** button to import the image file used to upgrade the ESXI hosts.
3. Select the ISO file to use for the upgrade by using the **Browse** button in the wizard, then click on **Next** to upload the image into VUM.
4. When the upload completes, click on **Close** to exit the import wizard. The uploaded image will be listed in the ESXi images.
5. Now, click on the **New Baseline** button from the **Hosts Baselines** tab. Type the name of the new baseline and select the **Host Upgrade** option under **Baseline Type**, then click **Next**.
6. Select the ESXi image to use for the upgrade and then click **Next**.
7. A review of the settings is displayed. Click on **Finish** to create the baseline.
8. To attach the created baseline to the hosts to upgrade, click on the **Go to compliance view** button.
9. In the **Update Manager** tab, click on the **Attach Baseline** button to specify the baseline to attach to the object level (cluster) that contains the ESXI hosts to upgrade, and then click on **OK**.
10. To verify the host's compliance with the attached baseline, click on **Scan for Updates**. In the **Confirm Scan** wizard, specify **Upgrades** under **Scan for** and then click **OK**.
11. To perform the upgrade, click on **Remediate**, selecting the correct baseline to apply to ESXI hosts. Click on **Next** to continue.

Before remediating hosts, back up the ESXi configuration to quickly restore the hypervisor in case something goes wrong with the upgrade.

12. Specify the hosts to remediate, then click **Next**.
13. Accept the EULA and click **Next** to continue with the upgrade procedure.
14. The remediation task can be scheduled to run during a maintenance window or at other times. Enable **Schedule this action to run later** to schedule remediation, then click **Next**.
15. Specify the **Host remediation options** and **Cluster remediation options**, and click on **Next** to continue.

16. When the remediation procedure has completed, the upgraded hosts will be marked as **Compliant**:

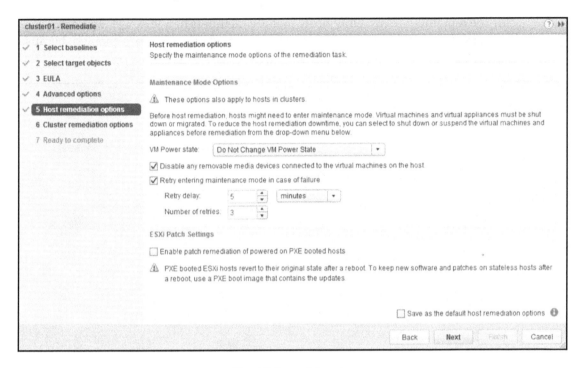

Figure 4.18: Host remediation options

Staging multiple ESXI host upgrades

The upgrade procedure has been simplified in version 6.5, and the host upgrade can be performed through different methods:

- **CD-ROM, USB drive**: This is the simplest method to use, making use of ESXi installer ISO images to upgrade hosts; it is useful for small environments.
- **Update Manager**: This is the recommended method for performing an upgrade of ESXI hosts. Clustered ESXI hosts are processed one by one by default, and DPM, HA admission control, and FT must be disabled.

Parallel remediation can be enabled for a cluster in order to process multiple ESXI hosts at the same time, and the number of concurrently remediated hosts can be limited. If a host fails, it will be ignored by VUM, and remediation will continue for the remaining hosts. Only hosts that are members of a vSAN cluster are processed sequentially, even if the parallel remediation option is enabled, because by design only one ESXi can be in maintenance mode at a time:

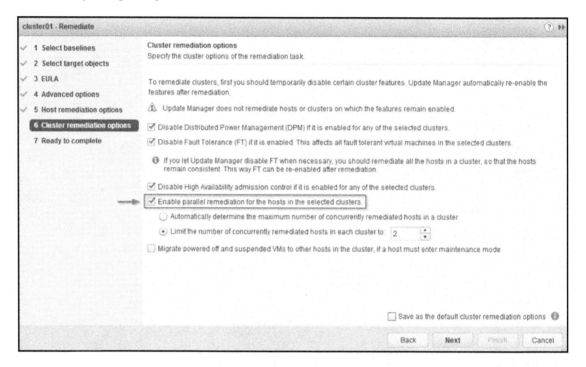

Figure 4.19: Enabling parallel remediation

 The remediation process for multiple clusters within a datacenter runs in parallel. If a remediation fails for one of the clusters, remediation continues for the remaining clusters.

- **Auto Deploy**: Based on the use of master images, Auto Deploy installation is a way to automate the upgrade process in large environments, through PXE booting ESXI hosts from a central Auto Deploy server.
- **esxcli commands**: Patches and updates for ESXi are combined in a bundle provided by VMware in ZIP format, including some VIBs (ESXi software packages) containing fixes and updates.

Once the bundle has been copied into a datastore reachable by the hosts to upgrade, make an SSH connection to the hypervisor to access the console.

To proceed with the upgrade, enter the host in maintenance mode with the following command:

```
esxcli system maintenanceMode set --enable true
```

Using the `esxcli` upgrade command, combined with the full path to the ZIP bundle file previously copied to the datastore, you will be able to upgrade the host as follows:

```
esxcli software vib update -d
/vmfs/volumes/datastore/patch_bundle.zip
```

To apply the newest VIBs, the host must be rebooted with the following command:

```
reboot
```

When the ESXi boots again, exit maintenance mode, as follows:

```
esxcli system maintenanceMode set --enable false
```

- **Scripts**: Scripts are used to perform unattended upgrades and help to avoid repeating the same steps.
  If the number of hosts to install increases dramatically, the installation process can be automated by using a script, providing an efficient way to deploy multiple hosts.

The installation script is a text file, often named `ks.cfg`, that contains supported commands useful for providing required installation options to the ESXi installer. The script can be saved on a USB flash drive or in a network location accessible through NFS, HTTP, HTTPS, or FTP.

For example, you could use the following command to specify the path to an installation script:

```
ks=http://ip_address/kickstart/ks.cfg
```

In the preceding code, the IP address refers to the machine that the script resides on.

Aligning appropriate baselines with target inventory objects

Baselines are used during the scan of the VM to determine the compliance level of scanned objects (hosts, VMs, and virtual appliances). While host baselines can be customized, you cannot create custom VM or VA baselines.

Some predefined baselines provided by VUM can only be attached or detached to/from the inventory objects, and cannot be edited or deleted:

- **Host Baseline**: It provides critical host patch and non-critical host patch options
- **VM/VA Baseline**: It provides a VMware Tools upgrade to match host, a VM hardware upgrade to match the host, and a VA upgrade to the latest version

During the creation of the host baselines, you can choose from the following two baseline types:

- **Static Baseline**: The baseline doesn't change, even if new patches are added to the repository; this can be used to ensure that a specific patch is applied to all of the hosts in your environment.
- **Dynamic Baseline**: Patches in this baseline change over time, and it is used to keep the environment up to date. Patches meet the criteria specified during the configuration, adding or removing some specific patches.

In vSphere 6.5 Update 1, VUM has been integrated into vSAN, providing an automated update process to ensure that a vSAN cluster is up to date with the best release available, keeping your hardware in a supported state:

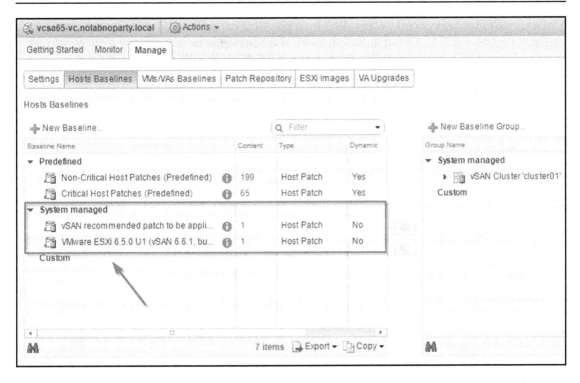

Figure 4.20: System managed baselines

 By default, when a vSAN cluster is created using an ESXI host version 6.0 Update 2 or later, some new system managed baselines are generated by vSAN.

Objective 4.2 – Perform vCenter Server Upgrades (Windows)

vCenter Server is a core component of the vSphere infrastructure service that centralizes the management of the ESXI hosts and the VMs that run on the hypervisor. vCenter Server also provides advanced features, such as sign-on server, centralized authentication, vMotion, DRS, HA, and FT. Also, management of resources, logs and stats, alarms, and events comes into play when vCenter Server is present in the infrastructure.

VMware vCenter Server can be installed on a physical or virtual Windows machine, or can be deployed as a vCSA. The installation of vCenter Server is now supported by Windows, macOS Sierra 10.12, and Linux OS. With version 6.5, both the Windows and vCSA deployments provide the same features, plus some additional capabilities that are available to the vCSA only. Hosts that you plan to connect to vCenter Server 6.5 must be running ESXi version 5.5 or later.

Comparing the methods of upgrading vCenter Server

vSphere 6.5 provides a Migration Tool, useful for easily and quickly upgrading from version 6.0 to 6.5. With the release of Update 1, vSphere 6.0 Update 3 installations can also be upgraded to vSphere 6.5 Update 1. The upgrade can be perform via GUI or CLI commands.

You cannot upgrade to vCenter Server 6.5 from vCenter Server 5.1 or earlier. Upgrade to vCenter Server version 5.5 or 6.0 first. vCenter Server 6.5 can manage ESXi version 5.5 or 6.0 hosts.

Before upgrading vCenter Server to version 6.5, there are some configuration aspects that you must consider to avoid potential problems.

Starting from version 6.0, vCenter Server is deployed with two core components, as follows:

- **Platform Services Controller (PSC)**
- **vCenter Server (VC)**

The PSC is a component used to provide common infrastructure services for VMware products, and it provides essential services for the vSphere functionality, such as the following:

- **Single Sign-On (SSO)**: A prerequisite for installing vCenter Server, it solves the problem of authentication in an environment with multiple ESXI hosts.
- **VMware License Service**: Centralizes the management of all of the information related to the licenses for products that support PSC.
- **Certificate Management**: Required to communicate with the vCenter and ESXI hosts in a secure way. vCenter Server services make use of SSL.

Other services provided by PSC are as follows:

- VMware Appliance Management Service (only in appliance-based PSC)
- VMware Component Manager
- VMware Identity Management Service
- VMware HTTP Reverse Proxy
- VMware Service Control Agent
- VMware Security Token Service
- VMware Common Logging Service
- VMware Syslog Health Service
- VMware Authentication Framework
- VMware Directory Service

PSC and vCenter Server can be deployed in two different ways, depending on the design of your infrastructure:

- **Embedded**: Both PSC and VC are installed on the same machine, making management simpler; however, this installation type is resource-consuming, because for each product, there is a PSC that is not always needed. An embedded deployment is an ideal solution for small environments:

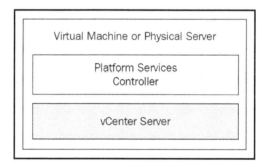

Figure 4.21: PSC and vCenter Server can be installed on the same machine

- **External**: This solution fits large environments best; PSC and vCenter Server are installed on different machines, with the advantage that shared services in the PSC instances consume fewer resources:

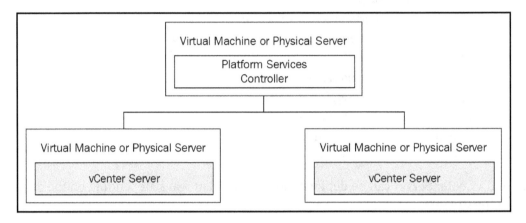

Figure 4.22: An external PSC can manage multiple vCenter Servers

The method used to upgrade to version 6.5 depends on the vCenter Server version installed in the environment. The upgrade can be performed from the following versions:

- vCenter 5.5, with an embedded vCenter SSO, on Windows
- vCenter 6.0, with an embedded PSC instance, on Windows
- vCenter SSO 5.5 on Windows
- PSC 6.0 on Windows
- vCenter 5.5 on Windows
- vCenter 6.0 on Windows

Upgrading vCenter Server 5.5 on Windows

The available upgrade configurations and options are determined by the running vCenter Server version. Common services, such as vCenter Single Single-On, are upgraded by the software in the Platform Services Controller instance, while remaining components, such as vSphere Web Client Inventory Service, are upgraded to 6.5 as a part of the vCenter Server group of services. The vCenter Server and all of its services are upgraded by the software processing the components with the correct order to the same version.

A vCenter Server running version 5.5 determines the following available upgrade configurations:

- If all vCenter Server 5.5 components are installed on the same system, the vCenter Server 6.5 software upgrades your system to vCenter Server with an embedded platform services controller instance. You cannot change the deployment type during the upgrade process:

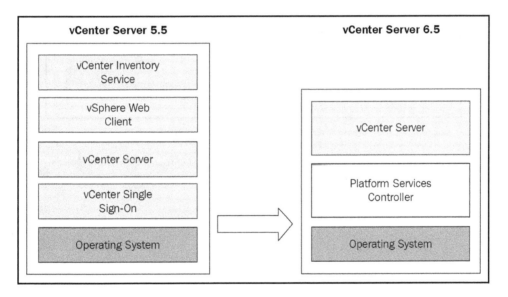

Figure 4.23: vCenter Server 5.5, with the embedded vCenter SSO upgrade

- If you have a vCenter Server 5.5 configured with an external vCenter SSO, the software upgrades your deployment to vCenter Server 6.5, with an external platform services controller instance:

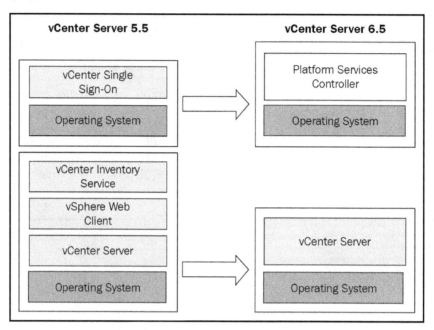

Figure 4.24: vCenter Server 5.5, with the external vCenter SSO upgrade

- If a vSphere Auto Deploy server is configured in your environment, the upgrade process upgrades it while upgrading the associated vCenter Server instance. You cannot use an earlier version of vSphere Auto Deploy with vCenter Server 6.5. If your vSphere Auto Deploy server is running on a remote system, it is upgraded and migrated to the same system as vCenter Server during the upgrade process:

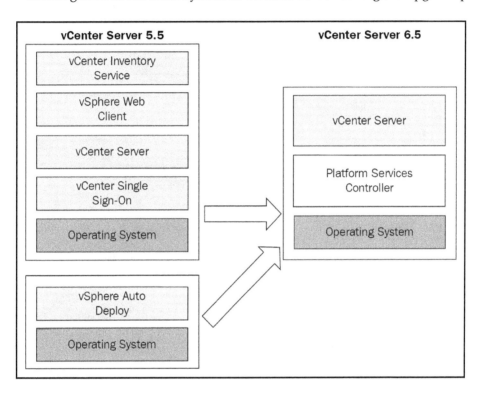

Figure 4.25: vCenter Server 5.5, with the remote vSphere Auto Deploy Server upgrade

- If vSphere Web Client is deployed remotely, it is upgraded along with the vCenter Server instance to which it is registered, and is migrated to the same location as the vCenter Server instance. Only the vCenter SSO instance remains remotely deployed as a part of the PSC instance:

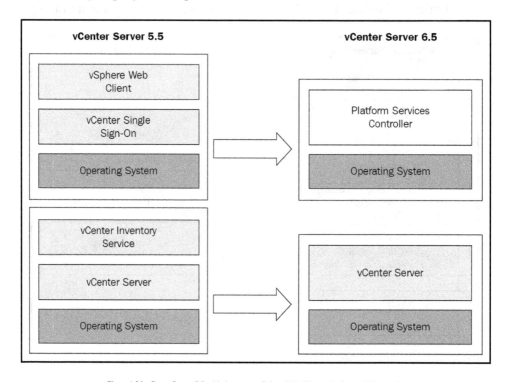

Figure 4.26: vCenter Server 5.5, with the remote vSphere Web Client and vCenter SSO upgrade

- If all of the components of the vCenter Server are deployed remotely, all of them are migrated to the vCenter Server, except for the vCenter SSO. The Inventory Service data is migrated to the vCenter Server, but the legacy version must be uninstalled manually, because it is no longer used:

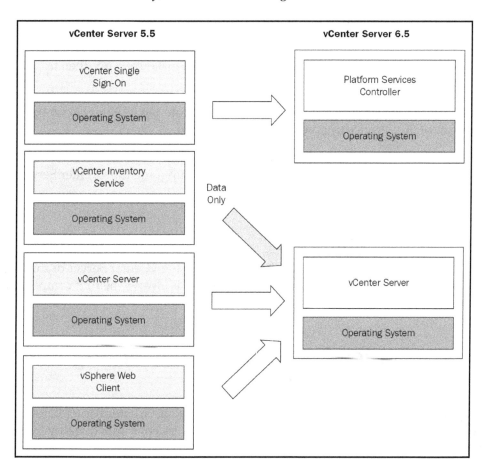

Figure 4.27: vCenter Server 5.5, with the All Remote Components upgrade

Upgrading vCenter Server 6.0 on Windows

If your environment has vCenter Server running version 6.0, the deployment type does not change during the upgrade to version 6.5.

The steps involved in the upgrade process depend on the deployment type, as follows:

- **vCenter with PSC embedded**: Only one upgrade step is required.
- **vCenter with PSC external**: Upgrade the PSC instance to 6.5, then upgrade the vCenter Server instance.

To avoid issues, all PSC instances must be upgraded before the vCenter Server instances, and concurrent PSC instance upgrades are not supported.

For multiple vCenter Server instances sharing the same PSC or vCenter SSO, you have to upgrade the vCenter SSO or the PSC first, then you can upgrade the vCenter Server instances concurrently.

Mixed platform upgrades

In a mixed environment scenario, regardless of whether the vCenter Server or the PSC instances run under Windows or as appliances, the PSC is always the first component that you must upgrade to version 6.5.

Backup vCenter Server database, configuration and certificate datastore

It is always a good practice to perform a full backup of your vCenter Server before proceeding with the upgrade, in order to quickly restore vCenter functionality in the case of a failure.

Backup the Windows vCenter Server

Regardless of the vCenter Server deployment in your environment (PSC embedded or external), you have to back up the vCenter database (external databases, such as SQL or Oracle, have dedicated backup tools), every external PSC server, and the vCenter Servers connected to a shared PSC.

The backup can be made by using any suitable backup solutions on the market that support the vCenter Server version to process (Veeam, Nakivo, Vembu, and Altaro, just to mention some).

Backup the vCSA

vSphere vCSA 6.5 introduces a new feature that allows a file-based backup of the vCSA and the PSC, performed through the **vCenter Server Appliance Management Interface (VAMI)**.

When you perform a backup via the VAMI, the backup file created includes the core vCSA configuration, inventory, and historical data of your choice. The backup file is not stored in the vCSA, but is streamed over FTP, FTPS, HTTP, HTTPS, or SCP to a remote system of your choice.

 If you back up a vCSA in an HA cluster, only the active node of the vCenter Server instance is backed up.

To create the vCSA backup, follow this procedure:

1. In your preferred browser, enter the address `https://<VCSA_IP>:5480` to access the VAMI, and log in as `root`.
2. From the **Summary** tab, click on the **Backup** button in the right-hand pane.
3. Specify the backup protocol (the available options are HTTP, HTTPS, SCP, FTPS, and FTP), then enter the details in the **Location** field, specifying the credentials required to access the target destination. If you want to encrypt the backup file, check the **Encrypt Backup Data** option and enter a password. The password will be requested during the restore process. Click on **Next**.
4. Specify the data to back up, selecting **common** parts (inventory and configuration) and **Stats, Events, Alarms, and Tasks** to back up additional historical data in the vCenter Server database. Click on **Next**.

5. Review the summary information and click on **Finish** to perform the backup:

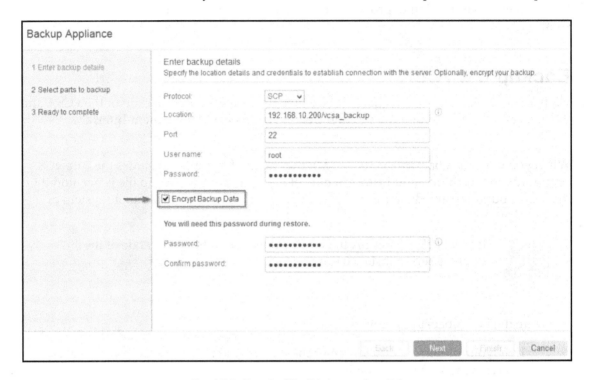

Figure 4.28: Backing up the vCSA, with backup encryption enabled

You can use the vCSA GUI installer to restore a failed vCSA from a file-based backup.

The restore process will be completed in the following two stages:

1. Deployment of a new vCSA
2. Copying data from the file-based backup to the appliance

A file-based restore can only be performed if the backup has been previously taken from the VAMI. Alternatively, you can deploy a new vCSA and restore the data from the file-based backup by using the VAMI.

If your environment uses vSphere Distributed Switches, it is recommended to export and restore the Distribute Switch config separately, after the vCSA restore process has completed.

To restore a vCSA, there are a few steps to perform:

1. From the vCSA ISO file, run the vCSA 6.5 installer and select the **Restore** option. Stage 1 of the restore process deploys a new vCSA to replace the failed appliance. The new vCSA will run on the target ESXi.

2. After the deployment has completed, click on **Next** (on the introduction page of stage 2) to complete the restore process by copying the data from the backup location.

3. On the **Review backup details** page, click on **Next** to finalize the procedure. Click on **Finish**, then **OK**, to complete stage 2. The vCSA will reboot to complete the restore process.

When the procedure has completed, the following configurations will be restored:

- Virtual machine resource settings
- DRS configuration and rules
- Cluster-host membership
- Resource pool hierarchy and settings:

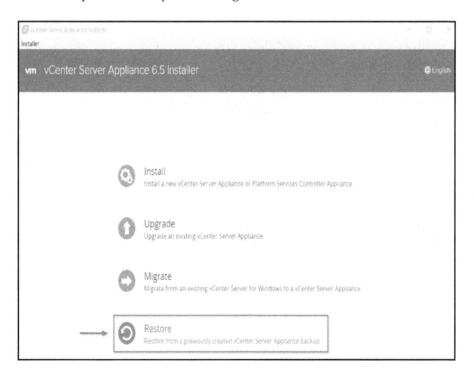

Figure 4.29: Restoring a vCSA

Performing updates as prescribed

Before proceeding with the upgrade, you will have to download the ISO installer for the vCenter Server or the vCSA from VMware's website at `https://my.vmware.com/group/vmware/downloads`. Mount the ISO file in a machine running Windows, macOS Sierra 10.12, or Linux OS to run the installer.

Upgrading vCenter Server

The upgrade process of Windows-based vCenter Server is pretty straightforward. After mounting the downloaded ISO image, run the installer and follow the instructions.

Check out the previous step for different configuration scenarios, and once again pay attention to the correct upgrade sequence.

Determining the upgrade compatibility of an environment

Before upgrading your vCenter Server, check whether your system meets specific hardware and software requirements.

During the deployment of the vCSA, the selected options determine the number of CPUs and the amount of memory required for the appliance. PSC appliance resource requirements are the same for all environment sizes:

	PSC	Tiny environment (up to 10 hosts, 100 VMs)	Small environment (up to 100 hosts, 1,000 VMs)	Medium environment (up to 400 hosts, 4,000 VMs)	Large environment (up to 1,000 hosts, 10,000 VMs)	X-large environment (up to 2,000 hosts, 35,000 VMs)
CPUs	2	2	4	8	16	24
RAM	4 GB	10 GB	16 GB	24 GB	32 GB	48 GB

Tabel 4.1: Minimum hardware requirements for vCenter Server and PSC on Windows

The vCenter Server services deployed on the machine, the upgrade deployment model, and the size of the vSphere inventory all determine the storage requirements per folder. The storage requirements are calculated by the installer during the upgrade, verifying that the machine has sufficient free disk space:

Default folder	vCenter Server with an embedded platform services controller	vCenter Server with an external platform services controller	External platform services controller
Program files	6 GB	6 GB	1 GB
Program data	8 GB	8 GB	2 GB
System folder	3 GB	3 GB	1 GB

Tabel 4.2: vCenter Server minimum storage requirements, depending on the deployment model

vCenter Server requires a 64-bit operating system and supports Windows Server 2008 SP2 or later. If an external database is used with vCenter Server, the 64-bit system DSN is required for vCenter Server to connect.

The vCSA or Platform Services Controller appliance can be deployed on an ESXI host 5.5 or later, or on an ESXI host or DRS cluster from the inventory of a vCenter Server instance 5.5 or later.

Determining correct order of steps to upgrade a vSphere implementation

The first step of the upgrade procedure is to check whether the systems used meet the minimum hardware and software requirements to avoid any problems.

If other software products are used in your infrastructure, such as a backup or additional VMware products, make sure that there are no compatibility issues.

 Before migrating, ensure that the backup solution used in your environment supports the new version, to protect your workloads. Take all necessary actions, such as upgrades or replacements, to ensure full support.

If any PSC is present in your environment, it must always be upgraded first.

The upgrade process needs to follow a specific sequence, as follows:

1. PSC
2. vCenter Servers
3. ESXI hosts
4. VMware Tools for the installed VMs

If you have more VMware products, the entire sequence is more complicated. Check out KB 2147289 at `https://kb.vmware.com/kb/2147289, for the correct update sequence for vSphere 6.5 and compatible VMware products.`

Make sure that the machine that you are going to install the vCenter Server on is not a domain controller, that it is time synced with your environment, and that the DNS name can be resolved.

If the vCenter Server service runs with a dedicated account, ensure that it has the permissions **Administrator**, **Log on as a service**, and **Act as part of the operating system** (for domain users).

In order to add Active Directory as the identity source, the machine must be connected to a domain.

Before proceeding with the upgrade, it is always recommended to make a backup of your environment, so that you can revert to it if something goes wrong during the upgrade process.

Objective 4.3 – Perform vCenter Server migration to VCSA

The **vCenter Server Appliance** (**vCSA**) is a prepackaged and preinstalled Photon Linux-based VM that provides vCenter and PSC services. vCSA 6.5, compared to the previous version, now offers the same capabilities provided by the Windows-based version, plus some exclusive services, such as native high availability, native backup and restore, a Migration Tool, and improved appliance management.

With version 6.5, the **client integration plugin** (**CIP**) is now deprecated and no longer required, since it has been replaced by the native web client.

Since VMware has deprecated the Windows-based version of vCenter Server, use of the vCenter Server vCSA option with an embedded deployment (good enough for a small environment) or external PSC (if you have multiple vCenter servers and you want to use the Linked Mode feature across them) is strongly recommended.

Migrating to vCSA

To simplify the migration process to vSphere 6.5, VMware has introduced a Migration Tool that allows easily upgrading an existing vCSA and PSC appliance 6.0 or a Windows-based vCenter Server to the newest version. The tool supports migration from a vCenter Server running version 5.5 Update 3 or 6.0, but migration from Windows vCenter Server 6.5 to vCSA 6.5 is not supported.

The upgrade procedure is a two-stage process, as follows:

1. vCSA deployment
2. Copying the configuration from the source vCenter Server

If you make use of the DRS feature in the clustered environment where the source vCenter Server resides, the automated upgrade process requires the DRS function not set to Fully Automated.

If an external vSphere Update Manager is used for migration in the vCenter Server, it is required to install the Migration Assistant on the source Update Manager machine, a tool that facilitates the migration of the two components and the database to the new, upgraded vCSA. If the tool is not running on the source vCenter Server, an error will be displayed and the migration will stop. To resume the upgrade, the procedure must be restarted from the beginning.

Before beginning the migration, log in to the source Update Manager machine as an administrator and copy the `migration-assistant` directory from the vCSA installer package.

Access the copied folder in the source Update Manager machine and double-click on the `VMware-Assistant-Migration.exe` file to execute the tool:

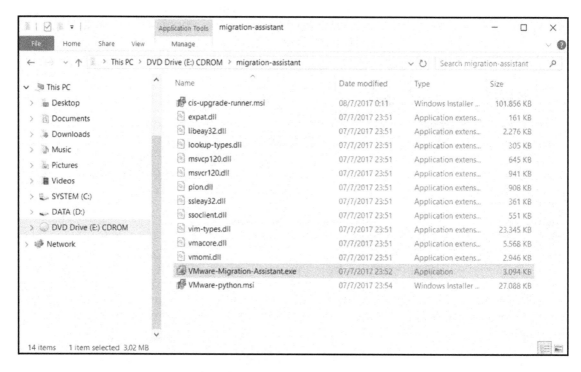

Figure 4.30: The executable file to run the Migration Assistant

Type the vCenter SSO administrator password, and if no errors are displayed after the pre-checks, the source Update Manager system will be ready for the upgrade. Leave the Migration Assistant window open until the upgrade of the vCSA has completed:

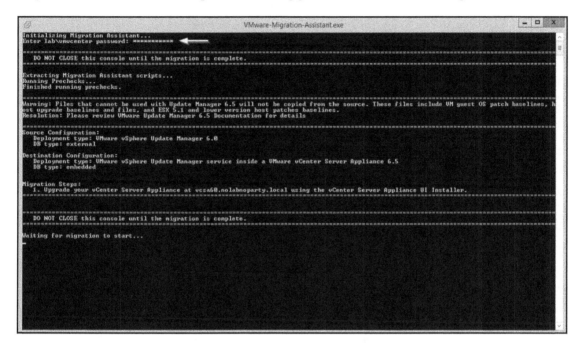

Figure 4.31: The Migration Assistant running in the source Update Manager machine

Mount the vCSA installer ISO file in a machine running Windows, Linux, or macOS Sierra, and access the `vcsa-ui-installer` folder. Select the correct OS version and run the `installer.exe` file.

From the vCSA installer, you have the options to upgrade an existing vCSA or migrate a Windows-based vCenter Server to vCSA version 6.5.

From the vCSA 6.5 installer, select the action that you want to perform, as follows:

- Click on **Upgrade** to upgrade an existing vCSA to version 6.5.
- Click on **Migrate** to perform an upgrade from an existing Windows-based vCenter Server to a vCSA. This is a two-stage process, as follows:

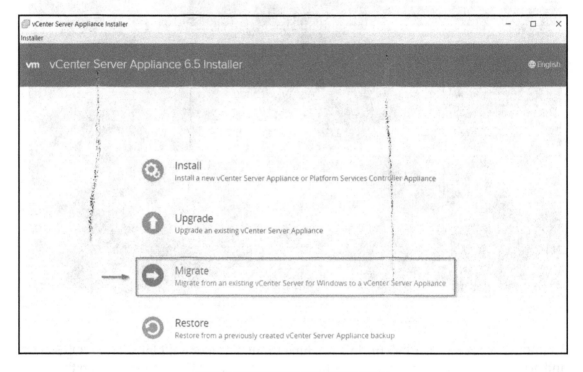

Figure 4.32: Migrating a Windows vCenter Server to vCSA 6.5

Stage 1 of the migration creates a new vCSA to the target host, assigning a temporary IP address specified in the Migration Tool wizard.

At this stage, the Migration Tool may be unable to connect to the Migration Assistant on the source vCenter Server. Connect to the source vCenter Server and make sure that the Migration Assistant is actually running:

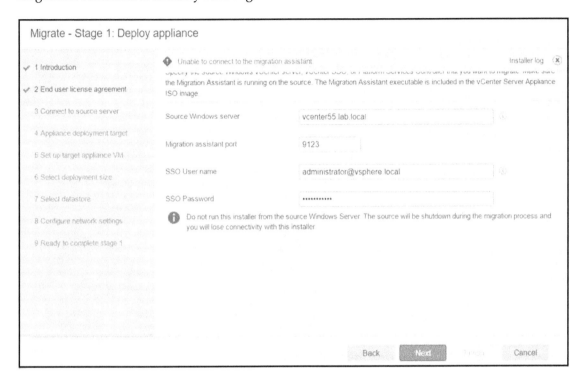

Figure 4.33: Migration Assistant not running in the source vCenter Server

During the configuration of the network settings, you will have to specify the temporary IP address used by the vCSA:

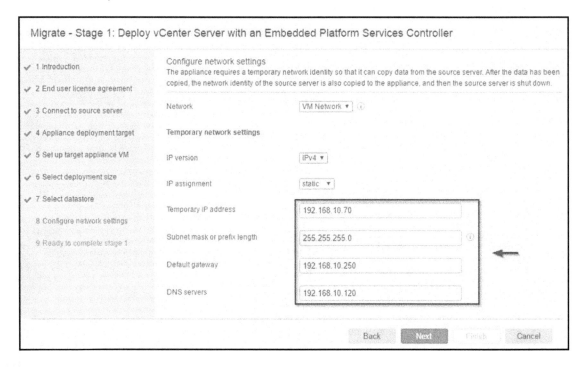

Figure 4.34: Network parameters assigned to the vCSA during migration

Once the vCSA has been deployed successfully, the Migration Tool will proceed with stage 2. During stage 2, the following data is copied from the source vCenter Server to the target vCSA 6.5:

- FQDN
- IP address
- UUID
- Certificates
- MoRef IDs

Before starting the data copying procedure, the system performs some pre-upgrade checks, to ensure that the prerequisites are met and the migration can be finalized. If the DRS feature is not set to **Manual** in the cluster where the source vCenter Server is located, the procedure will stop, showing an error:

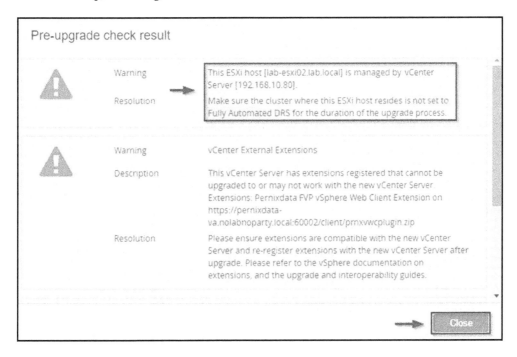

Figure 4.35: The error displayed when DRS is not set to Manual

At the end of the migration, the new vCenter Server will have the same hostname and IP address as the source vCenter Server, without any service disruption. This will allow you to quickly restore the old vCenter Server if the upgrade process fails.

> The migration process doesn't delete the old vCenter Server and its configuration, but simply copies the data to the new vCSA and then powers the source vCenter Server off.

Understanding the migration paths to the vCSA

Migration is supported from a vCenter Server version 5.5 or version 6.0 instance on Windows to a vCSA 6.5 deployment on a Linux-based OS.

Migrating from 5.5 to 6.5 with embedded PSC

You can migrate a vCenter Server instance with an embedded vCenter SSO (version 5.5) or PSC (version 6.0) to a vCSA 6.5 instance with an embedded PSC appliance. Both the vCenter Server instance and the embedded vCenter SSO instance or PSC are migrated at the same time:

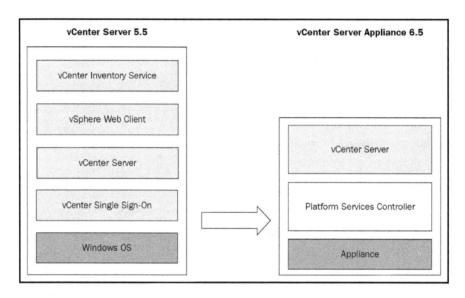

Figure 4.36: vCenter Server 5.5 with embedded vCenter SSO installation migration

Also, when migrating from version 6.0 to version 6.5 the behavior is the same:

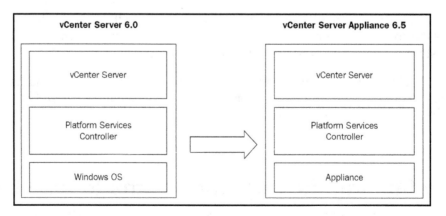

Figure 4.37: vCenter Server 6.0 with embedded PSC installation migration

Migrating from 5.5 to 6.5 with external PSC

You can migrate a vCenter Server instance with an external vCenter SSO (version 5.5) or PSC (version 6.0) to a vCSA 6.5 instance with an external PSC appliance. The external vCenter SSO instance or PSC instance must be migrated first, followed by the vCenter Server:

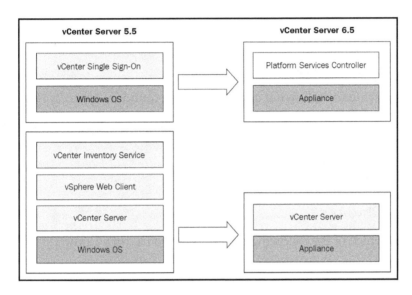

Figure 4.38: vCenter Server 5.5 with external vCenter SSO installation migration

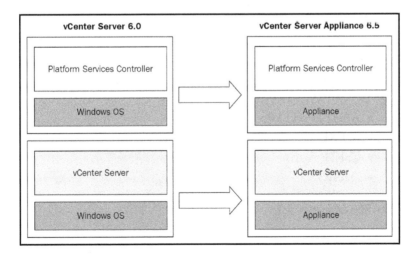

Figure 4.39: vCenter Server 6.0 with external PSC installation migration

For multiple systems configured for high availability, vCenter Server enables you to incorporate your common services into an external PSC configuration as a part of your upgrade process.

For a multi-site setup configured with replication, you can use vCenter Server to incorporate your common services into an external PSC configuration as a part of your upgrade process.

Review questions

The correct answers to the following questions can be found in *Appendix A*:

1. Migration from vCenter Server to vCSA 6.5 requires DRS in the target cluster to be set to **Manual**:
    - A: True
    - B: False

    B - See *Objective 4.2*.

2. From which of the following operating systems can you run the vCSA 6.5 installer?
    - A: Windows, macOS Sierra 10.12, Linux
    - B: Windows, Linux
    - C: Windows, Linux, Solaris
    - D: Windows only

    A - See *Objective 4.2*.

3. Which of the following protocols are supported for an upgrade script (select three)?
    - A: HTTP/HTTPS
    - B: PXE
    - C: FTP
    - D: NFS

    A, C, D - See *Objective 4.1*.

4. Which of the following services is not provided by the Platform Services Controller?
  - A: Single-Sign On
  - B: License Service
  - C: Certificate Managemnt
  - D: High Availability

  D - See *Objective 4.2.*

5. Which of the following actions is not required to upgrade an ESXI host using the Update Manager?
  - A: Importing the host upgrade image
  - B: Remediating the host
  - C: Staging the upgrade
  - D: Attaching the host baseline

  C - See *Objective 4.1.*

6. Which vCenter Server version can you migrate to vCSA 6.5 Update 1 by using the Migration Tool?
  - A: Windows vCenter Server 6.5
  - B: vCenter Server 5.1 Update 3
  - C: vCenter Server 5.5 Update 3b
  - D: vCenter Server 6.0 Update 3

  A, C, D - See *Objective 4.2.*

7. When you perform a backup via the VAMI, where is the backup file stored?
  - A: USB drive
  - B: Network share
  - C: In the vCSA
  - D: Local drive

  B - See *Objective 4.2.*

Summary

This chapter covered the part of the exam related to the upgrading and migration of vSphere from version 5.5 or 6.0 to version 6.5. Make sure that you understand Objectives 4.1, 4.2, and 4.3, as well as all of the required steps to perform a successful upgrade/migration.

Chapter 5, *Administer and Manage vSphere 6.x Resources*, will cover the creation and management of a Resource Pool (*Objective 5.1*), a vSphere object used to allocate resources to a group of virtual machines. The configuration of the vSphere DRS feature, as well as the management of both VM-VM and VM-Host affinity rules, will be covered in detail as a part of Objective 5.2, illustrating the different configuration procedures. Last but not least, the following chapter will cover the new Predictive DRS feature that was introduced in vSphere 6.5.

5
Administer and Manage vSphere 6.x Resources

The ability to properly manage available resources for VMs is a key point for the global performance of the infrastructure because a bad design will negatively affect VM behavior and the whole environment. An ESXi can host a limited number of VMs and a good optimization of the available resources ensures best performance. Compared to the physical world, where servers are often equipped with more resources than they need, in a virtualized environment you allocate resources to a VM based on its role and function.

Resource pools are special vSphere objects used to allocate resources to a group of VMs. The use of resource pools allows you to prioritize resources for business-critical VMs when resources are constrained. You can also use resource pools to limit or guarantee access to resources.

This chapter will cover the creation and management of resource pools and how you can assign resources to VMs. In addition, as part of the exam, we will discuss the configuration of vSphere **Distributed Resource Scheduler** (**DRS**) clusters and Storage DRS clusters.

 To fully understand the configuration steps for specific settings, it is recommended to build a small lab environment to test and practice what you read in this chapter.

What will the reader learn to do in this chapter?

- Manage resource pools
- Determine appropriate shares, reservations, and limits
- Manage the DRS affinity/anti-affinity rules and configure the DRS automation level
- Understand how the DRS affinity rules affect virtual machine placement
- Understand network DRS and predictive DRS

Objective 5.1 – Configure multilevel Resource Pools

When the resource demand exceeds the available resource capacity, attributes such as shares, reservations, and limits can be used to determine the amount of CPU, RAM, and storage resources to be provided to VMs. This method is not always the most efficient solution you can use, especially if you are managing a large environment where the number of VMs could be high.

The management of resources can be performed through the use of the shares, reservation, and limit attributes:

- **Shares**: Specifies the priority of a VM to get resources during a period of contention. When resources in an ESXi host are limited and the VMs compete to access resources, the VMs configured with higher shares will have higher priority to access more of the host's resources. Shares can be specified as **High**, **Normal**, or **Low** with a ratio of 4:2:1 and should be used for resource pools or sibling VMs (sibling VMs have the same parent in the resource pool hierarchy). By default, shares are set to **Normal** for both VMs and resource pools:

Settings	CPU share values	Memory share values
High	2,000 shares per virtual CPU	20 shares per megabyte of configured virtual machine memory
Normal	1,000 shares per virtual CPU	10 shares per megabyte of configured virtual machine memory
Low	500 shares per virtual CPU	5 shares per megabyte of configured virtual machine memory

Table 5.1: Default CPU and memory share values for a virtual machine

- **Reservation**: Specifies the minimum allocation guaranteed to a VM. When the VM is powered on, the server assigns resources based on the specified minimum reservation regardless of whether the physical server is heavily loaded. Resources are allocated only when requested by the VM and if the host's unallocated resources don't meet the reservation requirements, the VM cannot be powered on. Resources reserved for a virtual machine can never be taken away and if too many reservations are configured and not used by the virtual machine, other VMs are not able to use any of those resources, limiting access to physical resources. Default reservation is set to 0.

- **Limit**: Specifies the maximum amount of resources a virtual machine can use. If the limit is not set, a VM cannot consume more resources than what is configured in its setup; if a VM is configured with 2 GB of RAM, it will be limited to consume no more than 2 GB. Too many limits prevents full resource utilization and actually limits access to physical resources. The default limit value is set to **Unlimited**.

Determining the effect of the expandable reservation parameter on resource allocation

When, in a resource pool, the reservation type field is set as **Expandable**, admission control checks whether the resource demands of powering on a new virtual machine can be satisfied with the available resources from the selected resource pool. If the requirements cannot be satisfied, admission control takes resources from the parent resource pool. This process continues until the resource demand is satisfied or the resources are not available any more:

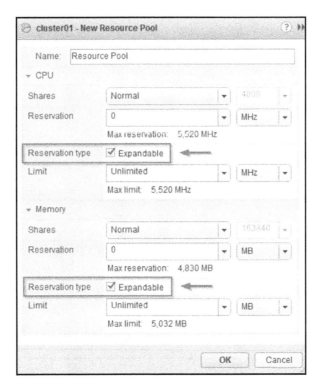

Figure 5.1: Resource pool with expandable reservation type

Although it provides more flexibility to the design, leaving the **Expandable** option enabled without a deep control provides less protection. Misconfigured VMs or resource pools could consume all unused resources, preventing other VMs from powering on.

Creating a Resource Pool hierarchical structure

Resource pools can be nested and assigned to different levels for specific configuration needs. You can use resource pools to limit or guarantee resources to a pool of VMs without configuring individual VMs. To simplify the management of resources in large environments, resource pools are the most suitable design approach to use. In VMware vSphere 6.5, a maximum tree depth of eight resource pools is supported.

For example, you might use a hierarchical structure to assign resources to different departments so that each department has a dedicated resource pool. To create this type of structure, it's important to understand how it works and how resources are actually provided to VMs:

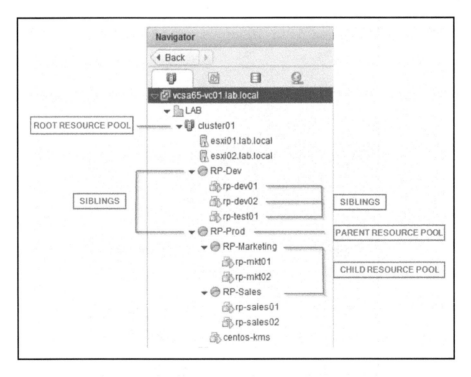

Figure 5.2: Resource pools in a hierarchical structure

You should limit the use of too many nested VMs and resource pools to keep the configuration simple.

Let's analyze how resource pools are organized and how they work.

Looking at *Figure 5.2*, **cluster01** is intended as the root resource pool while **RP-Dev** and **RP-Prod** are child resource pools and siblings of each other. Two or more resource pools are defined as siblings when they have the same parent in the resource pool hierarchy.

For example, you can add VMs in **RP-Prod** (child of the root resource pool) and they will get resources from **RP-Prod** depending on configured shares, limits, and reservations. Underneath **RP-Prod**, you can also add new resource pools (**RP-Sales** and **RP-Marketing,** for example) that will become children of **RP-Prod**, making **RP-Prod** the parent.

Don't use resource pools to logically group VMs (as an organizational tool) use folders instead.

You should always double-check whether you have enough available resources before creating a new child resource pool or before powering on a virtual machine, to avoid issues due to lack of resources.

You can check resource availability by selecting the resource pool object and navigating to the **Monitor** I **Resource Reservation** tab. The **Available Reservation** value for **CPU** and **Memory** displays resources that are unreserved:

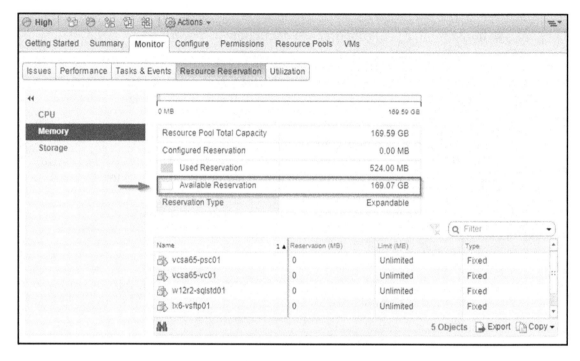

Figure 5.3: Resource reservation

Whether actions are performed and how CPU and memory are computed depends on the **Reservation Type**, which can be fixed or expandable.

Preconfigured reservation or limit settings cannot be violated since the system doesn't allow this action. The system validates all parameters to guarantee service-level compliance each time a resource pool is reconfigured or a virtual machine powered on.

 While optimizing resource assignment, you should avoid adding some VMs to resource pools and leaving other VMs at the root level of the resource pool hierarchy. This way, VMs and resource pools will be sibling each other, competing for resources and negatively affecting the performance of the VMs.

Configuring custom Resource Pool attributes

In addition to the default shares (high, normal, low), limits, and reservations available in the resource pools, you can customize these parameters by changing the different assigned values. When you customize resource pools, you should consider the total shares between resource pools that may compete for resource demand and the number of VMs in each pool.

Although you can assign memory and CPU shares from 0 up to 1 million, the given values must be configured accordingly to avoid some resource pools being oversized and others being inadequate, affecting the performance of VMs.

To customize resource pool parameters, select the **Inventory** view from vSphere Web Client, right-click the resource pool to modify, and select the **Edit Resource Settings...** option:

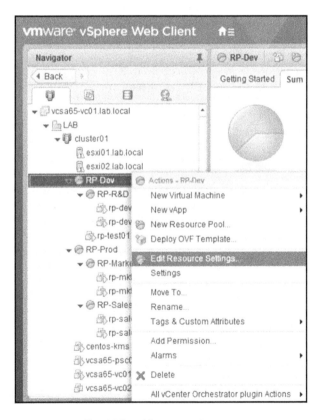

Figure 5.4: Customizing resource pool parameters

In the configuration window, you can specify the **Shares**, **Limit**, and **Reservation** settings for the CPU and memory assigned to the resource pool, specifying whether the **Reservation type** is **Expandable**.

Determining how Resource Pools apply to vApps

As seen for resource pools, vApps have the same shares, reservation, and limit parameters you can configure to allocate resources for VMs.

 Reservations on vApps and all their child resource pools, child vApps, and child VMs count against the parent resources only if those objects are powered on.

To create a vApp in the **Inventory**, from vSphere Web Client, right-click the cluster object and select the **New vApp** | **New vApp** option. In terms of permissions, the vApp creation requires the **vApp** | **vApp resource configuration** privileges.

To modify resource allocation for a vApp, right-click an existing vApp object and select the **Edit Settings** option. Expand the **CPU resources** and **Memory resources** items to configure allocation parameters:

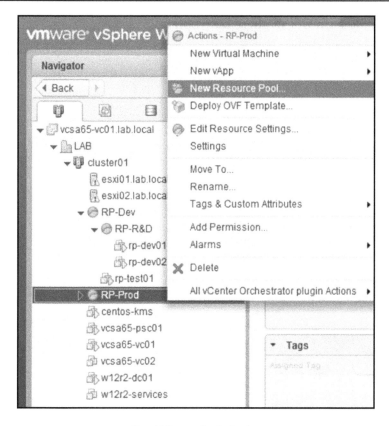

Figure 5.5: Resource allocation for vApps

Creating/removing a Resource Pool

Resource pools can be created and removed in a similar way in both ESXi hosts and clusters. To create resource pools in a cluster, the vSphere DRS feature must be enabled first.

To enable DRS for a cluster, proceed as follows:

1. From vSphere Web Client, right-click the cluster object from the **Inventory** view and select **Settings**.
2. Select the **vSphere DRS** tab and click **Edit** in the right-hand pane.

3. Check the **Turn ON vSphere DRS** option:

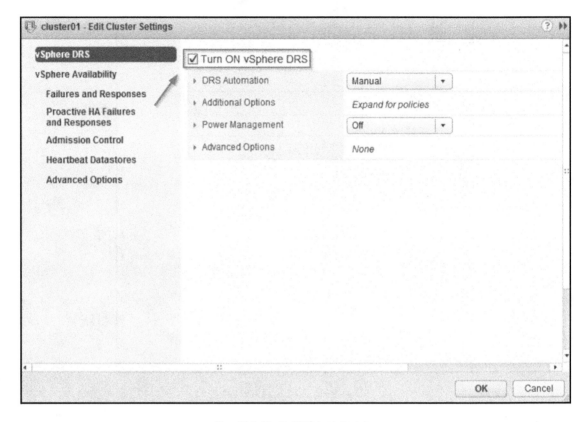

Figure 5.6: Enabling the DRS feature in the cluster

Once the DRS feature has been enabled in the selected cluster, to create a resource pool you should perform the following steps:

1. From vSphere Web Client, right-click the cluster object and select the **New Resource Pool...** option:

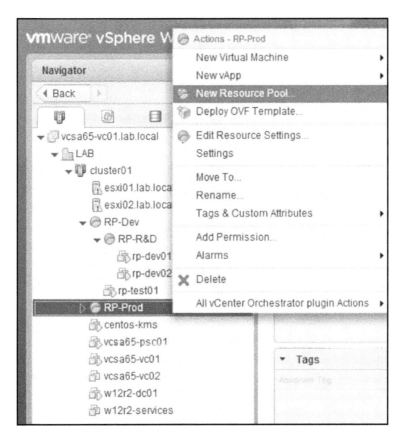

Figure 5.7: Creation of a new resource pool

2. In the **New Resource Pool...** wizard, specify the resource pool **Name** by entering a meaningful name to better identify the resource scope.

3. Specify the resource allocation in terms of CPU and RAM, then click **OK**. When the resource pool has been created, you can start adding VMs to it. Share values set as **High**, **Normal**, or **Low** specify share values in a 4:2:1 ratio:

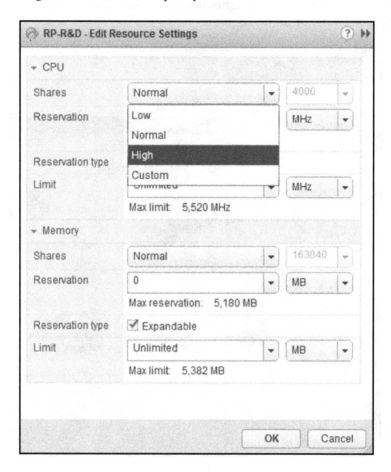

Figure 5.8: Configuring resource shares in a resource pool

If a created resource pool is no longer required, you can easily remove it from the **Inventory** in just one click:

1. From vSphere Web Client, right-click the resource pool to remove and select the **Delete** option.
2. Click Yes to confirm deletion:

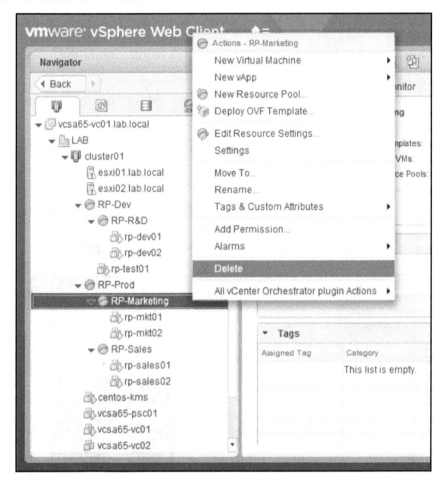

Figure 5.9: Removing a resource pool from the system

 Deleting a resource pool doesn't delete the VMs it may contains but they are placed in the parent resource pool.

Adding/removing VMs from a Resource Pool

The procedure to add or remove VMs from resource pools is pretty simple and intuitive. One or multiple VMs can be added to a resource pool using the **Migrate** or drag and drop features.

To add a single virtual machine to a resource pool, select the VM to move and drag and drop the VM to the target resource pool. If the target resource pool doesn't have enough resources available to satisfy the new virtual machine's requirements, the move will fail if the VM is powered on.

A VM can be also added to a resource pool during its creation from the creation wizard when you have to specify the computing resources.

When a virtual machine is added to a resource pool, the VM will assume the following configuration:

- Reservations and limits do not change.
- Shares adjust to reflect the total number of shares in use in the new resource pool if shares are set to high, medium, or low.
- If custom shares have been assigned, the share value is maintained:

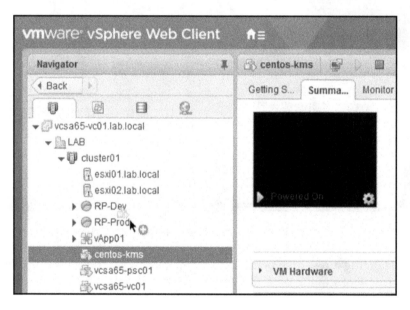

Figure 5.10: Adding a single VM to a resource pool with the drag and drop feature

To add multiple VMs, from vSphere Web Client perform the following steps:

1. Select the inventory object (data center, cluster, or another resource pool) that contains the VMs to move.
2. Go to the **VMs** tab in the right-hand pane and select the VMs to move.
3. Click **Action** and select **Migrate....**

4. Select the **Change compute resource only** option and click **Next**.
5. Select the **Resource Pools** tab in the compute resource window and select the resource pool to use. Click **Next**:

Figure 5.11: Resource pool used to add VMs

6. Select the destination network to use and click **Next**.
7. Click **Finish** to move the specified VMs to the selected resource pool.

Using the drag and drop feature, you can move a single VM off the resource pool. To remove multiple VMs from a resource pool, select the VMs to remove (select the **Resource Pools** first, then go to **VMs** tab), then click on **Actions** | **Migrate** to move VMs to another resource pool or location.

When a virtual machine is removed from a resource pool, the associated total number of shares with the resource pool decreases, so that each remaining share represents more resources.

Determining appropriate shares, reservations, and limits for hierarchical Resource Pools

To better understand how a resource pool with expandable reservations works, take a look at *Figure 5.12*, where a resource pool hierarchy has been configured as follows:

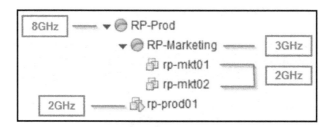

Figure 5.12: Admission control allows the VM to power on

A resource pool named **RP-Prod** has been configured with a reservation of 8 GHz, with a running virtual machine, **rp-prod01**, which reserves 2 GHz.

A new child resource pool, **RP-Marketing**, is created underneath **RP-Prod** with a reservation of 3 GHz and with the **Expandable Reservation** option selected. Two VMs (**rp-mkt01** and **rp-mkt02**) are added to the child resource pool with a reservation of 2 GHz each.

Are you able to power on both the **rp-mkt01** and **rp-mkt02** VMs? In this example, the resources for the VMs are provided as follows:

- **rp-mkt01** gets resources from **RP-Marketing** (it has a 3 GHz reservation) while **rp-mkt02** needs to borrow resources from the parent **RP-Prod** since no local resources are available (only 1 GHz available).
- **RP-Prod** has 8 GHz minus 2 GHz reserved by the **rp-prod01** virtual machine, minus 3 GHz reserved by the child resource pool **RP-Marketing**. 3 GHz are left unreserved. With 3 GHz available, the virtual machine with the 2 GHz reservation can be powered on.

Let's have a look at the following scenario:

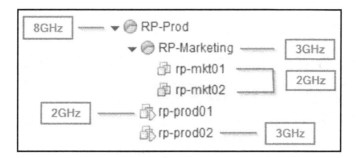

Figure 5.13: Admission control prevents the VM from powering on

In **RP-Prod**, there are now two running VMs with a total reservation of 5 GHz.

Are you still able to power on both the **rp-mkt01** and **rp-mkt02** VMs? In this example, the resources for the VMs are provided as follows:

- **rp-mkt01** gets resources from **RP-Marketing** (it has a 3 GHz reservation) while **rp-mkt02** needs to borrow resources from the parent, **RP-Prod**, since no local resources are available (only 1 GHz available).
- **RP-Prod** has 8 GHz minus 5 GHz reserved by the **rp-prod01** and **rp-prod02** VMs, minus 3 GHz reserved by the child resource pool **RP-Marketing**. 0 GHz are left unreserved. The virtual machine **rp-mkt02** with the 2 GHz reservation does not have enough resources to power on.

To determine how the cluster's CPU is shared between resource pools, just remember that shares can be specified as high, normal, or low with a ratio of 4:2:1 and are applied to resource pools and sibling resource pools (sibling resource pools have the same parent in the resource pool hierarchy).

Looking at *Figure 5.14*, what are the CPU values assigned to the resource pools?

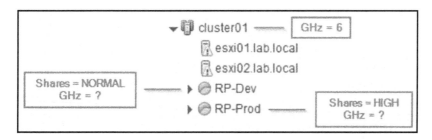

Figure 5.14: Shares assigned to resource pools

Applying the ratio 4:2:1 (high, normal, low), if the cluster provides 6 GHz, **RP-Dev** will get 2 GHz while **RP-Prod** gets 4 GHz.

Objective 5.2 – Configure vSphere DRS and Storage DRS clusters

A cluster is a collection of ESXi hosts and associated VMs with shared resources and a shared management interface. To benefit from cluster-level resource management, you must first create a cluster and enable the vSphere DRS feature.

Adding/removing Host DRS Group

A host DRS group is used to create a VM-Host affinity rule to establish an affinity or anti-affinity relationship between a VM DRS group and a host DRS group.

To create a host DRS group, proceed as follows:

1. From vSphere Web Client, select the cluster in the **Inventory** view.
2. Go to **Configure** tab in the right-hand pane and select **VM/Host Groups** under **Configuration**.
3. Click **Add...** to open the **Create VM/Host Group** wizard.
4. Enter a **Name** for the group and select **Host Group** from the **Type** drop-down menu.
5. Click **Add** to specify the ESXi hosts to add.
6. From the available hypervisors in the list, select the ESXi hosts you want to add, and click **OK** to confirm.

7. Click **OK** to save the configuration of the new host DRS group:

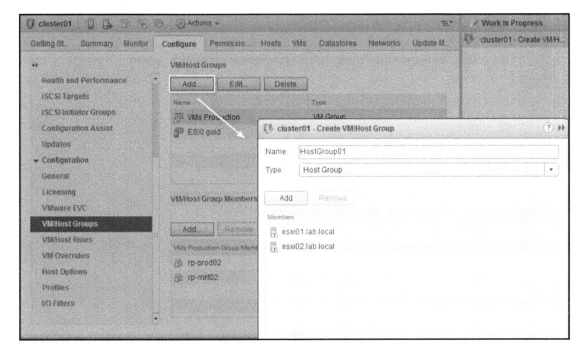

Figure 5.15: Configuring a host DRS group

Removing a host DRS group is pretty simple. Select the group to remove from the **Configure** | **VM/Host Groups** section and click **Delete**. In the warning window, click **Yes** to confirm the group deletion:

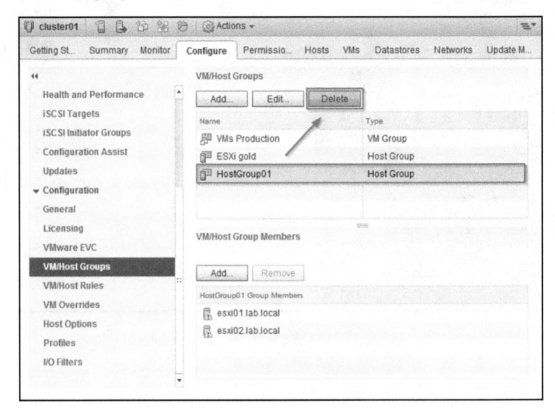

Figure 5.16: Removing a host DRS group

Adding/removing a virtual machine DRS group

A virtual machine DRS group is used to establish a relationship with a host DRS group to define a VM-Host affinity rule.

To create a virtual machine DRS group, you should perform the following steps:

1. From vSphere Web Client, select the cluster in the **Inventory** view.
2. Navigate to the **Configure** tab and select the **VM/Host Groups** item under **Configuration**.

1. Click **Add** to open the **Create VM/Host Group** wizard.
2. Enter a **Name** for the group and select **VM Group** from the **Type** drop-down menu.
3. Click **Add** to specify the VMs to add.
4. From the available list, select the VMs you want to add then click **OK** to confirm.
5. Click **OK** to save the configuration of the new VM DRS group:

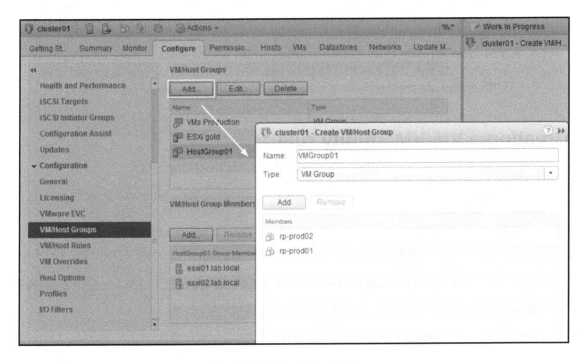

Figure 5.17: Configuring a virtual machine DRS group

To remove a virtual machine DRS group, you act in the same way as for host DRS group removal. Select the group to remove from the **Configure** | **VM/Host Groups** section and click on the **Delete** button. In the displayed warning window, click **Yes** to confirm group deletion.

Managing DRS affinity/anti-affinity rules

By enabling the DRS feature on your vSphere cluster, you can manage the placement of VMs within that cluster through the use of affinity rules.

The DRS supports the following affinity rule types:

- **VM-VM affinity rule**: Used to specify that selected VMs should run on the same host. The anti-affinity rule behaves in the opposite way, instead ensuring that VMs are kept on different hosts.
- **VM-Host affinity rule**: Allows you to control which hosts in the cluster can run which VMs and requires that at least one VM DRS group and at least one host DRS group are created before managing host affinity rules.

Creating a VM-VM affinity rule

To create a VM-VM affinity rule, you should perform the following steps:

1. From vSphere Web Client, right-click the cluster to configure and select the **Settings** options.
2. Under **Configuration**, select the **VM/Host Rules** item and click the **Add...** button.
3. Type a **Name** for the rule and select one of the available options from the **Type** drop-down menu:
   - **Keep Virtual Machines Together**: The specified VMs are kept together on the same host
   - **Separate Virtual Machines**: The specified VMs are kept separate on different hosts
4. Click the **Add...** button to specify the VMs (at least two) that must run with the specified rule.
5. Click **OK** to save the configuration:

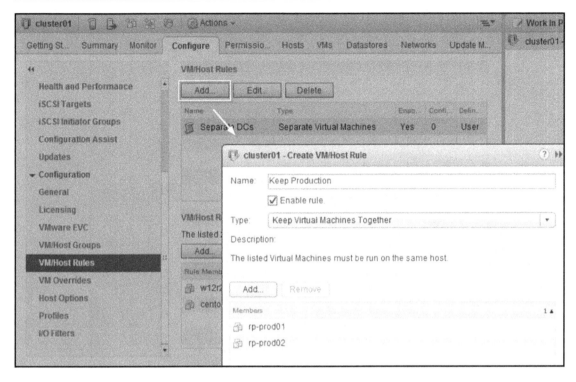

Figure 5.18: Configuring a VM-VM affinity rule

Creating a VM-Host affinity rule

Before creating a VM-Host affinity rule, at least one VM DRS group and at least one host DRS group must be created before managing host affinity rules.

To create a VM-Host affinity rule, proceed as follows:

1. From vSphere Web Client, right-click the cluster to configure and select **Settings**.
2. Under **Configuration**, select **VM/Host rules** and click on the **Add...** button.
3. Enter a **Name** for the new rule and select the **Virtual Machines to Hosts value** from the **Type** drop-down menu.
4. Specify a **VM group** and the rule to use, for example, **Should run on hosts in group**.

5. Select the **Host Group** to associate and click **OK** to save the rule:

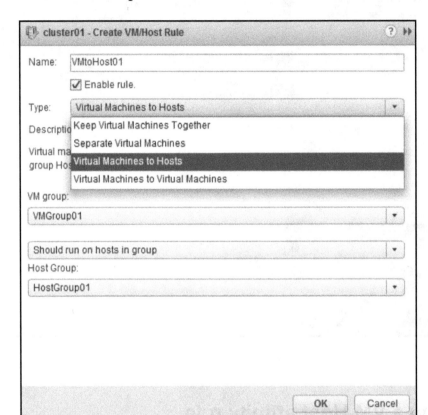

Figure 5.19: Configuring a VM-Host affinity rule

The options available for the rule are the following:

- **Must run on hosts in group**: VMs in the selected VM group must run on host members of the specified host group
- **Should run on hosts in group**: VMs in the VM group should run on hosts of the specified host group but it is not required
- **Must not run on hosts in group**: VMs in the VM group must never run on host members of the specified host group
- **Should not run on hosts in group**: VMs in the VM group should not, but might, run on hosts of the specified host group

Configuring the proper DRS automation level based on a set of business requirements

One of the vSphere features available to balance loads across the ESXi hosts of the cluster is called vSphere DRS, which provides two main functions:

- Executing the placement of the just-powered-on VM on a specific host in the cluster
- Periodically (every 5 minutes by default), the DRS checks the load on the cluster, providing recommendations for migration or automatically performing a vMotion of the VM to ensure a balanced cluster

 The vSphere DRS feature is available only when a cluster is created.

When a virtual machine in a DRS-enabled cluster is powered on, the admission control checks whether the cluster has enough resources to support the VM and displays a warning if the available resources in the cluster are not sufficient to power on the VM.

With sufficient resources, a recommendation as to which host the VM should run on is generated by the DRS and, based on the automation level configured in the cluster, one of the following actions is taken:

- Placement recommendation is executed automatically
- Placement recommendation is displayed, leaving the user with the option to accept or override

Placement recommendations are provided only when the DRS feature is enabled in the cluster and VMs are not moved between the cluster's hosts.

When the service is enabled, DRS provides three levels of automation:

- **Manual**: Placement and migration recommendations are displayed, but must be applied manually.
- **Partially Automated**: The initial placement is performed automatically but migration recommendations are only displayed without running.

- **Fully Automated**: Placement and migration recommendations run automatically:

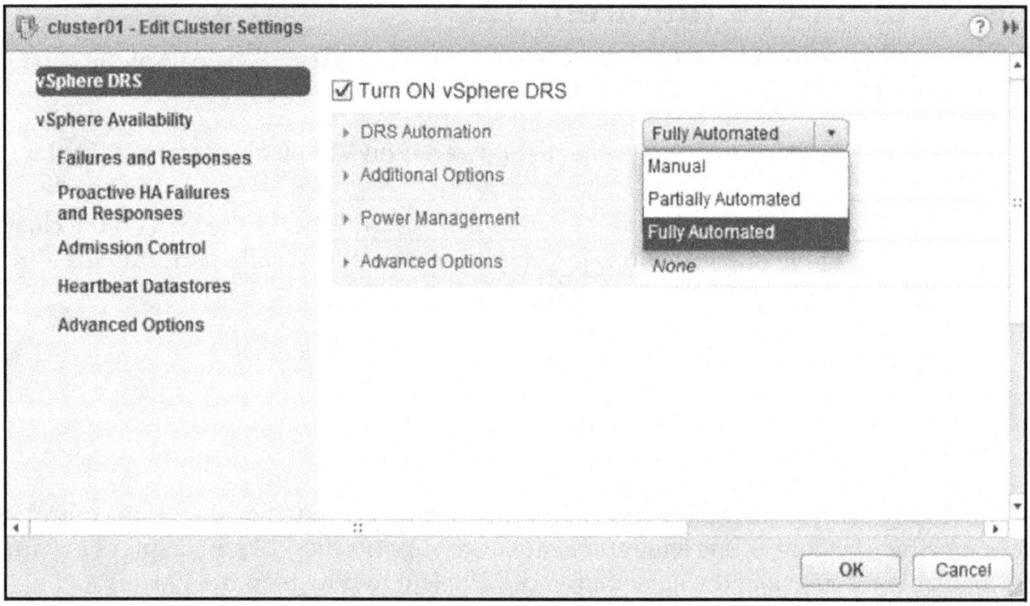

Figure 5.20: Configuring the DRS automation level

To enable the DRS in a cluster, proceed as follows:

1. From vSphere Web Client, right-click the cluster in which you want to enable the DRS and select the **Settings** option
2. Under **Services**, select **vSphere DRS** and click the **Edit...** button
3. Enable the **Turn ON vSphere DRS** option and select the level of automation you want to apply to the cluster from the **DRS Automation** drop-down menu

Backup a resource pool tree

If a resource pool's hierarchy and affinity rules are configured in the cluster, when the DRS service is disabled, the resource pools and the affinity rules are not re-established when the DRS is re-enabled. When the DRS is disabled, configured resource pools are removed from the cluster.

By saving a snapshot of the resource pool tree on your local machine, resource pools are not lost and can be restored from the snapshot when DRS is enabled once again.

To save a resource pool snapshot, follow these steps:

1. From vSphere Web Client, right-click the cluster and select **Settings**.
2. Under **Services**, select **vSphere DRS** and click the **Edit...** button.
3. Uncheck the **Turn ON vSphere DRS** option and click **OK**.
4. Click **Yes** to save a snapshot of resource pool tree:

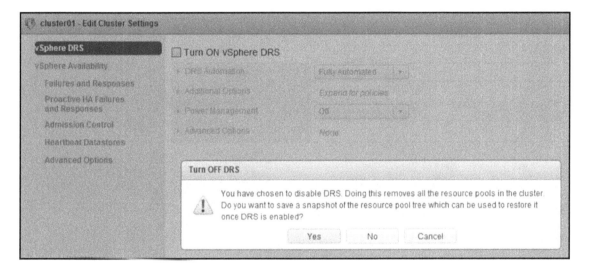

Figure 5.21: Saving a snapshot of the resource pool tree

5. Select the folder in which to store the snapshot and click **OK**. The system creates a file named `clustername.snapshot` in the specified folder.

As a result, the vSphere DRS feature is disabled for the selected cluster and all resource pools are removed:

Figure 5.22: Resource pools removed after disabling the DRS feature

Restoring a resource pool tree

A saved resource pool tree snapshot can be restored at any time in the processed cluster if the following prerequisites are met:

- vSphere DRS must be enabled
- The snapshot can be restored only on the same cluster from which it was taken
- No other resource pools are present in the cluster

To restore a resource pool tree, the procedure is pretty simple:

1. From vSphere Web Client, select the cluster to restore, go to **Configure** | **vSphere DRS**, and click the **Edit...** button.
2. Check the **Turn ON vSphere DRS** option and click **OK**.
3. Once DRS is enabled, right-click the cluster and select the **Restore Resource Pool Tree...** option.
4. Click **Browse** and locate the snapshot file previously saved on your local machine.
5. Once you have selected the snapshot file, click **Open**, then **OK**, to restore the resource pool tree:

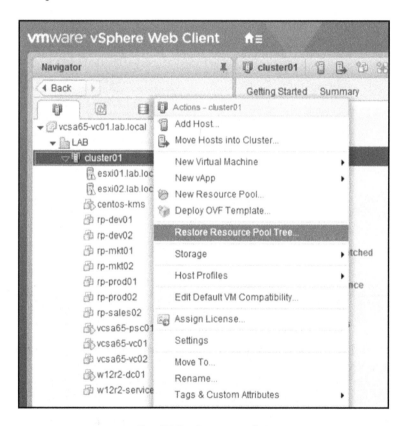

Figure 5.23: Restoring a resource pool tree

To retain the resource pool tree in case you need to temporarily disable the DRS service, you should configure the DRS automation level to **Manual** instead of disabling DRS. Automatic actions are not performed but the resource pool hierarchy is preserved.

The DRS automation level can be configured also on a per-VM basis by enabling the **Enable individual virtual machine automation levels** option from the configuration window of the vSphere DRS service:

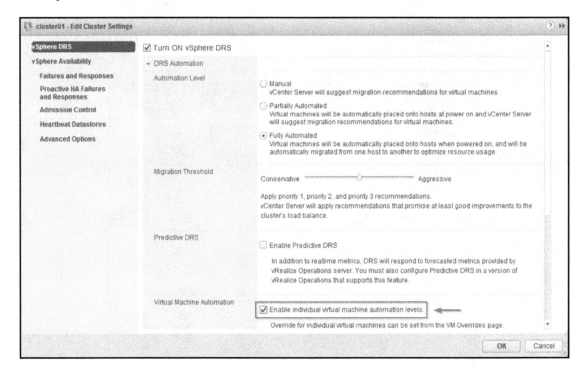

Figure 5.24: Enabling the DRS automation level on a per-VM basis

To disable individual virtual machine overrides, you must uncheck this option. When enabled again, the VMs settings are restored.

Explaining how DRS affinity rules effect virtual machine placement

To manage and control virtual machine placement on hosts within a cluster, the use of affinity rules allows you to define where specific VMs should be placed.

VM-Host affinity rule

The VM-Host affinity rule specifies an affinity relationship between a group of VMs and a group of hosts. By creating an affinity rule, you can specify that members of a specific virtual machine DRS group can or must run on members of a specific host DRS group.

To act exactly in the opposite way, you create an anti-affinity rule to specify that members of the selected virtual machine DRS group cannot run on members of a specified host DRS group.

To create a VM-Host affinity rule, take a look at the *Managing the DRS affinity/anti-affinity rules* section:

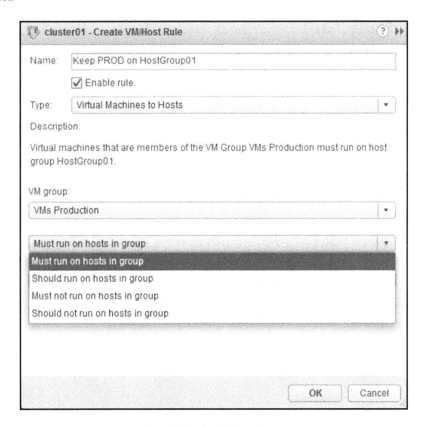

Figure 5.25: Creating a VM-Host affinity rule

A VM-Host affinity requires that at least one virtual machine DRS group and at least one host DRS group are created before managing host affinity rules.

No actions are taken by the DRS, vSphere HA, and vSphere DPM if their execution results in the violation of required affinity rules.

Cluster functions not performed may include the following:

- VMs are not evacuated to place a host in maintenance mode
- VMs are not placed for power-on or load balance VMs
- vSphere HA does not perform failovers
- vSphere DPM does not optimize power management by placing hosts into standby mode

VM-VM affinity rule

The VM-VM affinity rule is used to specify that certain VMs should run on the same host, for example, to improve performance. The anti-affinity rule ensures that selected VMs are kept on different hosts instead. For example, anti-affinity rules can be used to keep active directory domain controllers on different hosts to avoid service disruption if a host fails.

The procedure to create a VM-VM affinity rule was covered in the *Managing DRS affinity/anti-affinity rules* section.

 If one rule is configured to keep VMs together and another rule keeps the same VMs separate, you can't enable both. In the event of a conflict between two affinity rules, the older rule takes precedence and the newer rule is disabled.

To disable VM/Host rules, proceed as follows:

1. Select the cluster object from the **Inventory** view and navigate to the **Configure** | **VM/Host Rules** tab under **Configuration**
2. Select the rule to disable and click the **Edit...** button
3. Uncheck the **Enable rule** option and click **OK**

If you need to re-enable a previously disabled VM/Host rule, the procedure is pretty much the same:

1. Select the cluster object from the **Inventory** view and navigate to the **Configure** | **VM/Host Rules** tab under **Configuration**
2. Select the rule to enable and click the **Edit...** button
3. Check the **Enable rule** option and click **OK**

If the cluster's current state is in violation of a just added or edited rule, the system tries to correct the violation and continues to operate. For the DRS clusters configured in **Manual** or **Partially Automated** mode, migration recommendations based on rule fulfillment and load balancing are presented for approval. Although is not mandatory to fulfill the rules, corresponding recommendations remain until the rules are approved.

From the cluster's **Monitor | vSphere DRS | Faults** tab, you can check whether any enabled affinity rules are being violated and cannot be corrected by DRS (violated rules have a corresponding fault in this page). To determine why DRS cannot satisfy a specific rule, read the reported message in the **Reason** column or the log event:

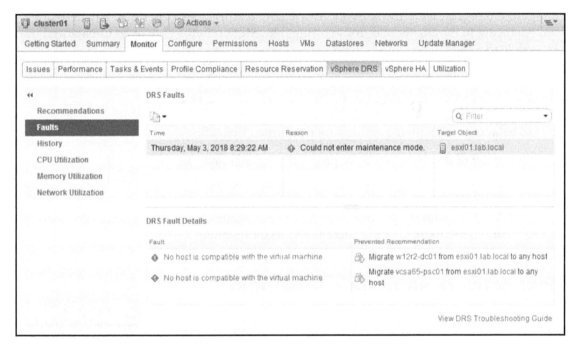

Figure 5.26: Affinity rule faults in the DRS cluster

Understanding network DRS

Virtual network-aware DRS is a new feature introduced in vSphere 6.5, where DRS now also considers network utilization when it generates migration recommendations. If a host has Tx and Rx rate utilization of connected physical uplinks greater than 80%, the virtual machine won't be placed on that host.

Network utilization is an additional check to evaluate whether a specific host is suitable for the VM and has sufficient network resources available. This additional input improves DRS placement decisions, which results in better VM performance.

The initial placement is performed by DRS in two stages:

1. ESXi host members of the cluster are ranked based on cluster constraints and compute resource availability
2. The host with the best rank and best network resource availability is chosen for placement

Compared to regular DRS, the network-aware DRS feature doesn't perform any network load balancing in the cluster and doesn't trigger a vMotion in the case of an imbalanced network load.

Differentiating load balancing policies

To load balance, the following actions are performed by DRS:

- A list of possible migration proposals is generated
- For destination hosts where the network is saturated, the proposals are eliminated
- The host with the maximum balance improvement in terms of compute resources and network resource availability is recommended

Host network saturation threshold

During the load balancing, the DRS doesn't consider as good candidates, in terms of network resource availability, hosts where network utilization is above 80% (threshold is set to 80% by default). DRS considers a host network saturated if the network utilization is at or above the saturation threshold.

If the host members of the cluster are all network saturated, DRS won't migrate VMs to avoid further performance degradation, with the result of having a possible cluster imbalance.

Monitoring host network utilization

The host network load distribution can be monitored in vSphere 6.5 from vSphere Web Client under the **Monitor | vSphere DRS | Network Utilization** tab. This value indicates the percentage of the host network utilization, given by the average capacity being utilized across all the **physical NICs (pNICs)** on that host:

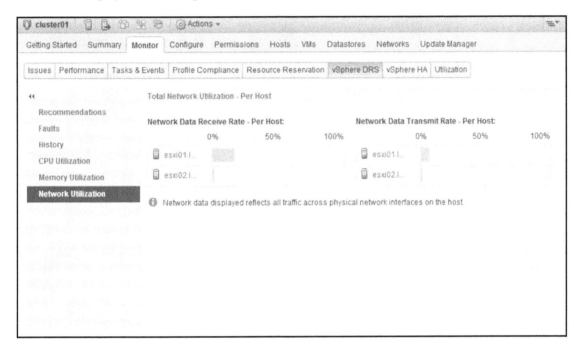

Figure 5.27: Network utilization per host

If a host is equipped with three pNICS and one of them is 90% utilized while the other two are 0% utilized, the percentage value of the network utilization is considered to be 30%.

Describing Predictive DRS

By default, vSphere DRS evaluates the state of the cluster every 5 minutes and in the case of resource congestion, a vMotion action is triggered in order to balance the workload.

What happens if resource congestion occurs every second? If DRS has already evaluated the cluster status and concluded that everything is ok, and a heavy batch job starts after this , workloads will be impacted by resource contention, affecting overall performance. To solve this, VMware developed the predictive DRS feature.

Predictive DRS is a new feature introduced in vSphere 6.5 that, combined with vRealize Operations Manager, allows you to balance workloads for certain VMs before resource utilization spikes occur. Based on metric history pulled from vCenter, vRealize Operations computes and forecasts virtual machine CPU and memory utilization, creating dynamic thresholds that make forecasts more accurate when more data points are introduced over time.

These forecasts from **vRealize Operations** (**vROps**) are then sent to DRS, which acquires these metrics in advance (by default, every 60 minutes starting from the current time) and balances the cluster based on forecasted utilization. This way ensures that predictable workload utilization spikes can be acknowledged and balanced before they occur, improving the overall performance for workloads.

To enable the predictive DRS feature in vSphere, follow these steps:

1. From vSphere Web Client, right-click the cluster object from the **Inventory** view and select **Settings**.
2. Select the **vSphere DRS** tab and click **Edit...** in the right-hand pane.
3. Expand the **DRS Automation** item.
4. Check the **Enable Predictive DRS** option and click **OK**:

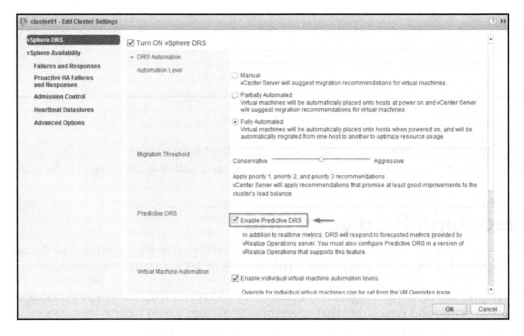

Figure 5.28: Enabling the predictive DRS feature

Storage DRS Cluster

Storage DRS is a feature of vSphere that is useful for managing the aggregated resources of a datastore cluster. This service allows you to keep space and I/O resources balanced in the datastore cluster, providing recommendations for best virtual machine disk placement and migration.

By enabling the Storage DRS feature, the following functions are enabled within the created datastore cluster:

- **Space load balancing among datastores**: You can set a custom threshold for space use. When the utilization exceeds the threshold, to keep space balanced across the datastore cluster, Storage DRS performs Storage vMotion migrations or generates recommendations depending on the automation level configured.
- **I/O load balancing among datastores**: To avoid bottlenecks, you can set an I/O latency threshold. When the I/O latency exceeds the threshold, Storage DRS performs Storage vMotion migrations or generates recommendations to balance the I/O depending on the automation level configured.
- **Initial placement of virtual disks based on space and I/O workload**: Recommendations for initial placement are evaluated, considering space constraints and space and I/O load balancing criteria, to avoid the overprovisioning of one datastore, storage I/O bottlenecks, and a negative impact on virtual machine performance.

Placements are evaluated by Storage DRS every 8 hours (by default) or when one or more datastores exceeds the threshold of space utilization and I/O latency set by the user. Storage I/O control automatically sets the latency threshold that corresponds to the estimated latency when the datastore is operating at 90% of its peak throughput.

Functions can be enabled or disabled all at once by enabling the Storage DRS checkbox and you can independently manage I/O-related functions and space balancing functions.

To enable Storage DRS, you must first create a datastore cluster. From vSphere Web Client, perform these steps:

1. Go to **Storage** view, right-click the data center object and select the **Storage ǀ New Datastore Cluster...** option.

2. Enter the **Datastore cluster name** and check the **Turn ON Storage DRS** option. Click **Next**:

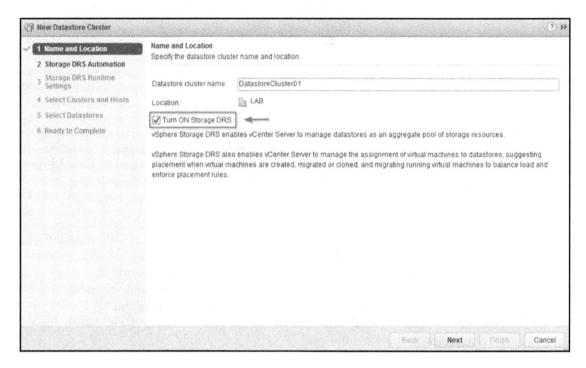

Figure 5.29: Enabling Storage DRS

3. Specify the Storage DRS automation level of available functions by choosing one of the available options:
    - **No Automation (Manual mode)**: Recommendations about placements and migrations are displayed, but are not applied until you manually apply the recommendation
    - **Fully Automated**: Recommendations about placement and migration run automatically

    Click **Next** when done.

4. To enable I/O-related functions, check **Enable I/O metric for SDRS recommendations**. On this page, you can also specify **Space** and **I/O latency** thresholds. Default values are suitable for most environments. Click **Next**:

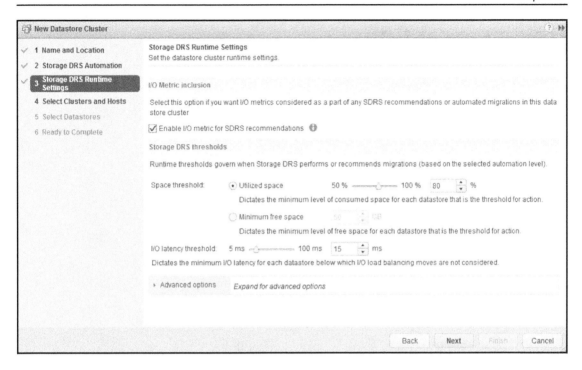

Figure 5.30: Configuring space and I/O latency thresholds

5. Specify clusters and hosts that require connectivity to the datastores in the datastore cluster and click **Next**.

6. Select the datastores to use for the datastore cluster, then click **Next**.

7. Click **Finish** to create the datastore cluster.

 If the Storage DRS feature is disabled on a datastore cluster, all settings are preserved. When you re-enable Storage DRS, all settings are restored to the point where Storage DRS was disabled.

Review questions

1. Which of the following is not a DRS automation level?
   - A: Fully Automated
   - B: Partially Automated
   - C: Disabled
   - D: Manual

   C - See *Objective 5.2*

2. What is the maximum resource pool tree depth supported?
   - A: 6
   - B: 8
   - C: 3
   - D: 10

   B - See *Objective 5.1*

3. When are two resource pools defined as siblings?
   - A: When they are both child resource pools in the resource pool hierarchy
   - B: When they are in the same cluster
   - C: When they have the same parent in the resource pool hierarchy
   - D: When they share the same resources

   C - See *Objective 5.1*

4. When the vSphere DRS feature is disabled, what happens to resource pools?
   - A: Resource pools are removed from the inventory
   - B: Resource pools are temporarily removed but restored once DRS is enabled again
   - C: Resource pools are not affected
   - D: Resource pools are moved outside the cluster

   A - See *Objective 5.2*

5. What is the default threshold percentage where DRS considers a host network saturated?

- A: 50%
- B: 80%
- C: 70%
- D: 90%

B - See *Objective 5.2*

Summary

This chapter covered exam topics related to resource pool management (*Objective 5.1*) and DRS configuration (*Objective 5.2*), describing the use of affinity and anti-affinity rules. Make sure you understand how resources are provided to VMs when resource pools are used and how to benefit from DRS affinity rules. To avoid performance issues, the new network DRS capability helps to prevent migration recommendations for a saturated host network.

6
Backup and Recover a vSphere Deployment

In each design, the protection of infrastructure is important to ensure all services are available with, but a working strategy to quickly recover vSphere components is needed in case of failure.

If the **vCenter Server Appliance** (**vCSA**) installed in your virtual infrastructure fails, advanced features available in vSphere can't be used without vCenter Server. You won't be able to provide services such as vMotion, DRS, HA, FT, and Update Manager, just to mention a few.

This chapter will walk through the configuration and management of some solutions, such as VMware Data Protection and vSphere Replication, to limit service disruption and enable failed components to be quickly restored.

To practice the installation processes and different configuration steps covered, download the products described and install them in your lab to have a look at the available options you may come across in the exam questions.

What will the reader learn to do in this chapter?

- Configure a backup of the vCSA using a file-based backup
- Restore a vCSA from a file-based backup
- Install and manage VMware Data Protection
- Create a backup job with VMware Data Protection
- Backup/restore a virtual machine with VMware Data Protection
- Install and configure vSphere Replication
- Recover a VM using vSphere Replication
- Perform a failback operation using vSphere Replication

Objective 6.1 – Configure and Administer vCenter Appliance Backup/Restore

vSphere 6.5 comes with a new feature introduced in the vCSA that allows a file-based backup of the vCSA and the PSC (embedded and external deployments are supported) through the **vCenter Server Appliance Management Interface** (**VAMI**). This new capability allows you to backup core vCSA configuration, inventory, and historical data of your choice, speeding up the restore process.

Configuring vCSA File-based backup and restore

To backup the vCSA, the procedure is pretty straightforward, with only a few steps to follow:

1. From your preferred browser, enter the address `https://<VCSA_IP>:5480` and log in as root to access the VAMI.
2. Select the **Summary** tab and click the **Backup** button to open the backup appliance wizard.
3. Specify the **Protocol** to use (select from **HTTP, HTTPS, SCP, FTPS**, and **FTP**), then provide the address and the **Location** with the format `Address/Folder/Subfolder`. If the target destination requires the credentials to be connected, specify the correct **User name** and the **Password** to use. Optionally, you can enable the **Encrypt Backup Data** option to encrypt (AES 256) the backup file, providing a password for the encryption. The password will be requested during the restore process. Click **Next**:

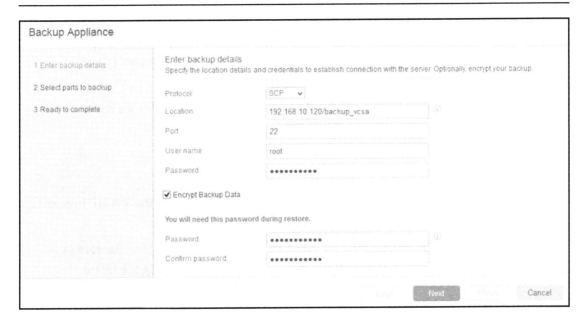

Figure 6.1: Configuring the vCSA backup

4. Specify the data to backup, selecting common parts (inventory and configuration) and stats, events, alarms, and tasks to backup additional historical data in the vCenter Server database. If a PSC is being restored, this second option is not available since all historical and performance data is kept in the vCSA database. Click **Next**.

5. Click **Finish** in the summary to run the backup. The ongoing status is displayed in the **Backup Progress** window once the backup is launched. When the procedure has completed, click **OK** to close the window.

The backup is not stored in the vCSA but streamed to a remote system. If, for any reason, the backup fails, cancel the backup job and start the process again.

Make sure to have a running server with the protocol specified in the wizard (FTP, FTPS, HTTP, HTTPS, or SCP) and sufficient disk space to store the backup. Each file-based backup should be stored in a dedicated folder.

> To add an additional layer of security, and to better protect vCenter Server, vSphere 6.5 introduced **vCenter Server High Availability** (**VCHA**), a new feature available to vCSA only that provides HA to vCenter Server.

With a valid backup, the restore of a failed vCSA is performed using the GUI installer of the appliance (stage 2) and it is a two-stage process:

1. Deploy a new vCSA
2. Copy the data from the file-based backup to the appliance

The restore works only if the backup has been previously taken from the VAMI. Proceed as follows:

1. From the vCSA media, run the vCSA 6.5 installer and select the **Restore** option.
2. Stage 1 of the restore process deploys a new vCSA, replacing the failed appliance. Once the deployment has completed, the new vCSA will run on the target ESXi specified during the setup, but no data has been copied from the backup yet.
3. When the deployment is complete, you are automatically redirected to stage 2, which finalizes the process by copying the data from the backup location.
4. Click **Next** in the introduction page of the stage 2 installer to proceed with the restore.
5. Once you have reviewed the backup details, click **Next** to go to the final step. If you have enabled backup encryption, you must enter the **Encryption password** to restore the vCSA successfully:

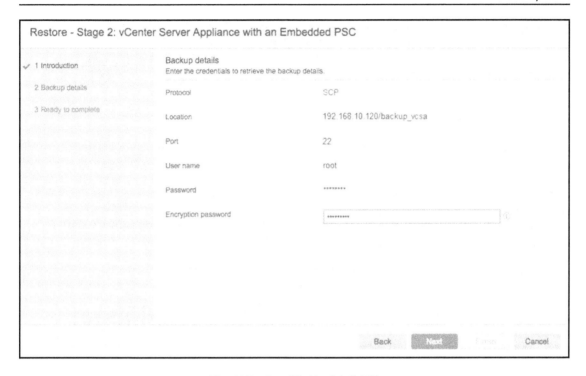

Figure 6.2: Restoring a vCSA with an Embedded PSC

6. Click **Finish** then **OK** to complete stage 2. To complete the restore process, the appliance will be restarted.

A file-based restore of the PSC should be performed only when the last PSC installed in the domain fails. If a PSC fails, you must decommission the failed PSC first, redeploy a new one, and join the existing SSO domain. The multi-master model of the PSC will allow the replication to update the new PSC.

Defining supported backup targets

When the file-based backup is performed, the backup file is not stored in the vCSA but streamed over to a remote system. This allows you to quickly restore the vCSA starting from a fresh deployment if the appliance gets corrupted.

The file-based backup supports the following protocols:

- FTP/FTPS
- HTTP/HTTPS
- SCP

The path to be specified for SCP, FTP, and FTPS is relative to the user's home directory, while for HTTP and HTTPS protocols, the path is relative to the web server's home directory.

Objective 6.2 – Configure and administer vCenter Data Protection

vCenter Data Protection is a pre-built, Linux-based virtual appliance provided by VMware to protect virtual machines configured in your vSphere environment, and requires vCenter Server in Windows or Linux versions. Managed through vSphere Web Client, the appliance is deployed with hardware version 7 and can be stored on VMFS, NFS, and vSAN datastores. Since the communication between **vSphere Data Protection** (**VDP**) appliance and ESXi host uses port 902, if there is a firewall in between, port 902 must be open.

You can deploy up to 20 VDP appliances per vCenter Server and, by default, each appliance is deployed with four virtual CPUs and 4 GB of memory with a data capacity you can configure from 0.5 TB up to 8 TB (available storage sizes are 0.5 TB, 1 TB, 2 TB, 4 TB, and 8 TB) depending on the number of virtual machines to protect, data quantities, backup data retention periods and data change rates, and so on.

In addition, you can optionally deploy up to eight external proxies (virtual appliances) to enable SCSI HotAdd transport backups of VMs running on datastores not directly accessible by the VDP:

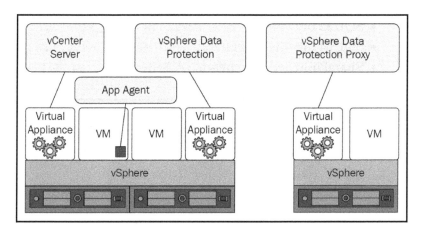

Figure 6.3: VMware Data Protection components

Deploying VDP application agents

VDP agents are used to support granular guest-level backup and recovery for Exchange, SharePoint, and SQL Server and require the installation of a VDP client on those application servers to support guest-level backups.

The VDP client is an MSI package in a format such as `VMwareVDPExchange-windows-x86_64.6.1.8.31.msi` installed from the target server's Command Prompt; you must open it with administrative privileges.

To install the VDP client, you have to download the MSI file from the VDP appliance in the following way:

1. Log in to Exchange, SharePoint, or SQL Server and from the web browser access vSphere Web Client, entering the correct credentials.
2. Select **Home** | **vSphere Data Protection 6.1** and click **Connect** on the welcome page to connect the VDP appliance.

3. Select the **Configuration** tab and, under **Downloads**, click the appropriate application server type to download the corresponding VDP client. There are four available VDP clients:

- **Exchange**: VMwareVDPExchange-windows-x86_64.6.1.8.31.msi
- **SQL 32 bit**: VMwareVDPSQL-windows-x86_32.6.1.8.31.msi
- **SQL 64 bit**: VMwareVDPSQL-windows-x86_64.6.1.8.31.msi
- **SharePoint**: VMwareVDPMoss-windows-x86_64.6.1.8.31.msi:

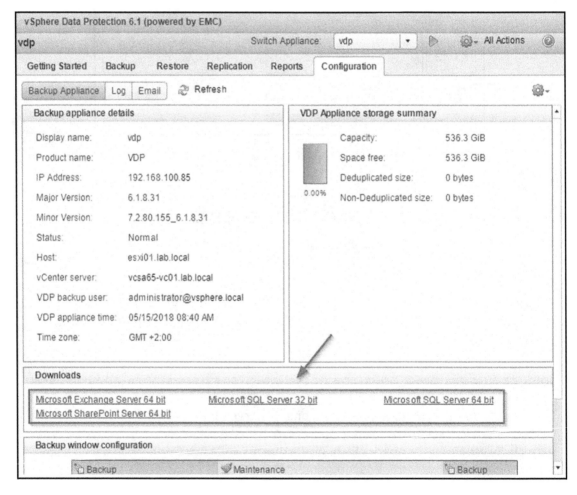

Figure 6.4: VDP client download area

4. Click on the corresponding server link and save the MSI file in a directory on the server to process.

5. From the Windows server, open Command Prompt with administrative privileges and navigate to the directory where the VDP client has been saved.

6. Run the following command:

```
msiexec /i VMwareVDP<servertype>-windows-x86_64-<version>.msi
```

Differentiating VMware Data Protection's capabilities

The VMware Data Protection solution performs image-level backups using snapshot technology. Data is deduplicated within the appliance and, if the internal proxy is used, each appliance can backup up to eight virtual machines simultaneously. It is possible to backup 24 virtual machines if external proxies are deployed instead.

VDP uses **Changed Block Tracking** (**CBT**) technology, allowing incremental backups to be taken and performing backup only of the blocks that have changed, rather than backing up every block of every VM in the infrastructure. This solution allows you to save disk space and requires less time to complete. Virtual machines restored to the same location take advantage of CBT technology, optimizing the process in terms of data transfer and RTO, but if the VM is restored to a different location, CBT is not used. Virtual machines can also be renamed during the restore process.

Backing up a vCenter Server by using an embedded platform service controller and an external platform service controller is supported by VDP, and filesystem quiescing is performed during backups to keep the filesystem consistent. If during the backup process the vCenter Server is heavily loaded, the backup may fail due to the failure to quiesce the VM. Although VMware VDP supports backup and restore for the vCenter Server, a successful restore is not guaranteed.

Generally, a full backup includes all disks of the processed virtual machine in a single image backup. VDP provides the capability to *backup individual disks* in order to backup only required disks. Due to snapshot limitations, unsupported disks installed in the virtual machine won't be included in the image-level backup.

When a restore procedure is performed by the VDP, virtual disks (.vmdk files) of the original virtual machine are created through the restored .vmx configuration file. If any of the virtual disks were not included in the backup, temporary VMDKs are created during the restore process, with the potential result of a malfunctioning virtual machine.

Additional application backup and restore support for Microsoft SQL, Microsoft Exchange, or SharePoint servers, is given by the VDP *guest-level backup* capability, which makes use of client agents (VDP clients) installed on Microsoft SQL, Microsoft Exchange, or SharePoint servers.

To reduce service disruption in the case of a failure in the production site, critical virtual machines can be replicated (an identical copy of the source VM is created on the target ESXi host) to the DR site and are ready to be powered on if needed. Through the replication jobs, VDP can manage backups to replicate specifying the schedule and the target location.

The supported replication targets for backups created with VDP 6.0 or later are as follows:

- Another VDP appliance
- EMC Avamar server
- Data Domain system

VDP also provides support for **File Level Recovery** (**FLR**), which allows you to recover individual files from a mounted backup of a protected virtual machine. The VDP Restore Client is required to perform FLR.

Explaining VMware data protection sizing guidelines

The appliance can backup up to 400 virtual machines per VDP and, if the internal proxy is used, each appliance can backup up to 8 virtual machines simultaneously. It is possible to backup 24 virtual machines if 8 external proxies are deployed.

VDP can be configured with the following capacity range:

- 0.5 TB
- 1 TB
- 2 TB
- 4 TB
- 6 TB
- 8 TB

These values indicate the amount of space available in the appliance to store the backups. After VDP deployment, the disk size can be increased. The required space to install the appliance is greater than the configuration size:

	0.5 TB	1 TB	2 TB	4 TB	6 TB	8 TB
Processors	Minimum four 2 GHz processors	Minimum four 2 GHz processors	Minimum four 2 GHz processors	Minimum four 2 GHz processors	Minimum four 2 GHz processors	Minimum four 2 GHz processors
Memory	4 GB	4 GB	4 GB	8 GB	10 GB	12 GB
Disk space	873 GB	1,600 GB	3 TB	6 TB	9 TB	12 TB

Table 6.1: Minimum system requirements for VDP

Before proceeding with the backup, make sure your virtual machines use supported disks.

 VDP does not support Independent, **Raw Device Mapping** (**RDM**) Independent—Virtual Compatibility Mode, and RDM Physical Compatibility Mode virtual hardware disk types. Also, backups and restores of virtual machines on **Virtual Volumes** (**VVOLs**) are not supported.

To determine the VDP appliance size and the number of appliances required, consider the following factors:

- Number and type of VMs
- Amount of data
- Retention periods
- Typical change rate

Creating/deleting/consolidating virtual machine snapshots

Snapshot technology (many software backup solutions, such as VDP, rely on this technology) allows you to capture the state of a virtual machine at a specific point in time, which you can revert from at any time. Taken on a per-VM basis, each virtual machine can have multiple snapshots, and changes that have occurred can be kept by deleting the saved snapshots or discarded by reverting to a previous snapshot.

Snapshot utilization has some limitations:

- Raw disks and RDM physical mode disks are not supported (virtual compatibility mode is supported instead)
- Independent disks are supported only for powered-off VMs
- VMs configured for bus sharing are not supported
- A maximum of 32 snapshots are supported in a chain, and keeping them for a long time may negatively impact the VM performance
- Snapshot creation can require a lot of time to complete if the VMs virtual disk is larger than 2 TB

 Don't use snapshots as backups because if the files of the VM are lost or the storage itself fails, the snapshot files are lost as well.

The manual creation of a virtual machine snapshot can be done by right-clicking the virtual machine to process and selecting the **Snapshots** | **Take snapshot** option.

In addition to **Name** and **Description**, you can enable the two available options:

- **Snapshot the virtual machine's memory**: If enabled, the snapshot will also include the RAM. If the VM is powered off, this option is grayed out.
- **Quiesce guest file system (Needs VMware Tools installed)**: This option is available only if the VMware Tools are installed or the VM is powered on. It ensures consistent backups, bringing the on-disk data into a state suitable for backups:

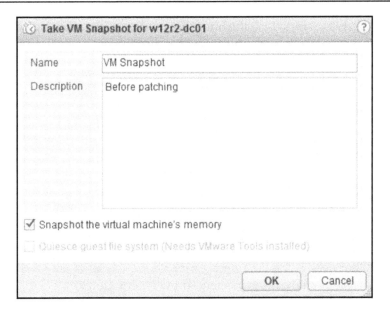

Figure 6.5: Snapshot options

 If you revert a virtual machine to a snapshot taken with the **Snapshot the virtual machine's memory** option disabled, the VM will be powered off.

When a snapshot is taken, the following files are created:

- `vmname-00000#.vmdk`: Contains information about snapshot and snapshot disks
- `vmname-00000#-delta.vmdk`: Contains the difference in terms of virtual disk changed blocks between the current state of the VM and the state at the time of snapshot creation
- `vmname.vmsd`: Contains snapshot information such as names, descriptions, and relationships between snapshots
- `vmname.snasphot#.vmsn`: Contains the memory state of the VM when the **Snapshot the virtual machine's memory** option is enabled

Using the available delete options in the Snapshot Manager, changes can be committed by merging delta disks with the base disks in the following ways:

- **Delete**: By deleting the selected snapshot from the chain, changes that occurred between the state of the snapshot and the previous disk state to the parent snapshot are consolidated
- **Delete all Snapshots**: All changes that occurred in the virtual machine between snapshots are consolidated by merging delta disks to base disks, deleting all snapshots from the VM

If the redundant delta disk deletion procedure fails for any reason, snapshots left in the virtual machine will impact negatively on the performance and precious space is taken from the storage with the risk of running out of space. To remove these snapshots, you need to perform a consolidation procedure that will keep the VM healthy.

Virtual machines that need consolidation are reported in the **VMs** tab of vCenter Server, cluster, or host objects in vSphere Web Client. If the **Needs Consolidation** column is not visible, right-click the column heading and select the **Show/Hide Columns** option then click **Needs Consolidation**:

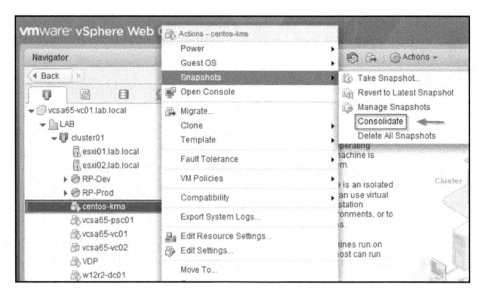

Figure 6.6: Consolidating a virtual machine from vSphere Web Client

Consolidation is a resource-consuming task since a large amount of data must be read and written to the disk, affecting the virtual machine performance while consolidating.

Installing and configuring VMware Data Protection

Before proceeding with the installation, there are some prerequisites that must be met in order to implement VDP:

- **DNS configuration**: The DNS server must support forward (A record) and reverse (PTR record) lookup for both VDP appliance and vCenter Server using the IP addresses and the FQDN. The VMware proxy nodes also require communication to DNS (port 53) over both TCP and UDP protocols. Make sure DNS configuration is properly working by running the nslookup command on the vCenter Server using the VDP and vCenter Server FQDN.
- **NTP**: Network time must be synced between vSphere components, such as VDP, vCenter Server, and ESXi hosts, to avoid potential issues related to authentication. Since VDP leverages VMware Tools to synchronize time through NTP, getting the correct time through vSphere, you must not configure VDP with NTP.

If you configure the NTP directly on the VDP appliance, you may experience time synchronization errors.

- **VMware vCenter Single Sign-On**: A user account from the SSO domain or from a domain configured as SSO identity source (Active Directory for example) must be configured to connect VDP and vCenter Server. Make sure you assign the correct permissions for the VDP service account used, such as the Administrator role.

Before proceeding with the deployment, you should verify that you meet at least the minimum requirements specified previously. Ensure your web browser is supported and Adobe Flash is installed.

To avoid a global failure, VDP should not be installed on the same datastore used by virtual machines you need to protect. To take advantage of **Change Block Tracking** (**CBT**) technology, virtual machines should run at least virtual hardware version 7 with VMware Tools installed to support some features such as file level restore and quiescing.

The deployment of the VMware Data Protection is composed of two main steps:

1. Deployment of the VDP from the OVA file
2. Initial configuration and storage setup

To deploy the VMware Data Protection appliance, perform the following steps:

1. From vSphere Web Client, right-click the object level in the Inventory view (data center, cluster) and choose **Deploy OVF Template**.
2. Click **Browse** to select the OVA file downloaded from VMware and click **Next**.
3. Enter the appliance **Name** and specify the location then click **Next**.
4. Specify the resource to locate the appliance and click **Next**.
5. In **Review details**, click **Next** to continue.
6. Click the **Accept** button to accept the EULA and click **Next**.
7. Select the disk type and the storage to use. Click **Next**.
8. Specify the appropriate network to connect and click **Next**.
9. Specify the network settings (**IP address**, **Netmask**, **DNS**, and **Gateway**) and click **Next**.
10. Click **Finish** to begin the deployment.
11. When the deployment procedure has completed successfully, power on the appliance.

To perform the initial configuration of the appliance, follow this procedure:

1. From your favorite browser, type the address `https://IP_VDP:8543/vdp-configure/` to access the configuration page of the appliance.
2. On the login page, enter the default credentials (`root/changeme`) then click **Login**.
3. The welcome page is displayed. Click **Next** to begin the configuration.
4. Enter the **Network settings** and server information for the VDP appliance and click **Next**.
5. Specify the **Time Zone** then click **Next**.

6. Enter a new password for the VDP appliance, making sure you meet the password requirements, then click **Next**.

7. Enter the credentials for a user with the privileges to add objects with the vCenter Server and specify the vCenter Server's FQDN. If the used vCenter Server has the embedded PSC, check the **Use vCenter for SSO Authentication** option. Deselect this option if the external PSC is used instead and specify the **SSO FQDN or IP**. Click **Test Connection** to verify the correct connection with the vCenter Server:

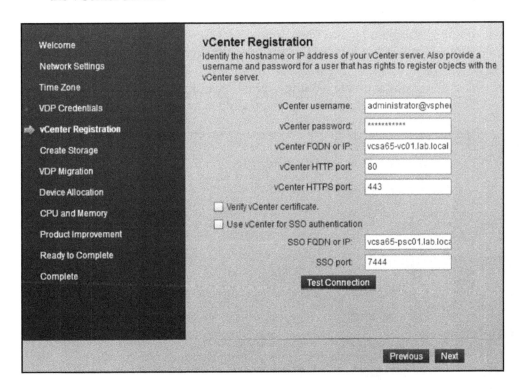

Figure 6.7: Registration of the VDP with vCenter Server with an external PSC

8. If the test succeeds, click **Next** to continue. If the test fails, double-check the user's permissions and credentials, and FQDN.

9. On the **Create Storage** page, select the **Create new storage** option and specify the **Capacity** value. Valid capacity values are 0, 5 TB, 1 TB, 2 TB, 4 TB, 6 TB, and 8 TB. Select the appropriate capacity value and click **Next**.

10. Specify the disk type to use from the **Provision** drop-down menu by choosing **Thick-Lazy Zeroed** (default), **Thick Eager-Zeroed**, and **Thin**. VMware recommends the use of **Thick-Lazy Zeroed** as provision type. Click **Next**.

11. Review **CPU** and **Memory** requirements for the specified capacity then click **Next**.

12. Optionally, check **Enable Customer Experience Improvement Program** then click **Next**.

13. On the **Ready to Complete** page, you can enable the **Run performance analysis on storage configuration** option (this process can take from 30 minutes to several hours to complete) if you wish to do performance analysis, and the self-explanatory option **Restart the appliance if successful**. Click **Next** to apply.

14. Click **Yes** in the warning message to proceed with the storage configuration. The ongoing status is displayed under previous options and when the process has completed, the appliance is automatically restarted:

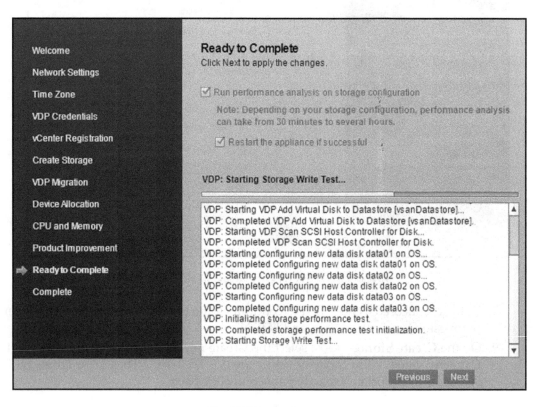

Figure 6.8: VDP configuration process

Once the installation procedure has completed successfully, you can access the VDP console from vSphere Web Client. A new VDP icon is displayed in the **Home** tab:

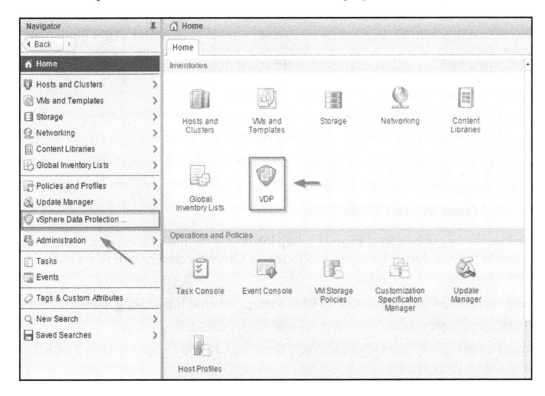

Figure 6.9: VDP in vSphere Web Client

Since VDP is deployed with hardware version 7, the Flash Read Cache capability (a feature introduced in vSphere 5.5 that makes use of host local flash devices as a cache to improve VM storage performance) cannot be used. The result is that during an image-level backup of a vSphere Flash Read Cache-backed disk, VDP will use the **Network Block Device** (**NBD**) protocol instead of HotAdd, affecting the backup performance.

Additional information can be found in the vSphere Data Protection Administration Guide (`https://docs.vmware.com/en/VMware-vSphere/6.5/vmware-data-protection-administration-guide-61.pdf`).

Creating a backup job with VMware Data Protection

Before proceeding with backup job creation, make sure to understand VDP's limitations.

The following virtual machines types are not backed up:

- VDP appliances
- **vSphere Storage Appliances** (**VSA**)
- **VMware Data Recovery** (**VDR**) appliances
- Templates
- Secondary fault tolerant nodes
- Proxies
- **Avamar Virtual Edition** (**AVE**) servers

Virtual machines can be added to any backup job only if the use of special characters in their names is limited to - (dash) or _ (underscore). Other special characters are not supported.

Backups performed with snapshots on VMs configured with bus sharing are also not supported.

To create a backup job, from vSphere Web Client, click **Home** | **vSphere Data Protection 6.1** and follow these steps:

1. From the VDP dashboard, click the **Create Backup Job** option:

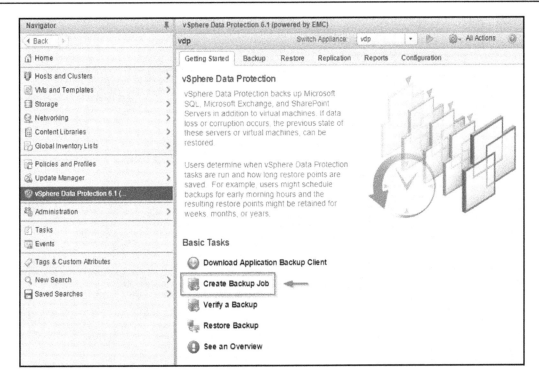

Figure 6.10: Backup job creation from the VDP dashboard

2. The **Create a new backup job** wizard is displayed.
3. Select **Guest Images** as Job type to backup virtual machines then click **Next**.
4. Select **Full Image** as **Data Type** to backup the full VM. Select **Individual Disks** if you need to backup only individual virtual machine disks. Click **Next**.
5. Select virtual machines to backup then click **Next**. You can select individual virtual machines or VMs contained in a specific container such as a resource pool, host, data center, or folder by checking the vSphere object. New virtual machines added to the selected container are automatically included in subsequent backups.
6. Specify a backup **Schedule** then click **Next**.
7. Specify the **Retention Policy** (how long backups are retained) to use and click **Next**.
8. Enter a backup job **Name** and click **Next**.
9. Click **Finish** to save the configured backup job.

10. Click **OK** when the information concerning the job is displayed:

Figure 6.11: Backup job listed in the Backup tab

If you need to adjust the backup versus maintenance timeline, from the VDP dashboard, go to the **Configuration** tab and, in the **Backup window configuration**, change the **Backup start time** and the **Backup duration** then click **Save**:

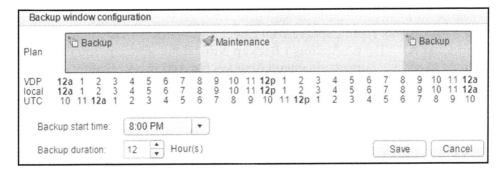

Figure 6.12: The backup window configuration

Backing up/restoring a virtual machine with VMware Data Protection

VDP allows you also execute a backup job immediately, without waiting for its schedule. You just need to select the backup job to run and click the **Backup now** button. Specify what virtual machines you want to process from these two options:

- **Backup all sources**: Select this option to backup all virtual machines configured in the backup job
- **Backup only out of date sources**: Only the virtual machines that were not successfully backed up during the last backup are processed.

The backup runs immediately if VDP is in the backup or the maintenance window:

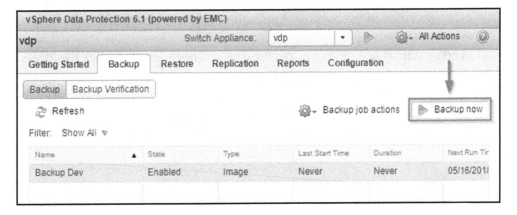

Figure 6.13: Starting the backup process immediately

You can also perform an immediate backup of a protected virtual machine if it is already a member of a backup job. From vSphere Web Client, right-click the virtual machine to backup and select **All VDP 6.1 Actions** | **Backup Now**. If the selected virtual machine doesn't belong to any backup job, the menu displays **No Actions Available**.

With VDP, backed-up virtual machines can be restored to the original location or to an alternate location. Restore operations are managed from the VDP's **Restore** tab and have some limitations:

- Multiple restore points for the same MSApp client cannot be selected.
- Restores to virtual machines with SCSI bus sharing configured are not supported.
- If a virtual machines contains snapshots, snapshots must be removed for a successful restore. If the target virtual machine contains snapshots, the restore job fails.

To restore the virtual machines to their original location, in vSphere Web Client, select **Home** | **vSphere Data Protection 6.1** and follow this procedure:

1. Navigate to the **Restore** tab.
2. A list of backed-up virtual machines is displayed and backups can be filtered to better identify the object to restore.
3. From the backup list, click on the virtual machine to recover to display available restore points then select the appropriate backup. To restore a specific virtual disk, click on the desired restore point and select the correct disk. In the **Name** column of the restore points list, for each restore point there is a specific icon for crash-consistent and application-consistent backups (Windows clients only; for Linux clients, a **Consistency level not applicable** icon appears) and the expiration date of the backup. Application-consistent backups apply only to Windows clients.
4. When a virtual machine or a specific disk has been selected, click **Restore**:

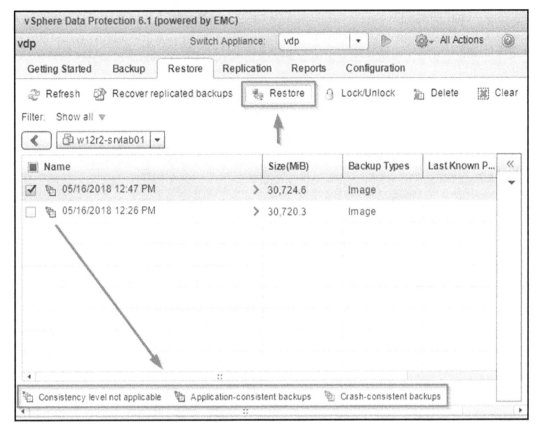

Figure 6.14: Restoring a virtual machine to source location

5. Verify whether the selected virtual machines to backup are correct and, if you need to exclude any, make the required modifications. Click **Next**.

6. Leave the **Restore to original location** option checked and configure the **Advanced** options if you wish to power on the VM when the restore has completed. Click **Next**.

7. Click **Finish** on the **Ready to Complete** page to run the restore.

8. Click **OK** in the **Info** window.

To restore a virtual machine to a different location, repeat the same procedure and, in step 6, uncheck the **Restore to original location** option. You must provide a **New name** for the virtual machine, the **Destination** and, under **Advanced options**, the **Datastore** used to restore the VM:

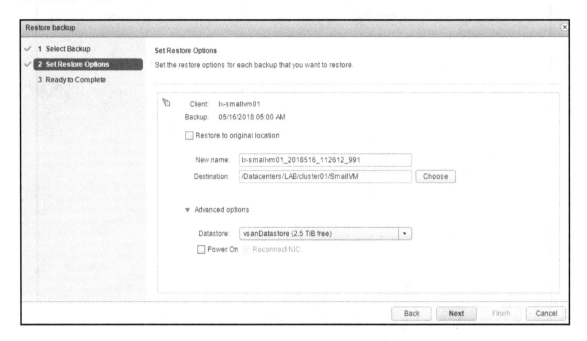

Figure 6.15: Options to restore a virtual machine to a new location

 The restore to original location option is not allowed if the original virtual disk of the virtual machine to restore has been removed. In this case, the virtual disk must be restored to a different location.

vMotion operations are not allowed to run on the VDP appliance during active backup or restore processes and you should wait until the backup operations have completed before performing vMotion to avoid backups or snapshot deletion failures.

Objective 6.3 – Configure vSphere Replication

vSphere Replication 6.5 (**VR**) is a host-based virtual machine replication solution distributed as an OVF virtual appliance. A replica allows the creation of an exact copy of a production virtual machine and it is stored on a DR site ready to be fired up in case of a disaster in the primary site. Through scheduled or manual replication jobs, you can specify which backups are replicated and target storage devices to use.

Comparing and contrasting vSphere Replication compression methods

vSphere Replication can be configured to compress transferred data to save network bandwidth, reducing the amount of buffer memory used on the **vSphere Replication server** (**VRS**). vSphere Replication uses the FastLZ compression library, which provides a balance of speed, minimal CPU overhead, and compression efficiency. Although compression is enabled during the replication configuration in a vSphere Replication appliance, compression is actually performed by the ESXi hosts.

The downside of using compression is that more CPU resources are required in the source site and the server that manages the target datastore.

To support full end-to-end compression (from source to target storage), source and target ESXi hosts must both run version 6.x. If an earlier than version 6.0 source ESXi host is used, the data compression is not supported and the **Enable network compression for VR data** option is disabled in the **Configure Replication** wizard. If the source site has an ESXi 6.x host but the target ESXi runs an earlier than version 6.0, data can't be decompressed in the target site. Data is decompressed from the vSphere Replication appliance and sent to the target host uncompressed.

Although vSphere Replication uses CBT technology to replicate only changed blocks to the DR site, the primary site and DR site are quite often connected over a slow WAN with a limited bandwidth. Enabling compression in the replication process saves bandwidth, improving performance.

Configuring a recovery point objective (RPO) for a protected virtual machine

During the configuration of a replication, the RPO settings for the virtual machine can be changed to a value suitable for the business needs.

vSphere Replication allows you to configure the RPO from 5 minutes up to 24 hours:

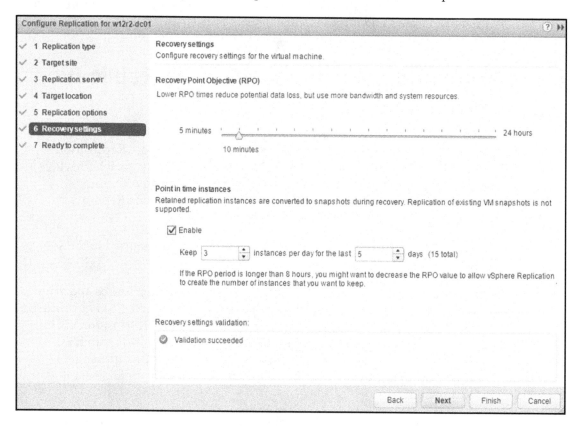

Figure 6.16: RPO configuration in the replication wizard

Managing snapshots on recovered virtual machines

During the configuration of a replication in vSphere Replication, the retention policy defines the snapshot instances (**Point in time instances** option) of the virtual machine that are retained on the target site (*Figure 6.16*).

When the replicated virtual machine is recovered, the replication instances are converted to snapshots. If you right-click the recovered virtual machine in the DR site and select **Snapshots | Manage Snapshots**, you are able to see the point-in-time snapshots created by vSphere Replication.

Select the desired snapshot (point in time) you want to use and select **All Actions | Revert to** option:

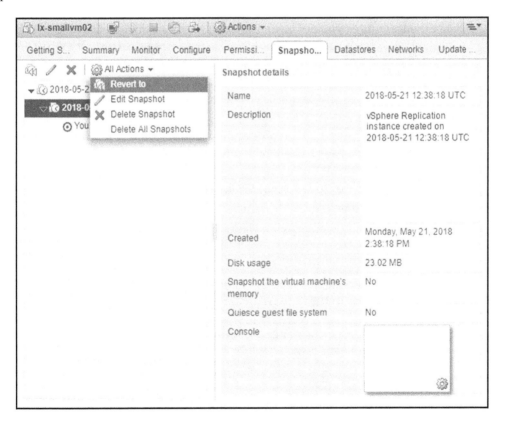

Figure 6.17: Point-in-time snapshots created by vSphere Replication

A maximum of 24 snapshot instances are supported by vSphere Replication.

If a retention policy is set to 30 days, the backup is retained for the specified period. When the retention expiration date is reached, the backup is deleted by the **garbage collection** process during the maintenance window, freeing up space in the storage.

Installing/configuring/upgrading vSphere Replication

Download the vSphere Replication appliance from the VMware website in ISO format and use vSphere Web Client to deploy the appliance by performing the following steps:

1. Mount the downloaded vSphere Replication ISO file.
2. From the **Inventory** view of vSphere Web Client, right-click the object level (data center, cluster, resource pool) you want to use and select **Deploy OVF Template**.
3. From the wizard, click **Browse** and make sure to select all the required files (vSphere_Replication_OVF10.ovf, vSphere_Replication_OVF10.cert, vSphere_Replication_OVF10.mf, vSphere_Replication-system.vmdk, and vSphere_Replication-support.vmdk) located in the \bin directory in the mounted ISO image. These files are required to deploy the first appliance, referred to as the **vSphere Replication Management Server (VRMS)**, on-premises that handles replications from source hosts. Click **Next**.
4. Type a **Name** and specify a folder. Click **Next**.
5. Select the computing resource in which to run the appliance and click **Next**.
6. On the **Review details** page, click **Next**.
7. Click the **Accept** button to accept the license agreement then click **Next**.
8. Specify the number of CPUs to use by choosing from the **Configuration** drop-down menu a value between 2 vCPU and 4 vCPU then click **Next**. If you are unsure on which configuration to use, select the 2 vCPU configuration.

To ensure better performance, a higher number of vCPUs should be chosen but replication speed might be affected if replicas run on ESXi hosts with four or fewer cores per NUMA node.

9. Specify the disk format and select the datastore in which to store the appliance then click **Next**.

10. Select the correct **Management Network** from the drop-down menu and, although the appliance supports both DHCP and static IP addresses, it is recommended to use a static IP. Set the **IP allocation** field as **Static-Manual**. Network parameters can be changed also from the VAMI once the installation has completed. Click **Next**.

> The vSphere Replication appliance supports both IPv4 and IPv6 addresses, but a single appliance cannot be configured with both IPv4 and IPv6 addresses because it is not supported.

11. Enter a **Hostname** providing the FQDN if a static IP address is used. Specify the **NTP Servers** to use and the root password (at least eight characters).

12. Click **Next** on the vService bindings page. If the **Binding status** shows a green check, the vSphere Replication successfully bound the vCenter Server used to deploy the replication appliance:

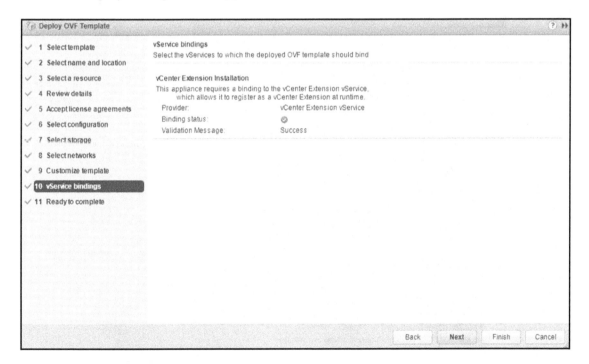

Figure 6.18: vSphere Replication successfully bound the vCenter Server

13. Click **Finish** to start the deployment of the vSphere Replication appliance.

Once the deployement procedure has been completed, power on the appliance. Using your favorite browser, type the address `https://IP_address_VR:5480` and log in with the root credentials to the VAMI in case you need to change the registration of the vSphere Replication with vCenter Single Sign-On.

In the **VR | Configuration** tab of the VAMI, you can configure or change the vCenter Server registration by modifying the **LookupService Address** in the following way:

- If the vCenter has an embedded PSC, enter the FQDN of the vCenter Server
- If the vCenter has an external PSC, enter the FQDN of the PSC
- Specify the SSO Administrator account and the password

Click **Save and Restart Service**:

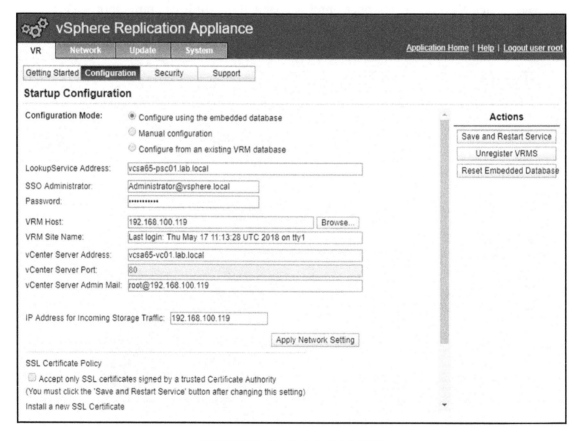

Figure 6.19: Configuration of LookupService in the VAMI

When the service has been restarted, the vSphere Replication icon is displayed in the **Home** tab of vSphere Web Client:

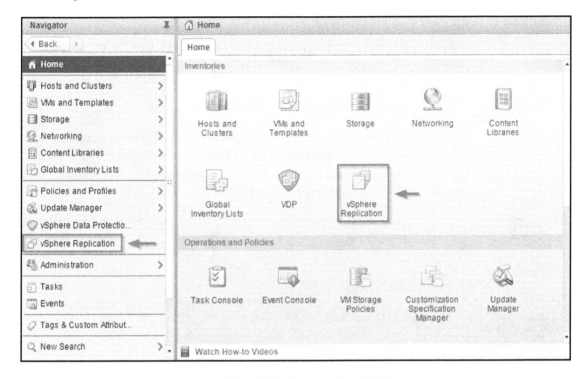

Figure 6.20: vSphere Replication plugin in vSphere Web Client

 In order to use vSphere Replication, you must deploy the VRMS appliance in each vCenter Server and only one VRMS appliance should be installed per vCenter Server.

Once the VRMS has been deployed, if the number of virtual machines to replicate grows, you can deploy up to nine VRS appliances per vCenter Server, which have the function of receiving replicas from source hosts. While the VRMS has the management service enabled, VRS provides only the replication service and it is managed by the VRMS.

VRS is deployed through the **Deploy OVF Template** option in vSphere Web Client and you should select the vSphere_Replication_AddOn_OVF10.ovf, vSphere_Replication_AddOn_OVF10.cert, vSphere_Replication_AddOn_OVF10.mf, vSphere_Replication-system.vmdk, and vSphere_Replication-support.vmdk files from the \bin directory in the mounted ISO image. Once the VRS has been deployed and powered on, it must be connected to the vCenter Server.

Proceed as follows to connect a VRS to the vCenter Server:

1. From vSphere Web Client, select the vCenter Server from the **Inventory** view and select **Configure | vSphere Replication | Replication Servers**.
2. Click the **Register a virtual machine as vSphere Replication server** icon and select from the list the appropriate VRS appliance. Click **OK**:

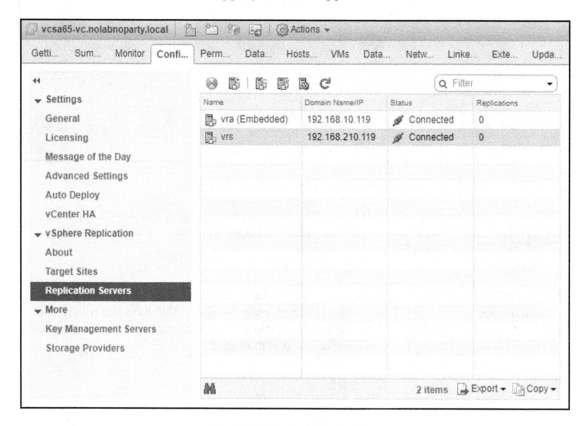

Figure 6.21: The VRS registered in the vCenter Server

Upgrading the vSphere Replication appliance can be performed in two different ways, depending on the installed versions to upgrade:

- Use the ISO image to upgrade the appliance to a major version (for example, from 6.0/6.1 to 6.5).
- Along with the ISO image, the Update Manager and the VAMI can be also used to perform updates (for example, from 5.5.0 to 5.5.1).

To upgrade the vSphere Replication Appliance from the VAMI using an ISO image, follow this procedure:

1. Download the latest available vSphere Replication update from the VMware website in ISO format and save it anywhere on your computer.
2. Mount the ISO image.
3. Open your favorite browser and type the address `https://IP_Address_VR:5480` to access the login page and enter the root credentials. Click **Login**.
4. Go to the **Update | Settings** tab and select the **Use CDROM Updates** option under Update Repository. Click **Save Settings**.
5. Go to **Status** and click **Check Updates**.
6. If a new update is found, click **Install Updates** to proceed with the update then click **OK**:

Figure 6.22: vSphere Replication upgrade from the VAMI

7. When the update procedure has been completed, reboot the appliance. Go to **System** | **Information** and click **Reboot**.

 Downgrading to an earlier version of vSphere Replication is not supported.

For more information, check out VMware vSphere Replication Installation and Configuration 6.5 (`https://docs.vmware.com/en/vSphere-Replication/6.5/vsphere-replication-65-install.pdf`).

Replication Configure VMware Certificate Authority (VMCA) integration with vSphere

If you need to replace the self-signed SSL certificate installed in the vSphere Replication appliance with a new SSL certificate issued by VMware Certificate Authority (VMCA), you can use the VAMI to configure a new SSL certificate.

Proceed as follows:

1. Using your favorite browser, log in to vSphere Replication VAMI and navigate to the **VR** | **Configuration** tab.
2. Check the **Accept only SSL certificate signed by a trusted Certificate Authority** option.
3. Click **Choose File** to select the new SSL certificate issued by the VMCA.
4. Click **Upload and Install** then **Save and Restart Service**:

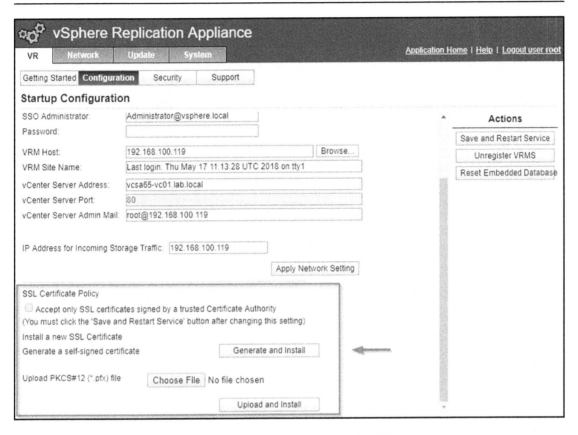

Figure 6.23: Installation of a new SSL certificate through the VAMI

Configuring vSphere Replication for single/multiple VMs

In order to replicate virtual machines, vSphere Replication should be deployed at the source and target sites and must be connected.

Although replication can also be configured for a powered-off virtual machine, data synchronization occurs only when the virtual machine is powered on.

To create a replication, the user must have the **VRM virtual machine replication user** role assigned.

The procedure to create a virtual machine replication is composed of the following steps:

1. To configure a replication for a single virtual machine, right-click the virtual machine to replicate and select **All vSphere Replication Actions | Configure Replication**. To replicate multiple virtual machines, select the vCenter Server from the **Inventory** view and click the **VMs** tab. Select the virtual machines to replicate and click **Actions | All vSphere Replication Actions | Configure Replication...**:

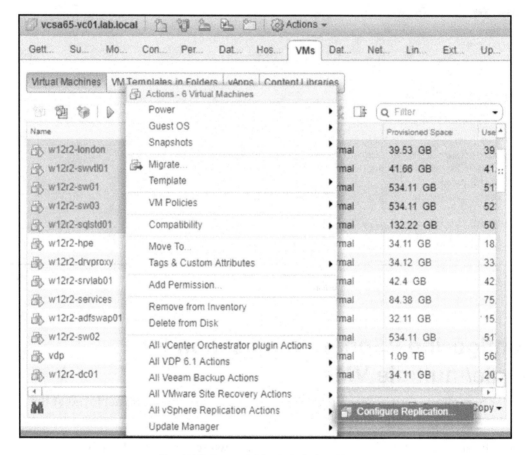

Figure 6.24: Configuration of vSphere Replication for multiple VMs

2. Select the **Replicate to a vCenter** option and click **Next**.
3. Select the target site where the virtual machine will be replicated. To add a remote site, the logged-in user account must have the **VRM remote.ManageVRM** privilege assigned. Click **Next**.

4. Specify the VRS used to handle the replication and click **Next**.

5. On the **Target location** page, click **Edit** and select from list the datastore used to store replicated files. Click **OK** to confirm the selected datastore then **Next** to continue the configuration.

6. Check the **Enable network compression for VR data** option to save network bandwidth. The **Enable quiescing** option should be checked if you need to ensure the application/database isn't corrupted after a disaster recovery. The Quiesce feature requires the VMware Tools installed on the virtual machine to replicate. Click **Next**.

 Don't use VSS quiescing if the application doesn't require it.

 VSS quiescing on Virtual Volumes is not supported in vSphere Replication.

7. Specify the RPO to configure using the slider (from 5 minutes up to 24 hours) and tick the **Enable** option under the **Point in time** instances to specify the replication instances to keep. During the recovery process, these instances will be converted to snapshots of the source virtual machine. Click **Next**.

 Up to 24 instances can be kept for a virtual machine.

8. Click **Finish** to save the configuration.

Recovering a VM using vSphere Replication

Once the virtual machines have been replicated successfully to the DR site with vSphere Replication, if a disaster occours at the primary site, you can recover replicated virtual machines using vSphere Web Client. Only one virtual machine at a time can be recovered. Before proceeding with the recovery, make sure the virtual machine at source is powered off to avoid an error during the recovery process.

Proceed as follows:

1. From vSphere Web Client, select the vCenter Server from the **Inventory** view and navigate to the **Monitor | vSphere Replication** tab.
2. Select **Incoming Replications** under **vSphere Replication**.
3. Right-click the virtual machine to recover and select the **Recovery...** option:

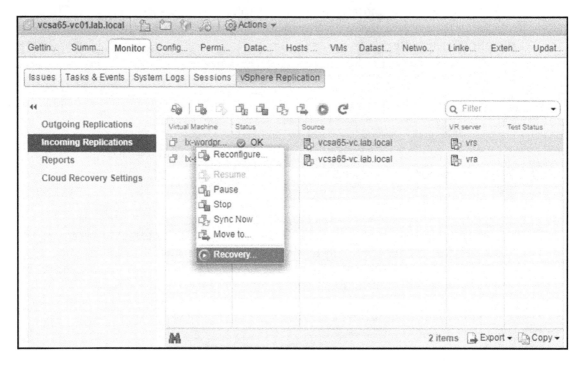

Figure 6.25: Recovering a virtual machine from vSphere Replication

4. In the recovery wizard, select the appropriate recovery option then click **Next**. Depending on the status of the source virtual machine, you have two options available:
   - **Synchronize recent changes**: If the source virtual machine is still accessible, the target is fully synchronized with latest changes, ensuring no data loss. This option is available only if the virtual machine is powered off.
   - **Use latest available data**: Use this option if the source virtual machine is inaccessible or corrupted. Data changed since the last replication is lost:

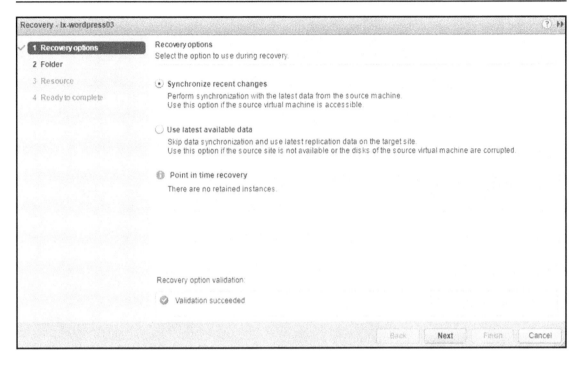

Figure 6.26: Recovery options from vSphere Replication

5. Specify the folder at the target site to store the recovered virtual machine and click **Next**.

6. Select the target compute resource (cluster, host, or resource pool) and click **Next**.

7. If the protected virtual machine contains some hard disks not included in the replication, the system displays a page where for each virtual disk you have to use the **Browse** button to attach an existing disk or click **Detach** button to detach the disk excluding disk files from the recovery.

8. On the **Ready to complete** page, optionally you can select the **Power on after recovery** option. Click **Next**.

9. Click **Finish** to start the recovery.

 When the procedure has completed, the network device of the recovered virtual machine is disconnected from the network to prevent potential issues. You must manually connect the virtual network adapters to the correct network.

When the recovery has completed successfully, the status of the virtual machine changes to **Recovered**:

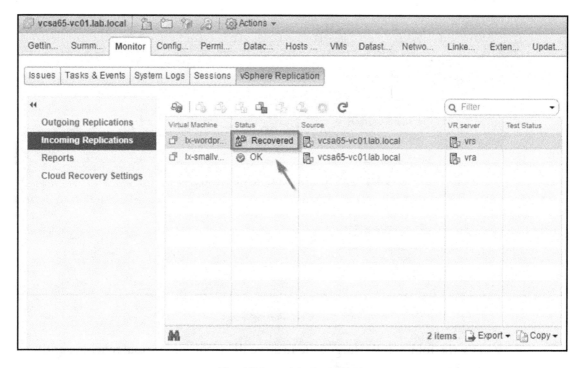

Figure 6.27: Recovered virtual machine status

The recovered virtual machine shows up in the **Inventory** of the target site.

Check out Using VMware vSphere Replication 6.5 (`https://docs.vmware.com/en/vSphere-Replication/6.5/vsphere-replication-65-user.pdf`) for additional information.

Performing a failback operation using vSphere Replication

vSphere Replication doesn't provide any automated action to perform failback of virtual machines, but it must be executed manually.

To perform a failback, basically you need to reconfigure a replication in the reverse direction in order to replicate the virtual machine from the target to the source site.

When configuring the replication in reverse direction, source disks are used as replication seeds and only changed blocks in the target site are used by vSphere Replication for the syncronization. Since you don't need to copy the entire virtual machines but only the changes, it allows you to save time and bandwidth.

 You need to unregister the virtual machine from the source inventory before configuring the reverse replication.

If the source virtual machine has been recovered and you don't need to keep changes from the target site, you can simply power off the recovered virtual machine at the target site and stop the replication. To stop a replication, select the vCenter Server from the **Inventory** view then navigate to the **Monitor | vSphere Replication** tab. Right-click the virtual machine with the **Status** reported as **Recovered** and select **Stop**. Once you click **OK** in the warning window, the replication of the selected virtual machine is permanently stopped:

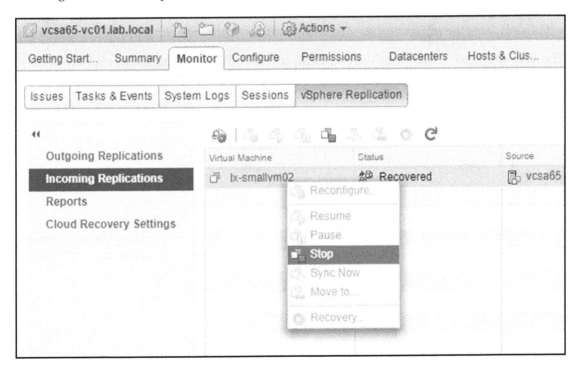

Figure 6.28: Disabling the virtual machine replication

Deploying a pair of vSphere Replication virtual appliances

As covered in the *Installing/configuring/upgrading vSphere Replication* section, you can deploy the first vSphere Replication appliance, referred to as VRMS, by selecting the following files located in the \bin directory in the mounted vSphere Replication ISO image:

- vSphere_Replication_OVF10.cert
- vSphere_Replication_OVF10.mf
- vSphere_Replication_OVF10.ovf
- vSphere_Replication-system.vmdk
- vSphere_Replication-support.vmdk

The installed appliance must be connected to the vCenter Server.

To support a larger number of virtual machines (scale up), you can also deploy the VRS, which only runs the replication service with the role of receiving replicas from source hosts.

The VRS appliance is deployed using the **Deploy OVF Template** option in vSphere Web Client and, from the \bin directory of the mounted vSphere Replication ISO image, you should select the following files:

- vSphere_Replication_AddOn_OVF10.cert
- vSphere_Replication_AddOn_OVF10.mf
- vSphere_Replication_AddOn_OVF10.ovf
- vSphere_Replication-system.vmdk
- vSphere_Replication-support.vmdk

You can deploy 1 VRMS appliance per vCenter Server instance and up to 9 VRS appliances per vCenter Server instance, providing a total of 10 appliances you can use as targets for replication.

Review questions

1. Which protocol is not supported in file-based backup?
    - A: FTP/FTPS
    - B: HTTP/HTTPS
    - C: SCP
    - D: TFTP

    D - See *Objective 6.1*

2. How is a VDP appliance deployed?
    - A: As an OVF/OVA
    - B: By running `Setup.exe` in the `/bin` folder in the ISO file
    - C: From the Update Manager
    - D: From vSphere Web Client **Home** | **VDP**

    A - See *Objective 6.2*

3. What is the maximum RPO you can configure in vSphere Replication?
    - A: 12 hours
    - B: 60 minutes
    - C: 24 hours
    - D: 5 minutes

    C - See *Objective 6.3*

4. What is the maximum supported number of VRS appliances per vCenter Server?
    - A: 5
    - B: 9
    - C: 10
    - D: 7

    B - See *Objective 6.3*

5. vSAN can be used by vSphere Replication as a destination datastore for replication.
    - A: True
    - B: False

A - See *Objective 6.3*

Summary

This chapter covered exam topics related to vCSA file-based backups (*Objective 6.1*) used to backup and restore the vCenter Server appliance, as well as the backup, recovery, and replication of virtual machines using VDP (*Objective 6.2*) and vSphere Replication (*Objective 6.3*). Chapter 7, *Troubleshoot a vSphere Deployment*, will cover the troubleshooting part of a virtual environment by providing a short overview of some topics and possible cases.

7
Troubleshoot a vSphere Deployment

This chapter will cover the approach and some tools that are used to troubleshoot a vSphere environment for performance or other issues.

Note that the basic install, configure, and manage course does not provide enough skill for this task, but there is a specific course that does (*VMware vSphere: Troubleshooting Workshop*).

The chapter focuses on analyzing different critical resources, such as computing, storage, and networking across the ESXi hosts, resource pools, and clusters.

Providing a complete troubleshooting approach is out of the scope of this book, and to pass the exam you can just learn the basics. Also, most troubleshooting skills come with practical experience in the field.

Practicing what you learn during this chapter is a key point so that you can enforce your skills and preparation for the exam. There are some VMware labs that are useful for this task, such as *HOL-1804-01-SDC*.

In this chapter, the reader will learn how to do the following:

- Troubleshoot vCenter Server
- Troubleshoot ESXi
- Troubleshoot VMs
- Troubleshoot cluster features

Objective 7.1 – Troubleshoot vCenter Server and ESXi hosts

Troubleshooting vCenter and ESXi hosts means analyzing different performance monitors, alerts, alarms, and log files. Most analysis can be performed with the vSphere Web Client, but sometimes you need direct access to ESXi or vCenter in order to collect logs or other specific information.

 Objective 7.1 for VCP65-DCV and VCP6-DCV are very similar just because there weren't big changes in the troubleshooting approach from vSphere 6.0 to vSphere 6.5. Just the first part of VCSA is new.

The vSphere 6.5 Troubleshooting guide contains in-depth information and examples, and can be found here: `https://docs.vmware.com/en/VMware-vSphere/6.5/vsphere-esxi-vcenter-server-651-troubleshooting-guide.pdf`.

Understanding the VCSA monitoring tool

You can monitor VCSA through the VAMI or the vSphere Web Client.

With VAMI, you can do the following:

- Reboot or shut down the appliance
- Upgrade or patch the appliance
- Create a vCenter Support Bundle
- Manage VCSA backup (as described in *Objective 6*)
- Check the health status of vCenter

The VAMI interface is quite simple:

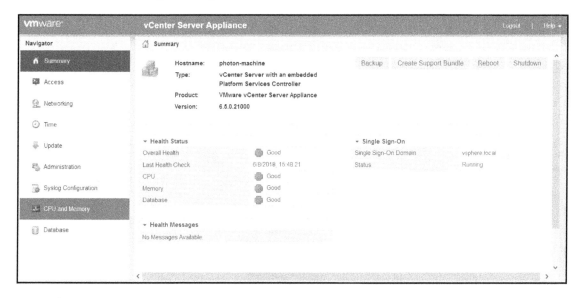

Figure 7.1: VAMI interface

With vSphere Web Client, you can check the alarms, events, and status of each service.

From the CLI, the VCSA provides a powerful monitor tool: `vimtop` (for more information, see this blog post: `https://virtualizationreview.com/articles/2018/04/03/ow-to-monitor-a-vcsa-using-vimtop.aspx`).

Monitoring status of the vCenter Server services

In the vSphere Web Client, you can view the health status of vCenter services and also for other nodes (including PSC).

You need an SSO admin privilege (as described in *Objective 1*) to do this. After you have acquired an SSO admin privilege, select the **Home** | **Administration** | **System Configuration** menu. You can also see the nodes and their status, as shown in the following screenshot:

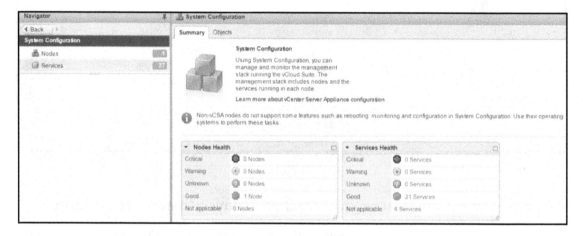

Figure 7.2: System Configuration—nodes and services

To include more details, you can also select the proper node and then click on the **Related Objects** tab:

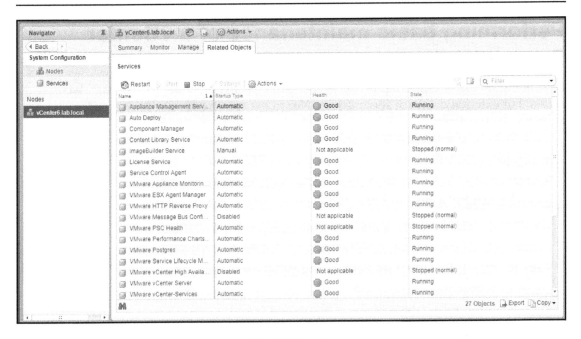

Figure 7.3: Node services

Each service is reported with a badge status as in the following table:

Badge icon	Description
	Good: The health of the object is normal
	Warning: The object is experiencing some problem
	Critical: The object is not functioning properly or will stop functioning soon
	Unknown: No data is available for this object

Table 7.1: Service status

To manage the different services, look at VMware KB 2109887 (`https://kb.vmware.com/s/article/2109887`)—Stopping, starting, or restarting VMware vCenter Server Appliance 6.x services.

Performing basic maintenance of a vCenter Server database

Depending on the vCenter deployment, you can have an embedded or external database server. For external database servers, just refer to the specific vendor's suggestions on how to manage the databases.

Usually, you have to perform some standard database maintenance processes, such as the following:

- Monitoring the growth of the database files, and compacting them as needed
- Backing up the database before any vCenter Server upgrade
- Scheduling regular backup tasks of the database

For the VCSA, an embedded database (PostgreSQL) is used and is auto-managed by VCSA, so no specific DB tasks are necessary.

You can monitor the database status using the VAMI:

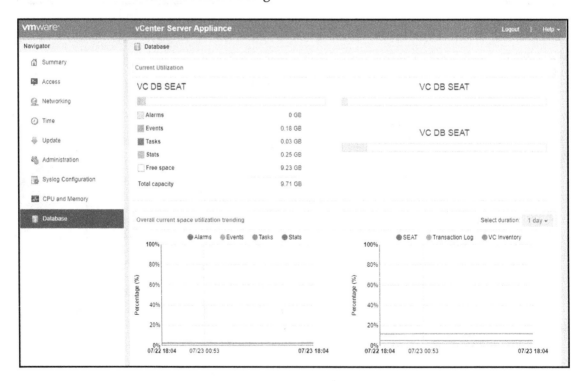

Figure 7.4: Database view in VAMI

For more information on this, go to `https://blogs.vmware.com/kb/2013/05/the-inside-scoop-maintenance-tips-for-your-vsphere-database.html`.

Monitoring status of ESXi management agents

You can monitor the ESXi services status in different ways: using the vSphere Web Client, using the host UI or other UIs, or with the CLI.

If you are using the vSphere Web Client, you will have a report like this:

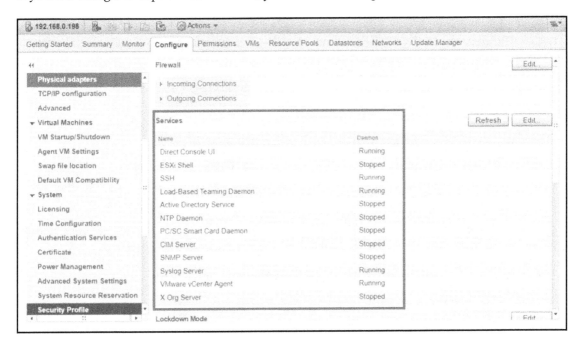

Figure 7.5: ESXi services

If you are using the host UI, you will have a report like this:

Figure 7.6: ESXi services

The colors that are used here are the same ones that we described previously for vCenter services.

TIP

From both UIs, you can also manage the services and try to restart them, but note that you cannot see all the services, as some are hidden in those interfaces.

From the DCUI, you can simply restart all the agent services, and this can be really useful in case of issues with the `vpxa` or `hostd` services (the first time it's used is by vCenter, the second time it's used is by the host UI).

To restart the services from the DCUI, connect to the console of the ESXi Host, press *F2* on the keyboard, and log in as the `root` user (or a user with admin privileges).

Choose the **Troubleshooting Options** | **Restart Management Agents** menu option, like so:

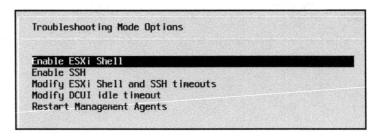

Figure 7.7: Restart management agents

For more information, see VMware KB 1003490 (`https://kb.vmware.com/s/article/1003490`)—Restarting the Management agents in ESXi.

Determining ESXi host stability issues and gather diagnostics information

There are several possible causes that can imply possible stability issues, and exploring all of them could be quite difficult. Sometimes, this depends on the type of services that are used.

But one of the most common issues that can cause the **ESXi Purple Screen of Death** (**PSOD**) is related to wrong drivers.

For more information, look at VMware KB 1007813 (https://kb.vmware.com/s/article/ 1007813)—Common ESX/ESXi host configuration issues which can cause virtual machines to become unresponsive.

Monitoring ESXi system health

ESXi uses the **Common Information Model** (**CIM**) to monitor the different hardware sensors. The ESXi health status can be monitored in the **Issues** and **Hardware Status** tabs.

The **Hardware Status** tab shows the health of a variety of host hardware components:

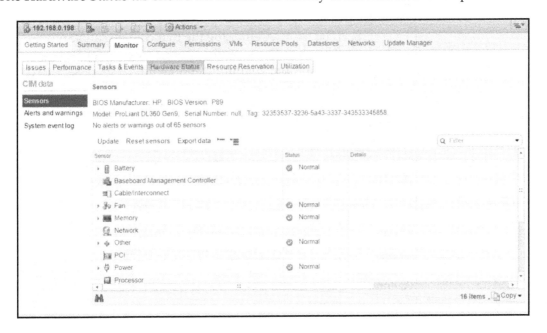

Figure 7.8: ESXi hardware sensors

Locating and analyze the vCenter Server and ESXi logs

VMware vSphere has different log files on the different infrastructural components.

For ESXi, the location of those logs is `/var/log/`.

For vCenter and PSC, the location depends on the deployment used:

- **Windows bases**: The log files will be located in `C:\ProgramData\VMware\VMware VirtualCenter\Logs`
- **VCSA**: The log files will be located in `/var/log/`

The log files also vary depending on the PSC deployment: there are some common log files, files specific to the PSC, and some files that are specific to the vCenter.

For more information on the log file's location, name, and content, see the vSphere 6.5 Troubleshooting guide (`https://docs.vmware.com/en/VMware-vSphere/6.5/com.vmware.vsphere.troubleshooting.doc/GUID-552CC9E8-441C-434A-88FC-3F50881245D7.html`).

Here is a short list of some log files:

Log file	Component	Description
`vpxd.log`	vCenter	The main vCenter log file that contains all vSphere Client and web services connections, internal tasks and events, and communication with the `vpxa` service on managed ESXi hosts.
`cim-diag.log` and `vws.log`	vCenter	The log file related to CIM monitoring information, including communication between the vCenter and all managed ESXi CIM interfaces.
`drmdump`	vCenter	The log file (in a compressed format) with all the actions proposed and actuated by the DRS, grouped by the DRS-enabled cluster that's managed by vCenter.
`vimtool.log`	vCenter	The log file with a dump of strings used during the vCenter's installation where information related to the DNS, username, and so on is hashed.
`stats.log`	vCenter	The log file that provides information about the historical performance data collected from the ESXi hosts.

sms.log	vCenter	The log file with the health reports for the Storage Monitoring Service extension, connectivity logs to vCenter Server, the vCenter Server database, and the xDB for vCenter Inventory Service.
eam.log	vCenter	The log file with the health reports for the ESX Agent Monitor extension and connectivity logs to vCenter Server.
auth.log	ESXi	The log file with all the ESXi Shell authentication successes and failures.
esxupdate.log	ESXi	The log file with a list of all ESXi patch and update installations.
lacp.log	ESXi	The log file related to LACP information.
hostd.log	ESXi	The log file about the host management service, which includes VM and ESXi tasks and events, communication with the vSphere Client and vpxa agent, or SDK connections.
usb.log	ESXi	The log file with USB device arbitration events, such as discovery and pass-through to VMs.
vobd.log	ESXi	The log file with VMkernel Observation events.
vmkernel.log	ESXi	The log file with Core VMkernel information, including device discovery, storage and networking device and driver events, and VMs startup.

Table 7.2

From the vSphere Web Client, you can see the vCenter log files. Just select the vCenter server (the root of each inventory), and go into the **Monitor** | **System Logs** tab:

Figure 7.9: vCenter log files

You can also export these files, which can be useful during VMware's technical support sessions.

VMware technical support may request diagnostic information from your infrastructure when a support request is handled. This diagnostic information contains product-specific logs, configuration files, and data appropriate to the situation.

Those collections of information are called the host support bundles (for ESXi) and vCenter Server support bundles.

 Note that data collected in a support bundle may be considered sensitive.

To generate ESXi and vCenter Server support bundles, in the previous window (*Figure 7.9*), do the following:

1. Click on the **Export System Logs** button.
2. Select the ESXi hosts from which you want to export the logs and, if you also need a vCenter bundle, select the **Include vCenter Server and vSphere Web Client logs** option.
3. Select **Gather performance data to include performance data information in the log files**. You can update the duration and reverse between which you want to collect the data.
4. When you click **Generate Log Bundle**, a ZIP file bundle containing the log files will be generated.

> For more information, see the VMware KB 653 (`https://kb.vmware.com/s/article/653`)—Collecting diagnostic information for VMware ESX/ESXi and KB 1011641 (`https://kb.vmware.com/s/article/1011641`)—Collecting diagnostic information for VMware vCenter Server 4.x, 5.x and 6.x.

Determining appropriate commands for troubleshooting

Troubleshooting using the CLI is quite difficult and require a lot of experience, but there are some local commands on ESXi that can help in this task:

- `esxtop`: Used for real-time ESXi performance monitoring
- `vmkping`: Useful for testing VMkernel adapter networking
- `esxcli`: Used to configure and monitor a lot of ESXi features (introduced in vSphere 5.0)
- `esxcfg-*`: A set of old commands that were used before vSphere 5.0, but some of them are still working today
- `vmkfstools`: Used to manage VMFS volumes and VMDK

For performance troubleshooting, see VMware KB 2001003 (`https://kb.vmware.com/s/article/2001003`)—Troubleshooting ESX/ESXi virtual machine performance issues.

Troubleshooting common ESXi/vCenter issues

There are several VMware KB articles that help with troubleshooting specific issues:

- **vCenter Server services**: Has already been discussed in the previous part of this chapter and also VMware KB 1003926 (`https://kb.vmware.com/s/article/1003926`)—Troubleshooting the vCenter Server service.
- **vCenter Server connectivity**: For a list of all required ports, see VMware KB 2106283 (`https://kb.vmware.com/s/article/2106283`)—Required ports for vCenter Server 6.x.
- **Platform Services Controller (PSC)**: See the VMware KB 2113115 (`https://kb.vmware.com/s/article/2113115`)—FAQ: VMware Platform Services Controller in vSphere 6.0.
- **Identity Sources**: See *Objective 1.1*.
- **vCenter Certification Authority**: See this blog post: `https://blogs.vmware.com/vsphere/2015/03/vmware-certificate-authority-overview-using-vmca-root-certificates-browser.html`
- **Virtual machine resource contention, configuration, and operation**: See VMware KB 1007819 (`https://kb.vmware.com/s/article/1007819`)—Troubleshooting a virtual machine that has stopped responding.
- **VMware Tools installation**: See VMware KB 1003908 (`https://kb.vmware.com/s/article/1003908`)—Troubleshooting a failed VMware Tools installation in a Guest Operating System.
- **Fault Tolerant network latency**: See VMware KB 1013428 (`https://kb.vmware.com/s/article/1013428`)—FAQ: VMware Fault Tolerance.
- **KMS connectivity**: See VMware KB 2147566 (`https://kb.vmware.com/s/article/2147566`)—Connect a vCenter Server System to a Key Management Server.
- **Problems with installation**: For AutoDeploy, see *Objective 8.1*, and for host profiles, see *Objective 8.2*.

For more information, see the vSphere 6.5 Troubleshooting guide (`https://docs.vmware.com/en/VMware-vSphere/6.5/com.vmware.vsphere.troubleshooting.doc/GUID-6F6CE545-58FA-490B-8C8A-3CB8196CAEA8.html`).

Objective 7.2 – Troubleshoot vSphere storage and networking

Troubleshooting storage and networking is usually more complex because they can be interconnected (for example, for IP-based storage) or the issue or the root cause could be completely outside the vSphere perimeter, such as in the storage fabric or in the network switches.

 Objective 7.2 for VCP65-DCV and VCP6-DCV are the same, just because there weren't big changes in the troubleshooting approach from vSphere 6.0 to vSphere 6.5.

The vSphere 6.5 Troubleshooting guide contains in-depth information and examples: `https://docs.vmware.com/en/VMware-vSphere/6.5/vsphere-esxi-vcenter-server-651-troubleshooting-guide.pdf.`

Identifying and isolating network and storage resource contention and latency issues

`Chapter 2`, *Configure and Administer vSphere 6.x Networking*, and `Chapter 3`, *Configure and Administer vSphere 6.x Storage*, already provided some information regarding storage or networking contention issues.

For the storage, the following are some possible problems:

Symptoms	Possible cause	Resolution
Slow ESXi storage performance on some operation on block storage	SCSI reservations that can lock the entire LUN and slow down some operation	Reduce the number of VMs per datastore and use storage with VAAI ATS
High storage latency peak on a SAN storage	Storage path thrashing or LUN trespass	Use the proper multipath policy
High command latency	LUN queue depth too big	Increase the queue depth on the adapter and VMs, following storage recommended practices

Table 7.3

To monitor storage performance, you can use the graph in the vSphere Web Client, but remember that most of those graphs are only in "real time" (you can change the stats level, but this will increase the database's used space). You can also use `esxtop` from the CLI to look at more information on the storage latency, as described in the following diagram:

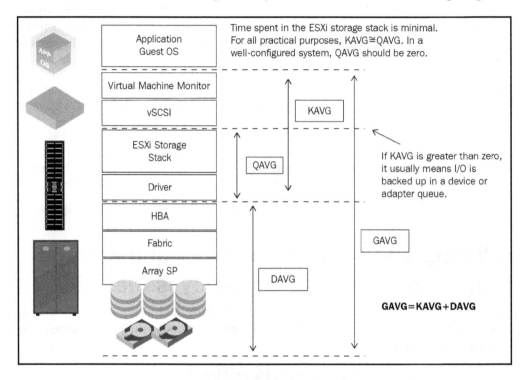

Figure 7.10: Storage latency

The most important parameters are as follows:

Disk Metric	Threshold	Description
DAVG	25	This is the average response time in milliseconds per command being sent to the device.
GAVG	25	This the response time as it is perceived by the guest operating system. This number is calculated with the formula DAVG + KAVG = GAVG.
KAVG	2	This is the amount of time the command spends in the VMKernel.

Table 7.4

To minimize storage latency and contention issues, you can use SIOC (see *Objective 3.5*).

For networking issues, latency could potentially be caused by one of the following infrastructure elements:

- External Switch throughput (usually not an issue with full speed switches)
- NIC configuration and bandwidth (1 G/10 G/40 G)
- ESXi CPU contention

To minimize network latency and contention issues, you can use NIOC (see *Objective 2.2*).

For more information, see the following sections of the vSphere 6.5 Troubleshooting guide:

- Resolving SAN Performance Problems (`https://docs.vmware.com/en/VMware-vSphere/6.5/com.vmware.vsphere.troubleshooting.doc/GUID-6A025132-6662-4A81-BFF5-775F2DA853F5.html`)
- Troubleshooting Storage Adapters (`https://docs.vmware.com/en/VMware-vSphere/6.5/com.vmware.vsphere.troubleshooting.doc/GUID-4B051670-531A-4CED-A048-B509A279C606.html`)

Verifyinging network and storage configuration

`Chapters 2`, *Configure and Administer vSphere 6.x Networking*, and `Chapter 3`, *Configure and Administer vSphere 6.x Storage*, have already provided several pieces of information on how to configure storage or networking, including how to check their configuration.

For more information, see the following sections of the vSphere 6.5 Troubleshooting guide:

- Resolving SAN Storage Display Problems (`https://docs.vmware.com/en/VMware-vSphere/6.5/com.vmware.vsphere.troubleshooting.doc/GUID-DA4A22C8-74C6-48C3-A20E-76BCB9FCDD71.html`)
- Software iSCSI Adapter Is Enabled When Not Needed (`https://docs.vmware.com/en/VMware-vSphere/6.5/com.vmware.vsphere.troubleshooting.doc/GUID-FF84B9AD-0C92-4E95-B947-CD1163CE9603.html`)
- Troubleshooting MAC Address Allocation (`https://docs.vmware.com/en/VMware-vSphere/6.5/com.vmware.vsphere.troubleshooting.doc/GUID-87366623-A211-4437-8AC2-563103279731.html`)
- Alarm for Loss of Network Redundancy on a Host (`https://docs.vmware.com/en/VMware-vSphere/6.5/com.vmware.vsphere.troubleshooting.doc/GUID-511D60CA-5AE2-427F-9DDB-CCEAFA2FE373.html`)

Verifying that a given virtual machine is configured with the correct network resources

Chapter 2, *Configure and Administer vSphere 6.x Networking*, provided some information on networking configuration, and for VMs, the most relevant aspects to consider are the vNIC type and the virtual switch configuration.

For recent OS's, the vmxnet3 adapter type is recommended (this is the same case if it isn't the default option for Windows OS).

For the virtual switch, you need to verify the proper port group configuration (and use the same name across the cluster), the teaming policy, the VLAN settings, the security settings, and so on.

For more information, see the following VMware KB:

- KB 1003893 (https://kb.vmware.com/s/article/1003893)—Troubleshooting virtual machine network connection issues
- KB 1007842 (https://kb.vmware.com/s/article/1007842)—Troubleshooting virtual machine TCP/IP connection issues

Monitoring/troubleshooting Storage Distributed Resource Scheduler (SDRS) issues

The SDRS may not work in some cases and will generate an alarm to indicate that it cannot operate.

There are different possible reasons why SDRS may not work on a datastore:

- **Datastore connected to an unsupported host**: SDRS is not supported on ESX/ESXi 4.1 and earlier hosts. Ensure that all hosts associated with the datastore cluster are ESXi 5.0 or later.
- **Datastore shared across multiple data centers**: This configuration is not supported by SDRS. When a datastore is shared across multiple data centers, SDRS I/O load balancing is disabled for the entire datastore cluster. However, SDRS space balancing remains active for all datastores that are not shared across data centers.
- The datastore is connected to a host that is not running SIOC.

But there are also some cases where SDRS may not work on a specific VM, for example:

- **Local VM's swap file**: The swap file is stored in a specified datastore that is on the host or it's not movable by SDRS
- **There is an independent disk**: Storage DRS is disabled, except in the case of relocation or clone placement
- The virtual machine is a template
- The virtual machine is vSphere Fault Tolerance-enabled

For more information, see the vSphere 6.5 Troubleshooting guide (`https://docs.vmware.com/en/VMware-vSphere/6.5/com.vmware.vsphere.troubleshooting.doc/GUID-142C5ED0-09E6-4EB3-BC7A-A93317E3156A.html`).

Recognizing the impact of network and storage I/O control configurations

As written in *Objective 2.2*, **Network I/O Control** (**NIOC**) provides vDS with a network QoS mechanism with shares, reservations, and limits.

You can create custom network resource pools for VMs traffic, but first, you need to reserve part of the traffic for them.

Note that, if you have NIOC v3 enabled with high-speed NICs (for example, 10 Gbps), you may not be able to add a low-speed NIC (for example, 1 Gbps) to the vDS if there are some bandwidth reservations. For more information, see the vSphere 6.5 Troubleshooting guide (`https://docs.vmware.com/en/VMware-vSphere/6.5/com.vmware.vsphere.troubleshooting.doc/GUID-13EA5047-CF81-472D-AAAA-98745A914126.html`).

Also, to guarantee that sufficient bandwidth is available for a VM, vSphere implements admission control at host and cluster levels based on the bandwidth reservation and teaming policy. For more information, see the vSphere 6.5 Networking guide (`https://docs.vmware.com/en/VMware-vSphere/6.0/com.vmware.vsphere.networking.doc/GUID-7B131191-D989-431A-99F7-BA3C27BD4F64.html`).

As written previously in *Objective 3.5*, **Storage I/O Control** (**SIOC**) allows cluster-wide storage QoS to manage proper I/O queue prioritization and provide storage shares, reservations, and limits. Note that virtual disk limits can also work without SIOC.

By default, all virtual machine disks have shares that are set to Normal (1,000) with unlimited IOPS. Storage I/O Control is enabled by default on Storage DRS-enabled datastore clusters.

Note that, with SIOC, you cannot have external workloads (for example, from another ESXi without SIOC connected to the same datastore). In this case, vCenter does not reduce the total amount of I/O sent to the array, but continues to enforce shares. See VMware KB 1020651 (https://kb.vmware.com/s/article/1020651)—Unmanaged workload is detected on datastore running SIOC for more information.

For more information on SIOC troubleshooting, see the vSphere 6.5 Troubleshooting guide (https://docs.vmware.com/en/VMware-vSphere/6.5/com.vmware.vsphere.troubleshooting.doc/GUID-BC5E7519-98B2-473D-B360-F01707106A71.html).

 Note that both NIOC and SIOC require the Enterprise Plus edition.

Recognizing a connectivity issue caused by a VLAN/PVLAN

Objective 2.1 describes virtual networking and also VLAN/PVLAN usage.

To avoid networking connectivity issues, verify the topology of the vDS and be sure that the VLAN IDs are assigned to all uplinks of the dvPort, both on the dvPort configuration and also on the physical switches.

Link discovery protocols such as CDP or LLDP can help verify the network topology. Also, the vDS health check feature can verify the proper VLAN (and MTU) configuration; for more information on this feature, see the VMware KB 2032878 (https://kb.vmware.com/s/article/2032878)—Enabling vSphere Distributed Switch health checks on the vSphere Web Client.

For PVLAN, be sure to learn the difference between promiscuous, community, and isolated PVLANs before try to implement a solution based on them.

For more information on troubleshooting VM connectivity issues, see the vSphere 6.5 Troubleshooting guide (https://docs.vmware.com/en/VMware-vSphere/6.5/com.vmware.vsphere.troubleshooting.doc/GUID-5324A0E4-AA7B-40CC-A975-D45328B5C434.html).

Troubleshooting common storage and networking issues

Troubleshooting storage and networking usually means analyzing the physical infrastructure. For IP-based storage, this also means correlating data because a network issue can mean a storage issue.

For networking, several problems can come from incorrect teaming configuration, especially for IP hash or LACP, where a proper configuration at physical switches is also needed.

For more information, see the following VMware KB:

- KB 1001938 (https://kb.vmware.com/s/article/1001938)—Host requirements for link aggregation for ESXi and ESX
- KB 1004048 (https://kb.vmware.com/s/article/1004048)—Sample configuration of EtherChannel/**Link Aggregation Control Protocol (LACP)** with ESXi/ESX and Cisco/HP switches

For a more general approach to networking troubleshooting, see VMware KB 1003893 (https://kb.vmware.com/s/article/1003893)—Troubleshooting virtual machine network connection issues.

For storage, there is too much to talk depending on the storage type, vendors, the used frontend protocols, and so on, but the exam guide suggests a specific topic: VMFS metadata consistency.

The VMware KB 2036767 (https://kb.vmware.com/s/article/2036767)—Using **vSphere On-disk Metadata Analyzer (VOMA)** to check VMFS metadata consistency explains how to use the VOMA tool to perform checks on the VMFS filesystem.

Basically, the command that can be used for this is as follows:

```
# voma -m vmfs -f check -d /vmfs/devices/disks/naa.Disk_ID:Partition#
```

Objective 7.3 – Troubleshooting vSphere Upgrades and Migrations

VMware vSphere upgrades were described in Chapter 4, *Upgrade a vSphere Deployment to 6.x*, and most of the issues can be prevented by following the proper documentation, best practices, KB articles, and compatibility matrix.

 Objective 7.3 for VCP65-DCV and VCP6-DCV are similar. It should be noted that the title has changed because there weren't big changes regarding the troubleshooting approach from vSphere 6.0 to vSphere 6.5.

The vSphere 6.5 Upgrade guide contains more information on this: https://docs.vmware.com/en/VMware-vSphere/6.5/vsphere-esxi-vcenter-server-652-upgrade-guide.pdf.

Collecting upgrade diagnostic information

For VCSA, you can collect diagnostic information with the vc-support.sh script, as described in VMware KB 1011641 (https://kb.vmware.com/s/article/1011641)—Collecting diagnostic information for VMware vCenter Server 4.x, 5.x, and 6.x.

Also, if the installation or the upgrade process fails, the setup interrupted page appears, with the log collection checkboxes selected by default.

The installation files are collected in a .zip file on your desktop, with the following syntax:

```
VMware-VCS-logs-TIMESTAMP.zip
```

Here, TIMESTAMP displays the year, month, date, hour, minutes, and seconds of the installation attempt.

For ESXi, you can use the vm-support command, as described in the VMware KB 1010705 (https://kb.vmware.com/s/article/1010705) (vm-support command in ESX/ESXi to collect diagnostic information).

 For more information, see the VMware vSphere 6.5 Installation guide (https://docs.vmware.com/en/VMware-vSphere/6.5/com.vmware.vsphere.install.doc/GUID-0F24A762-F7AE-4B8F-A433-FDD226AB8408.html).

Recognizing common upgrade and migration issues with vCenter Server and vCenter Server Appliances

Be sure to plan the upgrade or migration process carefully by verifying the hardware and software compatibility matrix.

Also, check the VMware KB 2147548 (`https://kb.vmware.com/s/article/2147548`)—Important information before upgrading to vSphere 6.5 for more information on this.

Note that the installation or upgrade process runs a precheck script to verify some conditions as well asto try to identify possible issues before starting the process.

If there is an issue during the interactive installation, upgrade, or migration process, the errors or warnings are displayed on the final panel of the installer. For a scripted process, the errors or warnings are written to the installation log file.

Creating/locating VMware log bundles

Objective 7.1 has already covered the log file's locations and how to collect VMware log bundles.

For ESXi hosts managed by vCenter, logs can be exported with the vSphere Web Client.

For standalone ESXi hosts, you can use VMware KB 653 (`https://kb.vmware.com/s/article/653`)—Collecting diagnostic information for VMware ESX/ESXi.

Determining alternative methods to upgrade ESXi hosts in the event of a failure

In case of any issues during the host upgrade phase, there are different methods that can be used to finalize an upgrade (but note that all of them may fail):

- **Interactive upgrade**: You can boot with the ESXi 6.5 installer and perform an interactive upgrade process.
- **Scripting upgrade**: Similar to the scripted installation, this can be used to perform an unattended upgrade. This can be used for multiple hosts.

- **CLI upgrade**: You can use the `esxcli` command and the upgrade bundle to perform a host upgrade via the command line.
- **VUM upgrade**: You can use VUM to perform an unattended upgrade of ESXi hosts.

Another option is to just perform a new reinstallation from scratch and use host profiles to reapply the host configuration.

Configuring vCenter Server logging options

The vCenter Server logs can be set with a different level of detail. To change this level, just use the vSphere Web Client with administrative privileges, select the vCenter Server and, in the **Configure** tab, choose the **Settings** | **General** menu and click on the **Edit...** button:

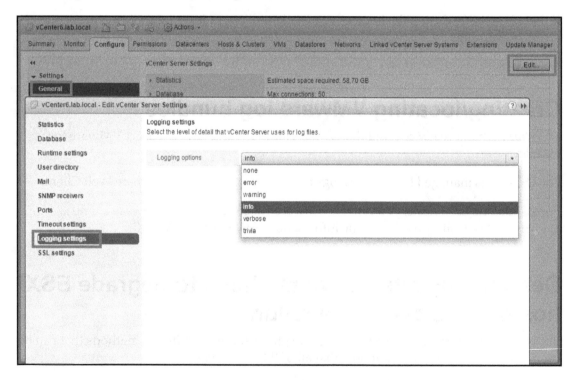

Figure 7.11: vCenter log settings

Choose the proper level from the **Logging options** drop-down menu.

The available log levels are as follows:

- **none (Disable Logging)**: Turns off all logging
- **error (Errors Only)**: Displays only error log entries
- **warning (Errors and Warnings)**: Displays warning and error log entries
- **info (Normal Logging – Default)**: Displays information, error, and warning log entries
- **verbose (Verbose)**: Displays information, error, warning, and verbose log entries
- **trivia (Extended Verbose)**: Displays information, error, warning, verbose, and trivia log entries

For more information, see the vSphere 6.5 Configuring Host and vCenter guide (`https://docs.vmware.com/en/VMware-vSphere/6.5/com.vmware.vsphere.vcenterhost.doc/GUID-0439D577-66F7-4584-AF05-5EB41A761873.html`).

Objective 7.4 – Troubleshooting virtual machines

VM troubleshooting in most cases means configuration checks on the VM's health or performance analysis. However, there can be several other possible issues, such as wrong drivers, wrong VMware Tools versions, virtual hardware options, and so on.

Objective 7.4 for VCP65-DCV and VCP6-DCV are similar. The title has also changed because there weren't big changes in the troubleshooting approach from vSphere 6.0 to vSphere 6.5. The part on how to troubleshoot virtual machine performance with vRealize Operations has been removed.

The vSphere 6.5 Troubleshooting guide contains in-depth information and examples on this topic: `https://docs.vmware.com/en/VMware-vSphere/6.5/vsphere-esxi-vcenter-server-651-troubleshooting-guide.pdf`.

Monitoring CPU and memory usage

For each VM, you can generate several performance graphs with different sets of counters.

For CPU, the default graph reports the overall CPU usage of the VM (both in MHz and in percentage).

However, you can change the settings in the **Monitor** | **Performance** tab, just by clicking on the **Chart Options** link:

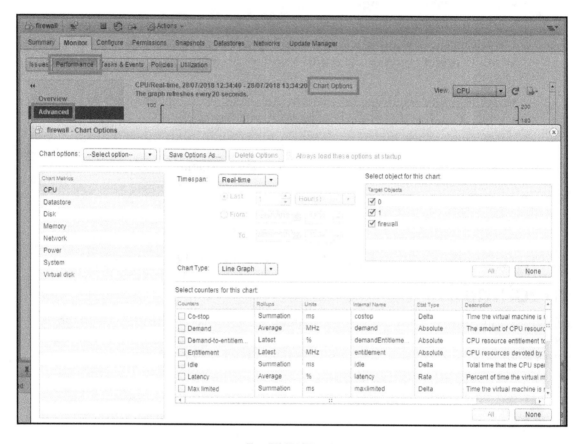

Figure 7.12: VM CPU graph

You can also monitor every single virtual CPU (for example, to see how multi-processing is working) instead of having to aggregate values for the entire VM. This is the behavior of the default **CPU** graph.

For VM memory, the default **Memory** graph shows the active, consumed, granted, and ballooned memory of the VM:

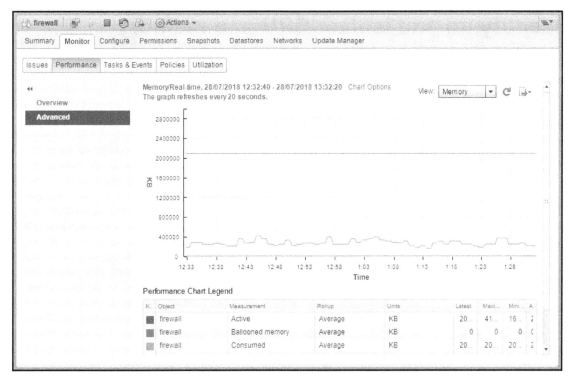

Figure 7.13: VM Memory graph

You can still change the counters using the **Chart Options** link.

For both CPU and Memory graphs, you can also choose a specific time period, but the farther you go, the fewer details you can gain.

For more information, see the vSphere 6.5 Monitoring and Performance guide (`https://docs.vmware.com/en/VMware-vSphere/6.5/com.vmware.vsphere.monitoring.doc/GUID-AA1F733C-1450-4437-AB0A-E5FA24CC386E.html`).

Identifying and isolate CPU and memory contention issues

VM contention issues appear when resource overprovisioning occurs, for example, at a specific time when there are too many running VMs with the total number of virtual cores bigger than the number of the host's physical cores.

In the case of CPU contentions, the primary counter to check is not the CPU usage. In the case of "low" CPU usage, you can have high CPU contentions and probably low VM performance.

The main counter to check is **Ready Time**, which measures the time that a VM was ready and waiting to be scheduled by the ESXi. With high CPU overprovisioning and contention, this value can increase, making the VM slow (it takes too long to run).

In a perfect world, the ready time would be zero, but in a virtualized world, this value is usually greater than zero and, until it's not too big, can be acceptable.

There are different ways to monitor a VM's ready time, but the best way is to use the esxtop command on each ESXi, and short the view on the ready time column using the *R* key. You can use the *V* key to limit the list an select only the running VM:

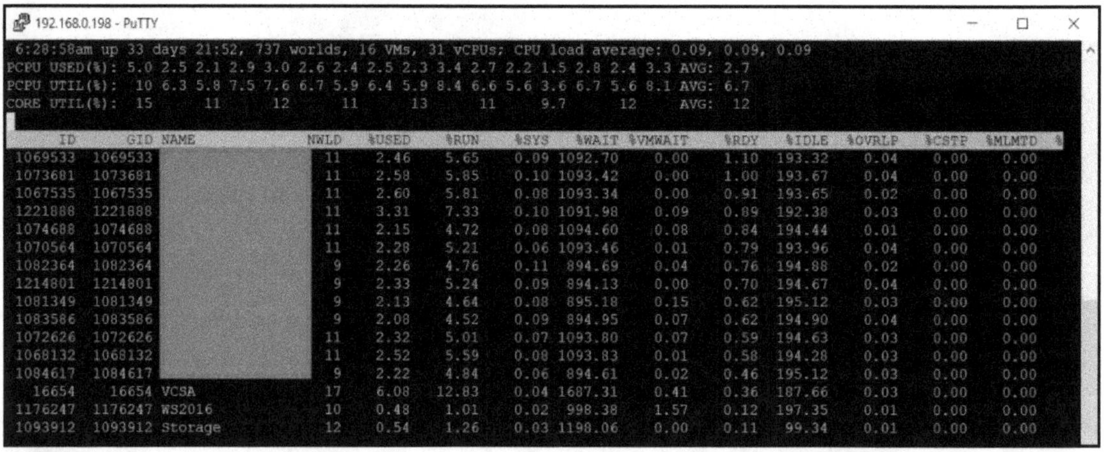

Figure 7.14: VM's ready time

Ready time values under the 5% mark could be considered acceptable. Values between 5% and 10% could be indicative of an oversubscribed host or a misconfigured VM (for example, too much vCPU), while greater than 10% usually means low overall performance.

For a VM's memory, there can be contention when the overall allocated memory exceeds the physical memory. This can be bad, considering that memory is overcommitted by default.

However, you need to monitor and check different memory parameters to ensure that there aren't any memory contention issues. The main parameters that you need to check are active memory, ballooning, and swapping. Of course, there are several other parameters that can be monitored so that you can identify possible memory contentions (see the Understanding Memory Management in VMware vSphere 5 document for more details (`https://www.vmware.com/content/dam/digitalmarketing/vmware/en/pdf/techpaper/mem_mgmt_perf_vsphere5.pdf`)).

The active memory could be something interesting to look into so that you can find which VM has a high memory usage, but for troubleshooting, high values in ballooning or swapping usually mean high memory contentions and potentially also an increasing level of storage I/O (both imply that disk is used instead of physical RAM).

In a perfect world, those two counters should be zero, but in a virtualized world, it could be acceptable have a small value, maybe during memory peaks.

 Note that only the ballooning value is shown in the default VM's memory graph. For the swap value, you need to customize the graph.

Depending on the memory state, ESXi uses different memory reclamation techniques, and are presented in the following table:

Memory state	High	Clear	Soft	Hard	Low
Memory threshold		<100% of minFree	<64% of minFree	<32% of minFree	<16% of minFree
Transparent Page Sharing (TPS)	Normal TPS cycle	ESXi actively calls TPS to collapse pages	X	X	X
Ballooning			X		
Compression				X	X
Swapping				X	X

Table 7.5

Note that "minFree" is a dynamic value and depends on the ESXi host's memory configuration:

- For the first 28 GB of physical RAM in the ESXi Host: minFree = 899 MB
- + Add 1 percent of the remaining RAM to your calculation

You can find several resources on this topic, such as the VMware KB 2001003 (`https://kb.vmware.com/s/article/2001003`)—Troubleshooting ESX/ESXi virtual machine performance issues.

> Remember that the ESXi also needs some physical memory (usually more than 2 GB). Instead, the CPU consumed by ESXi in most cases could be considered minimal and not relevant for the overall considerations.

Recognizing the impact of using CPU/memory limits, reservations, and shares

ESXi can manage CPU and memory resources with three specific parameters that can change the priority or the effective amount of resources assigned to a VM:

- **Limits**: This is the maximum set of resources assignable to a VM. Note that there is an implicit limit for each VM, defined by the number of virtual cores and the amount of the virtual RAM configured for the VM.
- **Reservations**: This is the minimum set of resources guaranteed for a VM. For the memory, it's also possible to flag the "reserve all guest memory" option to pre-allocate the entire VM's memory.
- **Shares**: This is the priority of the resources, and each VM has an implicit priority depending on the configured resources. Shares are only applied and honored during resource contention.

For more information about resource allocation, see `Chapter 5`, *Administer and Manage vSphere 6.x Resources*.

Using limits, reservation, or shares in a wrong way can limit the ESXi resource allocation and cause performance issues.

Usually, it's not recommended to use a VM's specific limits or reservations, so it may be better to work with shares or use resource pools instead of setying specific VM resources.

Note that vSphere HA admissions control or vSphere DRS (see *Objective 7.5*) can also limit the resource allocation.

Describing and differentiate critical performance metrics

For CPU and memory, we have already commented on the most important performance metrics.

For CPU, this can be another useful parameter (%CSTP) to measure how multi-CPU or multi-core VMs are working and distributing the load on the different resources.

For storage, the latency could be the first parameter to check. See *Objective 7.2* for more information on the different types of latencies that are available.

The default VM virtual disk graphs show, for each virtual disk, the read and write latencies:

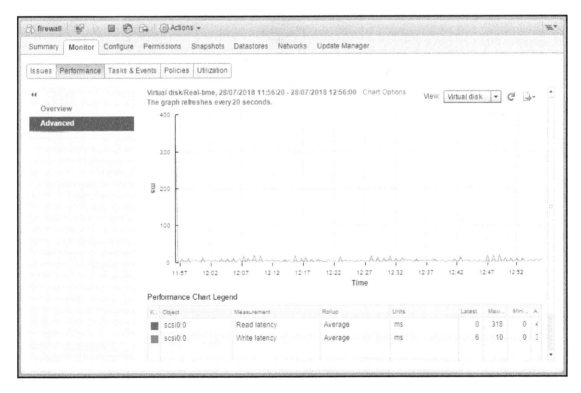

Figure 7.15: VM storage latencies graphs

The `esxtop` command can provide more information and more metrics, for example, the size of the storage queue.

For the network, usually, the throughput is the first metric. However, details about the packet errors, retransmissions, and so on can also be useful.

Describing and differentiate common metrics

As we stated previously, vCenter provides several default graphs for the VM and also for the ESXi objects with a lot of different metrics.

The most important metrics have already been discussed, but for more information see the vSphere 6.5 Monitoring and Performance guide (`https://docs.vmware.com/en/VMware-vSphere/6.5/com.vmware.vsphere.monitoring.doc/GUID-FF7F87C7-91E7-4A2D-88B5-E3E04A76F51B.html`).

It would be even more interesting to understand how data is collected and stored on vCenter.

Historical data can have different levels of details, depending on the vCenter Server settings (which can be found under **Configure** | **Statistics**):

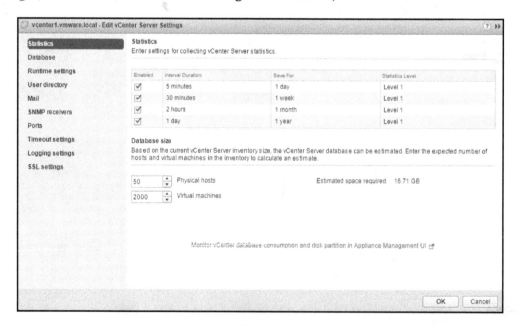

Figure 7.16: vCenter Server statistics

The collection level determines the number of counters for which data is gathered during each collection interval. The default level (1) limits some historical data, especially for storage and networking. Increasing the collection level will also increase the vCenter database size.

The collection interval determines the time period during which statistics are aggregated, calculated, rolled up, and archived in the vCenter Server database. Changing the collection interval will also change the vCenter database size.

Together, the collection interval and collection level determine how much statistical data is collected and stored in your vCenter Server database.

The following table shows the default configuration of the collection intervals:

Interval	Configuration
Past day	5 minute intervals that are kept for 1 day
Past week	30 minute intervals that are kept for 1 week
Past month	2 hour intervals that are kept for 1 month
Past year	1 day intervals that are kept for 1 year

Table 7.6

Note that the highest disk latency metric can be analyzed with the default VM disk graph. You can also do this for historical data without increasing the collection level.

Monitoring performance through esxtop

As we already discussed, the `esxtop` command can be used to gather some useful metrics directly from an ESXi host.

The syntax of this command is as follows:

```
esxtop [-h] [-v] [-b] [-s] [-a] [-c config file] [-R vm-support_dir_path]
[-d delay] [-n iterations]
```

For more details on all of the available options, see the VMware KB 1008205 (https://kb.vmware.com/s/article/1008205)—Using `esxtop` to identify storage performance issues for ESX/ESXi (multiple versions).

Using interactive mode is quite easy and there are some useful keyboard commands, as follows:

- *q*: Quits the interactive mode
- *h* **or** *?*: Displays a help menu for the current panel, giving a brief summary of commands and the status of secure mode
- **Space**: Immediately updates the current panel
- *f* **or** *F*: Displays a panel for adding or removing statistics columns (textboxes) to or from the current panel
- *o* **or** *O*: Displays a panel for changing the order of statistics columns on the current panel
- *c*: Switches to the CPU resource utilization panel
- *p*: Switches to the CPU power utilization panel
- *m*: Switches to the memory resource utilization panel
- *d*: Switches to the storage (disk) adapter resource utilization panel
- *u*: Switches to storage (disk) device resource utilization screen
- *v*: Switches to storage (disk) virtual machine resource utilization screen
- *n*: Switches to the network resource utilization panel

Troubleshooting Enhanced vMotion Compatibility (EVC) issues

Before performing a VM migration operation, vCenter performs compatibility checks to ensure that the VM or the host or other resources are compatible with the destination.

For vMotion migration, to ensure that the running state of a VM can be migrated between two different ESXi, the target CPU must provide the same instructions to the source CPU.

Only the processor instruction set is relevant; the clock speed, the cache size, and the number of cores can be different.

To improve compatibility between different physical server models (for example, old and new generations), it's possible to hide some host CPU features from the VM by using a specific vSphere cluster feature: **Enhanced vMotion Compatibility** (**EVC**).

EVC automatically configures server CPUs with Intel FlexMigration or AMD-V Extended Migration technologies so that they are compatible with older servers.

However, with EVC enabled, the processors must be in the same vendor class (AMD or Intel) to ensure vMotion compatibility.

For more information, see the VMWare KB 1003212 (`https://kb.vmware.com/s/article/1003212`)—**Enhanced vMotion Compatibility (EVC)** processor support.

Comparing and contrast the Overview and Advanced Charts

VMware vCenter provides two different sets of graphs:

- **The overview performance charts**: These display the most common metrics for an object in the inventory. Use these charts to monitor and troubleshoot performance problems.
- **The advanced charts**: These display detailed metrics and also permit the building of customized charts.

For more information about the overview performance charts, see the vSphere 6.5 Monitoring and Performance guide (`https://docs.vmware.com/en/VMWare-vSphere/6.5/com.vmware.vsphere.monitoring.doc/GUID-FF7F87C7-91E7-4A2D-88B5-E3E04A76F51B.html`).

Objective 7.5 – Troubleshoot HA and DRS configurations and Fault Tolerance

The vSphere HA and DRS troubleshooting topics provide solutions to potential problems that you might encounter when using those specific vSphere cluster functions.

Note that vSphere FT is related to vSphere HA and, generally, it's related to the availability topic, but it's a function at VM level.

Objective 7.5 for VCP65-DCV and VCP6-DCV are the same since there weren't big changes in the troubleshooting approach from vSphere 6.0 to vSphere 6.5.

The vSphere 6.5 Troubleshooting guide contains in-depth information and examples on this topic: `https://docs.vmware.com/en/VMware-vSphere/6.5/vsphere-esxi-vcenter-server-651-troubleshooting-guide.pdf`.

Troubleshooting common HA and DRS issues

It's really important to understand the requirements for vSphere HA and vSphere DRS first:

- **License**: All hosts must be licensed for vSphere HA (Essential Plus or greater) or vSphere DRS (Enterprise plus).
- **Cluster nodes**: For vSphere HA, you need at least two hosts in the cluster.
- **Network configuration**: For vSphere HA, each ESXi must maintain the same IP addresses for the management network (used by default by vSphere HA, except in VSAN's case, where the VSAN VMkernel adapter is used). Also, the network must be redundant (with more than one uplink in the virtual switch, or more VMkernel adapters on different virtual switches).
  For VM networks, to ensure that any VM can run on any host in the cluster, all hosts should have access to the same virtual machine networks.
- **Shared storage**: To ensure that any VM can run on any host in the cluster, all hosts should have access to the same datastores. For vSphere HA, at least two different shared datastores are recommended.
- **Processor compatibility**: For vSphere DRS, CPU of both the source and destination host must be compatible, as described in *Objective 7.4* in the EVC section.
- **vMotion requirements**: For vSphere DRS, there are several other requirements related to the vMotion feature. Note that enhanced vMotion (without shared storage) or cross vCenter vMotion are not used by vSphere DRS.
- **VMware Tools**: For vSphere HA VM Monitoring, VMware Tools must be installed.

For more information, see the following sections of the vSphere 6.5 Troubleshooting guide:

- Troubleshooting Availability (`https://docs.vmware.com/en/VMware-vSphere/6.5/com.vmware.vsphere.troubleshooting.doc/GUID-A20072AD-0B6C-4FB1-AD6F-EA68AE8F8CCF.html`)
- Troubleshooting Storage DRS (`https://docs.vmware.com/en/VMware-vSphere/6.5/com.vmware.vsphere.troubleshooting.doc/GUID-142C5ED0-09E6-4EB3-BC7A-A93317E3156A.html`)

HA configuration

vSphere HA configuration will be described in `Chapter 9`, *Configure and Administer vSphere and vCenter Availability Solutions*, with several details on the requirements, host states, monitoring options, and so on.

Other aspects of vSphere HA related to the storage part (such as VMCP) have already been described in `Chapter 3`, *Configure and Administer vSphere 6.x Storage*.

You will have a summary of the vSphere HA configuration and its status in the **Monitor** | **vSphere HA** tab of the cluster:

Figure 7.17: vSphere HA monitoring

For more information, see the vSphere 6.5 Troubleshooting guide regarding the different sections:

- Troubleshooting vSphere HA Host States (`https://docs.vmware.com/en/VMware-vSphere/6.5/com.vmware.vsphere.troubleshooting.doc/GUID-DF7CEF44-98EC-458A-8614-50CCAEC0A7C5.html`)
- Troubleshooting Heartbeat Datastores (`https://docs.vmware.com/en/VMware-vSphere/6.5/com.vmware.vsphere.troubleshooting.doc/GUID-6A3DC483-55F8-43F5-90A2-8C1F5F1EE09D.html`)
- Troubleshooting VM Component Protection (`https://docs.vmware.com/en/VMware-vSphere/6.5/com.vmware.vsphere.troubleshooting.doc/GUID-21D4E343-3753-4886-B654-1D2F4027BAF5.html`)

HA Admission Control

Admission control is a specific vSphere HA configuration option used to ensure that there are always enough free resources in a vSphere HA cluster. Those resources are reserved for a VM's recovery in the event of host failure.

When admission control is enabled, you may have some possible issues:

- **At cluster level**: The cluster status might become invalid (red) due to insufficient failover resources. This problem could occur when hosts in the cluster are disconnected, in maintenance mode, not responding, or have a vSphere HA error.
- **At VM level**: You might get a *not enough failover resources* fault when trying to power on a virtual machine in a vSphere HA cluster. This prevents you from powering on a VM if allocated resources violate the reserved resourced for HA.

For more information, see the vSphere 6.5 Troubleshooting guide (`https://docs.vmware. com/en/VMware-vSphere/6.5/com.vmware.vsphere.troubleshooting.doc/GUID-A20072AD- 0B6C-4FB1-AD6F-EA68AE8F8CCF.html`).

HA networking

In a vSphere HA cluster, the network communications, by default, are through the ESXi VMkernel Management adapters.

Network path redundancy between ESXi nodes is important for vSphere HA reliability, and is highly recommended (but for the production environment, we can consider it a requirement).

As we stated previously, one way to implement network redundancy is at the virtual switch level with more physical uplink and the use of the NIC teaming feature (see `Chapter 2`, *Configure and Administer vSphere 6.x Networking*). The recommended parameter settings for the VMkernel adapter used by HA are as follows:

- Default load balancing = route based on originating port ID
- Failback = No

An alternative way to provide HA network redundancy is to create another management VMkernel adapter that's connected to a different virtual switch.

Note that you must reconfigure vSphere HA on each ESXi if you change the network redundancy settings.

Another interesting aspect of vSphere HA networking is the network isolation address used to identify if a host can reach the other hosts or not and avoid the split brain scenario. By default, it's the default gateway for the host, and the ICMP protocols are used to test the isolation address (this means that the default gateway must be pingable). You can use the **das.isolationaddressX** advanced option to add other isolation addresses.

DRS configuration

The vSphere DRS feature was described in Chapter 5, *Administer and Manage vSphere 6.x Resources*, and its configuration is usually quite simple. However, using too many DRS rules (anti-affinity or affinity) may reduce the effectiveness of DRS or the ESXi resource scheduler.

You will have a summary of the vSphere DRS's configuration and status in the **Monitor | vSphere DRS** tab of the cluster.

DRS workload balancing

DRS clusters may become imbalanced or overcommitted for several reasons:

- A cluster might become overcommitted in the case of a host failure.
- A cluster becomes invalid if vCenter is unavailable and you power on VMs using the ESXi host UI or other direct host tools that bypass vCenter Server. When vCenter becomes available again, the cluster will turn red or yellow because cluster requirements are no longer met.
- A cluster becomes invalid if the user reduces the reservation on a parent resource pool while a VM is in the process of failing over.

Fault Tolerance configuration

The **VMware Fault Tolerance (vSphere FT)** feature has totally changed starting with ESXi version 6.0, and now supports multiprocessor VMs.

The requirements have also changed:

- **License requirements**: At least the Standard edition (max 2 vCPU), or even better, the Enterprise Plus edition (max 4 vCPU).
- **CPU requirements**: Physical CPUs must be compatible with EVC, but also similar in speed to avoid VM slowdown. CPUs must support hardware MMW virtualization (Intel EPT or AMD RVI). Used CPU resources are doubled.
- **Memory requirements**: No more than 64 GB for VMs. The used memory is doubled.
- **Network requirements**: Use a dedicated 10 GB network for the VMkernel adapter with the FT logging service.
- **Storage requirements**: A shared datastore for some common files, but also different locations (not necessary on shared datastores) for the other VM's files. Each VMDK cannot be greater than 2 TB. The VMDK used space is doubled.
- **Host limitations**: No more than 4 VMs with vSphere FT per host, or no more than 8 virtual CPUs (associated to VMs protected with vSphere FT) per host.

While FT provides a higher level of availability, there are some features that are not supported with FT-enabled VMs:

- Virtual machine snapshots, but it's possible to have VM snapshots managed by native backup programs
- Storage vMotion
- **VM Component Protection (VMCP)**
- Linked clones
- **Virtual SAN (VSAN)** with a stretched cluster
- Virtual Volume datastores
- I/O filters

For more information about vSphere FT, see the vSphere 6.5 Availability guide (`https://docs.vmware.com/en/VMware-vSphere/6.5/com.vmware.vsphere.avail.doc/GUID-7525F8DD-9B8F-4089-B020-BAA4AC6509D2.html`).

Explaining the DRS Resource Distribution Graph and Target/Current Host Load Deviation

We have already described that the monitor tab (see *Figure 7.18*) provides some information about the DRS configuration, with CPU, memory, and networking metrics for each host in the cluster.

But in the **Summary** tab of a vSphere cluster, you can also find another DRS chart that can show you how the cluster is balanced:

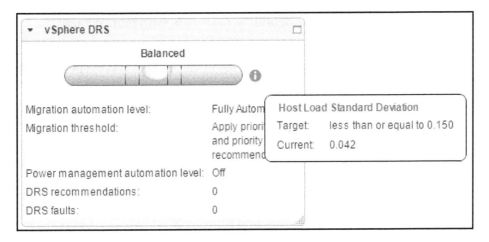

Figure 7.18: vSphere DRS distribution graph

 The target and current host load deviation is a representation of the balance of resources across the hosts in the vSphere cluster. Also, remember that the DRS process runs every 5 minutes (so it's not a real-time process).

Explaining vMotion Resource Maps

This seems a totally unneccesary section, related to the older versions of VMware vSphere products.

A resource map provides a visual representation of hosts, datastores, and networks associated with the selected virtual machine.

But those maps were only accessible with the legacy vSphere Client (C# Windows client), which is no longer available in vSphere 6.5!

The vMotion resource map indicates which hosts in the virtual machine's cluster or datacenter are compatible with the virtual machine and are potential migration targets.

What is missing

The official VCP65-DCV Exam Preparation Guide covers a lot of security topics, but the vSphere 6.5 Troubleshooting guide is definitely more rich, with more content.

For example, there are several missing parts, such as some possible examples of wrong VMs configuration, not related to the allocated resources, but related to specific VMware functions (for example, device passthrough).

Also, some common issues are totally ignored, like the way you recover Orphaned Virtual Machines (`https://docs.vmware.com/en/VMware-vSphere/6.5/com.vmware.vsphere.troubleshooting.doc/GUID-BFD8C9BC-30FB-4A92-AFEC-2FC9FF387920.html`).

The VMware vSphere: Troubleshooting Workshop course is recommended so that you can learn more about these specific tasks.

> For the VCP-DCV exam, you just need basic knowledge. Deeper knowledge will be useful for the VCAP exams that are related to the DCV path.

For performance aspects, see the Performance Best Practices for VMware vSphere 6.5 guide (`https://www.vmware.com/content/dam/digitalmarketing/vmware/en/pdf/techpaper/performance/Perf_Best_Practices_vSphere65.pdf`).

Review questions

For more questions, see `Chapter 11`, *Mock Exam 1*, and `Chapter 12`, *Mock Exam 2*:

1. A VM has configured more virtual RAM than the available ESX physical RAM. Other VM memory-related settings are with default values. Is it possible to power on this VM?
    - A: Yes
    - B: No

   A - See *Objective 7.4*

2. On a specific VM, vSphere FT could be enabled. Which could be a possible cause of this?
    - A: Guest is operating Windows Server 2003
    - B: VM configured memory is 128 GB
    - C: VMware Tools are not installed
    - D: VMware Tools are not updated

    B - See *Objective 7.5*

Summary

This chapter is dedicated to the troubleshooting part of a virtual environment, but only provides a short overview of some topics and possible cases. Real-world troubleshooting could be quite difficult and complex and requires a lot of experience.

Chapter 8, *Deploy and Customize ESXi Hosts*, and objective will provide information on how to deploy and customize ESXi hosts.

8
Deploy and Customize ESXi Hosts

One of the main tasks required during the vSphere environment implementation is the deployment of the ESXi hosts. Depending on the size of the environment to configure, there are different deployment methods available to successfully deploy the required components.

This chapter will cover the ESXi host deployment procedure using the Auto Deploy and Host Profiles features available in vSphere 6.5 to speed up and optimize the deployments, thereby especially in large environments, simplifying the overall management. As you will see, it is extremely important to understand the components involved and their configuration.

 As suggested several times in earlier chapters, practicing what you read throughout the chapter will help you to remember the concepts and understand the information you may find in the exam questions.

In this chapter, we will be studying the following:

- Installing and configuring Auto Deploy
- Deploying multiple ESXi hosts using Auto Deploy
- Creating/editing/removing a host profile from an ESXi host
- Importing/exporting a host profile
- Attaching and applying a host profile to ESXi hosts in a cluster

Objective 8.1 – Configure Auto Deploy for ESXi hosts

Auto Deploy installation is a way to PXE boot your ESXi hosts from a central Auto Deploy server. This method relies on the use of master images with a set of rules to deploy ESXi with the desired specifications. Auto Deploy can also be used along with the **vSphere Host Profiles** feature to customize all ESXi hosts, ensuring a consistent configuration within the infrastructure. The vSphere Auto Deploy feature is the most efficient and suitable method to use to deploy ESXi hosts, especially in large environments.

To take advantage of the Auto Deploy feature, you need the Enterprise Plus license.

Describe the components and architecture of an Auto Deploy environment

The Auto Deploy environment relies on several components for its functionality, and it requires a vCenter Server already present in the vSphere infrastructure to provide the Auto Deploy feature. Let's take a look at the following diagram:

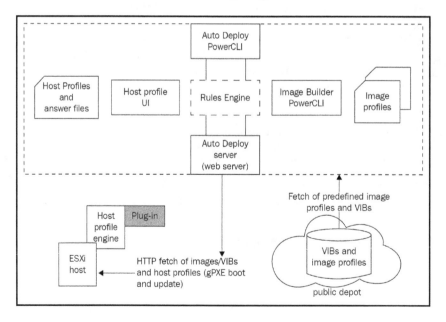

Figure 8.1: Auto Deploy components

The following services must be available and are prerequisites for successfully deploying ESXi hosts using the Auto Deploy capability:

- **PXE boot**: This must be configured in the new host to connect to a TFTP server.
- **Trivial File Transfer Protocol (TFTP)**: Used to retrieve the files used to get boot images. You need to retrieve the TFTP Boot Zip file and copy the file to the `TFTP server root` folder. To download the required file, select the vCenter Server from vSphere Web Client and navigate to **Configure** | **Auto Deploy** under the **Settings** area. Then, click on the **Download TFTP Boot Zip** link, as shown in the following screenshot:

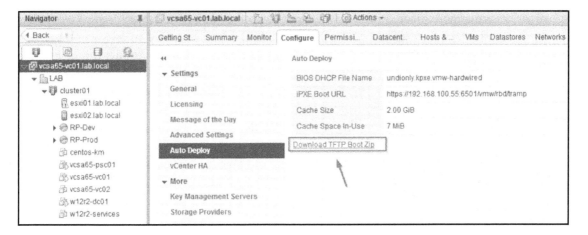

Figure 8.2: TFTP Boot Zip download link

- **DHCP server**: This provides the IP addresses to newly booted hosts. Along with the configuration of basic settings to define the DHCP scope, you need to specify two additional parameters:
    - `Option 66`: Specifies the **Boot Server Host Name** to be used
    - `Option 67`: Specifies the **Bootfile Name** `kpxe.vmw-hardwired` in the scope options used for Auto Deploy
- **Auto Deploy server**: Provides images and Host Profiles.

Although the configuration is more complex, this method is recommended for large environments, because ESXi hosts can be deployed in a matter of minutes, ensuring a consistent configuration.

To avoid errors with Auto Deploy, a working DNS must be present in the network and a forward (A record) and reverse (PTR record) zone entry for each target host must be configured properly.

> The Auto Deploy feature is part of the vCSA installation, but the service must be enabled because by default it is disabled.

When the Auto Deploy feature is used to boot an ESXi host, the following steps are involved:

1. When a new server boots, a PXE boot sequence begins. An IP address is provided by the DHCP server to the host containing the info specified in `Option 66` and `Option 67`, defined in the DHCP configuration, on how to contact the TFTP server.
2. Once the connection with the TFTP server has been established, the host downloads the executable boot loader (named `undionly.kpxe.vmw-hardwired`) and the configuration iPXE files, then it performs the iPXE execution.
3. An HTTP boot request to the vSphere Auto Deploy server is made by the host while executing iPXE to retrieve hardware and network information.
4. Once the Auto Deploy server has queried the rules engine to get host info, it then streams the components specified in the image profile.
5. The host boots using the assigned image profile. If Auto Deploy is combined with the Host Profiles feature, settings are applied to the host at this stage.
6. When the boot has completed, the new ESXi host is added to the vCenter where Auto Deploy is registered.
7. Virtual machines can be migrated to the new ESXi host only when the host is added to the vCenter Server if it is part of a **Distributed Resource Scheduler (DRS)** cluster.

Image profiles used to boot ESXi hosts through Auto Deploy are composed by a set of **vSphere Installation Bundles** (**VIBs**) that make the distribution process easier, allowing the creation of custom images. Existing image profiles are generally cloned to build custom images provided with additional VIB packages (drivers, patches, and third-party software) used for a specific hardware type or server role requirements.

To create an image profile, at least one software depot must be configured in the vCenter Server. These ready-to-use images, provided by VMware or VMware partners, are available as two public software depot types:

- **Online**: The image is provided as a structure of folders and files stored on an HTTP server
- **Offline**: The image is provided as a ZIP file

Until vSphere 6.0, the customization of ESXi images was possible only through the use of PowerCLI. In vSphere 6.5, the Image Builder GUI was introduced, simplifying the image building procedure.

Released VIBs come with an acceptance level that cannot be altered and that determines which VIBs can be installed to a host. There are four acceptance levels supported by VMware:

- **VMware Certified**
- **VMwareAccepted**
- **PartnerSupported**
- **Community supported**

VIBs can be installed on a host only if the ESXi host has the same or a higher acceptance level set.

Use the following command to determine the current host acceptance level:

```
esxcli --server=server_name software acceptance get
```

To change the acceptance level of the host, run the following command:

```
esxcli --server=server_name software acceptance set --
level=acceptance_level
```

where, `acceptance_level` is one of the four supported values:

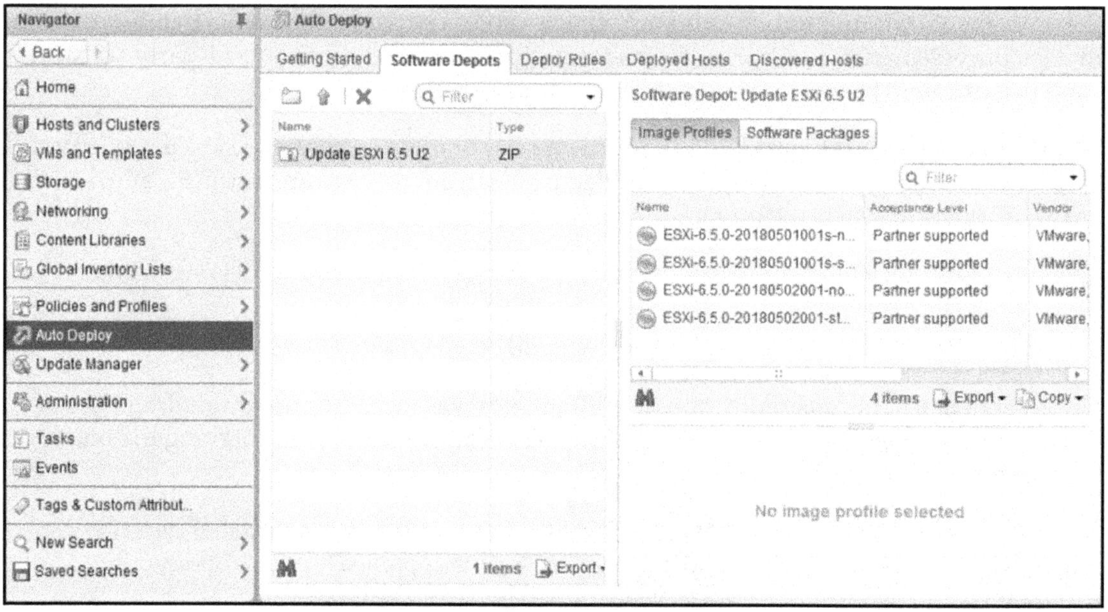

Figure 8.3: An image profile stored in the vCenter Server

No configuration (virtual switches, security settings, and so on) is stored within the image profile. To provide the desired ESXi configuration, the Host Profiles feature should be used instead.

To link available image profiles and specific VIBs to hosts, the deployment rules can be defined in the vCenter Server. To provision a new host with Auto Deploy, you have to specify the deployment rule to apply.

Implement Host Profiles with an Auto Deploy of an ESXi host

vSphere 6.5 provides the Host Profiles feature, which allows you to include an ESXi configuration in a profile (referred to as a *template*) to ensure all newly provisioned hosts have the same configuration across the infrastructure. To benefit from the Host Profiles feature, the Enterprise Plus license is required.

In a large environment, the manual setup of deployed hosts is not only time-consuming, but configuration errors may also occur at any time. A Host Profiles template is created by profiling an existing ESXi host (reference host) containing its configuration, and applying it to any host of the infrastructure to ensure consistency. You can edit a host profile to modify, enable, or disable its properties.

 By applying a Host Profiles template to a cluster, all ESXi members of the selected cluster get the same settings, ensuring a consistent configuration.

A host profile is created within vSphere Web Client with the following procedure:

1. From the **Inventory** view, right-click the hypervisor used as a reference host and select **Host Profiles | Extract Host Profile...**, as shown in the following screenshot:

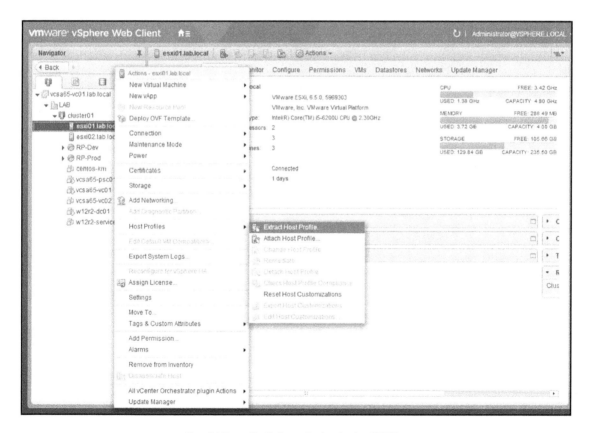

Figure 8.4: Create a Host Profiles template from the selected ESXi host

2. Specify a profile **Name** and a **Description** to identify the profile scope. Click **Next**.

3. To start profile creation, click **Finish**.

4. Created profiles can be found in the **Home** | **Host Profiles** section, as you'll see in the following screenshot:

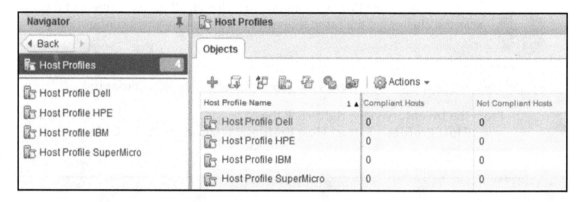

Figure 8.5: Host Profiles repository

Once the template has been created, new hosts can be provisioned using this template and keeping the same configuration as the reference host. The created host profile must be attached to the host to apply the settings:

1. In vSphere Web Client, right-click the desired host and select **Host Profiles** | **Attach Host Profile**.

2. Next, select the host profile to attach and click **Next**, as shown in the following screenshot:

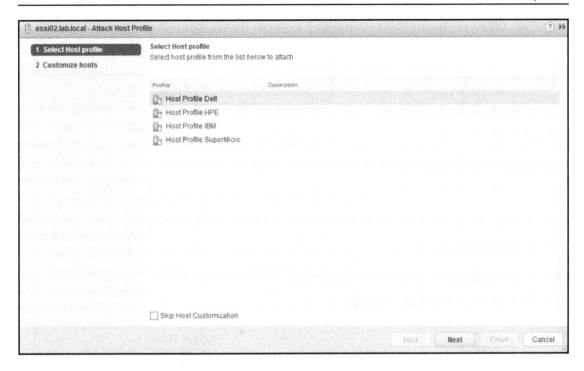

Figure 8.6: Host Profiles available to be attached to the selected ESXi

3. Click **Finish**.

4. When the host profile is attached, to apply the configuration right-click the ESXi host to configure and select **Host Profiles** | **Remediate...**, as follows:

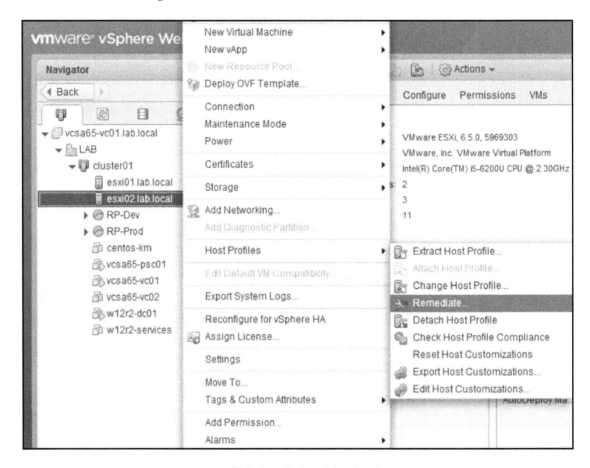

Figure 8.7: Host is remediated to apply the configuration

Combining the Host Profiles and Auto Deploy features, you can provision a large number of new ESXi hosts in a few minutes.

Three different installations can be performed depending on the business requirements:

- **Stateless**: The ESXi image is loaded directly into the host's memory as it boots.
- **Stateless caching**: The ESXi image is cached on the local disk, remote disk, or USB. When the ESXi is powered on, if no Auto Deploy servers are available, the host boots from the local cache. When the host has booted successfully, the Auto Deploy image loaded in memory is saved to the local disk, allowing the host to boot properly in case the Auto Deploy server is experiencing congestion that affects the deployment process.

  Stateless caching mode is configured as follows:

  1. From **Home** | **Host Profiles** in vSphere Web Client, edit or create the host profile to use, then select **System Image Cache Configuration** under **Advanced Configuration Settings**.
  2. Next, select **Enable stateless caching on the host** from the drop-down menu and click **Finish** to save the configuration, as shown in the following screenshot:

Figure 8.8: Configuring the Host Profiles deployment method

- **Stateful**: The image is cached on the local disk, remote disk, or USB, similar to stateless caching, but the host boots first from the cache, then from the network. After completing the first boot from the network, the Auto Deploy service is no longer required. To perform a stateful deployment, the server's BIOS must be configured to boot from the local disk first, then from the network. Stateful mode is configured as follows:
  1. From **Home** | **Host Profiles** in vSphere Web Client, edit or create the host profile to use, then select **System Image Cache Configuration** under **Advanced Configuration Settings**.
  2. Then, select **Enable stateful install on the host** from the drop-down menu and click **Finish** to save the configuration.

More information is available in the vSphere Host Profiles 6.5 Guide (`https://docs.vmware.com/en/VMware-vSphere/6.5/vsphere-esxi-vcenter-server-65-host-profiles-guide.pdf`).

Install and configure Auto Deploy

The installation of the Auto Deploy feature differs if the vCenter Server is the Windows-based version or the vCSA.

In the Windows-based vCenter Server, the Auto Deploy service is installed as an additional component, and it can reside on the same machine as the vCenter Server or be deployed on a separated physical or virtual machine. The installation option does not show up in the installer GUI, but you must execute the `VMware-autodeploy.msi` installer file located in the `\vCenter Server\Packages\` folder from the vCenter installation media. When running the `.msi` installer, no wizard is displayed, but instead a new service called **VMware vSphere Auto Deploy Waiter** is created in the vCenter Server, which, by default, is disabled and must be enabled to benefit from this feature:

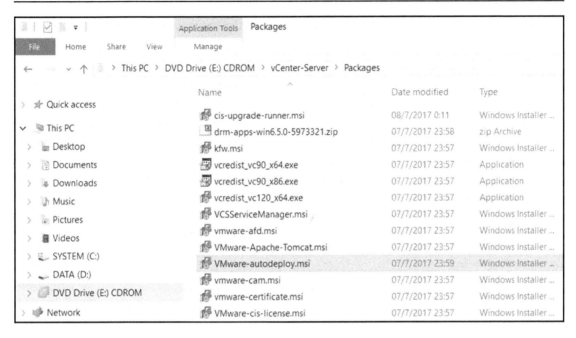

Figure 8.9: Auto Deploy installer file for the Windows version of vCenter Server

To enable the Auto Deploy feature in the vCSA, open vSphere Web Client and perform the following steps:

1. Navigate to **Home** | **Administration** | **System Configuration**.
2. Under **System Configuration**, select **Services** to display the list of available services.
3. Right-click the **Auto Deploy** item and select **Edit Startup Type**.
4. Choose **Automatic** and click **OK**.

5. Select **Start** from the **Actions** menu to start the service, as shown in the following screenshot:

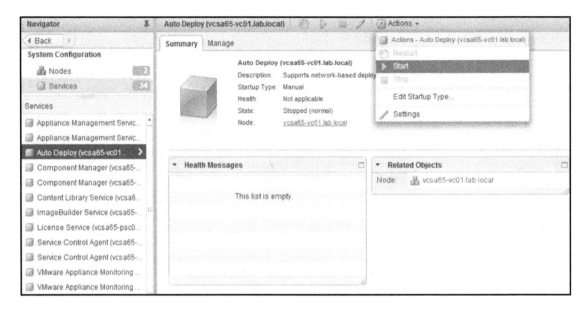

Figure 8.10: Auto Deploy feature enabled in the vCSA from vSphere Web Client

To display the Auto Deploy UI in vSphere Web Client, both the Auto Deploy and Image Builder services must be started.

If the Auto Deploy service has already started, follow these steps to start the Image Builder service:

1. Log in to vSphere Web Client as `administrator@vsphere.local`.
2. Go to **Administration** | **System Configuration** | **Nodes**, select the vCenter Server node, and select the **Related Objects** tab on the right pane.
3. Next, right-click **ImageBuilder Service** and select **Edit Startup Type**.
4. Choose **Automatic** and click **OK**.
5. Select **ImageBuilder Service** and choose **Start**.

The Auto Deploy feature is now enabled and ready to provision new ESXi hosts.

Deploy multiple ESXi hosts using Auto Deploy

As covered in the previous topic, a large number of ESXi hosts can be deployed in a virtual environment, keeping the configuration consistent by using the vSphere 6.5 Auto Deploy and Host Profiles features.

When the ESXi host reboots, the installation and all changes that have occurred since the deployment are lost, because the image provided by the Auto Deploy server is stored in the RAM. Each time a host is rebooted, an installation procedure takes place again. If the Auto Deploy server is unavailable, the host can't be installed, causing potential service disruption in the network.

To solve this, you have the option to install ESXi hosts by configuring the Host Profiles with three different deployment methods:

- **Stateless**: The ESXi image is loaded into the host's memory as it boots
- **Stateless caching**: The ESXi image is cached on the local disk, and if no Auto Deploy servers are available, the host boots from the local cache
- **Stateful**: The ESXi image is cached on the local disk, but after the first successful installation, the host boots first from the local disk and then from the network

Explaining the Auto Deploy deployment model needed to meet a business requirement

To install an ESXi host through the Auto Deploy service, a prerequisite is to have an Auto Deploy server up and running to provide the required image to the hypervisor to boot. If the Auto Deploy server is not available for any reason, the ESXi host to install is not provided with the image to load in memory, so it can't boot from the network.

Since the Auto Deploy service is part of the vCenter Server, to ensure high availability for the Auto Deploy server, configuring the vCenter Server in HA could be an option to avoid service disruption.

Alternatively, if the stateless method is considered unreliable, ESXi hosts can be deployed using the other two methods available: stateless caching or stateful. Although these two deployment types require a local disk—a small local disk, actually—you can also use USB drives.

Stateless caching could be an option to use if Auto Deploy is not always available in the network. The ESXi host can boot the cached image if it is not able to boot from the network. Anyway, to ensure ESXi host availability, the stateful deployment method could be a better solution to adopt. It requires the Auto Deploy server just for the first successful boot, then Auto Deploy availability is no longer required.

Additional info can be found in the vSphere Installation and Setup 6.5 document (`https://docs.vmware.com/en/VMware-vSphere/6.5/vsphere-esxi-vcenter-server-65-installation-setup-guide.pdf`).

Objective 8.2 – Create and Deploy Host Profiles

The Host Profiles feature available in vSphere 6.5 allows you to create a host profile template that includes the ESXi configuration, ensuring all deployed hosts have the same configuration across the network and providing a configuration standard in respect of the setup policy an organization may have. Recommended especially in large environments, Host Profiles can be combined with the Auto Deploy feature to automate the provisioning process, ensuring deployed host services match your infrastructure.

If you have to manually set up a large number of hosts, the procedure takes a lot of time and a mistake during the configuration may be made at any point. For example, a wrong IP address assigned or a wrong switch setup may cause service disruption.

To ensure all host members of a cluster have a consistent configuration, apply the Host Profiles at the cluster level.

The steps involved in the Host Profiles process are the following:

1. Since a Host Profiles is basically a template, make sure the ESXi host used as a reference is properly configured
2. From the reference host, extract the configuration to create the profile
3. Attach the profile to hosts or a cluster
4. Check hosts to process for compliance
5. Remediate hosts to apply the attached profile

> The configuration and management of the Host Profiles can be done through vSphere Web Client and via PowerCLI.

Editing answer file to customize ESXi host settings

In vSphere 6.5, the **answer file** is now referred to as **host customization**, and it is used to specify configuration settings such as IP address, hostname, syslog, and other parameters to apply to specific groups of ESXi hosts or clusters that share the same setup.

> Host customization management is done through the Host Profiles GUI accessible from the vSphere Web Client.

To create a host customization, go to the **Home** area and click **Host Profiles**. Then, go through the following steps:

1. From the available list, right-click the desired host profile and select the **Edit Host Customizations...** option, as shown in the following screenshot:

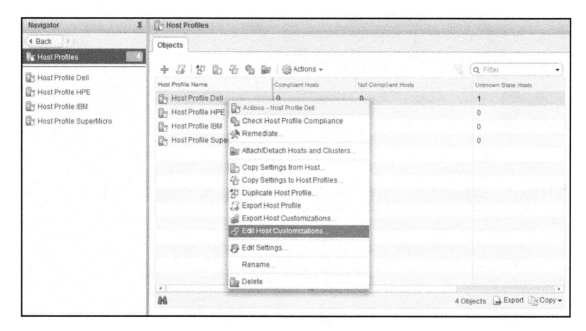

Figure 8.11: Editing the host customization from the GUI

2. Select the host you want to edit in the configuration settings, then click **Next**. Clicking on the **Browse** button gives you the option to import a CSV file previously created, containing the settings to apply. Once the file has been imported, fields in the window are automatically updated with the imported values.
3. Click **Finish** to save the customization.

Once the host customization process has been completed, you can export the profile in CSV format. To export a host customization, right-click the desired profile and select the **Export Host Customizations** option.

 When a host customization is exported, sensitive data such as passwords is not exported.

Additional information is available in the vSphere Host Profiles guide at the following address: `https://docs.vmware.com/en/VMware-vSphere/6.5/vsphere-esxi-vcenter-server-65-host-profiles-guide.pdf`.

Modifying and applying a storage path selection plugin (PSP) to a device using host profiles

To specify ESXi storage settings such as the PSP to use for a particular array type or for a particular device, to apply to a group of hosts with specific storage requirements, the use of the Host Profiles feature is extremely useful for this scenario, and also ensures consistency.

By editing a host profile, you can specify which PSP should be used and define the required parameters.

To make changes in the Host Profiles configuration, go to the **Home** | **Host Profile** section and right-click the profile to modify from the available list. Select the **Edit Settings** option to open the **Edit Host Profile** wizard. Make your changes, then click **Finish** to save the configuration, as you can see in the following screenshot:

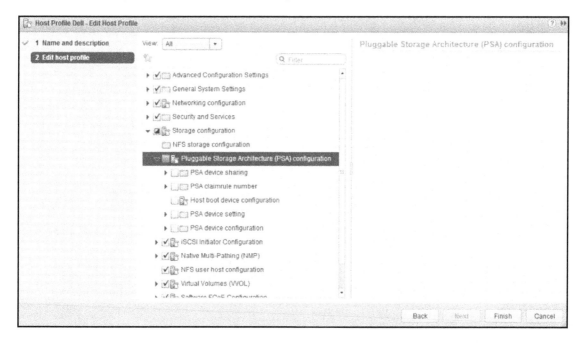

Figure 8.12: Configuration of the PSP parameters in the Host Profiles

From the same wizard, you can also configure **iSCSI Initiator Configuration** or **Native Multi-Pathing (NMP)**.

Modifying and applying switch configurations across multiple hosts using a host profile

Once a host profile has been created and extracted from the reference host, you may need to specify or modify settings for the virtual switches. Parameters such as **Link configuration**, **Number of ports**, **Network policy Configuration**, and so forth must be defined for each virtual switch used in your environment.

To modify the configuration settings, edit the desired host profile and, under the **Networking configuration** area, modify the parameters accordingly, as shown in the following screenshot:

Figure 8.13: Modify the virtual switch configuration in a host profile

From the list shown in the preceding screenshot, you can find and define the following options:

- **vSwitch**
- **Virtual machine port group**

- Host port group
- Physical NIC configuration
- vSphere Distributed Switch
- Host virtual NIC
- NetStack Instance
- Network Coredump Settings

Creating/editing/removing a host profile from an ESXi host

The creation of a host profile is a pretty simple procedure and requires the identification of a hypervisor to be used as a reference host.

The following steps are required to create a host profile:

1. From vSphere Web Client, access the **Inventory** view and right-click the host chosen as the reference host. Select the **Host Profiles | Extract Host Profile...** option, as shown in the following screenshot:

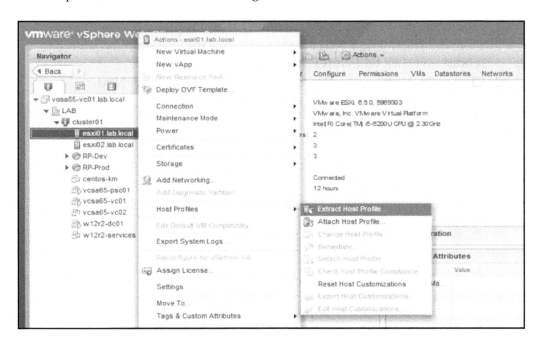

Figure 8.14: Creation of a host profile in vSphere Web Client

2. Give the profile a name and type a meaningful description to easily identify the profile's purpose, then click **Next**.
3. To begin host profile creation, click **Finish**.
4. When the process has been completed successfully, the created profile can be found in **Home** | **Host Profiles**.

The created profile contains parameters and services configured in the host used as a reference, and you may need to modify these parameters to better match your infrastructure, for example:

- **Networking configuration**: VMkernel and VM port groups, NIC-teaming, IP address, and so on
- **Storage configuration**: NFS configuration, software iSCSI adapters, port bindings
- **Time synchronization**: NTP server parameters
- **Enable services**: SSH
- **Firewall configuration**: Port used by some services

If you need to modify the configuration of an existing host profile, you can edit the profile to process and make modifications as follows:

1. From vSphere Web Client, go to **Home** | **Host Profiles**.
2. From the available list, select in the right pane the host profile you need to modify and click **Edit Host Profile**.
3. Change the **Name** or the **Description** if required, then click **Next**.
4. Modify the configuration parameters and click **Finish** to save changes, as shown in the following screenshot:

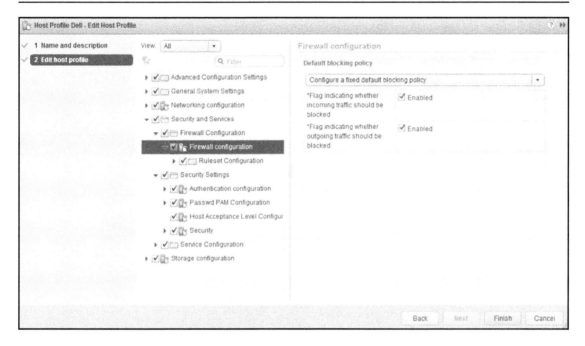

Figure 8.15: Modifying a host profile from vSphere Web Client

To simplify host profile management, vSphere 6.5 introduced a new feature that gives the user the ability to copy a host profile to a new profile. The procedure is pretty straightforward, as follows:

1. From vSphere Web Client, go to the **Home** | **Host Profile** section.
2. From the list, right-click the profile to copy and select the **Copy Settings to Host Profiles** option.

3. Specify the settings to copy and then click **Next**:

> In vSphere 6.5, host profile settings can now be copied from one profile to another, or to many others, and differences can be verified during the process.

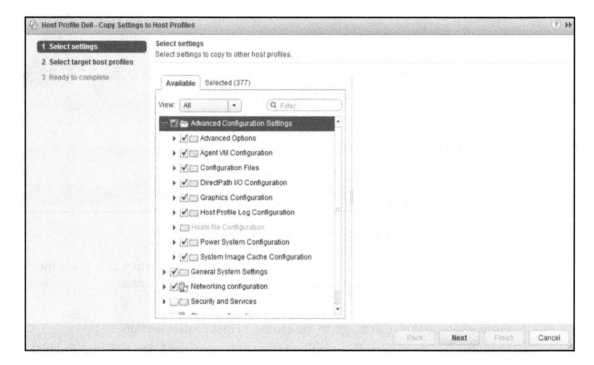

Figure 8.16: Host profile settings copied to another profile

4. Next, specify the target host profile and click **Next**.
5. Finally, click **Finish** to save the profile.

To remove a host profile from the list, simply right-click the profile to remove and select **Delete**, as you can see in the following screenshot:

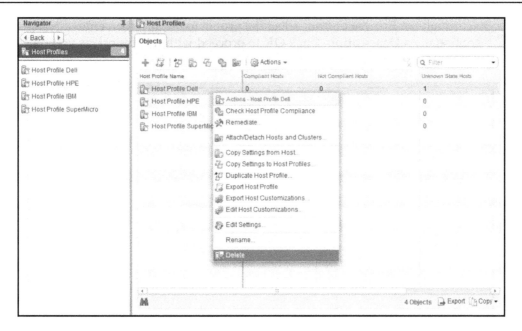

Figure 8.17: Removing a host profile

Importing/exporting a Host Profile

Depending on the business requirements, you may need to import or export a host profile. This task can be achieved in a very easy way, as explained in the following steps:

1. From vSphere Web Client, go to the **Home | Host Profile** section.
2. Click on the Import Host Profile icon, as shown in the following screenshot:

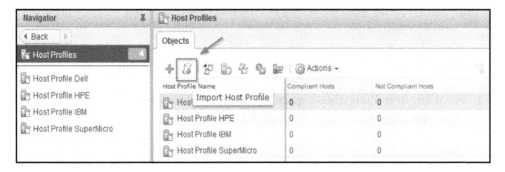

Figure 8.18 Importing a host profile

3. Through the **Browse** button, select the profile to import, then enter a **Name** and optionally a **Description**. Click **OK** to proceed with the import, as you can see in the following screenshot:

Figure 8.19: Importing a host profile

4. The imported host profile is displayed in the profiles list with the name previously assigned.

If your working environment has multiple physical locations or vCenter Servers and you want to keep the same ESXi configuration in your infrastructure, you can export the desired host profile in order to import the profile in other vCenter Servers.

 When you export a profile, administrator passwords are not exported for security reasons. When the profile has been imported and the password applied to a host, you are requested to re-enter the password.

To export a profile, proceed as follows:

1. From vSphere Web Client, go to the **Home | Host Profile** section.
2. From the available profiles, right-click the desired profile to export and select the **Export Host Profile** option, as you can see in the following screenshot:

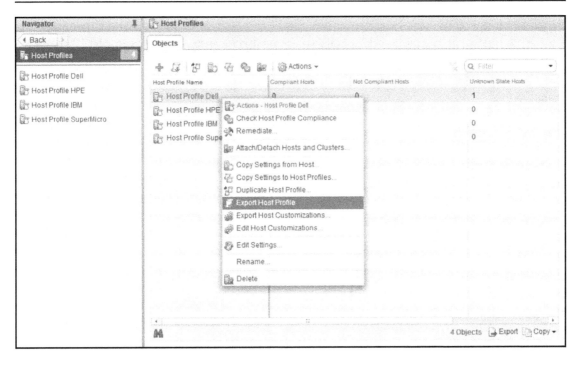

Figure 8.20: Exporting a host profile

3. Finally, click **Save** to save the file in VPF format anywhere on your computer.

Attaching and apply a Host Profiles to ESXi hosts in a cluster

When a Host Profiles has been extracted from the reference host, configured settings stored in the profile can be applied to other hosts or clusters by attaching the created Host Profiles, as explained in the following steps:

1. From vSphere Web Client, right-click the host or the cluster to process and select the **Host Profiles | Attach Host Profile** option.
2. Specify the Host Profiles to attach and click **Next**. Tick the **Skip Host Customization** checkbox if you don't want to customize the host settings in this step.

3. If the **Skip Host Customization** checkbox was left unchecked, the **Customize host** page is displayed. Specify the appropriate settings (for example, IP address or hostname), then click **Finish**, as shown in the following screenshot:

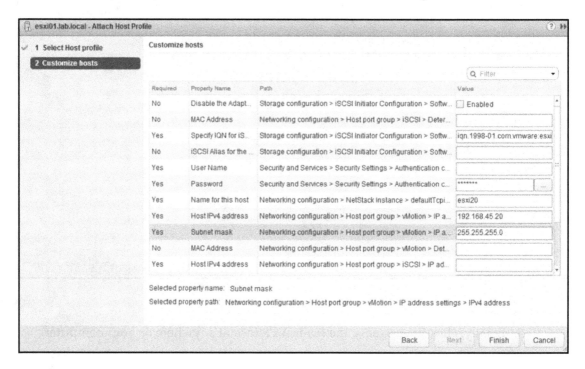

Figure 8.21: The configuration window for the Host Profiles to attach

If you need to apply a Host Profiles to multiple hosts that are members of the same cluster, by attaching the Host Profiles directly at the cluster level, all ESXi hosts will get the specified profile automatically attached.

When the Host Profiles has been attached, to apply the configuration you must perform a compliance check operation that compares the current host configuration with the configuration stored in the attached profile.

In the **Home** | **Host Profiles** section, you can determine the number of hosts attached to this profile and their current status. If the compliance check has not been performed yet, hosts are listed in the **Unknown State Host** column, which you can see in the following screenshot:

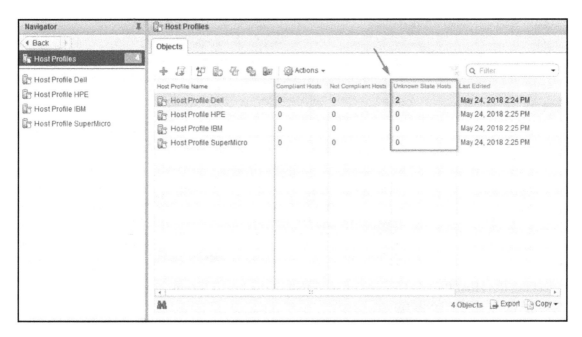

Figure 8.22: Hosts not scanned for compliance against the attached Host Profiles

Performing compliance scanning and remediation of ESXi hosts and clusters using Host Profiles

To apply the configuration stored in the Host Profiles attached to a host or cluster, you must perform a compliance check in order to determine the compliance of the host against the attached profile.

To perform the compliance check, right-click the host or cluster to check and select the **Host Profiles** | **Check Host Profile Compliance** option. If the scanned host is found to be non-compliant, in the host's **Summary** tab a warning message is displayed, as shown in the following screenshot:

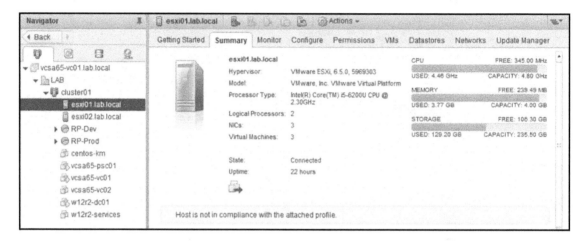

Figure 8.23: The scanned host is reported as non-compliant with attached Host Profiles

Checking the **Host Profile Compliance** widget in the host's **Summary** tab, you can verify settings that are not conforming.

You can have three types of compliance status:

- **Compliant**: Host is compliant with the attached profile.
- **Not Compliant**: Host and attached host profile are inconsistent, and host remediation is required to fix the issue.
- **Unknown**: Host compliance cannot be verified, and host remediation through the Host Profiles fixes the problem:

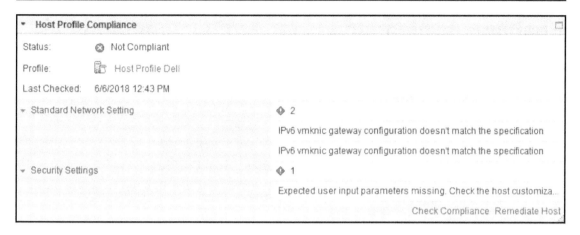

Figure 8.24: Scanned host status

 Offline or unpresented devices are not captured by the Host Profiles. After extracting a host profile, if any changes are made to offline devices, compliance check results won't be affected.

If the host status is reported as non-compliant, the remediation procedure must be performed in order to apply the Host Profiles settings to the host.

Before proceeding with remediation, the host must be put in **Maintenance Mode**. Here are the steps to achieve this:

1. First, right-click the host or cluster you want to remediate and select **Host Profile | Remediate**. Alternatively, from the **Home | Host Profile** section, right-click the profile to apply and then select **Remediate**.

2. If you are remediating from the Host Profiles area, you need to specify the hosts to remediate. Click **Next**.

3. Specify the parameter's values to apply or import a host customization file by clicking the **Browse** button. Click **Next**.

4. Finally, click **Finish** to remediate.

Enabling or disabling Host Profiles components

As an administrator, you may need to decide whether specific components configured in a Host Profiles should be considered and/or applied to hosts. If the hosts to provision are slightly different, you may decide to exclude some critical components that may cause issues or affect the installation procedure.

To modify a profile, follow this procedure:

1. From vSphere Web Client, go to the **Home** | **Host Profile** section.
2. From the available profiles, right-click the profile to modify and select the **Edit Settings** option.
3. Modify the **Name** and **Description** if requested, and then click **Next**.
4. Then, select the component to disable (it is enabled by default) by deselecting the checkbox, in order for it to be ignored during the profile compliance check and excluded during host remediation. You can see this in the following screenshot:

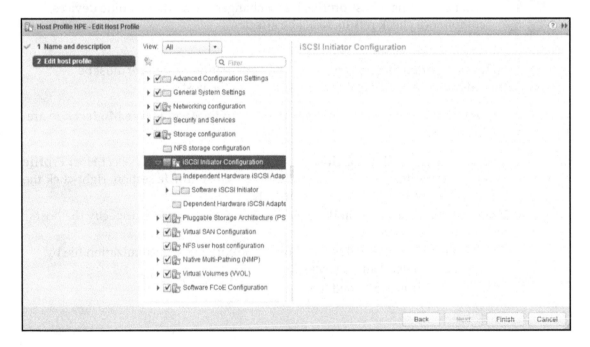

Figure 8.25: Enable and disable Host Profiles components

5. Finally, click **Finish** to save changes.

Review questions

1. If a Host Profiles is applied to a cluster, all ESXi members of the selected cluster get the same settings.
    - A: True
    - B: False

A - See *Objective 8.1*

2. The ESXi image is cached on the local disk and if no Auto Deploy servers are available, the host boots from the local cache. Which deployment method is described?
    - A: Stateless caching
    - B: Stateless
    - C: Stateful
    - D: PXE

A - See *Objective 8.1*

3. What is the file extension for an exported Host Profiles?
    - A: .vpf
    - B: .pfv
    - C: .cfg
    - D: .pro

A - See *Objective 8.2*

4. What are the valid acceptance levels? Select two answers:
    - A: VMwareCertified
    - B: VMwareSupported
    - C: PartnerAccepted
    - D: CommunitySupported

A, D - See *Objective 8.1*

5. When a Host Profiles is exported, administrator passwords are not exported for security reasons.
    - A: True
    - B: False

A - See *Objective 8.2*

Summary

The management and configuration of vSphere's Auto Deploy and Host Profiles features were covered in detail in this chapter, as part of *Objective 8.1* and *Objective 8.2* of the certification exam.

In `Chapter 9`, *Configure and Administer vSphere and vCenter Availability Solutions*, we will be covering the new vSphere HA cluster feature (*Objective 9.1* and *Objective 9.2*) introduced in vSphere 6.5 and available for the vCSA only.

9
Configure and Administer vSphere and vCenter Availability Solutions

Having workloads and vCenter Servers always available to avoid service disruption is the main responsibility of every vSphere Administrator. This chapter will explain the vSphere Availability feature (formerly known as vSphere HA) and the configuration settings used in a cluster to ensure virtual machine availability in the case of an expected host failure event.

The vCenter Server is the core component of the infrastructure because it provides all the main services and features that are available in vSphere, such as vSphere Availability, DRS, vDS, and so on, and its availability must be ensured to keep the infrastructure healthy. This chapter will also cover the configuration of **vCenter Server Appliance** (**vCSA**) HA, a new feature that became available in vSphere 6.5 (vCSA only) to ensure vCenter Server HA.

In this chapter, we will walk you through the available options so that you better understand how to configure available features and the logic behind them. In the exam, you may find some questions related to vSphere Availability and vCSA HA.

In this chapter, we will cover the following topics:

- Installing and configuring the vSphere HA feature
- Applying an admission control policy
- Configuring heartbeat datastores
- Configuring **Virtual Machine Component Protection** (**VMCP**) settings
- Implementing vSphere HA on a vSAN cluster
- Enabling and configuring vCSA HA
- Understanding and describing the architecture of vCSA HA

Objective 9.1 – Configure vSphere HA cluster features

vSphere HA is a feature that's available in vSphere and is applied to a pool of monitored ESXi hosts. It allows you, in the case of host failure, to restart the virtual machines that are detected as down on another host within the cluster.

Modify vSphere HA cluster settings

vSphere HA's responses to failure conditions on a cluster can be customized depending on your business requirements. In order to configure failures and responses, you must edit the cluster and enable the **Enable Host Monitoring** option, like so:

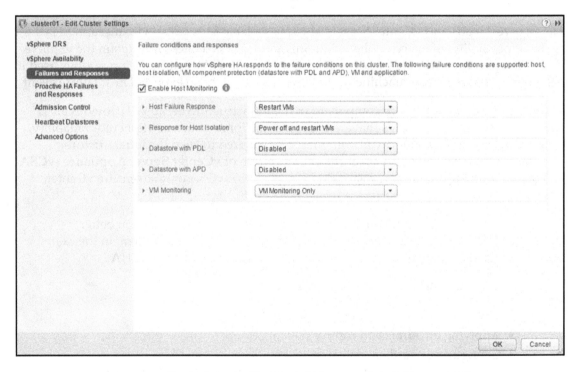

Figure 9.1: Configuration of the vSphere Availability parameters for the cluster

Here, you can configure the following parameters:

- **Host Failure Response**: You can configure host monitoring and failover to the selected cluster. Two options are available:
    - **Disabled**: Host monitoring is disabled
    - **Restart VMs**: The start order is determined by the VM's restart priority
- **Response for Host Isolation**: In the case of the network isolation of the host, you can configure different actions for running virtual machines in the cluster:
    - **Disabled**: No actions taken
    - **Shutdown and restart**: VMs are restarted on online hosts
    - **Power off and restart VMs**: VMs are restarted on hosts that still have network connectivity
- **Datastore with PDL**: In the case of **Permanent Device Loss** (PDL) datastore failures, configurable actions for the affected VMs are as follows:
    - **Disabled**: No actions taken
    - **Issue events**: Only events will be generated to notify the administrators about the issue
    - **Power off and restart VMs**: Affected VMs will be terminated and restarted on hosts that still have connectivity to the datastore
- **Datastore with APD**: In the case of **All Paths Down** (APD) datastore failures, configurable actions for the affected VMs are as follows:
    - **Disabled**: No actions taken
    - **Issue events**: Only events will be generated to notify the administrators about the issue
    - **Power off and restart VMs – Conservative**: Affected VMs will be powered off and restarted on hosts that still have connectivity to the datastore
    - **Power off and restart VMs – Aggressive**: Affected VMs will be powered off and vSphere HA will always attempt to restart the VMs
- **VM Monitoring**: You can enable heartbeat monitoring to reset individual virtual machines if specified heartbeats are not received within a specific time:
    - **VM Monitoring Only**: The VM is reset if VMware Tools heartbeats are not received within a specific time
    - **Application Monitoring**: The guest OS is restarted if application heartbeats are not received within a specific time

The **Application Monitoring** option is grayed out if VM monitoring is disabled.

Advanced cluster settings, such as the isolation address, can be configured in the **Advanced Options** area, as shown in *Figure 9.6.*

Configure a network for use with HA heartbeats

When the vSphere Availability feature is enabled in a vSphere cluster, a HA agent called **Fault Domain Manager** (**FDM**) is uploaded to host members and configured to communicate with other agents in the cluster. When the HA cluster is enabled, a master host is elected based on the most datastores that are connected. Only one master host can be elected per cluster, while all other hosts act as slaves. The master host has the duty of monitoring the state of slave hosts through heartbeats sent over the heartbeat network between master and slave hosts. For agent heartbeats, vSphere HA uses the management network as well as datastore heartbeats (datastore heartbeats will be covered later). If vSAN is enabled in the cluster, HA will use the vSAN network instead.

If you need to do some network maintenance in the HA cluster, make sure to disable host monitoring first. This is needed to avoid virtual machine failover attempts due to the interruption of heartbeats that vSphere HA uses to detect host failures. Make your changes and then turn host monitoring on again.

If a host is disconnected from the cluster, registered VMs in the host will not be protected by vSphere HA.

By default, vSphere HA heartbeats are sent over the management network, which requires the creation of a VMKernel with the appropriate service (**Management** or **vSAN**) selected:

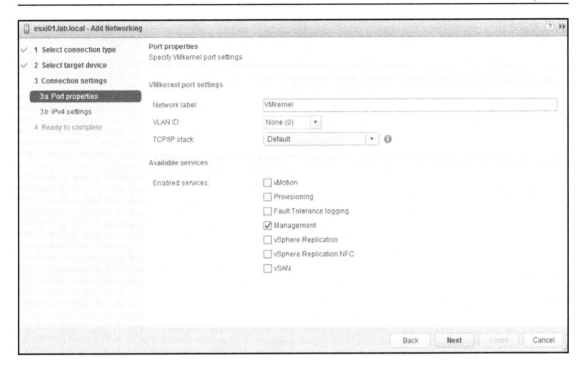

Figure 9.2: Management option enabled in the VMKernel setup

To keep the heartbeat network resilient, the configuration of an additional management network can prevent isolation or partition events since vSphere HA can send heartbeats on both networks. If one network fails, heartbeats can be sent through the other network. Having two management networks is also a best practice.

Additional information can be found in the vSphere Availability document available at the following URL: https://docs.vmware.com/en/VMware-vSphere/6.5/vsphere-esxi-vcenter-server-65-availability-guide.pdf.

Apply an admission control policy for HA

To ensure that a cluster has enough failover capacity, vSphere HA uses the admission control policy to determine how many host failures your cluster can tolerate, that is, the amount of resources the system should reserve to power on virtual machines in case a host fails.

When admission control has been enabled, actions that may violate the applied policy are not permitted. Powering on, migrating, or increasing the CPU or memory reservation of a virtual machine may be prevented if the cluster doesn't have enough resources available, that is, the admission control policy is violated.

Once the maximum host failures the cluster can tolerate has been specified, there are three ways to define the host failover capacity:

- **Slot Policy (powered-on VMs)**: A slot size defines the CPU and RAM resources required to satisfy the requirements for any powered on virtual machine in the cluster:

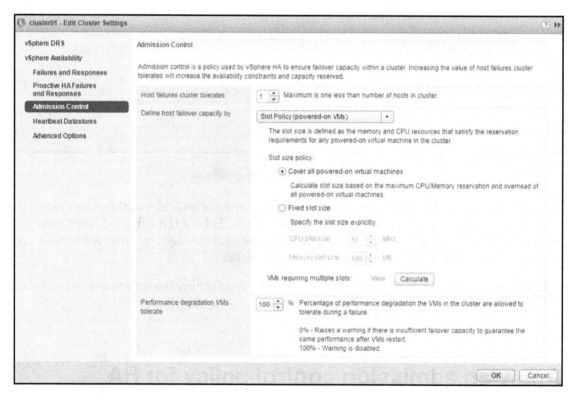

Figure 9.3: Admission control "slot policy" configuration

- **Cluster resource percentage**: Admission control can be configured by reserving a specific percentage of cluster CPU and memory for recovery from host failures. The total resource requirements for the powered on virtual machines are calculated by summing up the CPU reservations (by default, this is 32 MHz if no CPU reservation has been specified. The advanced setting `das.vmcpuminmhz` allows you to change this default) and the memory reservation (0 MB if not specified, plus memory overhead) of each powered on virtual machine.

Once specified the host failures the cluster can tolerate, unless you want to specify custom values through the **Override calculated failover capacity** option, the math is done automatically by the system with no need to manually enter the percentage value as we used to do in previous versions (if you have 4 hosts in a cluster, for 1 host failure, CPU and RAM will be set to 25% failover capacity):

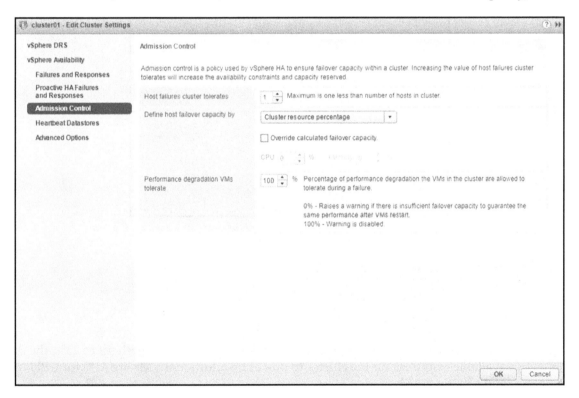

Figure 9.4: Admission control "Cluster resource percentage" configuration

The total failover capacity for CPU or RAM (the calculation method is similar) is calculated as follows:

(Total cluster host CPU – All cluster VM CPU required)/Total cluster host CPU

For example, we have a cluster composed of three hosts with the total available resources being 36 GHz and 28 GB, and five powered on virtual machines running in the cluster with total resource requirements of 12 GHz and 9 GB:

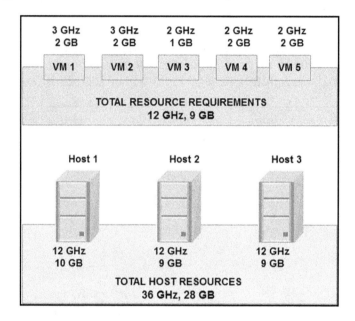

Figure 9.5: Admission control example

The total failover capacity is calculated as follows:

- **CPU**: *(36 GHz – 12 GHz)/36 GHz = 66%*
- **RAM**: *(28 GB - 9 GB)/28 GB = 68%*

If the configured failover capacity for CPU and memory are both set to 25%, the available resources for the cluster to power on additional VMs are 41% for CPU and 43% for RAM:

- **CPU**: *66% - 25% = 41%*
- **RAM**: *68% - 25% = 43%*

If the reserved percentage is 25% but 30% is required to power on all of the required virtual machines, some VMs may not be restarted.

- **Dedicated failover hosts**: A host is completely dedicated to being used for virtual machines that need to be restarted in the event of a host failure. The host is not used for production and acts as a spare. You can't power on virtual machines or perform vMotion on the failover host. DRS won't use the host for load balancing, and VM-VM affinity rules won't be applied for VMs running on failover hosts:

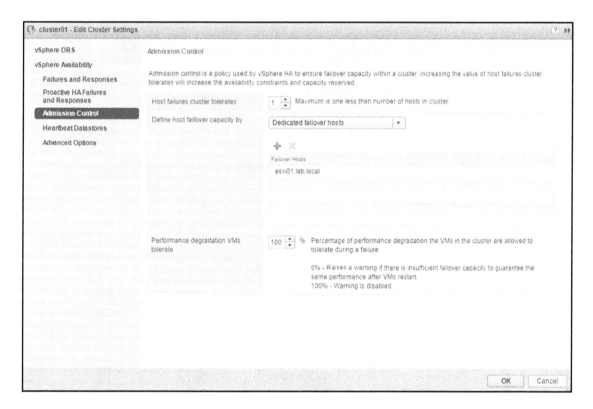

Figure 9.6: Admission control "Dedicated failover host" configuration

You also have the option to set a percentage from 0% (insufficient failover capacity to ensure the same performance after restart) up to 100% (warning disabled) in the **Performance degradation VMs tolerate** option so that you get a warning message if performance issues may occur on a particular virtual machine after a HA event.

Enable/disable vSphere HA settings

vSphere HA features can be enabled via vSphere Web Client. Right-click the cluster to modify it and select **Settings** | **vSphere Availability** under **Services**. After clicking the **Edit** button, tick **Turn ON vSphere HA** to enable this functionality.

On the left side, you can access the available configuration settings areas to enable/disable the individual parameters. The advanced HA settings can be modified by selecting the **Advanced Options** tab, and then clicking on the **Add** button to add parameters and their values.

Some parameters you may need to add/modify are as follows:

- **das.isolationaddress[X]**: This is used to configure the IP address to ping if a host is isolated from the network. Up to 10 multiple isolation addresses can be specified for the cluster (that is, `das.isolationaddress0`, `das.isolationaddress1`, and so on).
- **das.ignoreRedundantNetWarning**: The missing HA network redundancy warning is ignored.
- **das.useDefaultIsolationAddress**: Determines whether the default gateway is used as the isolation address.
- **das.iostatsInterval**: Determines the I/O stats interval for VM monitoring, which is set at 120 seconds by default.
- **das.ignoreInsufficientHbDatastore**: If the host doesn't have enough heartbeat datastores, the configuration issue warning is suppressed. The default is set to `false`.
- **das.heartbeatDsPerHost**: This is used to specify if more than 2 heartbeat datastores should be used. The default is 2 and the valid range is from 2 to 5:

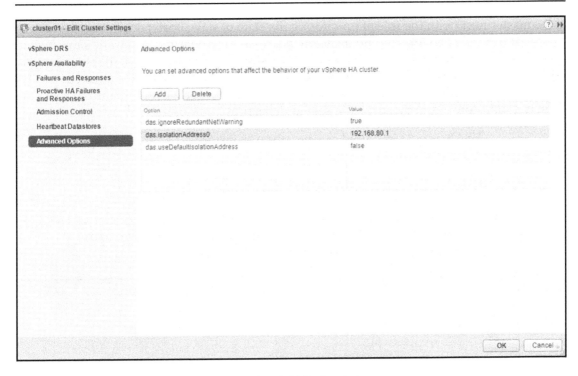

Figure 9.7: vSphere Availability advanced options

Configure different heartbeat datastores for a HA cluster

A heartbeat datastore is a feature that was introduced in vSphere 5.0, and is used by the host master to determine whether a host has failed or has just been isolated from others. There are three types of host failure that can be detected in a vSphere HA cluster:

- **Failure**: A host failed.
- **Isolation**: A host is network isolated.
- **Partition**: A host has lost network connectivity with the master host. The host is not isolated but the HA master host is not able to communicate with the host using the management network, and can only do so through the heartbeat datastores that have been configured.

If the master host (with the role of monitoring the state of slave hosts) doesn't receive any heartbeat from the network and no datastore heartbeats are detected, a specific slave host is considered **failed**. If the master receives only datastore heartbeats instead, the slave host is considered to be **isolated** from the network. At least two shared datastores must be accessible by all nodes in the cluster. By default, vCenter Server will automatically select at least two datastores from the available shared datastores.

VSAN is not supported as a heartbeat datastore.

To specify heartbeat datastores, from the inventory view, right-click the cluster and select **Settings**. In the **vSphere Availability** tab, click the **Edit** button and then go to the **Heartbeat Datastores** section to access the configuration page:

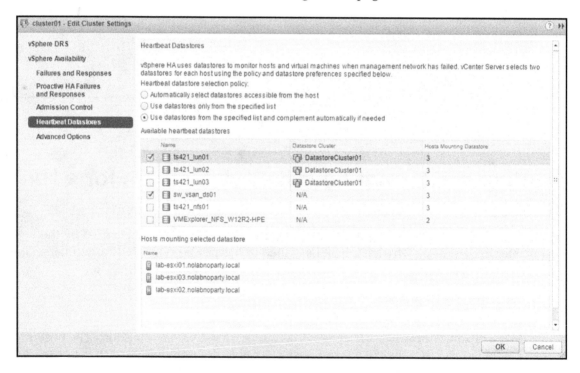

Figure 9.8: Configuration of heartbeat datastores for vSphere Availability

Apply virtual machine monitoring for a cluster

VM monitoring resets individual virtual machines if VMware Tools heartbeats are not received within a specific time. When a cluster is created, the VM monitoring feature is disabled by default.

To enable virtual machine monitoring, proceed as follows:

1. From vSphere Web Client, right-click the cluster to configure it and select **Settings**.
2. Access the **vSphere Availability** tab unders **Services** and then click the **Edit** button.
3. In the **Failures and Responses** section, select **VM Monitoring Only** from the **VM Monitoring** drop-down menu:

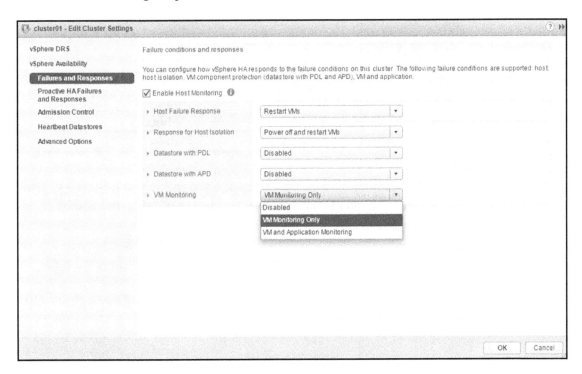

Figure 9.9: Enabling the VM monitoring feature in vSphere Availability

The VM monitor requires VMware Tools to be installed in the guest OS of the virtual machine.

To check whether the virtual machine is still running and avoiding unnecessary resets in the event the virtual machine's guest OS stops sending heartbeats to HA, the VM monitoring service also performs an I/O activity check on the virtual machine to verify there is disk or network activity within the I/O stats interval, which is set to 120 seconds by default.

If no heartbeats are received, VM monitoring checks the I/O stats interval. If no disk or network I/O activity occurred during the previous 120 seconds, the VM is considered failed and then reset.

The I/O stats interval's default value (120 seconds) can be changed through the advanced option **das.iostatsinterval**. The following tables shows the default settings for monitoring sensitivity:

Setting	Failure interval (seconds)	Reset period
High	30	1 hour
Medium	60	24 hours
Low	120	7 days

Table 9.1: Default settings for monitoring sensitivity

Power the virtual machine off and then back on, or vMotion to another host to clear the reset statistics.

Configure Virtual Machine Component Protection (VMCP) settings

VMCP is a feature of vSphere HA that is used to detect PDL (permanent device loss) and APD (all paths down) datastore accessibility failure events. When a failure is detected, running virtual machines are restarted accordingly.

The VMCP response type in the event of a PDL or APD datastore accessibility failure is configured in the **Failure and Responses** section of vSphere Availability. Check out the previous topic, *Modify vSphere HA cluster settings*, for additional details:

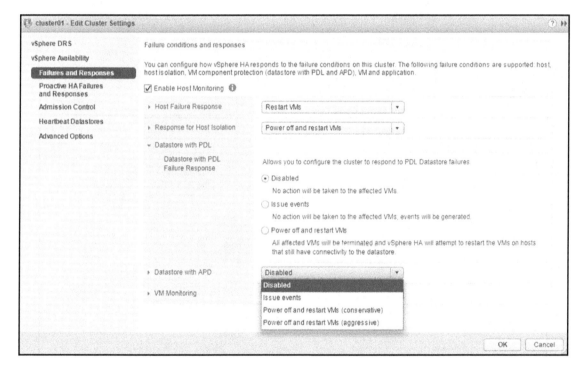

Figure 9.10: Configuration of PDL and ADP responses

 The VMCP feature is supported for ESXi hosts from version 6.0.

Implement vSphere HA on a vSAN cluster

By default, vSphere HA uses the management network for agent heartbeats when vSAN is disabled. Since vSAN has its own network, when the vSAN service is enabled in the same cluster, HA traffic flows through the vSAN network instead of the management network. The following table shows the differences in vSphere HA networking when the vSAN network is enabled or disabled:

	Virtual SAN enabled	Virtual SAN disabled
Network used by vSphere HA	Virtual SAN storage network	Management network
Heartbeat datastores	Any datastore mounted to > 1 host, but not Virtual SAN datastores	Any datastore mounted to > 1 host
Host declared isolated	Isolation addresses not pingable and vSAN storage network inaccessible	Isolation addresses not pingable and management network inaccessible

Table 9.2

To enable Virtual SAN, you must disable vSphere HA first, otherwise you will receive a warning error:

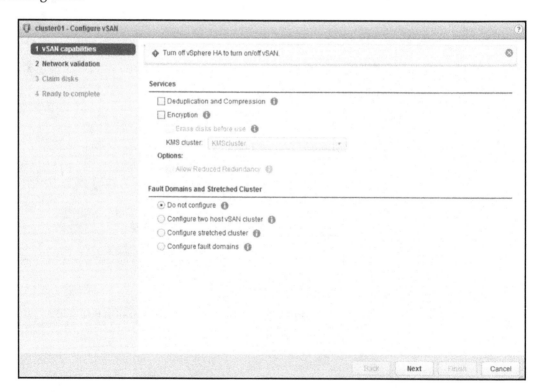

Figure 9.11: Enabling vSAN without disabling vSphere HA first will result in a warning error

The requirements for using Virtual SAN with a vSphere HA are as follows:

- ESXi hosts members of the cluster must be version 5.5 or later
- The cluster must have a minimum of three ESXi hosts

If the admission control policy is used to reserve resources for the vSphere HA cluster, the number of failures tolerated and configured in the vSAN rule must not be lower than the capacity reserved by the vSphere HA admission control setting.

 The vSAN datastore cannot be used for HA datastore heartbeats.

Explain how vSphere HA communicates with distributed resource scheduler and distributed power management

vSphere HA can be combined with vSphere DRS in the same cluster to provide a cluster with automated failover and load balancing. In the event of a host failure, vSphere HA's main duty is to restart the virtual machines for other available hosts. Once all VMs have been restarted, DRS load balances the cluster if necessary.

CPU and memory reservation and overhead memory are evaluated by vSphere HA to determine whether a host has enough available resources to power on the virtual machine.

Resource constraints may prevent vSphere HA to failover virtual machines. For example, VM-Host affinity rules may prevent some virtual machines from being placed in specific hosts. If a host member of the cluster with DRS and vSphere HA with admission control turned on is put in maintenance mode, VMs may not perform the automated vMotion to other hosts due to resources that are reserved for failure. A manual migration is then necessary using vMotion.

Distributed Power Management (**DPM**) is a feature used by DRS to reduce power consumption, turning on and off host members of a cluster, based on cluster resource utilization.

vSphere DPM monitors the resource demand (CPU and memory) of the virtual machines in a cluster, placing one or more hosts in standby mode if the available capacity exceeds the resource demand. When the capacity is not adequate, DRS powers on one or more hosts and migrates virtual machines to these hosts using vMotion instead:

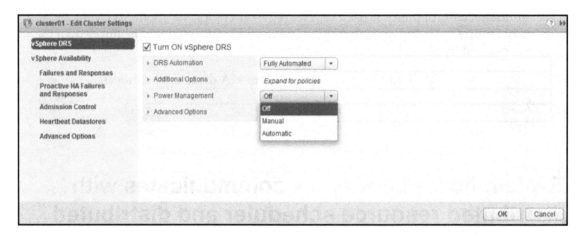

Figure 9.12: Enabling power management in the cluster

If HA admission control is disabled and DPM is enabled, running virtual machines in the cluster may be placed onto some hosts, leaving other hosts empty. DPM will place these empty hosts on standby, leaving insufficient resources to perform a failover.

Objective 9.2 – Configure vCSA HA

vCenter Server High Availability (**VCHA**) is a new feature that was introduced in vSphere 6.5, which eliminates the single point of failure of the vCenter Server by creating a three-node cluster (active, passive, and witness nodes), and it is available for vCSA only.

Enable and Configure vCSA HA

The configuration and management of the VCHA cluster is performed through vSphere Web Client. Before starting vCenter HA deployment, make sure that you have configured a dedicated network for node communication.

vCenter HA and the management networks must be configured on different subnets (the three nodes can be configured on different subnets) and the vCenter HA network must have a latency less than 10 milliseconds.

The VCHA cluster can be deployed in two ways:

- **Basic**: This requires a HA network to be available. This is a deployment type that's suitable for medium to small businesses. The wizard takes care of active/passive/witness node creation as well as vNIC interfaces. Only a little bit of information must be manually entered, such as the IP address.
- **Advanced**: The three active, passive, and witness nodes must be manually created, configuring the network settings accordingly. Although it is a more complex setup, the advanced deployment provides more flexibility in the design (a VM can be placed on a different datacenter or SSO domain).

To perform VCHA cluster deployment, the account used must be a member of the SSO Admin group.

To deploy a VHCA cluster, follow these steps:

1. Open vSphere Web Client and, from the inventory view, right-click the vCenter Server, selecting the **vCenter HA Settings** option:

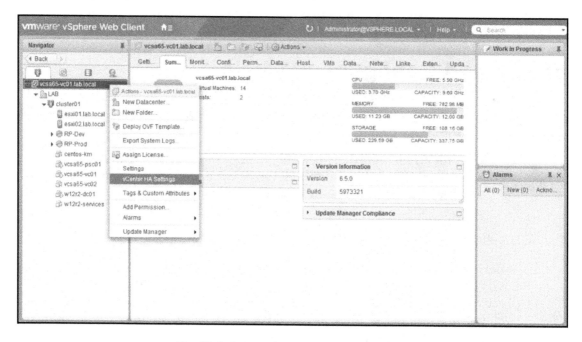

Figure 9.13: Configuring the VCHA cluster from the vSphere Web Client

2. From the **Configure | vCenter HA** section, click on the **Configure** button.
3. Select the deployment type by selecting the **Basic** or **Advanced** option. In this example, the **Basic** deployment type has been selected:

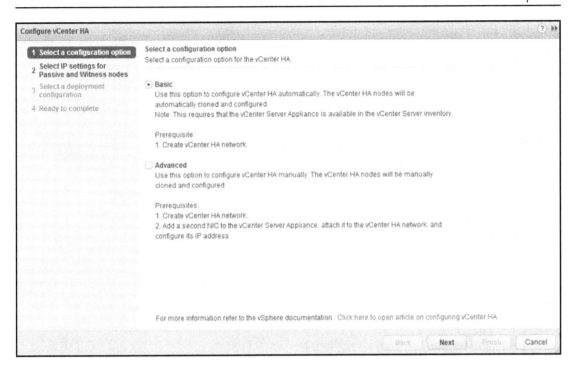

Figure 9.14: VCHA cluster deployment type

4. Specify the **IP address** and the **subnet mask** for the active node. Click on the **Browse** button and select the dedicated network to use for node communication. Click **Next**.

5. Specify the **IP address** for the passive and witness nodes and then click **Next**.

6. If the prerequisites are not met, the passive and witness nodes will be marked with a red error icon. Click the **Compatibility errors...** link to check the issues detected by the system. A window with a list of the all issues to fix will be displayed. Just remember that the three nodes must be stored in separate datastores, running on separated hosts, with a dedicated network that's used for nodes communication:

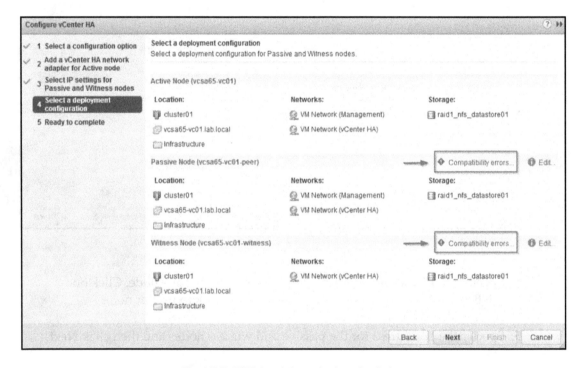

Figure 9.15: The VCHA cluster deployment detecting configuration issues

7. When the detected issues with the affected nodes have been fixed, the wizard will mark the nodes with a green icon. When no red icons are displayed in the wizard next to the node's names, click **Next** to continue with the deployment.

8. Review all configuration settings and click **Finish** to proceed with VCHA cluster creation.

9. The system deploys the passive node (cloning the vCSA) and the witness node (a lightweight VM), and creates the cluster.

To allow the placement of the VCHA in less than three nodes, you can disable the DRS affinity rule that blocks the deployment, as explained in virtuallyGhetto's blog post (`https:\\www.virtuallyghetto.com`). From the vCenter Server, go to the **Configure** | **Advanced Settings** section and configure the **config.vpxd.vcha.drsAntiAffinity** item as **false**. The use of this workaround is not recommended for production:

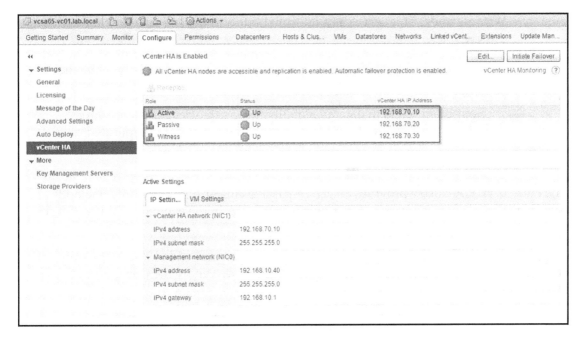

Figure 9.16: The VCHA cluster status in vSphere Web Client

Understand and describe the architecture of vCSA HA

To configure a VCHA cluster, only a single vCenter license is requested (a Standard license is sufficient) and both external PSC (vCenter and PSC installed on different VMs) and embedded PSC (vCenter and PSC reside on the same VM) deployment models are supported.

To enable VCHA, it is recommended that you select a time period with a low workload to avoid PostgreSQL DB issues in the passive node.

The VCHA architecture is composed of three main components:

- **Active node**: Runs the vCenter Server active instance serving the client requests.
- **Passive node**: Runs as the passive instance of the vCenter Server receiving state updates from the active node in synchronous mode constantly. If the active node fails, it takes over the role of active node.
- **Witness node**: This serves as a quorum node and doesn't take over the active or passive roles.

Data is continuously replicated between active and passive nodes, but only while the witness node provides a quorum to prevent a split-brain situation.

 Split-brain refers to data/availability inconsistencies due to network failures within distributed systems that are maintaining replicated data.

The created VCHA cluster provides an active-passive cluster type since only one node at a time can take over the active role. To protect vCenter HA in the event of a failure, the active node is the component you have to back up.

The deployment of a VCHA cluster using a vCSA with an embedded PSC is the simplest configuration since the entire process is automated and driven by the **Configure vCenter HA** installation wizard:

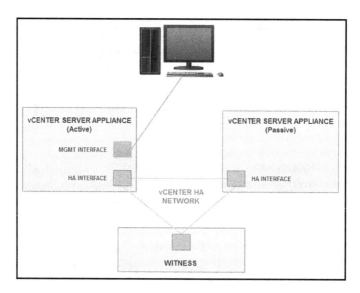

Figure 9.17: vCenter Server HA architecture with an embedded PSC

Deploying a VCHA cluster with an external PSC is also a supported setup but raises a single point of failure scenario. To ensure PSC fault tolerance, two external PSCs must be deployed and configured to replicate vCenter SSO and other PSC information to each other. The use of a load balancer, such as F5 or NSX, and Netscaler allows you to protect the PSC against service failures. In the event of a PSC failure, the load balancer redirects the vCenter Server to a different PSC, avoiding service disruption. This deployment type is more complex but solves the single point of failure issue. When the deployment is complete, the vCSA is the only component that's protected:

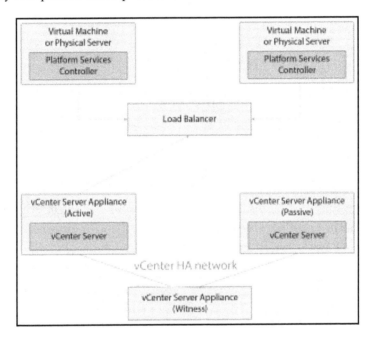

Figure 9.18: vCenter Server High Availability architecture with an external PSC

To support VCHA clusters spanning multiple datacenters, the use of a shared storage-based deployment is not supported. To avoid possible vCSA issues, it's important to configure the VCHA cluster, avoiding single points of failure. VMware recommends the use of three different hosts and three different datastores to store the active, passive, and witness VMs. In addition, each node must reside on a different host.

 To guarantee the same performance of the passive node when taking over the active role, the VM settings such as CPU, memory, and disk should be identical between nodes.

To ensure a zero **Recovery Point Objective (RPO)**, VCHA requires a low latency (up to 10 milliseconds), high bandwidth, and isolated network connectivity between the active and passive nodes, and must be separated from the management network. The vCSA is accessed through the management network interface.

The VCHA cluster can be shut down at any time, but a specific order must be followed to avoid vCSA service disruption.

Shut down the nodes in the following order:

- Passive node
- Active node
- Witness node

 To restart the VCHA cluster, you can restart the nodes in any order.

If you need to remove the vCenter HA configuration, proceed as follows:

1. From the active node, right-click **vCenter Server** and select **vCenter HA Settings**.
2. Under **Settings**, select **vCenter HA** and click the **Edit** button.
3. Select the **Remove vCenter HA** option:

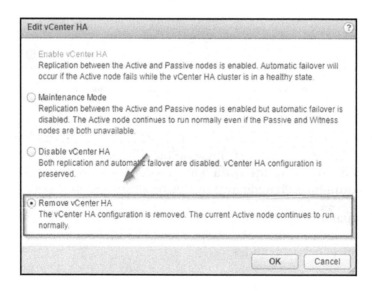

Figure 9.19: Removing the vCenter HA configuration

4. Click **OK** to confirm.

The HA configuration is removed from all of the cluster's nodes and the active node continues to run as a standalone vCSA. Former passive and witness nodes must be deleted since they cannot be reused for a new VCHA deployment.

 If the vCenter Server active node uses a certificate that must be replaced, you have to remove passive and witness nodes, install the new certifcate, and recreate the cluster.

Review questions

1. What options can be configured in vSphere Availability? (select two)
    - A: Admission controls
    - B: Failure and responses
    - C: Health and performance
    - D: VM overrides

   A, B - See *Objective 9.1*

2. If vSAN is enabled in the same cluster, what network is used by vSphere HA?
    - A: Management network
    - B: vSphere HA is not supported on a vSAN cluster
    - C: vSAN network
    - D: Datastore heartbeats

   C - See *Objective 9.2*

3. The vSAN datastore can be used as a heartbeat datastore.
    - A: True
    - B: False

   B - See *Objective 9.2*

4. What is the maximum accepted latency for the vCenter HA network?
   - A: 1 second
   - B: 10 milliseconds
   - C: 150 milliseconds
   - D: 50 milliseconds

B - See *Objective 9.2*

5. The correct sequence to shut down nodes in a VCHA cluster is passive, witness, active.
   - A: True
   - B: False

B - See *Objective 9.2*

Summary

This chapter explained the configuration settings for the vSphere HA feature as part of *Objective 9.1*, covering admission control policies and heartbeat datastores. *Objective 9.2* covered a new feature introduced in vSphere 6.5 that is only available for the vCenter Server appliance: vCSA HA. During the exam, you should expect some questions about these two topics, so make sure that you understand the different configuration scenarios.

Chapter 10, *Administer and Manage vSphere Virtual Machines*, will walk you through the administration and management of virtual machines as part of *Objective 10*.

10
Administer and Manage vSphere Virtual Machines

In Chapter 9, *Configure and Administer vSphere and vCenter Availability Solutions*, we covered the HA capabilities that are available in vSphere 6.5, and explained the configuration of the vSphere HA cluster and the vCSA HA setup. The deployment of virtual machines is the final step in vSphere 6.5 infrastructure configuration. Understanding the available settings and configuration options of virtual machines is a key point that's covered in *Objective 10.1* to ensure that you have the correct VMs deployment.

This chapter will also explain the concept and configuration of the content library feature, pointing out its benefits and the new capabilities introduced in vSphere 6.5 to ensure consistency and compliance of the network when deploying workloads, especially in large environments.

The consolidation of physical machines using the VMware vCenter Converter tool is the final topic of this chapter, which provides you with some useful information to properly perform **physical to virtual (P2V)** conversions as part of *Objective 10.4* of the certification exam.

 The content library feature is not only a useful capability available in vSphere 6.5, but it is also a topic that may have some questions related to the configuration options in the certification exam.

In this chapter, the reader will cover the following topics:

- Configuring virtual machine advanced settings
- Managing content libraries
- Synchronizing content library contents
- Publishing and subscribing content libraries
- Adding and removing content libraries
- Using the VMware Converter to consolidate physical machines
- Resizing and configuring the virtual disk format

Create and manage vSphere Virtual Machines and templates

The configuration of the virtual machine's advanced settings, such as vGPUs and SR-IOV, are covered in this objective as part of the exam preparation.

Additional information can be found in the guide *vSphere Virtual Machine Administration*, which is available at the following URL: `https://docs.vmware.com/en/VMware-vSphere/6.5/vsphere-esxi-vcenter-server-651-virtual-machine-admin-guide.pdf`.

Determine how using a shared USB device impacts the environment

In vSphere 6.5, a virtual machine can access multiple USB devices, such as mass storage devices and security dongles that are attached to the ESXi host on which the VM resides, relying on USB passthrough technology.

Only one virtual machine at a time can connect to a USB device and until the virtual machine is powered on, the connected USB device is not available to other virtual machines running in the host. To access a USB device from a virtual machine, the VM requires a USB controller in the configuration settings.

USB passthrough technology allows the virtual machines direct access to USB devices that are attached to the hosting ESXi and requires the following components:

- **USB arbitrator**: Enabled by default, the USB arbitrator has the role of scanning the host to detect new USB devices, and routes the USB device traffic to the correct virtual machine. This prevents access to the devices from other virtual machines until they are released.
- **USB controller**: To use USB devices, a virtual machine must have a USB controller. In vSphere 6.5, up to 8 virtual controllers can be added to a virtual machine and a controller must be presented before adding a USB device to the VM. A maximum of 15 USB controllers can be monitored by the USB arbitrator.
- **USB devices**: Up to 20 USB devices can be added to a virtual machine, and this is the maximum number of simultaneous connections supported.

To add USB support to a virtual machine, you must first install the USB controller and then specify which version to use (available values are 2.0 and 3.0).

To add the USB controller to a virtual machine, from the vSphere Web Client, right-click the virtual machine to edit it and follow these steps:

1. Select **Edit Settings**.
2. From the **Edit Settings** view, select **USB Controller** from the **New device** drop-down menu and then click **Add**.
3. Expand the **New USB Controller** and specify the controller type from the **Settings** drop-down menu (**USB 2.0** by default).

4. Click **OK** to install the USB controller:

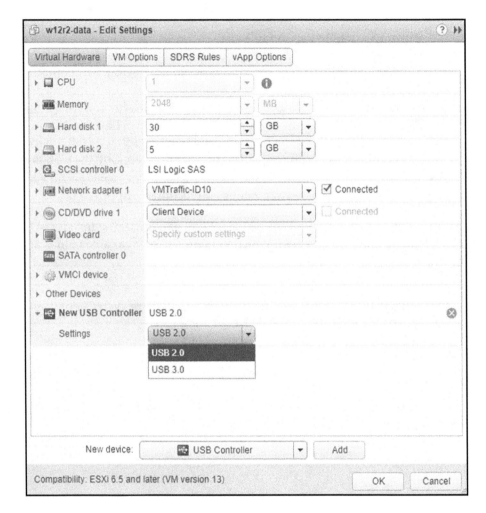

Figure 10.1: Adding the USB controller in the VM settings

 Starting from vSphere 5.5 Patch 3, to support USB 3.0 passthrough from a host to a virtual machine, the virtual machine must be configured with an xHCI controller and have Windows 8 or later, Windows Server 2012 or later, or Linux with a 2.6.35 or later kernel.

Since not all available vSphere features are supported by USB passthrough technology, make sure that you understand what capabilities are actually supported, as pointed out in the following table:

Feature	Supported with USB device passthrough
vSphere Distributed Power Management (DPM)	No
vSphere Distributed Resource Scheduler (DRS)	Yes
vSphere Fault Tolerance	No
vSphere vMotion	Yes

Table 10.1: vSphere features supported with USB device passthrough

When a virtual machine with an attached USB device is migrated with vMotion to a different host, the VM remains connected with the USB device until it is powered off or suspended. To restore the virtual machine USB device connection, you need to migrate the VM back to the host where the USB device is attached.

When a virtual machine is connected to a USB device, some functions can affect the USB's behaviour, with the risk of losing data.

To avoid data loss, follow these recommendations:

- Remove any USB device prior to hot adding memory, CPU, or PCI devices
- Make sure no data transfers are in progress before suspending a virtual machine
- Make sure USB devices are not attached to virtual machines before changing the state of an ESXi host USB arbitrator

Hot adding USB CD/DVD-ROM devices is not supported.

Configure virtual machines for vGPUs, DirectPath I/O and SR-IOV

If an NVIDIA GRID GPU graphics device is installed in an ESXi host, you can take advantage of NVIDIA GRID **virtual GPU** (**vGPU**) technology by configuring the virtual machine accordingly.

As prerequisites, the host must have an NVIDIA GRID GPU graphics device and the related driver installed, and the virtual machine needs to be compatible with ESXi 6.0 and later.

To allow the virtual machine to access the NVIDIA GRID GPU graphics device, proceed as follows:

1. From vSphere Web Client, right-click the virtual machine to configure it and select **Edit Settings**.
2. Select the **Shared PCI Device** item from the **New device** drop-down menu and then click **Add**.
3. Expand the **New PCI device** and specify the **GPU Profile**.
4. Click the **Reserve all memory** button and then click **OK**:

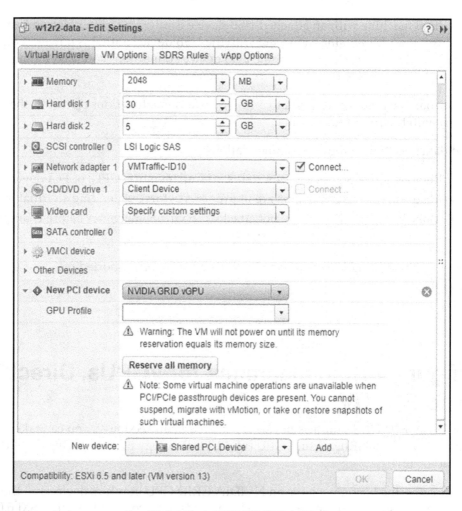

Figure 10.2: Configuring the NVIDIA GRID GPU in the VM settings

To configure the NVIDIA GRID GPU graphics device, the virtual machine must be powered off. If virtual machine compatibility is not 6.0 or later, the **Shared PCI Device** item will not be available.

DirectPath I/O is a configuration option that's available to virtual machines that allows you to directly access physical PCI and PCIe components connected to a host, such as high performance graphics or sound cards. Up to 6 PCI devices can be connected to a virtual machine.

With DirectPath I/O configuration, the virtual machine gains access to the dedicated device by bypassing the VMKernel, reducing the CPU demanded by the VMkernel itself. For example, a situation of high network demand can benefit from using DirectPath I/O.

When DirectPath is configured for a virtual machine, some features are no longer available. A virtual machine cannot be suspended, snapshots cannot be taken, and vMotion cannot be performed. Only those virtual machines that are not affected by these limitations are configured with DirectPath I/O on Cisco **Unified Computing Systems** (**UCS**) through Cisco **Virtual Machines Fabric Extender** (**VM-FEX**).

To enable DirectPath I/O for a virtual machine, the first step is to configure the DirectPath I/O passthrough for a device on a host:

1. From the vSphere Web Client, right-click the host to configure and select **Settings**.
2. Under **Hardware**, select **PCI Devices**.
3. Click the pencil icon (Edit) to enable passthrough for a PCI device on the host.
4. Select the device to be configured for passthrough and then click **OK**.

5. Reboot the host:

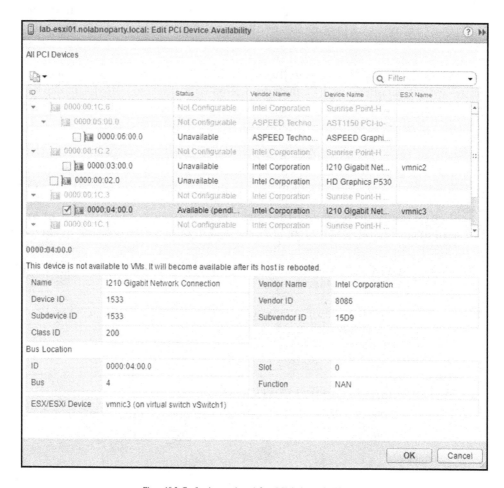

Figure 10.3: Configuring passthrough for a PCI device on the ESXi host

Once the passthrough for the PCI device on the host has been configured, select the virtual machine to edit. Make sure that the virtual machine is powered off and proceed as follows:

1. Right-click the virtual machine and select **Edit Settings**.
2. Expand **Memory** and set the **Limit** option as **Unlimited.**
3. Select **PCI Device** from the **New device** drop-down menu and then click **Add**.
4. Expand the **New PCI device** and select the passthrough device to use from the drop-down menu. Click **OK**.

5. Power on the virtual machine:

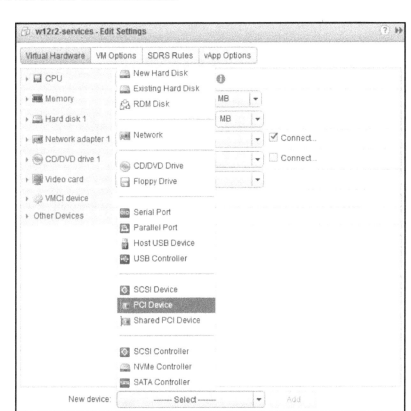

Figure 10.4: Configuring passthrough for a PCI device on the virtual machine

Compared to DirectPath I/O where you can only map one physical device to one virtual machine, Single Root I/O Virtualization (SR-IOV) allows you to share a single physical device between multiple virtual machines.

SR-IOV allows you to directly exchange data between the virtual machine and the physical adapter (the VMKernel is not used as an intermediary), reducing latency and improving CPU efficiency. Virtual machines that require low latency or more CPU resources can benefit from SR-IOV.

Appropriate BIOS and hardware is required to support PCI devices with SR-IOV enabled, and the device driver of the physical device must be installed in the guest operating system of the virtual machine.

Some of SR-IOV's core features, such as vMotion, are not available.

SR-IOV is mainly used for virtual machines with high network demands, and the configuration of this capability is a two-stage process.

The first step is the configuration of the physical device in the ESXi host:

1. From the vSphere Web Client, right-click the host to configure and select **Settings**.
2. Select **Physical adapters** under the **Networking** area.
3. Select the physical adapter to configure and click on the pencil icon (Edit adapter settings).
4. Under **SR-IOV**, set the **Status** as **Enabled.**
5. In **Number of virtual functions**, specify the number of virtual functions to configure for the adapter.
6. Click **OK** and reboot the host:

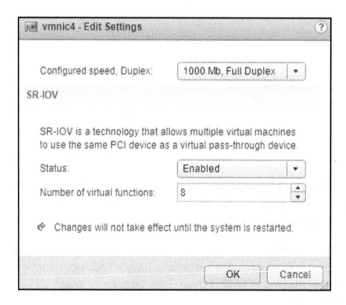

Figure 10.5: Configuring SR-IOV on the ESXi host

Now that you have configured the host, make sure that the virtual machine that you are going to set up is powered off and then follow these steps:

1. Right-click the virtual machine and select **Edit Settings**.
2. Select **Network** from the **New device** drop-down menu and then click **Add**.
3. Expand **New Network** and select **SR-IOV passthrough** from the **Adapter Type** drop-down menu.
4. Select the physical adapter that you previously configured from the **Physical function** drop-down menu.
5. From the **Guest OS MTU Change** drop-down menu, you can change the MTU.
6. Expand **Memory** and select **Reserve all guest memory (All locked)**, and then click **OK**.
7. Power on the virtual machine:

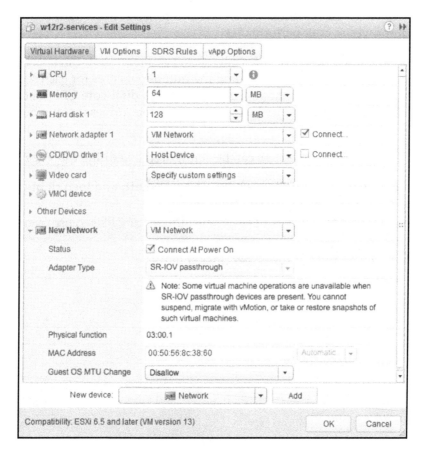

Figure 10.6: Configuring SR-IOV for a virtual machine

Configure virtual machines for multicore vCPUs

In vSphere 6.5, you can configure the number of cores per virtual socket to not only increase the virtual machine's performance, but also make it compliant with the requirements of the guest operating system EULA, which may limit the number of sockets that can be used.

The maximum number of vCPUs you can configure in a virtual machine is **128**, and the number of assigned vCPUs cannot exceed the physical cores available on the host if hyper-threading is disabled. By enabling hyper-threading on the host, the number of logical CPUs available to virtual machines is doubled. For example, if a host is equipped with 64 logical CPUs, the maximum number of vCPUs you can configure for a virtual machine is 64.

Hyper-threading is an Intel technology that's used to improve processor resource efficiency, allowing a single physical processor core to behave like two logical processors. It increases processor throughput and improves overall performance.

The vCPUs are assigned in terms of cores and cores per socket. You can specify the CPU cores to configure for the virtual machine and the number of cores for each socket, depending on the desired configuration (single-core CPU, dual-core CPU, and so on). The number of vCPU sockets specified in the configuration determines the number of cores that are available.

Multicore vCPUs for a virtual machine can be configured by editing the VM's settings:

1. Make sure that the virtual machine is **powered off**, and then right-click the virtual machine and select **Edit Settings**.
2. Expand the **CPU** section and select the number of CPUs to use from the drop-down menu.
3. Specify the number of **Cores per Socket** to use.
4. Click **OK**:

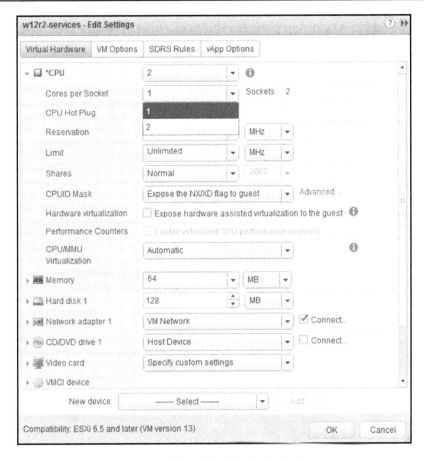

Figure 10.7: Configuring multicore vCPUs for a virtual machine

   You can't add or modify CPU resources while the virtual machine is powered on unless the **Hot add** option is enabled.

If you have more than 8 vCPUs, Virtual Non-Uniform Memory Access (vNUMA) is enabled and the ESXi host distributes the virtual machines to more NUMA nodes if one doesn't suffice. vNUMA is a memory-access optimization method used to prevent memory bandwidth bottlenecks for virtual machines.

If the **CPU Hot Add** option is enabled for a virtual machine, vNUMA support is disabled and the uniform memory access with interleaved memory access will be used instead (VMware KB 2040375: `https://kb.vmware.com/s/article/2040375`).

Differentiate virtual machine configuration settings

To configure the virtual machine settings, from the vSphere Web Client, you have to right-click on the virtual machine and select the **Edit Settings** options. There are several settings you can configure through the GUI, depending on your business requirements.

In the **VM Options** tab, you can access the advanced settings of the virtual machine by expanding the **Advanced** section. Clicking on **Edit configuration**, you can enter specific parameters to fine-tune the virtual machine's configuration:

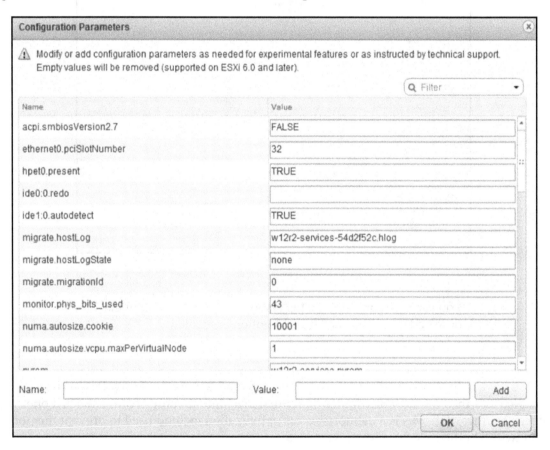

Figure 10.8: The virtual machine's advanced settings

To insert a new parameter, type a **Name** and its **Value** at the bottom of the window and then click **Add**. Click **OK** to save the new configuration. A typical use case of the advanced settings is to control the **Virtual Non-Uniform Memory Access (vNUMA)**, as reported in the following table:

Option	Description
cpuid.coresPerSocket	Determines the number of virtual cores per virtual CPU socket. If this value is greater than 1 for virtual machines with a virtual NUMA topology, this determines the size of virtual NUMA nodes. The default value is 1.
numa.vcpu.maxPerVirtualNode	Specifies, as a power of two, the maximum number of virtual cores per virtual node and can be used instead of the cpuid.coresPerSocket option. The default value is 8.
numa.vcpu.min	Specifies the minimum number of virtual CPUs in a virtual machine required to generate a virtual NUMA topology. The default value is 9.
numa.vcpu.maxPerClient	Determines the maximum number of vCPUs in a NUMA client, a group of virtual CPUs that are NUMA-managed as a single entity. This parameter is used when a virtual NUMA node is larger than a physical NUMA node. The default value is the same as numa.vcpu.maxPerVirtualNode.

Table 10.2: Advanced settings to control the vNUMA

Interpret virtual machine configuration file (.vmx) settings

The .vmx file stores all virtual machine settings you configure through the vSphere Web Client and, in most of situations, you don't need to manually edit this file.

If you need to add or modify configuration parameters in the .vmx file (for troubleshooting purposes, for instance), from vSphere Web Client, right-click on the virtual machine and select the **Edit Settings** option. Access this section to edit and configure the parameter as needed.

> Because a mistake in the configuration of the .vmx file will break the virtual machine's functionality, make a copy of the .vmx file before editing it.

To modify the .vmx file, proceed as follows:

1. Power off the virtual machine.
2. Right-click the virtual machine and select **Remove from Inventory**.
3. Edit the .vmx file using a text editor.

4. Browse the datastore on which the virtual machine's files are stored and right-click the `.vmx` file. Select **Register VM**:

```
w12r2-dc01.vmx
1    .encoding = "UTF-8"
2    config.version = "8"
3    virtualHW.version = "13"
4    nvram = "w12r2-dc01.nvram"
5    pciBridge0.present = "TRUE"
6    svga.present = "TRUE"
7    pciBridge4.present = "TRUE"
8    pciBridge4.virtualDev = "pcieRootPort"
9    vmci0.present = "TRUE"
10   hpet0.present = "TRUE"
11   floppy0.present = "FALSE"
12   svga.vramSize = "8388608"
13   memSize = "4096"
14   tools.upgrade.policy = "manual"
15   scsi0.virtualDev = "lsisas1068"
16   scsi0.pciSlotNumber = "160"
17   scsi0.present = "TRUE"
18   scsi0:0.deviceType = "scsi-hardDisk"
19   scsi0:0.fileName = "w12r2-dc01.vmdk"
20   scsi0:0.present = "TRUE"
21   vmci0.pciSlotNumber = "32"
22   ethernet0.virtualDev = "vmxnet3"
23   ethernet0.networkName = "VM Network"
24   ethernet0.addressType = "generated"
25   ethernet0.pciSlotNumber = "192"
26   ethernet0.uptCompatibility = "TRUE"
27   ethernet0.present = "TRUE"
28   displayName = "w12r2-dc01"
29   guestOS = "windows8srv-64"
30   disk.EnableUUID = "TRUE"
```

Figure 10.9: Some sample entries stored in the .vmx file

Make sure you are logged in with an account with the appropriate permissions. You can check out the required virtual machine configuration privileges at the following URL: `https://docs.vmware.com/en/VMware-vSphere/6.5/com.vmware.vsphere.security.doc/GUID-FEAB5DF5-F7A2-412D-BF3D-7420A355AE8F.html`.

Enable/disable advanced virtual machine settings

To enable or disable advanced settings for a virtual machine, the virtual machine must be powered off and you need to access the **Advanced** section of the **VM Options** tab in the virtual machine settings.

Generally, a parameter can be enabled by setting its value to TRUE or disabled by setting its value to FALSE:

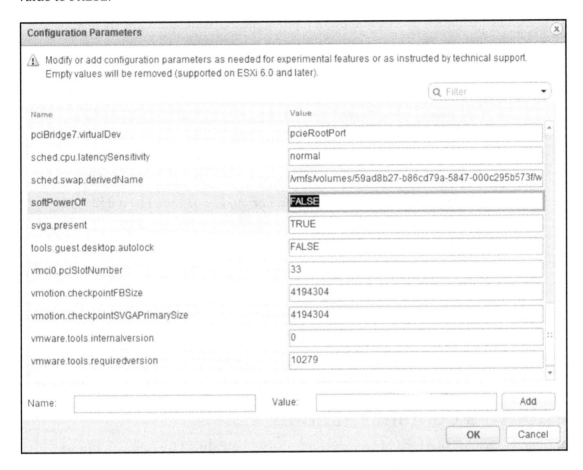

Figure 10.10: Enabling/disabling advanced settings in a virtual machine

Create and manage a content library

A content library is a feature available in vSphere 6.5 that acts as a container for objects so that you can store VM templates, vApp templates, ISOs, and files you need to share across multiple vCenter Server instances belonging to the same SSO domain. Content libraries can be used to ensure compliance and consistency within the network when deploying workloads.

A content library can be useful for the deployment of new virtual machines from a stored template or so that you can mount an ISO image directly from the library.

VM templates, vApp templates, and other types of file in a content library are defined as library items that can contain single or multiple files, such as OVF, ISO, and so on.

Two types of content library object can be created in vSphere 6.5:

- **Local**: Items are stored on a single vCenter Server instance and can be published to allow users from different vCenter Servers to access them via a subscription.
- **Subscribed**: Subscribing to a published library creates a subscribed library. A subscribed library can be created in the same vCenter as the published library or in a different vCenter Server instance. The content of a subscribed library is kept up to date through an automated or on-demand synchronization to the source's published library. Subscribers can't edit or modify its contents, but they can utilize them.

The new features introduced in vSphere 6.5 content libraries allows administrators to perform the following tasks:

- Mount ISO files directly from the library
- Update existing templates
- Apply guest OS customization

A content library must be published to make the content available to other vCenter Servers.

Publish a content catalog

During the creation of a local library, you can enable the **Publish this content library externally** option to make the content available to other vCenter Server instances. Optionally, you can enable authentication by checking the enable **Authentication** checkbox so that it asks for a password to access the library. Select **Optimize for syncing over HTTP** to create an optimized published library if the library resides on a remote vCenter Server system and enhanced linked mode is not used.

To publish an existing content library, from the vSphere Web Client, access the **Home** | **Content Library** section and right-click on the library to publish. Select **Edit Settings** and check the **Publish this content library externally** option. You also have the option to enable authentication. Click **OK** to publish the library:

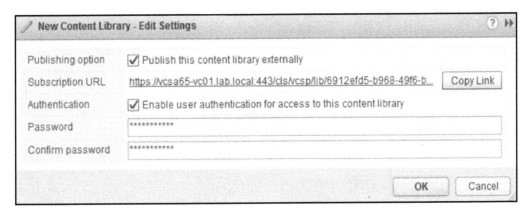

Figure 10.11: Publishing a created local library

You can't unpublish a content library if the library has been published with the option to synchronize the content over HTTP.

Subscribe to a published catalog

Once the content library has been created and published, content can be shared across vCenter Servers within the same SSO domain. To subscribe to a library, you need to create a subscribed library that can reside on the same vCenter Server instance or a different one.

To create a subscribed library, proceed as follows:

1. From vSphere Web Client, access the **Home ∣ Content Libraries** section and click on the **Create a new content library** button:

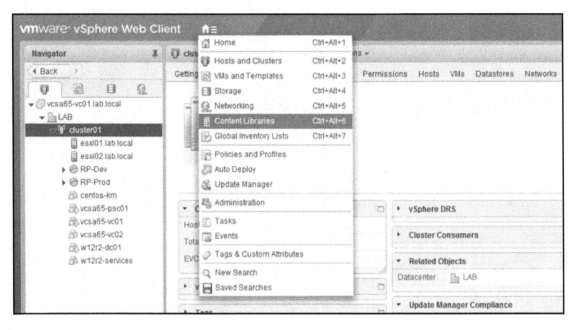

Figure 10.12: Accessing the content library section

2. Type a **Name** for the library and then click **Next**.
3. Select **Subscribed content library** and enter the **Subscription URL**.
Specify whether **Authentication** is required and the download type (immediately or on-demand). Click **Next**.
4. Specify the storage used for the library and click **Next**.

5. Click **Finish**:

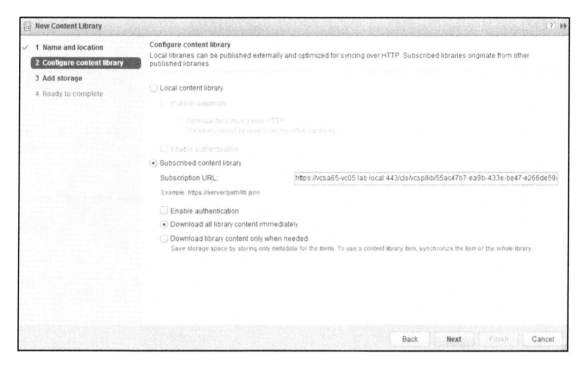

Figure 10.13: Subscribing to a content library

A content library can be configured to optimize synchronization over HTTP in order to reduce CPU usage so that you have faster streaming, but cannot be used to deploy virtual machines.

 Users in other vCenter SSO domains cannot subscribe to the library.

Determine which privileges are required to globally manage a content catalog

Content libraries are not direct children objects of the vCenter Server, but their direct parent is the global root. Permissions set at a vCenter level and propagated to the children objects won't be applied to content libraries. Permissions on a content library must be granted to users as a **global permission**.

To manage a content library, a user should be granted the content library administrator role (a sample role in vSphere Web Client) as a global permission. If the assigned role is defined as a global permission, the user is able to manage content libraries and the content in all vCenter Server instances. A user with the role of Administrator at the vCenter level can manage libraries that belong to this vCenter Server instance if the read-only privilege has been defined as a global permission:

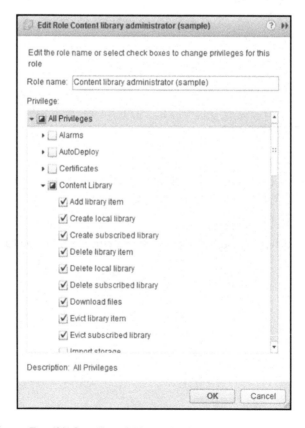

Figure 10.14: Content library administrator role available in vSphere Web Client

Compare the functionality of automatic sync and an on-demand sync

Published libraries with content shared across multiple vCenter Servers need to be synchronized in order to keep subscribed libraries' content up to date. Synchronization occurs by downloading the content from a published library to the subscribed library.

You can manually synchronize a subscribed library or automate the process by enabling the **Enable automatic synchronization with the external content library** option in the library settings:

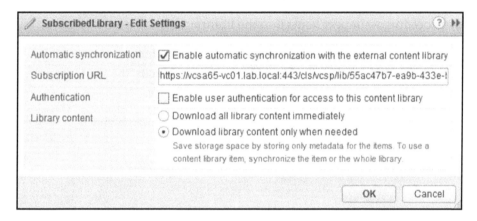

Figure 10.15: Enabling automatic synchronization

To synchronize a subscribed library on-demand, from the **Home** | **Content Library** menu, right-click the library to process and select **Synchronize**.

Library content can be synchronized in two different ways:

- **Download all library content immediately**: A full synchronization is performed immediately (data and metadata), and all of the content is actually downloaded to the subscribed library so that all of the data is available immediately.
- **Download library content only when needed**: When selecting this option, only metadata that contains information about content data is immediately transferred to the subscribed library, allowing the user to view the content list. Only when objects are demanded from the subscribed library is the actual data synced. Although this option allows you to save some storage space, you need to wait until the synchronization completes before data is available to use.

To perform the library synchronization, you need **Content library | Sync subscribed library** permissions on the library.

Configure content library to work across sites

Content libraries can be shared across different vCenter Servers, and the procedure is nothing more complicated than publishing a created library. When a library has been created, you can import VM templates, vApps templates, ISO files, and so on.

Follow this procedure to import items into the library:

1. Right-click the desired library and select **Import item**.
2. Enter the **URL** or click the **Browse...** button to specify the file to import.
3. Click **OK** to import the selected file into the library:

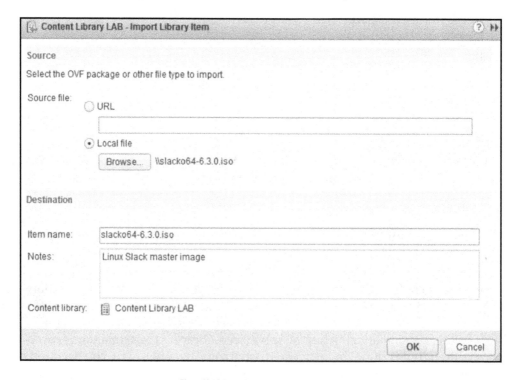

Figure 10.16: Importing items into a content library

To view the library items available in a content library, click on the desired library from the content library section. Inside the library, files are grouped as **Templates** and **Other Types**.

To make a library's content accessible from other vCenter Servers, you need to publish the library, enabling the **Publish externally** option by editing a configured library (right-click the library and then select **Edit Settings**) or during the library creation procedure. You can also enable authentication by checking the corresponding checkbox and entering its password:

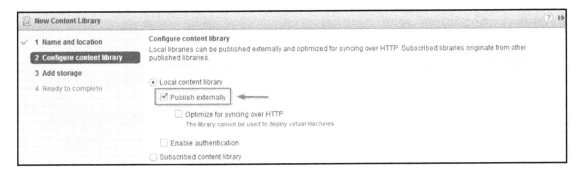

Figure 10.17: Library items available in the select content library

Configure content library authentication

In a content library, you have the option to enable authentication so that it asks for a password when the library is accessed. Authentication can be enabled during the creation of the library or by editing the library settings:

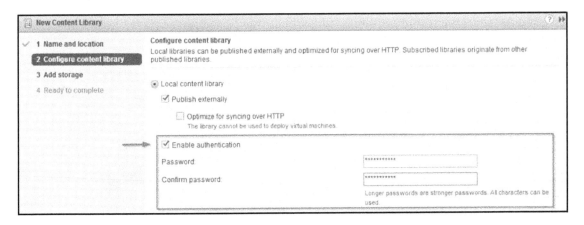

Figure 10.18: Enabling authentication for a library

The password is the only parameter you can set for the predefined *vcsp* username (you can't change the name) that's used to publish a content library.

Set/configure content library roles

In vSphere Web Client, there is a predefined **Content library Administrator** role you can use to assign permissions in order to manage content libraries and their content. Since content libraries are at the global root, privileges cannot be assigned directly to a library, but they must be defined as global permissions.

To assign permissions to manage content libraries, follow this procedure:

1. From vSphere Web Client, navigate to the **Home** | **Administration** | **Global Permissions** section.
2. Click the + (plus) icon to add a new permission.
3. Select the **Content Library Administrator (sample)** role from the drop-down menu.
4. Click **Add** and select the account or group to grant the selected role.
5. Click **OK** to save the configuration.

You can also create a custom role by cloning the Content library Administrator role and then specifying the permissions needed to perform only requested operations on libraries objects. For example, you can create a custom role to manage only the library items but no other actions, such as creating or publishing content libraries:

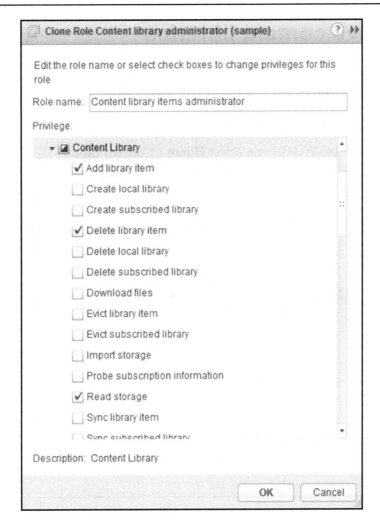

Figure 10.19: The set of permissions required to manage library items

Additional information can be found on the Content library Privileges page at VMware's website (`https://docs.vmware.com/en/VMware-vSphere/6.5/com.vmware.vsphere.security.doc/GUID-D490C499-8D68-42A1-AEB2-781F1DDA8A93.html`).

Add/remove content libraries

As described previously, content libraries can be added by clicking the **Create a new content library** icon from **Home** | **Content Library**. From there, you can configure library items such as library name, library type (local or subscribed), and storage to use.

To remove a content library, proceed as follows:

1. From vSphere Web Client, select **Home** | **Content Library** from the main menu.
2. Right-click the library to remove and select **Delete**.
3. Click **Yes** to confirm library deletion:

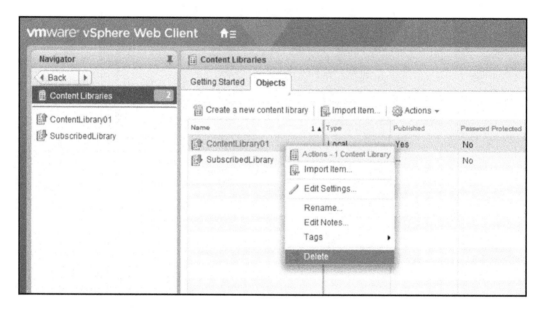

Figure 10.20: Removing a content library

Consolidate physical workloads using VMware vCenter Converter

VMware vCenter Converter is a tool by VMware that's used to import a physical or virtual machine into the vSphere environment. Conversion from P2V can be considered if the network has some old physical machines or physical machines with specific applications that require a long time for a fresh installation, and an excessive downtime period is not tolerated.

More information on this is available in the *VMware vCenter Converter Standalone User's Guide* (`https://docs.vmware.com/en/vCenter-Converter-Standalone/6.2/convsa_62_guide.pdf`).

Install vCenter Converter standalone instance

The vCenter Converter standalone is a Windows-based free tool used to convert physical machines to virtual machines and can be installed on physical or virtual machines.

The tool can be downloaded from the VMware website (`https://my.vmware.com/en/web/vmware/info/slug/infrastructure_operations_management/vmware_vcenter_converter_standalone/6_2_0`) and the installation is performed by launching the `.exe` installer file.

The installation of the vCenter Converter standalone includes the following steps:

1. After launching the executable file, click **Next** at the **Welcome** window.
2. Click **Next** in the **End-User Patent Agreement** window.
3. Agree with the EULA and click **Next** to continue.
4. Leave the default installation folder and click **Next**.
5. Select the installation type and then click **Next**. You have two options you can choose from:
    - **Local installation**: A Converter Standalone server, Converter Standalone agent, and Converter Standalone client are installed locally and the conversion process only takes place in the machine on which the application is installed.

- **Client-Server installation**: This option allows you to create and manage conversion tasks remotely, and the components of the Converter Standalone components can be selected during the installation:

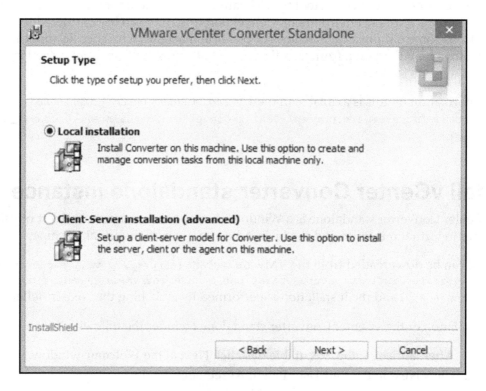

Figure 10.21: Available setup types in the vCenter Converter standalone

6. Leave **Join the VMware Customer Experience Improvement Program** selected if you want to join the CEIP.
7. Click **Install** to proceed with the installation.
8. When the installation has completed, click **Finish** to exit the wizard.

Convert physical workloads using vCenter Converter

The P2V procedure is used to convert a physical machine into a virtual machine. Machines running Windows and Linux (desktop and server editions) operating systems are both supported.

vCenter Converter supports the following operating systems:

- **Windows**: Windows Vista, 7, 8, 8.1, 10 (32-bit and 64-bit), and Windows Server 2008 SP2 and later
- **Linux**: CentOS 6.x, 7.0, RHEL 4.x, 5.x, 6.x, SUSE 10.x, 11.x, Ubuntu 12.04 LTS, 14.04 LTS, 16.04 LTS (32-bit and 64-bit)

 With the supported hot cloning feature, you can convert a running machine in a non-disruptive way, with no downtime or reboot requirements.

Before proceeding with the conversion, make sure that source machine has installed volumes and disks supported by vCenter Converter (see the following table for more information):

Source	Supported volumes and disks	Unsupported volumes and disks
Virtual machine	• Basic volumes • All types of dynamic volumes • **Master boot record (MBR)** disks • **GUID partition table (GPT)** disks	• RAID • GPT/MBR hybrid disks • RDM disks
Powered on machine	• All types of source volumes that the OS recognizes • **GUID partition table (GPT)** disks • **Master boot record (MBR)** disks	• RAID • GPT/MBR hybrid disks • Linux volumes mounted by Device Mapper multipath

Table 10.3: Volumes and disks supported by vCenter Converter

To convert a physical machine, proceed as follows:

1. Open the vCenter Converter Standalone and click the **Convert Machine** button.
2. Select **Powered on** or **Powered off** to specify the status of the machine to convert and whether the machine is local or remote. Enter the **IP address**, **User name**, and **Password** if the remote machine option is chosen, and then click **Next**. The vCenter Converter agent is deployed for the machine to convert. From the **Select source type** drop-down menu, you have the following options available:
   - **Powered on selected**: Remote Windows machine, Remote Linux machine, This local machine.

- **Powered off selected**: VMware Infrastructure virtual machine, VMware Workstation or other VMware virtual machine, Hyper-V Server:

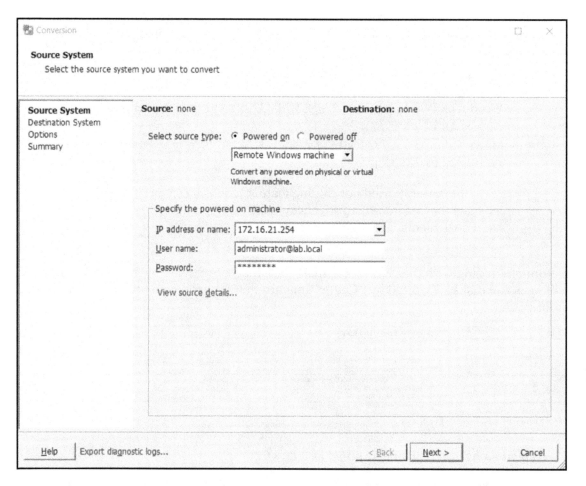

Figure 10.22: Parameters to configure for source machines

3. From the **Select destination type** drop-down menu, select the **VMware Infrastructure virtual machine** option. Enter the **IP address** of the vCenter Server and the **User name** and **Password**. Click **Next**:

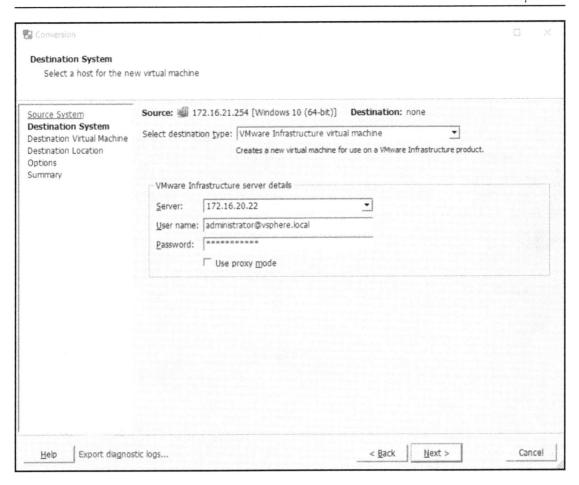

Figure 10.23: Specifying the destination system in the vCenter Converter

4. Type in a meaningful **Name** for the converted virtual machine and specify the destination folder. Click **Next**.

5. Specify the destination location by choosing a data center, cluster, or resource pool to place the converted virtual machine. Also select the datastore to use and the virtual hardware to install. Check out the following table for virtual hardware compatibility:

Virtual hardware version	Destination
7	ESXi 4.x or later
8	ESXi 5.0 or later
9	ESXi 5.1 or later
10	ESXi 5.5 or later
11	ESXi 6.0 or later

Table 10.4: Virtual hardware version compatible with destination location

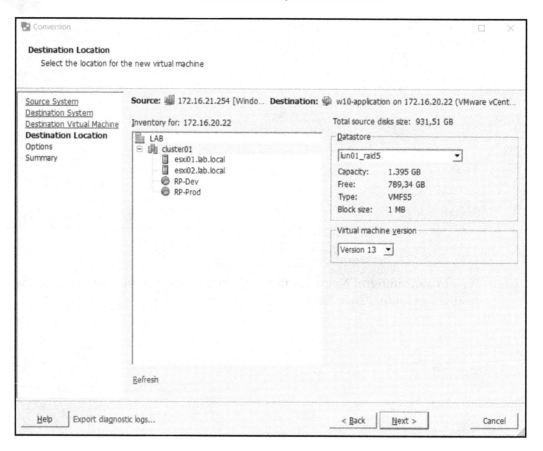

Figure 10.24: Specifying the destination's location for the virtual machine

vCenter Converter 6.2 doesn't support virtual hardware versions above 11 and limits the features to what's available for version 11 if a version above 11 is selected.

6. On the **Options** page, you have the option to modify parameters so that they're configured for the conversion task. There are different items you can change:
   - **Data to copy**: By default, all disks are selected
   - **Devices**: Disk controller, vCPUs, and RAM
   - **Networks**: Network settings
   - **Advanced options**: Install VMware Tools, synchronization, and so on

At this stage, you can also specify the disk type (available formats are **Thick** or **Thin**), as well as change the hard drive's size. If a hard drive size is modified, the copy process occurs at the file level and not at the block level. Click **Next** to continue:

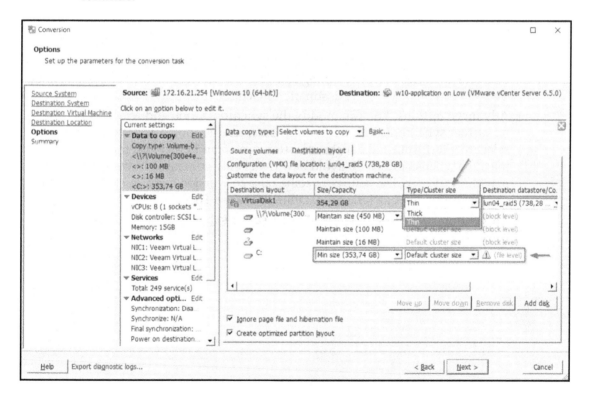

Figure 10.25: Configuration of the disk type during conversion

7. In the **Summary** window, click **Finish** to proceed with the virtual machine conversion.

Modify server resources during conversion

The **Options configuration** page that's available in the vCenter Converter wizard allows you to modify existing parameters such as vCPU, RAM, hard drive size, and so on. There are six sections where you can modify resources and parameters for the destination virtual machine:

- **Data to copy**: By default, all disks are selected. The advanced configuration allows you to change the disk format (**Thick** or **Thin**), add/remove hard drives, and modify the hard drive's size. For each disk, you can also specify the target datastore. Page and hibernation files are excluded from copies by default.

- **Devices**: The number of vCPU and cores per socket can be increased or decreased, as well as memory allocation. From this section, you can also modify the disk controller type.

- **Networks**: Network adapters can be added or removed with the option of specifying the port group to which the NICs will connect.

- **Services**: Includes a list of running and enabled services on the source machine that you can modify for the destination machine.

- **Advanced options**: You can modify the synchronization and related schedule. If no further synchronizations will occur between the source and the destination, select the **Perform final synchronization** option and power off the source machine when complete to avoid new data being generated in the source machine. You can also configure some post-conversion tasks, such as powering on the destination machine or installing VMware Tools.

- **Throttling:** This allows you to control resources that are being used for the current task:

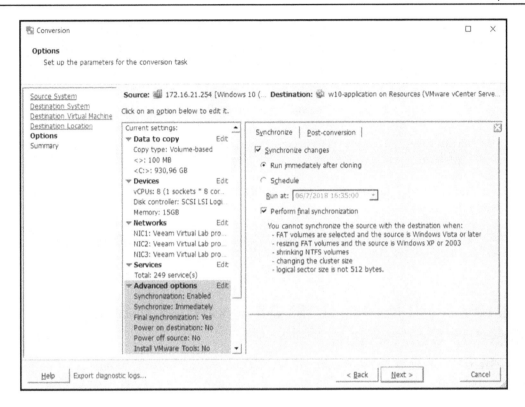

Figure 10.26: Configuration of the final synchronization task

To improve conversion speed, you can specify the number of concurrent tasks, from 1 up to 12 (select **Administration | Maximum concurrent tasks** from the main menu). By default, the number of concurrent tasks is set to 12.

Interpret and correct errors during conversion

During the conversion process, you may face some issues that result in conversion failure. Typical problems that may arise are often due to misconfiguration. Here are some examples:

- If vCenter Converter is not able to connect to a remote machine, it could be a typical communication error due to the Windows Firewall. Ensure that the firewall is disabled or that the required ports are open (TCP/IP and UDP port requirements for conversion can be found at the following URL: `https://docs. vmware.com/en/vCenter-Converter-Standalone/6.2/com.vmware.convsa. guide/GUID-4814B6B2-12A4-4E66-9B43-F1394F9E7433.html`).

- Another issue you can experience is that the virtual machine is unable to boot. Double-check whether the correct disk controller is configured in the vCenter Converter wizard and try changing IDE controllers with SCSI.

When you experience an error, the first thing you should do is troubleshoot the issue so that you can check the logs. The log's path may vary, depending on the OS that's installed on the machine used for the vCenter Converter. Typically, logs for vCenter Converter 5.x or 6.x are located in the `C:\ProgramData\Application Data\VMware\VMware Converter Standalone\Logs` folder.

Check out the *Collecting diagnostic information during the conversion operation* section for additional log locations.

To troubleshoot issues with the vCenter Converter, take a look at Vmware KB 1016330 (`https://kb.vmware.com/s/article/1016330`).

Deploy a physical host as a virtual machine using vCenter Converter

All the steps involved in the deployment of a virtual machine using vCenter Converter have been already covered in the *Converting physical workloads using vCenter Converter* section.

Collect diagnostic information during the conversion operation

Diagnostic information is often required by VMware support in order to provide assistance in the case of a support request.

There are different locations where logs are placed depending on used version. In vCenter Converter 5.x and 6.x, logs can be found in the following locations:

- In the vCenter Converter GUI, select the **Task** | **Export Logs** menu.
- From the **Job** view, select **Job** | **Export logs**.
- On the computer where the vCenter Converter is installed, logs are stored in `C:\ProgramData\Application Data\VMware\VMware Converter Standalone\Logs`.

- On the computer that is being converted, go
  to `C:\ProgramData\VMware\VMware vCenter Converter Standalone Agent\logs` or `%ALLUSERSPROFILE%\Application Data\VMware\VMware vCenter Converter Standalone Client\logs`.

Resize partitions during the conversion process

While inside the vCenter Convert wizard, select the **Data to copy** tab in the **Options** page. Besides adding or removing disks, you can resize partitions for the destination virtual machine. In the **Destination layout**, you can also specify the datastore for each hard drive and the disk provisioning type (**Thin** or **Thick**):

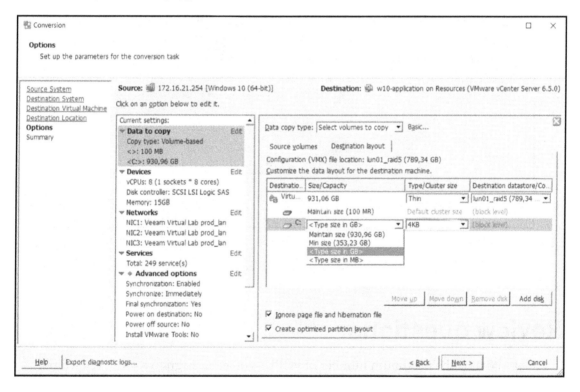

Figure 10.27: Resizing a hard drive for the destination machine

Determine which virtual disk format to use

While in the vCenter Converter wizard, on the **Options** page, you can specify the disk type to use for the converted virtual machine by choosing between the **Thin** and **Thick** formats.

For large volumes or disks, thin provisioning allows you to save some storage space:

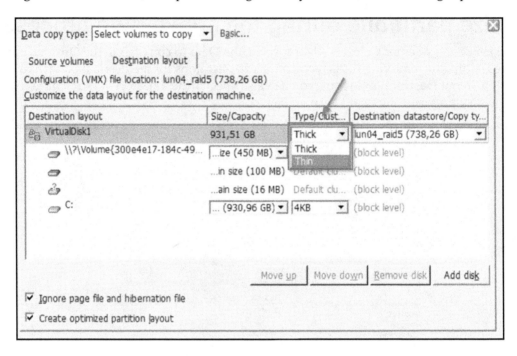

Figure 10.28: Configuring the disk format for the converted machine

Review questions

1. What is the maximum number of vCPUs you can assign to a virtual machine?
   - A: 256
   - B: 64
   - C: 128
   - D: 8

   C - See *Objective 10.1*

2. What feature must be defined for low latency and more CPU resource requirements to be given to a virtual machine?
   - A: DirectPath I/O
   - B: SR-IOV
   - C: VM-FEX
   - D: Shared PCI

B - See *Objective 10.1*

3. What is a possible reason why an administrator is not able to deploy a virtual machine from content libraries?
   - A: The account doesn't have read-only permission at vCenter level
   - B: Synchronization must be performed first
   - C: The library is optimized to synchronize the content over HTTP
   - D: The library is not published

C - See *Objective 10.2*

4. At what level must permissions to manage a content library be defined?
   - A: vCenter level
   - B: Cluster level
   - C: Global permission
   - D: Specific content library

C - See *Objective 10.2*

5. What are the supported disks in vCenter Converter? (choose two)
   - A: **GUID partition table (GPT)** disks
   - B: **Master boot record (MBR)** disks
   - C: RDM disks
   - D: RAID

A, B - See *Objective 10.3*

Summary

This chapter covered the final part of the *VCP6.5-DCV Exam Preparation Guide*. *Objective 10.1* explained the advanced configuration of virtual machines, covering the pro and cons of some features such as DirectPath I/O and SR-IOV. Configuration, synchronization, publication, and the subscription of content libraries was covered as part of *Objective 10.2*, explaining use cases and optimization settings. *Objective 10.4* covered the final section of the exam, walking you through the installation and use of the vCenter Converter tool used to convert physical machines to virtual machines.

11
Mock Exam 1

This chapter contains one mock exam, to test your knowledge of the content in all of the previous chapters.

The mock test exam will contain **70 questions** (like the real 2V0-622 exam), and readers should try to complete it in **105 minutes**, simulating the real exam's duration.

Note that the questions can also be used in preparation for the VCP6.5-DCV delta exam (the 2V0-622D exam), which also has 70 questions and a 105-minute duration.

The vSphere 6.5 Foundations exam (the 2V0-602 exam) is a little more general (and less deep, technically), but covers several other products from VMware, including vRealize Log Insight, vRealize Automation, and NSX.

The appendix of this book will provide more details on the different VCP65-DCV exams.

 VMware no longer provides free mock exams. Instead, they redirect users to Measure Up for online exam simulations; the price of each exam is US $109 (as of July 2018).

The following activities will be covered in this chapter:

- Testing your knowledge in preparation for the VCP65-DCV exam
- Simulating the VCP-DCV exam

Mock exam 1

This mock exam is structured in the same order as the book's chapters, in order to group questions on the same topic together; however, remember that in the real exam, the questions will be sorted randomly.

Also, in the real exam, the number of questions will not necessarily be equally distributed across the topics and contents of the different chapters.

 Note that some questions may have multiple answers. In this case, it will be indicated with a "Select all correct answers" sentence. In the real exam, the number of answers (in the case of a multiple-choice question) is usually specified.

The correct answers will be included at the end of each section.

Configure and administer vSphere 6.x security

1. What is the purpose of vCenter roles?
     • A: Roles help administrators to see which users are logged into virtual machines.
     • B: Roles are predefined sets of privileges.
     • C: Roles are used to ensure that a VM gets the correct amount of computing resources.
     • D: Roles are not used within vSphere.

2. To assign permissions in a vSphere environment, what attributes are mandatory? (Select two)
     • A: A firewall setting
     • B: A resource pool
     • C: A user or a group
     • D: A role
     • E: A share

3. What is the purpose of the PSC?
     • A: The PSC is not required for vCenter Server 6.5.
     • B: The PSC provides the cryptographic keys needed for VM encryption.
     • C: The PSC provides common infrastructure services to the vSphere environment.
     • D: The PSC provides an additional security level.

4. Which of the following are deployment options for the Platform Services Controller? (Select all correct answers)
    - A: vCenter Server appliance with an embedded Platform Services Controller
    - B: Platform Services Controller `.VIB` file deployed to each ESXi host in the vSphere environment
    - C: Standalone Platform Services Controller appliance
    - D: Standalone Platform Services Controller installed on a Windows server
    - E: Platform Services Controller deployed directly from the OVA file

5. Which of the following methods can be used to help improve the security of an ESXi host? (Select all correct answers)
    - A: Disabling SSH access
    - B: Disabling the ESXi firewall
    - C: Changing the password of the default administrator account
    - D: Enabling lockdown mode

6. What types of files are encrypted if VM encryption is enabled? (Select all correct answers)
    - A: Virtual machine configuration files (`.vmx`)
    - B: Virtual disk files (`.vmdk`)
    - C: VM log files
    - D: ESXi log files
    - E: ESXi core dump files

7. What is the default option for encrypted vMotion?
    - A: None
    - B: Opportunistic
    - C: Required
    - D: Enabled

The following list provides all of the correct answers to the preceding questions:

Q1: A

Q2: C, D

Q3: C

Q4: A, C, D

Q5: A, C, D

Q6: A, B, D

Q7: B

Configure and administer vSphere 6.x networking

1. When NIOC is enabled, which of the following settings can be used to reserve or limit bandwidth? (Select all correct answers)
   - A: Reservations
   - B: Shares
   - C: Limits
   - D: QoS
   - E: VLAN

2. What type of VLAN configuration is possible for a port group on a standard virtual switch? (Select all correct answers)
   - A: VLAN trunking on selected VLAN IDs
   - B: VLAN trunking for all VLAN IDs
   - C: VLAN tagging on a specific VLAN ID
   - D: Private VLAN

3. What vSphere distributed switch feature enables you to detect misconfigurations in the ESXi host management network?
   - A: Network Health Check
   - B: Network Restore
   - C: Automatic Rollback and Recovery
   - D: Network Reset

4. Which of the following actions requires a reboot of an ESXi host?
   - A: Disabling the IPv6 stack
   - B: Changing the number of ports on a standard virtual switch
   - C: Implementing VLANs for a (standard or distributed) virtual switch
   - D: Configuring an NIC team for a (standard or distributed) virtual switch

5. At which two levels can blocking policies be applied on a distributed virtual switch? (Select all correct answers)
   - A: Virtual switch
   - B: Virtual adapter
   - C: dvUplink
   - D: dvPort group
   - E: Physical adapter

6. Which of the following security policies must be configured if you have a network-based intrusion detection system running on a virtual machine that must capture analyses network packets?
   - A: Setting MAC address changes to `Reject`
   - B: Setting promiscuous mode to `Accept`
   - C: Setting forged transmits mode to `Accept`
   - D: Setting forged transmits mode to `Reject`

7. In order to monitor the VM network traffic, what are the best possible options when using a distributed virtual switch? (Select all correct answers)
   - A: Using promiscuous mode at the port group level
   - B: Using Netflow
   - C: Using Port Monitoring
   - D: Using SNMP

The following list provides all of the correct answers to the preceding questions:

Q1: A, B, C

Q2: B, C

Q3: C

Q4: A

Q5: C, D

Q6: B

Q7: B, C

Configure and administer vSphere 6.x storage

1. What kind of virtual disk provisioning is possible in NAS storage?
    - A: Only thin provisioning
    - B: Thin and thick provisioning
    - C: Usually thin, but with VAAI, thick is possible
    - D: Only thick provisioning

2. What network component usually provides support for IP storage?
    - A: VMkernel adapters with no specific services
    - B: VMkernel adapters for management traffic
    - C: VMkernel adapters for vMotion traffic
    - D: VMkernel adapters for provisioning traffic

3. What are the functions of multipathing? (Select all correct answers)
    - A: Managing the **all path down** (**APD**) condition
    - B: Managing path failover
    - C: Managing load balancing on different paths
    - D: Checking path speed

4. Which vSphere API is required to provide VVOLs support?
    - A: VASA 1.0
    - B: VASA 2.0
    - C: VAAI
    - D: VDAP

5. What is the minimum number of disks (for each ESXi host) required to build a VSAN hybrid cluster?
    - A: 1 SSD, 1 HDD
    - B: 1 SSD, 2 HDD
    - C: 2 SSD, 2 HDD
    - D: 2 SSD, 3 HDD

6. Which of the following statements are true about SIOC? (Select all correct answers)
   - A: Datastores that are SIOC-enabled must be managed by a single vCenter Server system.
   - B: SIOC is not supported on FC-connected storage.
   - C: SIOC supports Raw Device Mapping.
   - D: SIOC does not support datastores with multiple extents.

7. Which of the following are valid authentication methods for iSCSI configuration in vSphere? (Select all correct answers)
   - A: Using unidirectional CHAP, if required by target
   - B: Using unidirectional CHAP, unless prohibited by target
   - C: Using mandatory authentication
   - D: Using ESXi authentication
   - E: Using storage authentication

The following list provides all of the correct answers to the preceding questions:

Q1: C

Q2: A

Q3: B, C

Q4: B

Q5: A

Q6: A, D

Q7: A, B

Upgrade a vSphere Deployment to 6.x

1. Which of the following can be updated by VUM? (Select all correct answers)
   - A: The VM guest OS
   - B: VM applications
   - C: ESXi host patches
   - D: VM virtual hardware
   - E: VMware Tools

2. How do you enable VUM on VCSA 6.5?
   - A: It's enabled by default.
   - B: By installing it on a Windows system.
   - C: By adding an RPM package.
   - D: By starting the service.

3. If VUM does not have direct access to the internet, which of the following options can be used to download the required patches? (Select all correct answers)
   - A: The only available option is to enable internet access.
   - B: It's possible to use a web proxy server.
   - C: It's possible to download them with UMDS and share them with VUM.
   - D: The only available option is to download the patches manually.

4. Which of the following migration paths are supported by the VCSA 6.5 migration tool? (Select all correct answers)
   - A: From VCSA 5.5 or 6.0 to VCSA 6.5
   - B: From vCenter Server for Windows 5.5U3 to VCSA 6.5
   - C: From vCenter Server for Windows 6.0 to VCSA 6.5
   - D: From vCenter Server for Windows 6.5 to VCSA 6.5

5. Which vSphere functions can be temporarily disabled by VUM during an ESXi host remediation? (Select all correct answers)
   - A: vSphere HA host monitoring
   - B: vSphere HA admission control
   - C: vSphere FT
   - D: DPM
   - E: DRS

6. What options are available to update VMware Tools automatically? (Select all correct answers)
   - A: Using the Check and upgrading VMware Tools before each power-on option
   - B: Using VUM
   - C: Using Download Manager
   - D: Using the interactive install

7. How is it possible to manage the software updates for the VCSA?
    - A: Using VAMI
    - B: Using VUM
    - C: Using yum
    - D: Using rpm

The following list provides all of the correct answers to the preceding questions:

Q1: C, D, E

Q2: A

Q3: B, C

Q4: B, C

Q5: B, C, D

Q6: A, B

Q7: A

Administer and manage vSphere 6.x Resources

1. What other VMware product is needed for the new vSphere 6.5 predictive DRS feature?
    - A: None; it's embedded in vCenter
    - B: vRealize Automation
    - C: vRealize Operations
    - D: vRealize Orchestrator

2. What can determine the maximum number of vCPUs that can be assigned to a VM on vSphere? (Select all correct answers)
    - A: The number of VMs already running on the ESXi host
    - B: The number of logical processors on the ESXi host
    - C: The number of physical processors on the ESXi host
    - D: The ESXi host license/edition
    - E: The number of hosts in a cluster

3. In which of the following cases will the sharing mechanism be invoked, and the share number become relevant?
   - A: When there's resources contention
   - B: When VM limits are reached
   - C: When the sum of the different VM reservations exceeds the physical host resources
   - D: When a VM is running

4. Which of the following defines a memory reservation on a VM?
   - A: The amount of VM memory that can be paged to the host swapfile
   - B: The maximum amount of physical memory that will be used by a VM
   - C: The amount of physical memory that is guaranteed to the VM
   - D: The memory priority that will be used by a VM

5. What type of resources can be used by DRS to balance a vSphere 6.5 cluster better? (Select all correct answers)
   - A: CPU
   - B: Memory
   - C: Network
   - D: Storage

6. Which of the following is true about memory TPS in vSphere 6.5?
   - A: It must be enabled on each host.
   - B: It is enabled by default.
   - C: It is enabled by default, but only intra-VM.
   - D: It cannot be disabled.

7. If DRS is set to partially automated, which of the following is true?
   - A: Placements and migration recommendations are displayed.
   - B: The initial placements are performed automatically, but only migration recommendations are displayed.
   - C: Only the initial placements are displayed, but migration recommendations are performed automatically.
   - D: The placements and migrations are performed automatically.

The following list provides all of the correct answers to the preceding questions:

Q1: C

Q2: B, D

Q3: A

Q4: C

Q5: A, B, C

Q6: C

Q7: B

Backup and recover a vSphere Deployment

1. Which of the following backup options are possible in VCSA 6.5? (Select all correct answers)
    - A: Backing up the configuration from the vSphere Web Client
    - B: Backing up the configuration from the VAMI
    - C: Backing up the configuration from the vSphere Client
    - D: Backing up the entire VM with a backup product

2. Which of the following are the appliance sizes of **vSphere Data Protection (VDP)**? (Select all correct answers)
    - A: 4 GB
    - B: 8 GB
    - C: 16 GB
    - D: 32 GB

3. How many VDP appliances can be deployed per vCenter?
    - A: 5
    - B: 10
    - C: 20
    - D: 40

4. Which of the following kinds of VM configurations are NOT supported by VDP? (Select all correct answers)
    - A: Physical RDM
    - B: Virtual RDM
    - C: Up to 32 VM snapshots
    - D: VMDK larger than 2 TB
    - E: Bus sharing

5. What is the RPO range in vSphere Replication 6.5?
    - A: From 5 minutes to 24 hours
    - B: From 15 minutes to 24 hours
    - C: From 5 minutes to 48 hours
    - D: From 15 minutes to 48 hours

6. Which of the following types of recovery options do you have with vSphere Replication? (Select all correct answers)
    - A: Synchronizing recent changes
    - B: Using the latest available data
    - C: Selecting an RPO
    - D: Promoting the VM

7. Which of the following is the first step to deploying a vSphere Replication appliance?
    - A: Deploying the OVF file
    - B: Mounting the ISO file
    - C: Running the installer
    - D: Deploying from a URL

The following list provides all of the correct answers to the preceding questions:

Q1: B, C

Q2: A, B

Q3: C

Q4: A, E

Q5: A

Q6: A, B

Q7: B

Troubleshoot a vSphere Deployment

1. Suppose that you have several Windows VMs running on a production DRS enabled cluster. On the last day, several VMs running on one ESXi host suddenly hang, with a blue screen. Which of the following is the most likely cause of the failure?
    - A: An ESXi VMkernel panic on the host running the failed VMs
    - B: A patch recently applied to Windows VMs
    - C: Resource contentions on the host running the failed VMs
    - D: A hardware problem on the ESXi host running the failed VMs

2. What ESXi command is useful for troubleshooting network connectivity problems with VMkernel adapters?
    - A: `esxcli network`
    - B: `esxcli troubleshoot`
    - C: `vmkping`
    - D: `net-status`

3. Which of the following conditions will cause a vMotion validation check to fail? (Select all correct answers)
    - A: VMware Tools not installed
    - B: Insufficient network bandwidth on the target virtual switch
    - C: Guest OS not supported
    - D: VM resources not available on the target host (for example, local ISO)
    - E: Different CPU families or EVC baselines not compatible

4. Which of the following troubleshooting tasks can you perform with the VAMI interface? (Select all correct answers)
    - A: Rebooting or shutting down the appliance
    - B: Creating a vCenter Support Bundle
    - C: Checking the status of each vCenter/PSC service
    - D: Checking the health status of vCenter/PSC
    - E: Resetting the SSO admin password

5. What kind of storage latency is measured by the DAVG parameter/adapters?
    - A: The average response time, in milliseconds, per command being sent to the device.
    - B: The response time, as it is perceived by the guest operating system.
    - C: This is the amount of time the command spends in the VMKernel.

6. Which of the following tools can be used to check VMFS metadata consistency?
   - A: VAMI
   - B: VIC
   - C: VMA
   - D: VOMA

7. In order to find possible CPU contentions, what metric should you check first?
   - A: CPU usage at the VM level
   - B: CPU ready time
   - C: CPU usage at the ESXi level
   - D: CPU CSTP

The following list provides all of the correct answers to the preceding questions:

Q1: D

Q2: C

Q3: D, E

Q4: A, B, D

Q5: A

Q6: D

Q7: B

Deploy and customize ESXi Hosts

1. Which of the following services are required for AutoDeploy? (Select all correct answers)
   - A: FTP
   - B: TFTP
   - C: DHCP
   - D: NTP
   - E: DNS

2. Which of the following installations can be performed by AutoDeploy 6.5? (Select all correct answers)
   - A: Stateless
   - B: Stateful
   - C: Persistent
   - D: Floating
   - E: Stateless caching

3. What status will be displayed on an ESXi when there is an inconsistency between the host configuration and the host profile configuration?
   - A: Compliant
   - B: Non-compliant
   - C: Unknown
   - D: Mismatch

4. What kind of setting is not saved when you export a host profile?
   - A: vSwitch MTU
   - B: Storage adapter queue
   - C: ESXi root's password

5. What is the minimum ESXi license to use the host profile feature?
   - A: Essential Plus
   - B: Standard
   - C: Enterprise Plus

6. What is the minimum ESXi license to use the AutoDeploy feature?
   - A: Essential Plus
   - B: Standard
   - C: Enterprise Plus

7. What are the main differences between applying a network configuration using a host profile and using the DVS? (Select all correct answers)
   - A: The host profile requires hosts in the maintenance mode to apply the configuration.
   - B: The DVS requires hosts in the maintenance mode to apply the configuration.
   - C: The host profile can also work with standard virtual switches.
   - D: The host profile has rollback features.

The following list provides all of the correct answers to the preceding questions:

Q1: B, C, E

Q2: A, B, E

Q3: B

Q4: C

Q5: C

Q6: C

Q7: A, C

Configure and administer vSphere and vCenter Availability Solutions

1. What happens in a vSphere HA cluster when the master host is placed in maintenance mode, or if it crashes? (Select all correct answers)
    - A: A new automatic election takes place to determine the new master
    - B: vCenter Server elects a new master
    - C: VMs that were running on the failed host are restarted
    - D: vSphere HA executes the Host Isolation Response

2. If your default gateway is not pingable, which of the following vSphere HA advanced settings can be used? (Select all correct answers)
    - A: **das.isolationaddress[X]**
    - B: **das.ignoreInsufficientHbDatastore**
    - C: **das.iostatsInterval**
    - D: **das.useDefaultIsolationAddress**

3. In a vSphere HA cluster, which of the following methods can be used when the master node cannot communicate with a slave host?
    - A: Network Heartbeating
    - B: Management Networking
    - C: Datastore Networking
    - D: Datastore Heartbeating

4. What happens if you have only one shared datastore in a vSphere HA cluster?
    - A: At least required two shared datastores.
    - B: You can use the **das.ignoreInsufficientHbDatastore** setting to remove the warning.
    - C: You must increase the **das.iostatsInterval** setting.
    - D: You must add the **das.isolationaddress** setting.

5. What are the requirements for using the VCHA configuration? (Select all correct answers)
    - A: You need the VCSA.
    - B: The vCenter version must be 6.5 or higher.
    - C: You need the Windows version of vCenter.
    - D: You need the Standard Edition of vCenter.

6. What is the maximum memory supported by vSphere Fault Tolerance?
    - A: 32 GB
    - B: 64 GB
    - C: 128 GB
    - D: 256 GB

7. Which of the following vSphere features can increase uptime and the availability of VMs? (Select all correct answers)
    - A: vSphere FT
    - B: vSphere HA
    - C: vSphere DRS
    - D: vSphere DPM

The following list provides all of the correct answers to the preceding questions:

Q1: A, C

Q2: A, D

Q3: D

Q4: B

Q5: A, B, D

Q6: B

Q7: A, B

Administer and manage vSphere Virtual Machines

1. Where can one find centralized information about all snapshots of a VM?
    - A: The `.vmx` file
    - B: The `.vmdk` file
    - C: The `.vmsd` file
    - D: The `.vswp` file

2. How many USB devices can be added to a VM?
    - A: 5
    - B: 10
    - C: 15
    - D: 20

3. Which option allows administrators to choose the format in which the virtual machine's virtual disks must be stored?
    - A: **Clone to Template**
    - B: **Clone to Library**
    - C: **Convert to Template**
    - D: **Convert to Virtual Machine**

4. Which of the following security settings are available for a published catalog in a content library?
    - A: User authentication with password only
    - B: User authentication with user and password
    - C: Certification authentication
    - D: IP authentication

5. In vSphere 6.5, is it possible for a VM to mount an ISO file in a content library?
    - A: Yes
    - B: No
    - C: Yes, but only if the catalog is published
    - D: Yes, but only if the catalog is not published

6. Which of the following vSphere features are unavailable for a VM configured with DirectPath? (Select all correct answers)
    - A: Hot adding and removal of virtual devices
    - B: vSphere FT
    - C: vSphere HA
    - D: Snapshots

7. Which of the following operations can be performed with the Standalone Converter? (Select all correct answers)
    - A: Changing the virtual hardware of a VM
    - B: Shrinking a virtual disk
    - C: Changing the disk layout from one disk with multiple partitions to multiple virtual disks
    - D: Installing VMware Tools

The following list provides all of the correct answers to the preceding questions:

Q1: C

Q2: D

Q3: A

Q4: A

Q5: A

Q6: A, B, C, D

Q7: A, B, C, D

Consider each right answer to be one point (for questions with multiple answers, consider partial points for each answer). A reasonable target for a first attempt is around 60 points.

Note that the formula used to score a VMware exam is not published. Some hints will be provided in the appendix of this book.

Summary

This mock exam was designed to be taken in a single attempt; if you already know the right answers, the scores for future attempts may be very high, but will not be useful.

Chapter 12, *Mock Exam 2*, will provide a different mock exam.

Some links to free resources are provided in the book's appendix.

12
Mock Exam 2

This chapter will contain one mock exam, to test your knowledge of the content in all of the previous chapters.

The mock exam will contain 70 questions (just like the real 2V0-622 exam), and readers should try to complete it in 105 minutes, simulating the real exam's duration.

Note that the questions can also be used in preparation of the VCP6.5-DCV delta exam (the 2V0-622D exam), which also has 70 questions and a duration of 105 minutes.

The vSphere 6.5 Foundations exam (the 2V0-602 exam) is a little more general (and less deep, technically), but covers several other products from VMware, including vRealize Log Insight, vRealize Automation, and NSX.

This book's appendix will provide more details on the different VCP65-DCV exams.

 VMware no longer provides free mock exams. Instead, they redirect users to Measure Up for online exam simulations; the price of each is $109 USD (as of July, 2018).

The following activities will be covered in this chapter:

- Testing your knowledge in preparation for the VCP65-DCV exam
- Simulating the VCP-DCV exam

Mock exam 2

In this second mock exam, the questions will be sorted randomly (like in the real exam), and will not follow the structure of the book.

Also, in the real exam, the number of questions will not necessarily be equally distributed across the topics and contents of the different chapters.

Note that some questions will have multiple answers. This will be indicated with a "Select all correct answers" sentence. In the real exam, the number of answers (in the case of multiple choice questions) is usually specified.

The correct answers will be included at the end of the chapter.

1. Is it possible to have multiple Active Directory identity sources configured on one PSC?
    - A: No; there can only be one AD source
    - B: Yes, but only if all AD domains are in a single forest
    - C: Yes, but only if there are multiple PSCs in an enhanced linked mode
    - D: Yes, but only if Active Directory over LDAP is used

2. Which of the following features is available for VMs configured with a network device passthrough on **Cisco Unified Computing Systems (UCS)**, through **Cisco Virtual Machine Fabric Extender (VM-FEX)** distributed switches?
    - A: Hot adding and removal of virtual devices
    - B: Recording and replaying
    - C: Fault tolerance
    - D: High availability
    - E: DRS

3. What type of vSphere storage integration requires an additional third-party plugin?
    - A: VASA 1.0
    - B: VAAI (SAN storage)
    - C: VAAI (NAS storage)
    - D: VASA 2.0

4. A VM has 2 CPUs, 4 GB of RAM, and 40 GB of disk space. If there are 2 GHz of CPU reservation, 2 GB RAM reservation, and thick provisioning, how much storage is provisioned when the VM is running?
    - A: 40 GB
    - B: 41 GB
    - C: 42 GB
    - D: 43 GB
    - E: 43 GB

5. What tool can be used to capture network traffic at the uplink, vSwitch, or virtual port levels?
    - A: `tcpdump`
    - B: `tcpdump-uw`
    - C: `pktcap`
    - D: `pktcap-uw`

6. Which of the following VMware vSphere 6.0.x features are interoperable with **Virtual Volumes** (**VVols**)? (Select three correct answers.)
    - A: High availability
    - B: Native Snapshots
    - C: Storage vMotion
    - D: Fault Tolerance
    - E: Storage Distributed Resource Scheduler
    - F: Storage I/O Control

7. What is the VMware-recommended best practice for Fibre Channel zoning?
    - A: Multiple initiator, multiple target zoning
    - B: Multiple initiator, single target zoning
    - C: Single initiator, multiple target zoning
    - D: Single initiator, single target zoning

8. In which of the following ways is it possible to populate the storage capabilities in vSphere? (Select two correct answers)
    - A: Manually, by using tags to describe capabilities
    - B: Automatically, by using VASA
    - C: Automatically, by using a VAAI
    - D: Manually, by using SATP custom rules

9. Is it possible to hot-extend (with the VM powered on) a VMDK larger than 2 TB?
   - A: No
   - B: Yes, with vSphere 5.5 or greater
   - C: Yes, with vSphere 6.0 or greater
   - D: Yes, with vSphere 6.5 or greater

10. What is the result of a Consolidate action on a VM?
    - A: All snapshots of the VM will be deleted
    - B: The VM will be reverted to its last snapshot
    - C: Redundant delta disks will be combined and deleted
    - D: A new VM snapshot will be created

11. If the VM Monitoring setting is **High**, what is the failure interval for the VM?
    - A: 20 seconds
    - B: 30 seconds
    - C: 60 seconds
    - D: 120 seconds

12. What is the minimum number of ESXi hosts required to build a VSAN cluster?
    - A: 1
    - B: 2
    - C: 3
    - D: 4

13. How many concurrent cross-host vSphere vMotion migration instances are allowed per host?
    - A: 1
    - B: 2
    - C: 3
    - D: 4

14. For security compliance requirements, you need to ensure that all service-related passwords are changed every 30 days. What do you have to do with the vCenter agent user account to enforce this requirement?
    - A: Manually change the passwords on all ESXi instances every 30 days
    - B: Change the **VirtualCenter.VimPasswordExpirationInDays** setting on vCenter Server
    - C: Change the PAM settings on each ESXi instance, to enforce a password expiration of 30 days
    - D: Nothing

15. When can you configure vCenter HA with the basic option? (Select two correct answers)
    - A: The VCSA has a static IP address
    - B: The VCSA has an FQDN
    - C: SSH is enabled on the VCSA
    - D: The local shell is enabled on the VCSA

16. How many local disk groups can be formed in a Virtual SAN?
    - A: Up to 3
    - B: Up to 4
    - C: Up to 5
    - D: Up to 7

17. What are the requirements for using Kerberos authentication on NFS datastores? (Select two correct answers)
    - A: ESXi must be 5.5 or later
    - B: NFS version 4.1
    - C: Enabling AES256-CTS-HMAC-SHA1-96 or AES128-CTS-HMAC-SHA1-96 encryption modes on AD
    - D: Enabling DES-CBC-MD5 or AES128-CTS-HMAC-SHA1-96 encryption modes on AD

18. Suppose that you are trying to build a Microsoft failover guest cluster, and you have configured the first VM with the physical RDM. Why can't you add the physical RDM to the second VM with the GUI?
    - A: Because `config.vpxd.filter.rdmFilter` is set to true
    - B: Because you are using an NFS datastore
    - C: Because `config.vpxd.filter.rdmFilter` is set to true
    - D: Because the vSphere edition is Essential Plus

19. Which of the following virtual switch features can be used to help find the upstream physical switch connections and topology? (Select two correct answers)
    - A: LLDP
    - B: LACP
    - C: CDP
    - D: NetFlow

20. What two types of ESXi iSCSI initiators require a VMkernel networking configuration? (Select two correct answers)
    - A: Hardware-dependent
    - B: Hardware-independent
    - C: Software initiator
    - D: Guest initiator

21. What three Path Selection Policies are supported in vSphere by default? (Select three correct answers)
    - A: **Most recently used** (**MRU**)
    - B: Round Robin
    - C: Fixed
    - D: Adaptive
    - E: Least Queue

22. Suppose that you have a VM with an independent disk. Is it possible to take a snapshot of the VM?
    - A: Never
    - B: Only if the VM is powered off
    - C: Only if the VM first disk is not independent
    - D: Always

23. When is a reboot of an ESXi host required? (Select two correct answers)
    - A: If you install or update a VIB package
    - B: If you change the license
    - C: If you disable IPv6 support
    - D: If you add the host to a distributed virtual switch

24. What is the minimum number of virtual NICs for a VM?
    - A: 0
    - B: 1
    - C: 2
    - D: 3

25. If strict lockdown mode has been enabled on an ESXi host, is it possible to have an administrator that can perform ESXi Shell or SSH access?
    - A: Only if you switch to normal **Lockdown Mode**
    - B: Yes, if you add the users to **Exception Users**
    - C: Yes, if you add the users to the **Global permission**
    - D: Yes, if the user is an SSO admin user

26. If you enable CPU hot-add on a VM with 1 socket and 2 cores per socket, what will happen when you hot-add a new CPU?
    - A: You can choose whether you want to add sockets or cores
    - B: A new socket with 2 cores will be added
    - C: A new core will be added
    - D: If you have multiple cores, you cannot use CPU hot-add

27. Suppose that you try to log in on the ESXi SSH, but you are unable to do so. The ESXi service is enabled. You find that the root password was wrong, but you also cannot log in with the new password. What is the issue?
    - A: The root user cannot get access through SSH
    - B: You have to wait two minutes and retry
    - C: You have to enable Lockdown Mode
    - D: You must change the password with DCUI

28. Suppose that you need to increase the security of VMs. Which of the following actions could you consider? (Select two correct answers)
    - A: Disabling unused hardware devices
    - B: Disabling unexposed features
    - C: Disabling VMware Tools
    - D: Keeping the virtual hardware version low

29. The size of a VSAN datastore depends on which of the following? (Select two correct answers)
    - A: The number of capacity disks per ESXi host
    - B: The number of caching disks per ESXi host
    - C: The numbers of VMDK files
    - D: The number of ESXi hosts in the cluster
    - E: The type of VMDK provisioning

30. Which of the following ESXi passwords match the default security policy? (Select two correct answers)
    - A: xQaTEhb!
    - B: xQaT3#A
    - C: Xqat3hi
    - D: xQaTEh2

31. When should ESXi software iSCSI port binding be used?
    - A: When the Array Target iSCSI ports reside in the same broadcast domain and IP subnet as the VMkernel port
    - B: When the VMkernel ports used for iSCSI connectivity exist in a different broadcast domain, IP subnet, and/or vSwitch
    - C: When routing is required to reach the iSCSI array
    - D: When LACP is used

32. What are some of the requirements for cross vCenter migration? (Select three correct answers)
    - A: vCenter Server 6.0 or later
    - B: ESXi 6.0 or later
    - C: A minimum of 250 Mbps bandwidth
    - D: The same SSO domain for vCenter Servers
    - E: Less than 10 ms of network latency

33. What is the usual provisioning type of VMDK on NAS storage?
    - A: It depends on the NFS version
    - B: Thin provisioning
    - C: Thick eager-zeroed
    - D: Thick lazy-zeroed

34. Suppose that you have an isolated VM that is attached to a standard switch, with no physical uplinks configured. You try to migrate it with vMotion, but it fails. What is the most likely cause?
    - A: By default, you cannot use vMotion to migrate a VM that is attached to a standard switch with no physical uplinks configured
    - B: You don't have the proper ESXi license
    - C: The vMotion interfaces are not configured, or related VMkernel adapters cannot communicate
    - D: The host CPUs are not compatible, and EVC is not enabled

35. Suppose that on an ESXi 6.5 host, you are performing one Storage vMotion operation. What is the maximum number of concurrent operations that you can perform on the host? (Select two correct answers)
    - A: One additional Storage vMotion
    - B: Two additional Storage vMotions
    - C: Two additional vMotions
    - D: Four additional vMotions

36. In order to boot from a SAN for ESXi, what is required? (Select two correct answers)
    - A: Each host must have the same shared disk, with LUN ID 0 (zero)
    - B: With FCoE, the network adapter must support the FBFT or FBPT format
    - C: For software iSCSI or dependent hardware iSCSI, the network adapter must support the iBFT format
    - D: For FC, multipath must be used

37. What happens to ESXi certificates during an upgrade? (Select two correct answers)
    - A: ESXi 6.x host upgrades do not preserve the SSL certificate, and reissue one from the VMCA
    - B: ESXi 6.x host upgrades preserve the existing SSL certificate
    - C: ESXi 5.x host upgrades do not preserve the default SSL certificate, and reissue one from the VMCA
    - D: ESXi 5.x host upgrades do not preserve a custom SSL certificate, and reissue one from the VMCA

38. What are the requirements for using Jumbo Frames for iSCSI traffic? (Select two correct answers)
    - A: The network must support Jumbo Frames end-to-end for Jumbo Frames
    - B: HBA iSCSI adapters must be used
    - C: Only software iSCSI can be used
    - D: Check with your vendors to ensure that your physical NICs support Jumbo Frames

39. Suppose that in a two-node vSphere cluster with vSphere HA enabled, VUM fails the host remediation, because the hosts can't be put into maintenance mode automatically. The following event is shown for the hosts: *"Cannot remediate host <hostname> because it cannot enter maintenance mode."* Which of the following can you do to perform the host remediation? (Select two correct answers)
    - A: Disable HA Admission Control
    - B: Manually place individual hosts into maintenance mode and perform the update via VUM per host
    - C: Disable HA for the duration of the VUM cluster remediation
    - D: Remove the host from the cluster

40. If the virtual machine system traffic has 0.5 Gbps reserved on each 10 GbE uplink on a distributed switch that has 10 uplinks, what is the total aggregated bandwidth available for VM reservation on the switch?
    - A: 0.5 Gbps
    - B: 1 Gbps
    - C: 5 Gbps
    - D: 10 Gbps

41. A vSphere 6.5 cluster with three hosts has vSphere HA enabled with the default parameters, and admission control configured to tolerate one host failure. Which of the following statements will be true if a fourth host is added?
    - A: CPU and memory capacity will be set to 20%
    - B: CPU and memory capacity will be set to 25%
    - C: CPU and memory capacity will be set to 30%
    - D: CPU and memory capacity will be set to 33%

42. Why would VDP performance analysis results have a **Conditionally Passed** status?
    - A: The read, write, and seek tests have failed
    - B: The read, write, and seek tests were successful
    - C: The read and write tests were successful, but the seek test failed
    - D: The read and write tests were successful, but the seek test was skipped

43. When does ESXi not require a VMkernel port for iSCSI?
    - A: ESXi always requires a VMkernel port for iSCSI
    - B: When a software iSCSI initiator is used
    - C: When dependent hardware iSCSI initiators are used
    - D: When independent hardware iSCSI initiators are used

44. Suppose that on an ESXi 6.5 host, you have four VMs, protected by vSphere FT. Can you protect another VM on the same host?
    - A: No, because four VMs is the limit per host (primary VMs and secondary VMs count toward that limit)
    - B: Yes, because the limit per host is eight
    - C: Yes, but you need to change the `das.maxftvcpusperhost` HA advanced parameters
    - D: Yes, unless the total vCPUs aggregated across all fault-tolerant VMs on the host is less than eight

45. What two permissions are required to migrate a virtual machine with Storage vMotion? (Select two correct answers)
    - A: **Network** | **Move Network**
    - B: **Virtual Machine** | **Inventory** | **Move**
    - C: **Resource** | **Relocate**
    - D: **Datastore** | **Allocate Space**

46. Which three prerequisites must be in place prior to enabling secure boot for a virtual machine? (Select two correct answers)
    - A: A TPM chip
    - B: Virtual hardware version 13 or later
    - C: ESXi 6.0 or later
    - D: EFI firmware

47. Suppose that you are configuring replication for a VM, but you are not able to select a **Recovery Point Objective** (**RPO**) value of 5 minutes. What could be the reason?
    - A: The **OS quiescing** option is selected under **Replication** options
    - B: There are already more than 50 VMs with an RPO of 5 minutes
    - C: The datastore is NFS 4.1
    - D: The virtual machine hardware version is not compatible

48. Which CHAP security level is not supported with independent hardware iSCSI? (Select two correct answers)
    - A: Using unidirectional CHAP, if required by target
    - B: Using unidirectional CHAP, unless prohibited by target
    - C: Using unidirectional CHAP
    - D: Using bidirectional CHAP

49. In which formats can you export a VM using the vSphere Web Client on vSphere 6.5?
    - A: OVF only
    - B: OVF and OVA
    - C: OVA, OVA, and VMX
    - D: There is no export function

50. What VMkernel adapter is used for network traffic with a long-distance vMotion migration?
    - A: vMotion only
    - B: vMotion or Replication
    - C: Management or Provisioning
    - D: vMotion, Management, or Provisioning

51. Can Virtual Volumes work with VMCA?
    - A: No
    - B: Yes; the SSL certificates from the VASA provider must be replaced with the one from VMCA
    - C: Yes; the SSL certificates can be generated by the VMCA, for use by the VASA provider
    - D: It depends on the VASA version

52. Which of the following deployments are supported in vSphere 6.5U1, in order to implement enhanced linked mode?
    - A: External PSC only
    - B: Embedded PSC only
    - C: External or embedded PSC
    - D: PSC only, with a load balancer

53. What is the correct procedure for using a custom certificate on an existing vCenter HA configuration? (Select two answers that are part of the solution)
    - A: Putting the vCenter HA in maintenance mode
    - B: Deleting the Passive and Witness nodes
    - C: Replacing the certificate on the Active node
    - D: Replacing the certificate on the Passive and Witness nodes
    - E: Deleting the Active node

54. Which of the following tasks cannot be performed on an encrypted VM? (Select two correct answers)
    - A: VM snapshot with quiescence
    - B: VM snapshot with capture the virtual machine memory
    - C: Migration with cross-vCenter vMotion
    - D: Migration with vMotion

55. Which guest operating system supports PVRDMA on vSphere 6.5?
    - A: All Linux guest operating systems
    - B: Only 64-bit Linux guest operating systems
    - C: Windows Server 2012 or later
    - D: Windows Server 2016 or later

56. Which network failure detection methods can be used by ESXi? (Select two correct answers)
    - A: Link status only
    - B: Beacon probing
    - C: LACP
    - D: Notify switch

57. Which of the following are requirements for claiming a disk for the vSphere Flash Read cache? (Select three correct answers)
    - A: The disk is supported by vSphere
    - B: The disk is detected as local
    - C: The disk is detected as an SSD disk
    - D: The disk has been formatted with VMFS, and it's not mounted as a datastore

58. Which backup method is supported for backing up VCSA 6.5?
    - A: Full image backups
    - B: Incremental backups
    - C: Differential backups
    - D: Individual disk backups

59. An ESXi host fails to boot after you have installed ESXi in UEFI mode. How can you fix this issue?
    - A: Reinstall the ESXi
    - B: Reinstall the ESXi on an SD card, instead of on a local disk
    - C: Add a new boot option in your server
    - D: Upgrade the server's firmware

60. What is the best method for sharing templates across multiple vCenters that are geographically distributed?
    - A: Exporting as OVF and importing another vCenter
    - B: Using a common NFS share
    - C: Using a Content Library
    - D: Using Enhanced Linked Mode

61. What are some of the required vCenter privileges for creating a virtual machine? (Select three correct answers)
    - A: **Virtual machine** | **Inventory** | **Create new**
    - B: **Datastore** | **Allocate space**
    - C: **Resource** | **Assign virtual machine to resource pool**
    - D: **Virtual machine** | **Snapshot management** | **Create snapshot**
    - E: **Virtual machine** | **Interaction** | **Answer question**

62. Why is it better to design storage with several small datastores, rather than one big datastore? (Select two correct answers)
    - A: Fewer storage contentions
    - B: Less wasted storage space
    - C: More flexibility in creating virtual machines
    - D: More flexibility in storage capabilities

63. Which of the following could not be maintained during migration from a Windows vCenter Server to VCSA 6.5? (Select two correct answers)
    - A: Local Windows OS users and groups
    - B: vCenter IP addresses
    - C: Custom ports for vCenter services
    - D: vCenter system name

64. What remediation options are available in proactive HA? (Select two correct answers)
    - A: Quarantine mode for moderate, and maintenance mode for severe failure
    - B: Enforced locked mode for all failures
    - C: Maintenance mode for all failures
    - D: Suspended mode for all failures

65. What is the right procedure for patching a vCenter HA cluster? (Select two answers that are part of the solution)
    - A: Place the vCenter HA cluster in maintenance mode
    - B: Delete the Standby and Witness node
    - C: Patch the Active node
    - D: Patch the Passive node

66. Which VMkernel adapter is used for vSphere HA traffic on a VSAN cluster?
    - A: Management
    - B: Provisioning
    - C: VSAN
    - D: Heartbeat

67. Suppose that you need to use VMCA as an Intermediate Certificate Authority. What is the first step of the procedure?
    - A: Replacing Machine SSL Certificates (Intermediate CA)
    - B: Replacing the Root Certificate (Intermediate CA)
    - C: Replacing Solution User Certificates (Intermediate CA)
    - D: Replacing the VMware Directory Service Certificate

68. What types of disk formats are supported in VMFS6? (Select two correct answers.)
    - A: 512n
    - B: 512e
    - C: 4Kn
    - D: 4Ke

Checking your answers

The following list provides all of the correct answers to the preceding questions. Because the answers are not structured in the same order as the book contents (like in the real exam), we will provide explanatory links and/or information:

- Q1: D
  The vCenter Single Sign-On supports multiple Active Directory instances over LDAP identity sources. See `https://docs.vmware.com/en/VMware-vSphere/6.5/com.vmware.psc.doc/GUID-1F0106C9-0524-4583-9AC5-A748FD1DC4C5.html`.

- Q2: A, D, E
  Usually, all of the features are not available with DirectPath I/O, but with Cisco VM-FEX, there are different support matrices. See `https://docs.vmware.com/en/VMware-vSphere/6.5/com.vmware.vsphere.networking.doc/GUID-BF2770C3-39ED-4BC5-A8EF-77D55EFE924C.html`.

- Q3: C
  Each NAS storage vendor that wants VAAI functionality must provide its own plugin.
- Q4: D
  You must consider the space allocated by the storage (40 GB, due to the thick provisioning), and the swapfile (that it's the memory minimum the reservation). We assume that there are no snapshots.
- Q5: D
  Starting with vSphere 5.5, you can monitor packets on an ESXi host by using the `pktcap-uw` console utility, without any additional components. See `https:// docs.vmware.com/en/VMware-vSphere/6.5/com.vmware.vsphere.networking. doc/GUID-5CE50870-81A9-457E-BE56-C3FCEEF3D0D5.html`.
- Q6: A, B, C
  See `https://kb.vmware.com/s/article/2112039`.
- Q7: D
  See `https://docs.vmware.com/en/VMware-vSphere/6.5/com.vmware.vsphere.s torage.doc/GUID-E7818A5D-6BD7-4F51-B4BA-EFBF2D3A8357.html`.
  Note that storage vendors can have specific (and different) best practices for FC zoning.
- Q8: A, B
  See `http://cormachogan.com/2015/02/17/vsphere-6-0-storage-features-par t-5-virtual-volumes/`.
- Q9: D
  This is one of the new features for vSphere 6.5; see `https://kb.vmware.com/s/ article/2058287`.
- Q10: C
  See `https://docs.vmware.com/en/VMware-vSphere/6.5/com.vmware.vsphere. vm_admin.doc/GUID-2F4A6D8B-33FF-4C6B-9B02-C984D151F0D5.html`.
- Q11: B
  See `https://docs.vmware.com/en/VMware-vSphere/6.5/com.vmware.vsphere. avail.doc/GUID-62B80D7A-C764-40CB-AE59-752DA6AD78E7.html`.
- Q12: C
  Also, in the two node configurations, there are two ESXi instances, plus one witness that is still an ESXi (usually virtualized).
- Q13: B
  The limit is the same as in vMotion without shared storage; see `https://docs. vmware.com/en/VMware-vSphere/6.5/com.vmware.vsphere.vcenterhost.doc/ GUID-25EA5833-03B5-4EDD-A167-87578B8009B3.html`.

- Q14: D
  The vCenter Server creates the `vpxuser` account on each managed host, and the password for this account is autogenerated and updated by default every 30 days. See `https://kb.vmware.com/s/article/1016736`.
- Q15: A, C
  See `https://docs.vmware.com/en/VMware-vSphere/6.5/com.vmware.vsphere.avail.doc/GUID-33AC12C8-EEB7-422D-831B-B1B5A7FECC44.html`.
- Q16: C
  There can be up to five disk groups, each with one caching disk and up to seven capacity disks; see `https://www.vmware.com/pdf/vsphere6/r65/vsphere-65-configuration-maximums.pdf`.
- Q17: B, C
  See `https://docs.vmware.com/en/VMware-vSphere/6.5/com.vmware.vsphere.storage.doc/GUID-BDCB7500-72EC-4B6B-9574-CFAEAF95AE81.html`.
- Q18: C
  By default, vCenter Server uses storage filters to prevent LUN filtering corruption, and also, RDM LUNs are filtered. You need to disable it temporarily to build a guest cluster with shared disks with the GUI. Note that RDMs are not supported with NFS datastore, but in this case, option B was not applicable, because one RDM was already configured!
- Q19: A, C
  Note that CDP is available on both standard and distributed virtual switches; LLDP is only available on distributed virtual switches.
- Q20: A, C
  See `https://docs.vmware.com/en/VMware-vSphere/6.5/com.vmware.vsphere.storage.doc/GUID-C476065E-C02F-47FA-A5F7-3B3F2FD40EA8.html`.
- Q21: A, B, C
  See `https://docs.vmware.com/en/VMware-vSphere/6.5/com.vmware.vsphere.storage.doc/GUID-AE95818C-0782-429B-9526-DF12673A63C7.html`.
- Q22: B
  Virtual machines with independent disks must be powered off before you take a snapshot. Snapshots of powered-on or suspended virtual machines with independent disks are not supported. See `https://docs.vmware.com/en/VMware-vSphere/6.5/com.vmware.vsphere.vm_admin.doc/GUID-53F65726-A23B-4CF0-A7D5-48E584B88613.html`.
- Q23: A, C
  Note that some VIB packages may not require a host reboot (for example, NSX VIBs). Also, note that on vSphere 6.5, it is recommended to leave IPv6 enabled.

- Q24: A

  A VM cannot have virtual networking at all, but in this case, it is isolated. The maximum vNICs for a VM remains at 10 with virtual hardware 13.

- Q25: B

  Also, in strict lockdown mode, you will still have some direct access to the ESXi, as described at `https://docs.vmware.com/en/VMware-vSphere/6.5/com.vmware.vsphere.security.doc/GUID-F8F105F7-CF93-46DF-9319-F8991839D265.html`.

  Of course, you also have to enable the services (by default, they are disabled).

- Q26: B

  CPU hot-add can only add new sockets. Also, it requires the Standard Edition and supported guest operating systems.

- Q27: B

  Starting with vSphere 6.0, account locking is supported for access through SSH and the vSphere Web Services SDK. The **Direct Console Interface** (**DCUI**) and the ESXi Shell do not support account lockout. By default, a maximum of ten failed attempts is allowed before the account is locked. The account is unlocked after two minutes, by default.

  See `https://docs.vmware.com/en/VMware-vSphere/6.5/com.vmware.vsphere.security.doc/GUID-DC96FFDB-F5F2-43EC-8C73-05ACDAE6BE43.html`.

- Q28: A, B

  Installing VMware Tools is a good practice. Virtual hardware 13 introduces specific security features (such as secure boot).

- Q29: A, C

  Caching disks does not provide capacity; the raw VSAN datastore capacity depends on the total number of capacity disks.

- Q30: A, B

  `xQaTEhb!`: Contains eight characters from three character classes.

  `xQaT3#A`: Contains seven characters from four character classes.

  `Xqat3hi`: Begins with an uppercase character, reducing the effective number of character classes to two. The minimum number of required character classes is three.

  `xQaTEh2`: Ends with a number, reducing the effective number of character classes to two. The minimum number of required character classes is three.

  See `https://docs.vmware.com/en/VMware-vSphere/6.5/com.vmware.vsphere.security.doc/GUID-DC96FFDB-F5F2-43EC-8C73-05ACDAE6BE43.html`.

- Q31: A
  Usually, port binding is used when you have a single virtual switch and a single logical network for iSCSI. If you have different logical networks, port binding is not needed, and it can also slow down the ESXi startup.
  See `https://kb.vmware.com/s/article/2038869`.

- Q32: A, B, C
  The same SSO domain is required to perform the operation through the GUI.
  See `https://kb.vmware.com/s/article/2106952` and `https://docs.vmware.com/en/VMware-vSphere/6.5/com.vmware.vsphere.vcenterhost.doc/GUID-3B41119A-1276-404B-8BFB-A32409052449.html`.

- Q33: B
  Without a VAAI plugin, NFS storage can only support thin provisioning. For block storage, the default is thick lazy-zeroed provisioning.

- Q34: A
  All are acceptable reasons why vMotion can fail, but in this case, the reason is related to the VM configuration, as described at `https://docs.vmware.com/en/VMware-vSphere/6.5/com.vmware.vsphere.vcenterhost.doc/GUID-3B41119A-1276-404B-8BFB-A32409052449.html#GUID-3B41119A-1276-404B-8BFB-A32409052449`.

- Q35: A, D
  Each operation, such as a migration with vMotion or cloning a virtual machine, is assigned a resource cost. Each host, datastore, or network resource has a maximum cost that it can support at any one time. For more information,
  see `https://docs.vmware.com/en/VMware-vSphere/6.5/com.vmware.vsphere.vcenterhost.doc/GUID-25EA5833-03B5-4EDD-A167-87578B8009B3.html#GUID-25EA5833-03B5-4EDD-A167-87578B8009B3`.

- Q36: B, C
  See `https://docs.vmware.com/en/VMware-vSphere/6.5/com.vmware.vsphere.storage.doc/GUID-8FAD881D-7A00-43C9-AB69-66DC7816968C.html`
  `https://docs.vmware.com/en/VMware-vSphere/6.5/com.vmware.vsphere.storage.doc/GUID-C1FD30A2-27C1-45A6-A736-E0AE76A0ADB2.html`
  `https://docs.vmware.com/en/VMware-vSphere/6.5/com.vmware.vsphere.storage.doc/GUID-2A66A330-A9E5-460B-8982-54A1B1C38C02.html`.

- Q37: B, C
  See `https://docs.vmware.com/en/VMware-vSphere/6.5/com.vmware.vsphere.security.doc/GUID-5D8D20A1-F79B-49DA-BC90-73FF9AC2ADA0.html`.

- Q38: A, D
  See `https://docs.vmware.com/en/VMware-vSphere/6.5/com.vmware.vsphere.storage.doc/GUID-0AB1E949-8A97-425B-96E1-DC1A2BC7DC29.html`.

- Q39: B, C
  This behavior is per design; if one host is placed into maintenance mode, there will be only one host left, and therefore HA won't be able to perform a failover for VMs. See `https://kb.vmware.com/s/article/53682`.
- Q40: C
  See `https://docs.vmware.com/en/VMware-vSphere/6.5/com.vmware.vsphere.networking.doc/GUID-8E957535-7969-4E12-BD11-DF746D6D5379.html`.
- Q41: B
  See `https://docs.vmware.com/en/VMware-vSphere/6.5/com.vmware.vsphere.avail.doc/GUID-53F6938C-96E5-4F67-9A6E-479F5A894571.html`.
- Q42: C
  Possible results are Passed, Failed, and Conditionally Passed, depending on the tests. See `https://docs.vmware.com/en/VMware-vSphere/6.5/vmware-data-protection-administration-guide-61.pdf`.
- Q43: D
  Independent hardware iSCSI initiators are fully hardware-based (HBA iSCSI).
- Q44: C
  See `https://docs.vmware.com/en/VMware-vSphere/6.5/com.vmware.vsphere.avail.doc/GUID-57929CF0-DA9B-407A-BF2E-E7B72708D825.html`.
- Q45: C, D
  See `https://kb.vmware.com/s/article/1011345`.
- Q46: B, C
  See `https://docs.vmware.com/en/VMware-vSphere/6.5/com.vmware.vsphere.security.doc/GUID-898217D4-689D-4EB5-866C-888353FE241C.html`.
- Q47: A
  See `https://docs.vmware.com/en/vSphere-Replication/6.5/com.vmware.vsphere.replication-admin.doc/GUID-9E17D567-A947-49CD-8A84-8EA2D676B55A.html`.
- Q48: A, D
  See `https://docs.vmware.com/en/VMware-vSphere/6.5/com.vmware.vsphere.storage.doc/GUID-3F97FB05-3C92-4040-84E7-D928555B3808.html`.
- Q49: A
  In vSphere 6.5, it's only possible to export in the OVF format. An import can be from OVF or OVA. See `https://docs.vmware.com/en/VMware-vSphere/6.5/com.vmware.vsphere.vm_admin.doc/GUID-AFEDC48B-C96F-4088-9C1F-4F0A30E965DE.html`.

- Q50: D
  Cold data goes through the management or provisioning interface (in all vMotions without shared storage). See `http://frankdenneman.nl/2013/02/07/why-is-vmotion-using-the-management-network-instead-of-the-vmotion-network/`.

- Q51: C
  See `https://docs.vmware.com/en/VMware-vSphere/6.5/com.vmware.vsphere.storage.doc/GUID-36F6CC52-833F-4F37-AB4E-7EA80145979C.html`.

- Q52: A
  Note that on vSphere 6.5U2 or 6.7, the embedded deployment is now supported. See `https://docs.vmware.com/en/VMware-vSphere/6.5/com.vmware.vsphere.install.doc/GUID-91EF7282-C45A-4E48-ADB0-5A4230A91FF2.html`.

- Q53: B, C
  See `https://docs.vmware.com/en/VMware-vSphere/6.5/com.vmware.vsphere.avail.doc/GUID-CDC20BD4-E0CE-45D9-B73B-9AA795DA5FDD.html`.

- Q54: B, C
  See `https://docs.vmware.com/en/VMware-vSphere/6.5/com.vmware.vsphere.security.doc/GUID-C0AF1F3A-67B4-41A6-A933-7E52A3603D9D.html`.

- Q55: B
  See `https://docs.vmware.com/en/VMware-vSphere/6.5/com.vmware.vsphere.networking.doc/GUID-4A5EBD44-FB1E-4A83-BB47-BBC65181E1C2.html`.

- Q56: A, B
  Link status and beacon probing are the two failure detection methods available on both standard and distributed virtual switches. Also, LACP can manage link redundancy, but it's a protocol feature, not a specific ESXi failure detection method.

- Q57: A, B, C
  A formatted local flash disk becomes unavailable for the virtual flash resource or VSAN, so it's not possible to try to claim. See `https://docs.vmware.com/en/VMware-vSphere/6.5/com.vmware.vsphere.troubleshooting.doc/GUID-6E75A727-C2D9-4B20-B47A-A243AEBE1881.html`.

- Q58: A
  In this case, we are considering the image-based backup. Of course, VCSA 6.5 has a specific backup feature, but it's not listed in the available answers. See `https://docs.vmware.com/en/VMware-vSphere/6.5/com.vmware.vsphere.install.doc/GUID-1C73996F-8312-4BBD-A16C-B2C8FC3C0D31.html`.

- Q59: C
  See `https://docs.vmware.com/en/VMware-vSphere/6.5/com.vmware.vsphere.install.doc/GUID-D1BD27AB-C432-454D-9B2B-DC04E7BA9979.html`.

- Q60: C
  Subscribed libraries are the best solution. Also, a common NFS share can work, but it's quite difficult to have it in a geographically distributed environment.
  See `https://docs.vmware.com/en/VMware-vSphere/6.5/com.vmware.vsphere.vm_admin.doc/GUID-254B2CE8-20A8-43F0-90E8-3F6776C2C896.html`.

- Q61: A, B, C
  See `https://docs.vmware.com/en/VMware-vSphere/6.5/com.vmware.vsphere.vm_admin.doc/GUID-4D0F8E63-2961-4B71-B365-BBFA24673FDB.html`.

- Q62: A, D
  For block storage, fewer VMs in a datastore means fewer SCSI reservation problems. Also, having more datastores allows for a better multipath distribution and different datastores with different storage capabilities. See `https://docs.vmware.com/en/VMware-vSphere/6.5/com.vmware.vsphere.storage.doc/GUID-2C8FAE1F-98F7-4E0B-AEA0-83A4FF16A252.html`.

- Q63: A, C
  See `https://docs.vmware.com/en/VMware-vSphere/6.5/com.vmware.vsphere.upgrade.doc/GUID-5E19B79A-AE4F-497A-9047-3E9AAC1D7767.html`.

- Q64: A, C
  There is also the Quarantine mode for the all failures option. See `https://docs.vmware.com/en/VMware-vSphere/6.5/com.vmware.vsphere.avail.doc/GUID-3E3B18CC-8574-46FA-9170-CF549B8E55B8.html`.

- Q65: A, D
  There are only two steps in an articulated procedure, as described at `https://docs.vmware.com/en/VMware-vSphere/6.5/com.vmware.vsphere.upgrade.doc/GUID-C27CD7DF-AB52-4A77-A6A6-A966498D5CA0.html`.

- Q66: C
  Usually, it's always the Management network (unless specific HA advanced settings are used), but on a VSAN cluster, the default becomes the VSAN network.

- Q67: B
  See `https://docs.vmware.com/en/VMware-vSphere/6.5/com.vmware.psc.doc/GUID-5FE583A2-3737-4B62-A905-5BB38D479AE0.html`.

- Q68: B
  Support for 4K native has been introduced in vSphere 6.7. See `https://docs.vmware.com/en/VMware-vSphere/6.5/com.vmware.vsphere.storage.doc/GUID-7552DAD4-1809-4687-B46E-ED9BB42CE277.html`.

Consider each correct answer as one point (for questions with multiple answers, consider partial points for each answer). A reasonable target for a first attempt is 55-60 points, considering that the questions in this second mock exam are a little more complex.

Read the correct answers carefully, and follow the links to better understand the reasons and theory behind the answers.

> Note that the formula used to score a VMware exam is not published. Some hints will be provided in the book's appendix.

Summary

This mock exam was designed to be taken in a single attempt; if you know the right answers, the scores for future attempts may be very high, but will not be useful.

Do you want more free mock exams? The following are some web resources that can help you:

- Simon Long's VCP 6.5 VCP practice exams: `http://www.simonlong.co.uk/blog/vcp6-5-dcv-practice-exams`
- Paul McSharry's VCP 6 VCP practice exams: `http://www.elasticsky.co.uk/practice-questions/`

Practicing for a VCP 6.0-based exam could also be valuable, because the two exams are at least 60% alike.

Some links and references to free resources are provided in the book's appendix.

Understanding VMware Certification Paths

VMware certifications provide for increased flexibility and career growth, and can enhance your credibility with employers, colleagues, and clients.

There are different certifications, covering multiple technological areas; they apply to different levels, from those that are new to the industry to those that are already experts in the field.

Most importantly, VMware certifications are recognized by the market and the industry; for this reason, they are a good investment for your career.

Additional information about certification can be found at the VMware website (`https://www.vmware.com/education-services/certification.html`).

Certification paths

VMware certification allows for the flexibility to find the path that suits your needs, because there are different paths based on different technologies, as indicated by the following diagram:

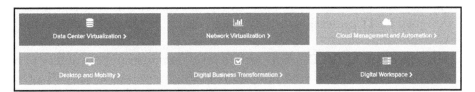

Figure A.1: Different areas of VMware certification

The four main paths are as follows:

- **Data Center Virtualization (DCV)**: These certifications are designed to gauge your level of skill in designing, installing, and managing VMware vSphere environments in real-world environments.
- **Network Virtualization (NV)**: These certifications are designed to gauge your level of skill in designing, installing, and managing VMware vSphere environments in real-world environments.
- **Cloud Management and Automation (CMA)**: These certifications are designed to gauge your level of skill in designing, installing, and managing VMware vSphere environments in real-world environments.
- **Desktop and Mobility (DM)**: These certifications are designed to gauge your level of skill in designing, installing, and managing a VMware Horizon with View environment deployed on a VMware vSphere implementation.

There are other paths, but they are limited to only one level of certification, or to the same badges (like the VSAN badge).

Certification levels

In each path described previously, there are different certification levels, based on your skills, roles, and knowledge level.

There are three main levels, as follows:

- **Professional (VCP)**: This first level demonstrates the ability to install, configure, and manage a specific set of VMware's products or solutions. This level is designed for IT professionals that install, configure, manage, and optimize VMware solutions.
- **Advanced (VCAP/VCIX)**: This second level demonstrates the ability to manage and troubleshoot (for the admin path) or design (for the design path) a specific set of VMware's products or solutions. The advanced levels are for those that design and build VMware Solutions (VCAP Design) and manage and optimize VMware solutions (VCAP Deployment).
- **Expert (VCDX)**: This high level of VMware certification demonstrates the ability to plan and design complex VMware-based projects. The highest level of certification, VCDX recognizes IT professionals that design, build, and manage VMware solutions and systems.

The following diagram displays the different levels as a pyramid, with the most important level at the top:

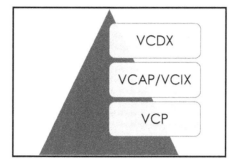

Figure A.2: Different levels of VMware certification

Which level should you choose? It depends on your skills and your role, but you do have to start with a VCP certification. For more information on the different purposes for the different levels of certification, see `https://searchvmware.techtarget.com/Which-VMware-certifications-are-right-for-you`.

In the past, there was also a lower level, the Associated level (VCA), but it no longer exists. Also, VCA is not mandatory for reaching the VCP. This entry-level certification is ideal for new IT professionals, as well as for executives making decisions about VMware solutions. There is still one VCA certification, but on a specific path, without any higher certifications.

Certification life cycle

The first entry point into VMware's certifications is the VCP level, and it usually takes two exams to acquire it (for the first time), as follows:

- The vSphere Foundation exam
- The specific VCP-XX exam for the selected path

The Foundation exam validates that you have the fundamental skills necessary to understand and begin deploying VMware environments based on vSphere and other VMware products (NSX, vRealize, and so on).

More details on the VCP6.5-DCV exam will be provided in the next appendix.

You can then gain a higher level (and those paths are not covered by this book). An interesting point is that you can start with the VCP on one path, then switch to the VCAP level of another path, without first gaining the VCP level of that specific path. This is an example of cross-path certification.

There are some specific cases of bridging upgrade certifications, as described in the post at https://blogs.vmware.com/services-education-insights/2018/01/new-bridge-upgrade-path-current-vcps.html.

 Note that the VCP certifications are, at this time, the only certifications with a recertification policy, and expire after 2 years.

The VCP recertification policy provides three ways to recertify, as follows:

- Advance to the next level by earning a **VMware Certified Advanced Professional** (**VCAP**) certification. For example, if you are a VCP5-DCV, you can earn a VCAP6-DCV Deploy certification.
- Take the current exam for your existing VCP certification solution track. For example, if you are a VCP4, you can take the current VCP6-Data Center Virtualization (VCP6-DCV) exam.
- Earn a new VCP certification in a different solution track. For example, if you are a VCP-Cloud, you can recertify by earning a VCP6-DTM certification.

For more information, see the official certification page at https://mylearn.vmware.com/mgrReg/plan.cfm?plan=49318ui=www_cert.

Some demographics data

Usually, VMware does not track the exact numbers of each certification and each path.

There is an exception for the VCDX level. Because it's an elite level, there is a certification portal called VCDX Directory (https://vcdx.vmware.com/), with all of the details of each VCDX.

Also, there is an interesting infographic about VCDX, available at `https://blogs.vmware.com/education/2018/02/15/vcdxs-around-world-wheres-nearest-vmware-certified-design-expert/`.

VMware sometimes publishes stats on the other certifications.

VCP-DCV is our most popular certification, with more than 120,000 professionals certified around the world, in more than 190 countries.

In the past, VMware has also published some infographics about the VCP and VCAP certifications, which can be seen in the following blog posts:

- `https://blogs.vmware.com/services-education-insights/2017/04/world-vcps-infographic-2.html`
- `https://blogs.vmware.com/services-education-insights/2017/07/around-world-vcaps.html`
- `https://blogs.vmware.com/services-education-insights/2016/04/where-in-the-world-are-vcaps-infographic.html`

Most required certifications

There has been research about the certification most requested by the industry market, but the analysis has continued to change over the different years, and the answer can vary by country and by role.

VMware's certifications remain still request and, in most cases, in the top 10-20 position.

Certification makes a difference by offering multiple benefits, including higher productivity, swifter troubleshooting, and fewer skill gaps.

For an example of some research on certification, see `https://blogs.vmware.com/services-education-insights/2017/10/3-key-takeaways-2017-skills-salary-report.html`.

Certification also provides indirect benefits, which can vary by the certification type and level. An interesting analysis can be seen in the blog post at `https://blogs.vmware.com/services-education-insights/2017/11/%C2%ADbenefits-vmware-certification-6-key-stats.html`.

Certification versus accreditation or awards

VCP, VCAP, VCIX, and VCDX certifications are the main certifications from VMware, but there are also some minor certifications, like the VCA (on digital business transformation).

Progress can be tracked (and shared) in different ways, such as through digital badges (`http://www.pearsonvue.com/vmware/badging/`).

Other than certification badges, there are also some specific badges, such as the following:

- **Specialist badges**: Such badges are built on VMware certifications and are issued to technical experts that understand select VMware technological architectures and feature sets, and can leverage best practices and advanced capabilities to optimize their VMware environments.
- **Co-skilled badges**: Such badges are awarded to individuals that successfully complete the requirements associated with the technology, solutions, or advanced/expert certifications of VMware and selected partners.

Both are outdated as of 2017, and there isn't a new version for 2018 as at the writing of this book.

Note that a specialist badge is not counted as a certification, and it's not a way to renew your VCP certification.

Finally, there is the **VMware vExpert** program, VMware's global evangelism and advocacy program. The program is designed to put VMware's marketing resources (such as promotion of your articles, exposure at global events, co-op advertising, traffic analysis, and early access to beta programs and VMware's roadmap) toward your advocacy efforts. The awards are for individuals, not companies, and they last for one year. Employees of both customers and partners can receive the awards.

For more information, visit the vExpert page at `https://vexpert.vmware.com/`.

In the last few years, this program has also been specialized for specific paths: VSAN, NSX, and Cloud.

Summary

In this appendix, we described the different VMware certification paths, as applied to data center virtualization, cloud management, network virtualization, and end user computing.

The VMware Certification Roadmap poster (`https://mylearn.vmware.com/lcms/web/portals/certification/PathDiagrams/VMware_Certification_Tracks.pdf`) provides a great overview of the different paths and levels.

Additional information about certification can be found on the VMware website (`https://www.vmware.com/education-services/certification.html`) and in the VMware Education blog (`https://blogs.vmware.com/services-education-insights`).

VCP6.5-DCV Certification

As described in the previous appendix, VCP6.5-DCV certification is for administrators and engineers, and it was designed for those that can install, configure, manage, and optimize VMware vSphere 6.5. It also represents the first level of the Data Center Virtualization path.

Keep in mind that to successfully pass the exams, you will need to gain some experience in the field, because studying books alone will probably not suffice. Exam questions are sometimes tricky, and the correct answer can often by discerned through experience.

Once you have obtained your certification, you will be entitled to a digital badge as proof of your accomplishment, providing valid verification of your VMware status for your employers:

Figure B.1: VCP6.5-DCV digital badge issued by VMware

For more information on VCP6.5-DCV certification, see the official VMware page at `https://www.vmware.com/education-services/certification/vcp6-5-dcv-exam.html`.

Certification paths

To obtain VCP6.5-DCV certification, you will need to follow a specific path, depending on your current certification status (including if you hold no VCP certifications).

A common first step is to gain experience with vSphere 6.5; it's better if it's practical experience.

Let's examine some different scenarios and their related paths.

No VCP certification

If a candidate starts without any VCP certification, the required path is as follows:

1. Attend one of the required training courses.
2. Pass the Foundation exam.
3. Pass the VMware Certified Professional 6.5 – Data Center Virtualization exam.

Required training courses

You must attend at least one of the following courses:

- VMware vSphere: Install, Configure, Manage [v6.5]
- VMware vSphere: Optimize and Scale [v6.5]
- VMware vSphere: Install Configure Manage plus Optimize and Scale Fast Track
- VMware vSphere: Skills for Public Sector Customers [v6.5]
- VMware vSphere: Fast Track [v6.5]
- VMware vSphere: Troubleshooting Workshop [v6.5]
- VMware vSphere: Optimize and Scale plus Troubleshooting Fast Track [v6.5]

There are different types of courses, depending on your knowledge level and your working role.

Note that there isn't really a course that covers 100% of the information required to gain VCP6.5-DCV certification; you will need to gain experience through the course labs and your own labs, covering any missing parts before taking the exam.

Exams to pass

You will have to pass both of the following required exams:

- The online vSphere 6.5 Foundation exam (105 minutes, 70 questions, online and not proctored)
- The VMware Certified Professional 6.5 - Data Center Virtualization exam (105 minutes, 70 questions, proctored)

Holding an active VCP5-DCV or VCP6-DCV

If you hold an old VCP5-DCV or VCP6-DCV certification, and the certification is still active (all VCP certifications expire after two years, as described in the previous appendix), then the course is not mandatory, and you can take one of the exams directly. Note that the Foundation exam is no longer mandatory.

The option to start with VCP5-DCV certification is something new, and it's called the bridge update path; in other words, previously, you were not allowed to skip a version (see the **Old Upgrade Path** in the following diagram), unless you wanted to start the track from the beginning, undergo training, and take the Foundation exam. Now if you hold a valid VCP certification who is two versions behind the latest, you can upgrade to current version only taking one exam:

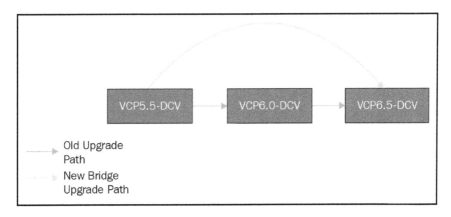

B.2: Bridge upgrade path

For more information, see the blog post at `https://blogs.vmware.com/services-education-insights/2018/01/new-bridge-upgrade-path-current-vcps.html`.

Recommended training courses

It is recommended, but not mandatory, to attend one of the following courses:

- VMware vSphere: Install, Configure, Manage [v6.5]
- VMware vSphere: Optimize and Scale [v6.5]
- VMware vSphere: Install Configure Manage plus Optimize and Scale Fast Track
- VMware vSphere: Skills for Public Sector Customers [v6.5]
- VMware vSphere: Fast Track [v6.5]
- VMware vSphere: Troubleshooting Workshop [v6.5]
- VMware vSphere: Optimize and Scale plus Troubleshooting Fast Track [v6.5]

Exams to pass

You will have to pass one of the following required exams:

- The proctored VMware Certified Professional 6.5 - Data Center Virtualization exam (105 minutes, 70 questions)
- The proctored VMware Certified Professional 6.5 - Data Center Virtualization Delta exam (105 minutes, 70 questions)

Holding an expired VCP-DCV

If your VCP-DCV certification has expired, you will need to take another mandatory course, as in the case of having no certification.

Required training courses

You must attend at least one of the following courses:

- VMware vSphere: What's New [v5.5 to v6.5]
- VMware vSphere: Install, Configure, Manage [v6.5]
- VMware vSphere: Optimize and Scale [v6.5]
- VMware vSphere: Install Configure Manage plus Optimize and Scale Fast Track
- VMware vSphere: Skills for Public Sector Customers [v6.5]
- VMware vSphere: Fast Track [v6.5]
- VMware vSphere: Troubleshooting Workshop [v6.5]
- VMware vSphere: Optimize and Scale plus Troubleshooting Fast Track [v6.5]

Exams to pass

You will have to pass both of the following required exams:

- The online vSphere 6.5 Foundation exam (105 minutes, 70 questions)
- The proctored VMware Certified Professional 6.5 - Data Center Virtualization exam (105 minutes, 70 questions)

Holding an active VCP in a different path

As described in the previous appendix, you can start with a VCP certification in one path, and then switch to another path.

Recommended training courses

It is recommended, but not mandatory, to attend one of the following courses:

- VMware vSphere: Install, Configure, Manage [v6.5]
- VMware vSphere: Optimize and Scale [v6.5]
- VMware vSphere: Install Configure Manage plus Optimize and Scale Fast Track
- VMware vSphere: Skills for Public Sector Customers [v6.5]
- VMware vSphere: Fast Track [v6.5]
- VMware vSphere: Troubleshooting Workshop [v6.5]
- VMware vSphere: Optimize and Scale plus Troubleshooting Fast Track [v6.5]

Exams to pass

You will have to pass one of the following required exams:

- The proctored VMware Certified Professional 6.5 - Data Center Virtualization exam (105 minutes, 70 questions)
- A VCAP exam in the DCV path: VCAP6.5-DCA or VCP6.5-DCD (in this case, you will get both VCAP and VCP certification with a single exam)

Order of the different steps

If your certification path includes a mandatory training course and passing one or two exams, you do not need to complete the requirements in the following order, although it is recommended to do so:

Figure B.3: Recommended order of certification requirements

For example, if your certification path includes attending a mandatory course and passing both the Foundation and VCP6.5-DCV exams, you can take the exams first (but not in a specific order), and then attend the course.

The glue for tracking your progress is your VMware mylearn ID (your email address), and it must match all of your registrations for exams and courses.

Following the suggested order is the most logical solution, allowing for your knowledge to grow.

 Note that if you fail a proctored VCP6.5-DCV exam, you have to wait at least seven days before retaking the exam. There is no wait time for the online Foundation exam.

Certification benefits

Once you have obtained VCP certification, VMware will come with the following benefits:

- Official transcripts
- VMware Digital Badges (badges available at Acclaim's website)
- Use of the certification logo
- Access to the exclusive portal and logo merchandise store
- Invitations to beta exams and classes
- Discounts from VMware Press
- Discounts for attending VMware events

What's next?

Obtaining VCP6.5-DCV certification can be the starting point of your certification path. You can then gain advanced certifications, such as VCAP and VCDX, as illustrated in the following diagram:

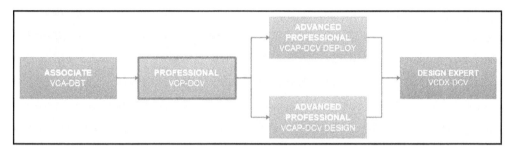

Figure B.4: Certification path

The VCP6.5-DCV certification opens up the entire Data Center Virtualization path, and can also be the starting point for other paths.

Note that, in the preceding diagram, VCA-DBT certification is also represented, but it's not mandatory for the DCV path.

Summary

The Data Center Virtualization path starts with VCP6.5-DCV certification, and there are different ways to gain that kind of certification, as described in this appendix.

Additional information about certification can be found at the VMware website (`https://www.vmware.com/education-services/certification.html`).

The next appendix will provide more information on the VCP6.5-DCV exam.

Before, During, and After the Exam

Like with any vendor's certification, a VMware exam can be challenging, and people that have been using the product for several years can fail it.

The main reason for failing an exam is a lack of preparation—mostly, a lack of time devoted to studying and a lack of appropriate preparation methods.

This chapter will provide specific information on the exam itself, such as its duration, language format, types of questions, registration process, and so on. We also have some tricks and suggestions for maximizing your exam results.

Additional information on certification can be found at the VMware website (`https://www.vmware.com/education-services/certification.html`).

Before the exam

If you are new to VMware certification, the first requirement for VCP6.5-DCV certification is to gain experience with vSphere 6.5 (the certification guide suggests a minimum of six months).

There are different ways to practice using a product: studying it, working on it in the field, and using labs.

Also, if you are new to VMware certification and this will be your first VCP, one of the mandatory requirements for VCP6.5-DCV certification is to attend at least one of the required training courses at a **VMware Authorized Training Center** (**VACT**).

Attending a course

There are different types of courses, depending on your knowledge level and your working role.

For new VCPs, the list of mandatory course (for VCP6.5-DCV) is as follows:

- VMware vSphere: Install, Configure, Manage [V6.5] (`https://mylearn.vmware.com/mgrreg/courses.cfm?ui=www_edua=oneid_subject=76648`)
- VMware vSphere: Optimize and Scale [V6.5] (`https://mylearn.vmware.com/mgrreg/courses.cfm?ui=www_edua=oneid_subject=76652`)
- VMware vSphere: Install, Configure, Manage plus Optimize and Scale Fast Track [V6.5] (`https://mylearn.vmware.com/mgrReg/courses.cfm?ui=www_edua=oneid_subject=79043`)
- VMware vSphere: Optimize and Scale plus Troubleshooting Fast Track [V6.5] (`https://mylearn.vmware.com/mgrReg/courses.cfm?ui=www_edua=oneid_subject=79181`)
- VMware vSphere: Skills for Public Sector Customers [V6.5] (`https://mylearn.vmware.com/mgrReg/courses.cfm?ui=www_edua=oneid_subject=79044`)
- VMware vSphere: Fast Track [V6.5] (`https://mylearn.vmware.com/mgrReg/courses.cfm?ui=www_edua=oneid_subject=79166`)
- VMware vSphere: Troubleshooting Workshop [V6.5] (`https://mylearn.vmware.com/mgrReg/courses.cfm?ui=www_edua=oneid_subject=79173`)

These kinds of courses have a five-day duration and can have different formats (classroom, live online, self-paced, vFlex-ILT, and onsite). Usually, the best option is to use the classroom format, because you can easily interact with the teacher and other attendees, in order to share experience, make the course more interactive, ask questions, and so on.

Note that none of the courses can 100% prepare you for the VCP exam, because all of the courses cover different aspects, and none of them provide total coverage of the knowledge required for the exam. For example, the Install, Configure, Manage course lacks some topics, such as distributed virtual switches (the coverage is too minimal) and troubleshooting.

VSAN is covered by other courses, but you only need a minimal overview of it for the VCP exam.

There are also other cases; for example, if you have an old VCP or you need a preparation course for the exam, consider the following:

- VMware vSphere: What's New [V5.5 to V6.5] (https://mylearn.vmware.com/mgrReg/courses.cfm?ui=www_edua=oneid_subject=76655)
- VMware Certification Exam Prep: VCP6.5-DCV Exams (2V0-622/2V0-622D) (https://mylearn.vmware.com/mgrReg/courses.cfm?ui=www_edua=detid_course=342946)
- VMware Certification Exam Prep: VCP6.5–DCV v6.5 Exams (2V0-622/2V0-622D) (https://mylearn.vmware.com/mgrReg/courses.cfm?ui=www_edua=detid_course=342946)
- VMware Certification Exam Prep: vSphere 6.5 Foundations Exam (2V0-602) (https://mylearn.vmware.com/mgrReg/courses.cfm?ui=www_edua=detid_course=342947)

The What's New course is a three-day course that introduces all of the new features of vSphere 6.5, walking you through the process of installing, upgrading, and migrating.

There are also some courses on the new vSphere 6.7 (more will likely be available in the next few months), as follows:

- VMware vSphere: Install, Configure, Manage [V6.7] (https://mylearn.vmware.com/mgrreg/courses.cfm?ui=www_edua=oneid_subject=84058)
- VMware vSphere: What's New [5.5 – 6.7] (https://mylearn.vmware.com/mgrReg/courses.cfm?ui=www_edua=oneid_subject=84063)

At this time, there isn't any certification for vSphere 6.7.

Studying by yourself

A course can be a good way to study theory (and to practice with labs), but what if you don't take the course (because you don't need it), or you want to learn more?

One solution is to study by yourself, with books, videos, and free resources; this will be covered in the following sections.

Books

There are actually a few books on vSphere 6.5, but one example is as follows:

- *Mastering VMware vSphere 6.5*: `https://www.packtpub.com/virtualization-and-cloud/mastering-vmware-vsphere-65`

Videos

If you prefer a video format over a book format, Packt has some videos on vSphere 6.5, as follows:

- *VCP6-DCV(6.5) Examination Preparation Guide*: `https://www.packtpub.com/virtualization-and-cloud/vcp6-dcv65-examination-preparation-guide-video`
- *Mastering VMware vSphere 6.5*: `https://www.packtpub.com/virtualization-and-cloud/mastering-vmware-vsphere-65-video`

Online resources

The following list has some additional useful resources for VCP-DCV preparation:

- `https://docs.vmware.com/en/VMware-vSphere/index.html`
- `https://www.vladan.fr/vcp65-dcv/`
- `https://vloreblog.com/2017/05/05/vcp6-5-dcv-exam-preparation/`
- `https://vbrownbag.com/2018/06/vcp6-5-dcv-study-guide/`
- `https://www.nakivo.com/it/resources/study-guide/`

Hands-on Labs

A **minimally qualified candidate** (**MQC**) for VCP6.5-DCV certification should generally have about six months of experience in working with a vSphere implementation, and more than one year of IT industry experience.

Typically, he should be capable of installing, configuring, monitoring, and managing a vSphere solution, and also capable of deploying and configuring other infrastructural parts, such as storage and networking. Some minimal skills in optimizing, securing, and troubleshooting all components of the implementation are also required.

What is the best way to get this kind of practice? If you already work on it, there is no problem; otherwise, you will need a lab to try the products.

The simplest method is to use the Hands-on Labs environment provided by VMware, located at `https://labs.hol.vmware.com/`.

There are labs on different products, including, of course, vSphere and VSAN. But, most importantly, each lab is not a simulated environment; it's a real, live environment (a nested environment), so you can use it as you please, even without following the suggested track.

You can build your own lab environment for practice, undergoing the installation and upgrade processes, allowing for a more flexible solution.

Which version should you use? VCP certification should be based on vSphere 6.5U1, so you can use this version; in most cases, it's similar to the U2 version.

Which management tool should you use? VCP certification uses the vSphere Web Client as a reference, in most cases. For this reason, in this book, most of the screenshots are with this client. The other reason is that the HTML5 client lacks some specific administrative tasks.

Checking your exam preparation

The first source of information for checking your preparation before taking the exam is the VCP6.5-DCV exam guide, at `https://www.vmware.com/content/dam/digitalmarketing/vmware/en/pdf/certification/vmw-vcp65-dcv-2v0-622-guide.pdf`.

This book is structured in the same way as the official exam guide, in order to simplify the process of finding specific information or filling the gaps of missing information. Note that there isn't a logical order to the chapters and topics; if you are at the beginning, it's better to start with a course, a book (for example, the *Mastering VMware vSphere* book), or the official vSphere documentation, and then use the exam guide (or this book) as a checklist for verifying your knowledge.

On the official course page, there are also other resources, such as the following:

- Prepare for your VCP6.x -DCV exam with these helpful tips (`https://onlinexperiences.com/Launch/QReg.htm?ShowKey=41188AffiliateData=ODweb`)

Mock exams

This book provides two mock exams to check your preparation.

The mock exams are designed to be taken in a single attempt; if you know the right answers, the scores for other attempts may be very high, but will not be useful.

VMware does not provide any free mock exams, but you can buy them at `http://www.vmwarecertificationmarketplace.com/VMware-Certified-Professional-6-5-p/mu_vcp6.5_dcv_p.htm`.

Do you want other free mock exams? The following web resources can help you:

- Simon Long's VCP 6.5 VCP practice exams: `http://www.simonlong.co.uk/blog/vcp6-5-dcv-practice-exams`
- Paul McSharry's VCP 6 VCP practice exams: `http://www.elasticsky.co.uk/practice-questions/`

You can also practice with VCP 6.0-based exams; they are still valuable, because the two exams are at least 60% alike.

During the exam

The VCP6.5-DCV exam tests candidates on their skills and abilities to install, configure, and manage vCenter Server, ESXi hosts, and virtual machines, using the appropriate VMware tools. Successful candidates demonstrate mastery of these skills and abilities.

Which exam to take

There are at least three different exams to gain the VCP6.5-DCV certification, and, depending on where you start (see *Appendix B*), you may need one or two single exams, as follows:

- **2V0-602**: VMware vSphere 6.5 Foundation exam
- **2V0-622**: VMware Certified Professional 6.5 - Data Center Virtualization exam
- **2V0-622D**: VMware Certified Professional 6.5 - Data Center Virtualization Delta exam

There are other options (such as directly taking the VCAP6.5-DCA or VCAP6.5-DCD exam), but we don't consider them.

In this book, we mainly consider the 2V0-622 exam.

Note that there are still exams for version 6.0 of vSphere, but they will be retired soon (probably when the new VCP exams based on vSphere 6.7 are released).

Foundation exam

This exam is mandatory for new VCP certification, and it's shared across the different VMware certification paths (see *Appendix A*).

It's an online, non-proctored exam, with a 105-minute duration and 70 questions. It costs $125 USD.

This exam validates that you have the fundamental skills necessary to understand and begin deploying VMware vSphere 6.5 environments.

Compared to the VCP6.5-DCV exam, the vSphere 6.5 Foundations exam (2V0-602) is a little more general (and less deep, technically), but covers several other products from VMware, including vRealize Log Insight, vRealize Automation, NSX, and so on.

The exam guide describes all of the products and the types of knowledge required for the exam, at https://www.vmware.com/content/dam/digitalmarketing/vmware/en/pdf/certification/vmw-vsphere65-foundation-2v0-602-guide.pdf.

This book may not help with Foundation exam preparation, due to the different products. However, if you have minimal experience with vSphere, NSX, and VSAN, you can pass the exam.

For more information, see the official page, at https://www.vmware.com/au/education-services/certification/vsphere6-5-foundation-exam.html.

VMware Certified Professional 6.5 - Data Center Virtualization exam

This is the exam considered in this book.

It's a proctored exam with a duration of 105 minutes (or more, for non-English-speaking people), with 70 questions and a cost of $250 USD.

The *Exam Preparation Guide* (Version 7.2, October 3, 2017) provides more details on the exam content, at https://www.vmware.com/content/dam/digitalmarketing/vmware/en/pdf/certification/vmw-vcp65-dcv-2v0-622-guide.pdf.

For more information, see the official page, at `https://www.vmware.com/education-services/certification/vcp6-5-dcv-exam.html`.

VMware Certified Professional 6.5 - Data Center Virtualization Delta exam

This exam is similar to the previous exam. It's still a proctored exam, with a duration of 105 minutes (or more, for non-English-speaking people), 70 questions, and a cost of $250 USD.

However, it's a Delta exam, so many questions are focused on vSphere 6.5, as compared to the previous exam. Also, it is a little simpler. This book can also be used to prepare for this kind of exam.

There is an exam guide at `https://www.vmware.com/content/dam/digitalmarketing/vmware/en/pdf/certification/vmw-vcp65-dcv-delta-2v0-622d_guide.pdf`.

Types of questions

All questions have closed answers, but several are multiple choice questions (with two, or, in a few cases, three answers). Also, note that sometimes, the best answer isn't available, so you should choose which provided option fits the best.

You can also work in a reverse mode. You can simply exclude some answers, and then focus on the remaining answers. Also, in some cases, the answer to one question might be in the text of another one. And some questions may be quite similar (asking the same thing in a different way). So, be sure to read all of the questions and answers carefully. Some answers are mutually exclusive, so be sure to always read both the question and the answers carefully.

Some questions might be related to maximum numbers, but fortunately, the number of questions is now lower than in previous VCP exams. However, it might be useful to look at those numbers at the following links:

- `https://configmax.vmware.com`
- `https://www.vmware.com/pdf/vsphere6/r65/vsphere-65-configuration-maximums.pdf`

Note that questions can change between different exam sessions, and may be upgraded from month to month. If you retake the exam, don't be too confident of seeing the same questions.

Also, note that at this time, the different questions should be based on vSphere 6.5U1, but this can change in the future. There are a few differences, but one big change is in the PSC-supported topology (the enhanced linked mode is now supported, with embedded PSC).

Time management

There are a total of 70 questions in 105 minutes. So, one big challenge is managing your time carefully.

One question per minute might be the right ratio for a VCP exam.

Spend your time carefully reading the questions and possible answers; some questions might not be clear, or may contain a very important term, such as must or should.

A good approach might be to move ahead if you are spending too much time on a single question; you can mark it and review it later. In this way, you can try to reach the maximum result by answering more questions.

Foreign language notes

The 105-minute exam is only available in English, but the exam is also available in English or Japanese.

If you take the exam in a country where English is not the primary language, as with other VMware exams, you will have 30 minutes added to the exam time.

This time extension is automatic; no additional action is required from the candidate. It should depend on the candidate, but the extension may not be automatically added if you take the exam in a testing centering in the UK or US. In that case, just ask before starting the exam.

After the exam

When you have finished your exam, you will get an immediate response and score. What should you do if you fail?

If you fail a proctored VCP6.5-DCV exam, you will have to wait at least seven days before retaking the exam. There is no waiting time for a Foundation exam taken online.

Note that no details will be provided on why you have failed.

If you pass the exam, you will receive a score and earn a VMware badge. When you accept your badge, you'll immediately be brought to a sharing workflow that will allow you to share to Facebook, Twitter, and LinkedIn, on a personal website, or over email.

Scoring in VMware exams

The following is quoted from the VMware Education site:

> *"Your exam may contain unscored questions in addition to the scored questions, this is a standard testing practice. You will not know which questions are unscored, your exam results will reflect your performance on the scored questions only.*
> *VMware exams are scaled on a range from 100-500, with the determined raw cut score scaled to a value of 300. Scaled scoring allows for raw scores from different VMware exams to be scaled to a consistent value. Raw passing scores differ between VMware exams based on different technologies or different levels of competency. A scaled score provides a standard range for test takers and permits direct and fair comparisons of results from one exam form to another."*

What does the preceding quote mean? It's not clear; nobody (except VMware Education) really knows how many questions you must get right to pass the exam. So, try to have a high target, and be prepared.

What's next?

What should you do next if you succeed? You can think of other certifications.

VCP, VCAP, VCIX, and VCDX certifications are the main certifications from VMware, but there are also some minor certifications, such as the VCA (on Digital Business Transformation) and specific exams on specific products (such as VSAN Specialist).

All progress can be tracked (and shared) in different ways, including through digital badges (http://www.pearsonvue.com/vmware/badging/).

One interesting aspect is that your VCP6.5-DCV certification will recertify any older VCP certifications! It will also open up all of the different certification paths.

Summary

That's it. You now have enough information to approach your VCP6.5-DCV certification, and we think that with this book, practice with a lab, a mandatory VMware official course (for the first certification), and at least three weeks of study, you will pass the exam and enter the VCP world.

The VMware Certification Roadmap poster (`https://mylearn.vmware.com/lcms/web/portals/certification/PathDiagrams/VMware_Certification_Tracks.pdf`) provides a great overview of the different paths and levels.

Additional information on certification can be found at the VMware website (`https://www.vmware.com/education-services/certification.html`) and on the VMware Education blog (`https://blogs.vmware.com/services-education-insights`).

Other Books You May Enjoy

If you enjoyed this book, you may be interested in these other books by Packt:

VMware vSphere 6.5 Cookbook - Third Edition
Abhilash G B, Cedric Rajendran

ISBN: 978-1-78712-741-8

- Upgrade your existing vSphere environment or perform a fresh deployment
- Automate the deployment and management of large sets of ESXi hosts in your vSphere Environment
- Configure and manage FC, iSCSI, and NAS storage, and get more control over how storage resources are allocated and managed
- Configure vSphere networking by deploying host-wide and data center-wide switches in your vSphere environment
- Configure high availability on a host cluster and learn how to enable the fair distribution and utilization of compute resources
- Patch and upgrade the vSphere environment
- Handle certificate request generation and renew component certificates
- Monitor performance of a vSphere environment

Mastering VMware vSphere 6.5
Andrea Mauro, Paolo Valsecchi, Karel Novak

ISBN: 978-1-78728-601-6

- Get a deep understanding of vSphere 6.5 functionalities
- Design and plan a virtualization environment based on vSphere 6.5
- Manage and administer a vSphere 6.5 environment and resources
- Get tips for the VCP6-DCV and VCIX6-DCV exams (along with use of the vSphere 6 documentation)
- Implement different migration techniques to move your workload across different environments.
- Save your configuration, data and workload from your virtual infrastructure.

Leave a review - let other readers know what you think

Please share your thoughts on this book with others by leaving a review on the site that you bought it from. If you purchased the book from Amazon, please leave us an honest review on this book's Amazon page. This is vital so that other potential readers can see and use your unbiased opinion to make purchasing decisions, we can understand what our customers think about our products, and our authors can see your feedback on the title that they have worked with Packt to create. It will only take a few minutes of your time, but is valuable to other potential customers, our authors, and Packt. Thank you!

Index

J

jumbo frames support
  enabling, on components 104

K

Kerberos
  authentication, options 186
  used, for connecting NFS 4.1 datastore 186
Key Management Server (KMS) 60
KMS for VM encryption
  configuring 60, 61
  managing 61

L

Large Receive Offload (LRO) 103
Large Send Offload (LSO) 104
Link Aggregation Control Protocol (LACP)
  about 363
  configuring, on vDS given design parameters 93,
  95
Link Aggregation Groups (LAG) 93
load balancing policies
  differentiating 288
  host network saturation threshold 288
  host network utilization, monitoring 289
load balancing
  configuring 97
  settings 97
logical unit number (LUN) identifier 127

M

Maximum Transmission Unit (MTU) 104
memory contention issues
  identifying 370
  isolating 370
memory usage
  monitoring 367
minimally qualified candidate (MQC) 554
multi-factor authentication (MFA) 50
multi-site PSC installation
  performing 51
multi-writer locking
  configuring 185
multi-writer option

  using 185
multilevel resource pools
  configuring 256
multiple ESXi Host upgrades
  staging 223, 224
multiple ESXi hosts
  stateful 401
  stateless 401
  stateless caching 401
multiple VMkernel default gateways
  configuring 110, 111

N

Native Multipathing Plug-In (NMP), components
  Multipathing Plugin (MPP) 164
  Path Selection Plugin (PSP) 164
  Storage Array Type Plugins (SATP) 164
Netflow
  configuring 114, 115
Network Block Device (NBD) 315
network DRS 288
Network File Copy (NFC) 113
Network I/O Control (NIOC)
  about 82, 361
  capabilities 116
  capabilities, differentiating 119
  configuring 115
  disabling 119
  enabling 119
  monitoring 120
  prerequisites, determining 118
  setting behavior 118
  shares/limits, configuring based on VM requisites
  116, 118
network security policies
  configuring 71
networking capabilities
  reference 80
networking issues
  troubleshooting 363
NFS 4.1 datastore
  connecting, Kerberos used 186
NFS datastore
  mounting 187
  proper use case, determining 191